ENVIRONMENTAL POLITICS

Domestic and Global Dimensions

ENVIRONMENTAL POLITICS

Domestic and Global Dimensions

Jacqueline Vaughn Switzer
Southern Oregon State College

St. Martin's Press   New York

Senior editor: Don Reisman
Manager, Publishing Services: Emily Berleth
Project management: Betsy Feist Resources
Cover design: Hothouse Design, Inc.
Cover art: R.R. Donnelley & Sons Company

Library of Congress Catalog Card Number: 92-62740
Copyright © 1994 by St. Martin's Press, Inc.
All rights reserved. No part of this publication may be reproduced, stored in a
retrieval system, or transmitted by any form or by any means, electronic, mechanical,
photocopying, recording, or otherwise, except as may be expressly permitted by the
applicable copyright statutes or in writing by the Publisher.
Manufactured in the United States of America.
8 7 6 5 4
f e d c b a

For information, write:
St. Martin's Press, Inc.
175 Fifth Avenue
New York, NY 10010

Paper ISBN: 0-312-08389-0
Cloth ISBN: 0-312-10238-0

For the members of my *karass*

Preface

Many people interested in the future of our nation and our planet may have only a "headline news" awareness of environmental problems. This book tries to provide a more comprehensive, objective view of issues that have been mired in controversy for decades, avoiding the rhetoric that often distorts the environmental protection debate.

This book uses the policy process as a framework for reviewing the broad spectrum of environmental problems facing political leaders today. Although much of the focus is on the development of environmental policy in the United States, there is also considerable attention paid to the globalization of environmental politics. The chapters refer to various environmental regimes—international agreements that may take the form of conventions or protocols—that have governed the solutions to many of the problems the book identifies. The key international body responsible for most regime formation in environmental issues is the United Nations, which has an alphabet soup of agencies to deal with these issues. After the Stockholm Conference, the UN General Assembly established the UN Environment Programme (UNEP), which has become the lead agency for many of the regimes discussed throughout this book. Other organizations and actors, such as the World Bank, the Group of 7 (and 77), and agreements, such as the General Agreement on Tariffs and Trade (GATT), are covered more effectively by other authors.[1]

Environmental Politics covers both the domestic environmental issues with which most Americans are familiar, as well as those global issues that have gained increasing prominence in recent years. The book is designed to serve as a complement to other books that can provide the reader with additional background on the nature of the public policy process, public administration, political history, or natural resources and environmental science.

Part 1 serves as an orientation, placing environmental politics in historical and political context. Chapter 1 begins with an overview of environmental history to provide background on the early beginnings of concern about the environment, followed by an explanation of the participants in the environmental debate in Chapter 2. Chapter 3 follows up with an introduction to the political process at the federal, state, and local levels, identifying the key agencies and nongovernmental organizations involved in the development of environmental protection legislation, regimes, and administrative rule making.

Parts 2, 3, and 4 introduce the essential issues related to protection of the land, water, and air. Although many of the problems of protection are overlapping and interrelated, these sections bring the reader up to date on the most critical aspects of political decision making in each area. Common to each chapter is a statement of the environmental protection problem, an analysis of the efforts made to solve the problem (legislatively and otherwise), an assessment of the most critical issues, and a status report as we enter the next century. Part 5 shifts the emphasis to those problems that are truly global in nature, such as transboundary pollution and the management of human population. The final section, Part 6, takes a look into the future to examine the environmental issues that are likely to dominate the political agenda as we begin the twenty-first century.

Any one of these topics merits a complete book-length treatment of its own, and the end of each chapter provides suggestions for further reading. Hopefully, this "taste" of the key environmental protection issues will lead the reader to develop an appetite for more comprehensive studies and research. But taken as a whole, it is hoped that all readers—whether students, citizen activists, or government officials—emerge with a better understanding of the totality and scope of environmental politics. Just as the emphasis of the 1972 Stockholm conference shifted from more localized concerns to international ones, this book should help its readers to understand how *all* environmental issues are, at their core, truly global ones.

ACKNOWLEDGMENTS

In preparing this manuscript, I was fortunate to have the benefit of advice, consultation, and support from a number of sources. Although I began writing this book assured that I had an excellent grounding in environmental history and politics, by the end of the project I was soundly assured that I had only begun to scratch the surface of what many of my colleagues and others in the field were doing. I am greatly indebted to the following individuals who generously agreed to read portions of the manuscript in preparation: William Ashworth, Kurt Austermann, David Baker, Claude Curran, Bob Headland, Wayne Linn, Frank Melone, Bill Perry, Denise Scheberle, Brian Shoemaker, and Vicky Sturtevant. I would also like to thank the following reviewers for St. Martin's Press: Roger Anderson, Bowling Green State University; James S. Bowman, Florida State University; Charles Davis, Colorado State University; Sheldon Kamieniecki, University of Southern California; Michael E. Kraft, University of Wisconsin–Green Bay; and Debra J. Salazar, Western Washington University. I must also acknowledge the assistance of the staff at the Southern Oregon State College Library, especially Anne Richards, who helped me wade through the maze of government publications. My colleagues in the Department of Political Science, Don Laws, Paul Pavlich, and Don Rhoades, were sensitive to my need for release time and picked up the slack left by my absence. From St. Martin's Press, I wish to thank Don Reisman and Frances Jones, along with Donna

Erickson, who first urged me to submit the manuscript. And lastly, I owe my husband, Steven, big time. He provided comments on the manuscript, prepared the tables and graphs, and continues to provide love, joy, and balance in my life.

NOTE

1. See Gareth Porter and Janet Welsh Brown, *Global Environmental Politics* (Boulder, CO: Westview Press, 1991), as an example of texts that provide background on regime formation and international environmental agreements.

Contents

Prologue

The Earth Summit should not be judged by the immediate results but by the process it sets in motion.
—Richard Benedict, U.S. Representative to the 1992 Earth Summit[1]

Two meetings, held on different continents and twenty years apart, have set the stage and the policy agenda for the overview of environmental politics that is the focus of this book. The political context and the issues negotiated at the two conferences were, however, dramatically different from each other.

In June 1972, the United Nations Conference on the Human Environment was convened in Stockholm to address the newly emerging issues related to the environment and was in fact the first global conference to focus exclusively on a single issue. The unprecedented meeting took place at a time when the United States was still deeply entrenched in an undeclared war in Vietnam and when detente had only begun to thaw cold war hostilities and old suspicions about the Soviet Union and China. The most controversial aspect of the meeting involved representatives of developing nations, who feared a proposed global environmental monitoring satellite system would be used as a tool for spying by the U.S. Central Intelligence Agency. The Soviet Union and most of the nations of Eastern Europe boycotted the conference over the postwar division of Germany. Still, it was at the time the largest meeting of its kind, attended by delegates from 114 nations, over 500 representatives from 250 nongovernmental organizations (NGOs), and 1,500 journalists. Most of the key issues discussed at the conference were largely local or regional, stemming from mounting public pressure to deal more effectively with air and water pollution and proposals to take additional measures for the preservation of special natural areas and endangered wildlife.[2] But the conference also produced the Stockholm Declaration, a compendium of twenty-six principles that serve as precedent for much of the environmental diplomacy for the next twenty years, including one that acknowledges state sovereignty over natural resources but stipulates that states have responsibility for controlling activities within their jurisdiction and their environmental impact on other states.[3]

In June 1992, 25,000 observers and delegates from 178 nations attending the United Nations Conference on Environment and Development in Rio de Janeiro, better known as the Earth Summit, tackled issues that were much more global in nature. More than 110 heads of state appeared at the meeting, along with thousands of representatives from environmental organizations attending a parallel nongovernmental Global Forum.[4]

The twenty-year interim had brought a virtual end to the cold war with the collapse of both the Soviet Union and the Berlin Wall, and a growing movement toward independence among the nations of Eastern Europe. The United States had ended its commitment in Vietnam but was involved militarily in the Middle East and Central America. Japan and a unified Germany took their place alongside the United States as world economic leaders. On the environmental front, the United Nations had brought together international agreements to control the export of hazardous waste, limits on the emissions of chlorofluorocarbons, control of ocean dumping, and prohibitions on trade in endangered species. Most industrialized countries of the Northern Hemisphere, in the twenty-year interim, made efforts to incorporate environmental protection into their policy-making apparatus. The developing nations of the South, however, have had only limited capacity to incorporate the environment as a policy priority. Their concern for economic development overshadows longer-term issues. Despite this fundamental difference between the nations of the North and South, many observers believe there has been a change in the international political atmosphere from 1972's confrontational politics to 1992's sense of cautious cooperation.

What the two UN conferences had in common, however, is that although the meetings themselves were a showplace for heads of state and political posturing, they represented only a small portion of the negotiations both before and after the conferences. Environmental protection may begin at such meetings, but the process of developing legislation and international regimes is a prolonged and complex one. In 1972, for example, a lengthy preparatory process allowed most of the nations to reach consensus on the issues, so only a limited number of questions needed to be resolved at the conference itself.[5] Preparations for the 1992 conference began more than two years in advance.

The two gatherings were also just the beginning steps for prioritizing the implementation of the decisions made there. In 1972, for example, the reconciled points of view were incorporated into a document called the Stockholm Action Plan for the Environment, which contained 109 recommendations with more than 150 proposals for action. Among the nine major recommendations were the convening of four UN conferences on Environmental Education, Human Settlements, Protection of the World's Cultural and Natural Heritage, and International Trade in Endangered Species; the establishment of an international fund to provide seed capital for housing improvement; the coordination of international programs for integrated pest control; and the development of a global atmospheric monitoring system, an International Registry of Data on Chemicals in the Environment, and an International Referral Service. Ten years later, nearly 30 percent of the proposals had been implemented, another 40 percent were partially implemented, 15 percent were not implemented at all, and information on the remaining 15 percent was unavailable.[6]

Early appraisals of the Earth Summit have been cautiously optimistic, citing the fact that the media attention, the level of participation, and the involvement of NGOs were all much greater in Rio than in Stockholm—evidence that the environment may be more firmly established on the international agenda. From a substantive standpoint, the conference produced five documents signed by heads of state: Agenda 21, a comprehensive eight-hundred-page statement of goals and objectives; the Rio Declaration (originally conceived of as an Earth Charter or statement of environmental principles); two treaties on climate change and biodiversity; and a statement on forest principles.[7] The parallel NGO event also produced two primary products: a treaty-writing project and a book on sustainable development initiatives in business and industry. Agenda 21 appears to be one of the most fragile of the documents since it is nonbinding and its work plan is dependent upon funding from the industrialized countries.[8] Critics of the summit (both environmentalists and conservatives) argue that the conference was just window dressing, or that it commits the United States to a cleanup program it cannot afford.[9]

What the Earth Summit spotlighted, perhaps more than any other issue, is the gap between the industrialized nations of the Northern Hemisphere and the developing nations of the South.[10] The negotiations and bitterness of Rio focused on whether the northern nations would be willing to help pay the cost of cleanup and environmentally responsible development in order to narrow the disparity of wealth and consumption between rich and poor nations. One component of that debate was control over a proposal to fund Third World development. The United States and other industrialized countries sought to have the funds disbursed through the Global Environmental Facility (GEF), controlled and dominated by the countries that were major donors. The southern nations sought to have a one-nation, one-vote "Green Fund" determine how the funds would be distributed. The end result was a compromise—the GEF was opened to greater participation by Third World representatives.[11]

Although the United States was considered the leader in environmental progress at the 1972 conference, that was not the case in 1992. Environmentalists harshly criticized President George Bush for his seeming lack of interest in even attending the Rio meeting, and argued that foot-dragging on the global warming and biodiversity conventions were signs that the president was no longer interested in retaining his title as "the environmental president." Other industrialized nations seemed eager to take the United States' place at the vanguard. Japan, for example, pledged $7.7 billion in aid to developing nations and agreed to eliminate the use of chlorofluorocarbons (which trigger destruction of the Earth's protective ozone layer) by 1996. Japan was also among the first to agree to reduce its emissions of carbon dioxide to 1990 levels by the year 2000 to reduce global warming, a goal also accepted by the twelve nations of the European Community.[12] France and Germany both pledged to increase development aid by the year 2000 to 0.7 percent of their nation's gross national product, a target sought by Third World nations. Although George Bush repeatedly stated that the United States remains a leader, not a follower, in environmental protection, the U.S. offer of $150 million to protect forests seemed inconsequential to some observers.

To place the Earth Summit and the contemporary environmental politics debate in perspective, the book begins by looking at the development of American environmental concerns. The middle chapters examine issues about which policy action continues to take place, primarily at the domestic or local level. Concluding chapters survey issues that require action that is more international in scope.

In order to put environmental politics in context, it is important to understand how the recognition of environmental conditions as "problems" and attempts to solve them make up the policy process. Public policies are those developed by government and are the focus of the remaining chapters of this book. The policy process follows a sequential pattern of activity that can be defined as follows:

1. *Problem identification and agenda formation*: In this stage, policy issues are brought to the attention of public officials in a variety of ways. Some are uncovered by the media; others become prominent through crisis or scientific study. Organized groups may demonstrate or lobby officials to focus attention on the problem, or may enlist celebrities to bring it to government's attention on their behalf.
2. *Policy formulation:* After a problem is identified as worthy of government attention, policymakers must then develop proposed courses of action to solve it. Groups may participate in this stage as well, lobbying officials to choose one alternative or proposal over another.
3. *Policy adoption:* The acceptance of a particular policy is a highly politicized stage that then legitimizes the policy, often involving legislation or rule making. This is often referred to as the authorization phase of policymaking.
4. *Policy implementation:* To put an agreed-upon policy into effect, this fourth stage involves conflict and struggle as the administrative machinery of government begins to turn. Affected groups must now turn their attention from the legislative arena to the bureaucracy and, in some cases, the judicial branch to get the policy to work.
5. *Policy evaluation:* An ongoing process, this stage involves various determinations as to whether or not the policy is effective. This appraisal may be based on studies of program operations, systematic evaluation, or personal judgment, but whatever the method, the evaluation may start the policy process all over again.[13]

Capitalizing on the weakened position of George Bush with environmentally minded voters, Bill Clinton and Al Gore pledged during their campaign to restore the environment to the top of the policy agenda, and they have supported elements of the Rio agreement that did not have the approval of George Bush. The ultimate success of Bill Clinton in translating campaign promises into substantive policy will depend not only on his good intent, but on his ability to deal with the actors, institutions, and processes that are examined in the chapters that follow.

NOTES

1. Quoted in William K. Stevens, "Lessons of Rio: A New Prominence and Effective Blandness," *New York Times*, June 14, 1992, 6.

2. *Report of the United Nations Conference on the Human Environment*, Document A/CONF.48/14/Rev.1 (New York: United Nations, 1973). See also Hans H. Lansberg, "Looking Backward: Stockholm 1972," *Resources* (Winter 1992): 2–3.

3. See Lynton K. Caldwell, *International Environmental Policy: Emergence and Dimensions*, 2nd ed. (Durham, NC: Duke University Press, 1990).

4. A guidebook to the Earth Summit can be found in Hal Kane and Linda Starke, *Time For Change: A New Approach to Environment and Development* (Washington, D.C.: Island Press, 1992). See also Peter M. Haas, Marc A. Levy, and Edward A. Parson, "Appraising the Earth Summit," *Environment* 34, no. 8 (October 1992): 7–11, 26–33.

5. See Louis B. Sohn, "The Stockholm Declaration on the Human Environment," *Harvard International Law Journal* 14 (1973): 423–515.

6. The Agesta Group AB, *Environment-International: Twenty Years After Stockholm 1972–1992* (Berlin: Erich Schmidt Verlag, 1982). The book is an excellent accounting of the actions taken during the first decade after the 1972 conference and the proposals for the second decade.

7. Edward A. Parson, Peter M. Haas, and Marc A. Levy, "A Summary of the Major Documents Signed at the Earth Summit and the Global Forum," *Environment* 34, no. 8 (October 1992): 12–15, 34–36.

8. See *The Global Partnership for Environment and Development: A Guide to Agenda 21* (92-1-100481-0) and *Draft Agenda 21* (92-1-100482-9) (New York: United Nations, 1991).

9. For a politically conservative view of the outcome of the Earth Summit, see "Yalta in Rio," *The National Review*, July 6, 1992, 14–16. The article argues that Senate ratification of the climate change and biodiversity agreements reached in Rio open the way to "green socialism—a suffocating regulation of American society enforced by federal agencies, the courts and environmental groups answerable not to the American voter but to international agencies acting on the authority of Rio."

10. For an explanation of the North/South, rich/poor split, see Shridath Ramphal, *Our Country, the Planet: Forging a Partnership for Survival* (Washington, DC: Island Press, 1992). The author explains why rich and poor countries see environmental issues from a totally different point of view that keeps them from cooperating with one another.

11. See Paul Lewis, "Negotiators in Rio Agree to Increase Aid to Third World," *New York Times*, June 14, 1992, A-1.

12. See James Brooke, "Japan Promises Lead Role in Battle against Pollution," *New York Times*, June 14, 1992, A-6.

13. Adapted from James E. Anderson, *Public Policymaking: An Introduction* (Boston: Houghton Mifflin, 1990).

PART 1

An Introduction to Environmental Politics

CHAPTER 1

A Historical Framework for Environmental Protection

Millions Join Earth Day Observances
—*New York Times* headline, April 23, 1979

Millions Join Battle for a Beloved Planet
—*New York Times* headline, April 23, 1990

Most contemporary observers focus the apex of the American environmental movement on Earth Day, 1970, and the events of April 22 were indeed historic, with an estimated twenty million Americans participating. New York Mayor John Lindsay closed Fifth Avenue to traffic for hours during the event, and a massive rally was held in Union Square. Speeches and songs were heard at the Washington Monument, and virtually every college town, from Berkeley to Madison, held teach-ins and demonstrations. Philadelphia held a week-long observance, with symposia by environmental leaders and scientists, including Maine's Senator Edmund Muskie, author Paul Ehrlich, and consumer activist Ralph Nader. The event was highlighted by the appearance of the cast of the Broadway musical *Hair*. In San Francisco, Earth Day was marked by symbolic protests, as a group calling itself Environmental Vigilantes dumped oil into the reflecting pool in front of Standard Oil. In Tacoma, Washington, nearly a hundred high school students rode down the freeway on horseback urging drivers to give up their automobiles.

But a review of American history shows concerns about the environment actually surfaced in the nation's infancy and have been a recurrent theme throughout the past three hundred years. One interesting aspect of that history is that some individuals or events appear to have had a momentary influence on policy development and then virtually disappeared from our historical consciousness. For example, Gifford Pinchot, an advisor to Theodore Roosevelt and leader of the conservation movement during the early twentieth century, had a tremendous impact on policymaking during that period, but his name is unknown to most contemporary members of the environmental movement. There is no Pinchot National Park or building in Washington, nor is the date of his birth celebrated. Like a shooting star, his role was transitory and ephemeral.

3

Similarly, although women's organizations were responsible for bringing urban environmental issues like solid waste and water quality to the policy agenda, that function ended, for the most part, when it was replaced by the struggle for suffrage. Women are now beginning to reemerge with the stirrings of the ecofeminist movement, which will be discussed in Part 6.

Equally perplexing are the effects of a number of environmental disasters and crises that made headlines. Some, like the thirty-million-gallon oil spill caused by the sinking of the supertanker Torrey Canyon off the coast of England in 1967, have been upstaged by more recent events such as the oil spill resulting from the grounding of the Exxon Valdez in Alaska. But the radiation leak at the Soviet Union's Chernobyl plant in April 1986 has become synonymous with concerns about nuclear power and is likely to serve as a catalyst for international protests for years to come.

The development of an environmental policy agenda can be viewed in two ways. One, it is a history of ideas, a philosophical framework about our relationship to nature and the world. This history is punctuated with names ranging from Thomas Malthus and Charles Darwin to Karl Marx and Francis Bacon, along with modern commentary from Barry Commoner, Garrett Hardin, and Paul Ehrlich.[1] Two, it is a factual history, made up of events, individuals, and conditions that are easier to identify. This chapter uses that second way of looking at history to identify five distinct periods in the development of policies to protect the environment.

GERMINATION OF AN IDEA: FROM THE COLONIAL PERIOD TO 1900

Even before the states were united there was an awareness of the need to limit the use of the new land's natural resources. As early as 1626, the members of the Plymouth Colony passed ordinances regulating the cutting and sale of timber on colony lands. Other colonial leaders recognized the importance of preserving the region's resources, prohibiting the intentional setting of forest fires and placing limits on deer hunting. In 1681, William Penn, proprietor of Pennsylvania, decreed that for every five acres of land cleared, one must be left as virgin forest.[2] In 1691, Massachusetts Bay leaders began to set aside "forest reservations"—large stands of pines that were valued strategically for their use as ships' masts. Forest preservation became a firmly entrenched principle of colonial land management as early as the seventeenth century.[3]

During the eighteenth century, the nation was consumed with the building of a new government, but individual states still made efforts to preserve the resources within their boundaries. Massachusetts began to protect coastal waterfowl in 1710 and banned the hunting of deer for four years in 1718. Other states, such as Connecticut (1739) and New York (1772), also passed laws to protect game.[4] Political leaders at the beginning of the nineteenth century expressed interest in studying soil erosion, and both Washington and Jefferson wrote of their concern about the lands at their estates. With the opening of the Erie Canal in 1825, bringing pine forests within the reach of eastern markets, states were forced to deal with the issue of timber poaching—one of the first environmental crimes.[5]

By mid-century, the public's interest in preservation of natural resources had begun to take shape. George Perkins Marsh's 1864 book *Man and Nature* captured attention with his call for protection of songbirds and the use of plantings to prevent soil erosion.[6] In 1866, German scientist and philosopher Ernst Haeckel coined the term *ecology*, and the subject became a thriving research discipline.[7] Still, there was no overall philosophy of protection that dominated either American or European thought. Studies of the popular literature of the 1870s have led some historians to conclude that the environmental movement really came alive with the advent of sportsmen's magazines. In October 1871, *The American Sportsman*, a monthly newspaper, marked a watershed in environmental history when it became the first publication to interrelate the subjects of hunting, fishing, natural history, and conservation as its primary concerns. Two years later, the debut of *Forest and Stream* called for the protection of watersheds, scientific management of forests, uniform game laws, and abatement of water pollution.[8] Diminishing supplies of fish in the Connecticut River resulted in the development of the fish culture industry and the formation of the first biological society to research a diminishing natural resource, the American Fisheries Society, in 1870. It was followed a year later with the creation of the U.S. Fish Commission—the first federal agency to deal with the conservation of a specific natural resource.[9]

Adventure and exploration enhanced the public's interest in the environment throughout the nineteenth century. Lewis and Clark's transcontinental journeys beginning in 1804, and John Wesley Powell's descent into the Colorado River in 1869, increased Americans' awareness of the undiscovered beauty of the frontier.[10]

Tremendous urban population growth between 1870 and the turn of the century led to a host of new environmental problems, characterized by piles of garbage, contamination of drinking water sources, and sewage dumping. The problems were most evident in the cities of the Northeast and Midwest, where the population increases were the most rapid. Although New York remained the nation's largest city, nearly tripling its population over the thirty-year period, Chicago had the biggest percentage increase, nearly sixfold. Philadelphia, St. Louis, and Boston nearly doubled the size of their population. Although industrial development did not reach the West Coast's cities as quickly, San Francisco, which served as the major shipping port, doubled its population between 1870 and 1890. Yet the biggest increase overall was in Los Angeles, which grew to over twenty times its size from 1870 to 1900. American cities became the center of industry, and industry and population growth meant pollution. By 1880, New York had 287 foundries and machine shops, and another 125 steam engines, bone mills, refineries, and tanneries. By the turn of the century, Pittsburgh had hundreds of iron and steel plants, and Chicago's stockyard stench combined with eight railroads and a busy port to produce odors and thick, black smoke.[11]

The pollution problems caused by rapid industrial growth resulted in numerous calls for reform, and women became the key actors in cleaning up the urban environment. Upper-class ladies with extended periods of leisure, believing "the housekeeping of a great city is women's work," formed civic organizations dedicated to monitoring pollution and finding solutions to garbage and sanitation problems. The first of these groups, the Ladies' Health Protective Association, was founded in 1884, with the goal of keeping New York's streets free of garbage. The Civic Club of Philadelphia, formed in 1894, began by placing trash receptacles at key intersections. Other groups were started in Boston (the Women's Municipal League) and St. Louis (Women's Organization for Smoke Abatement).[12]

Certainly there is some truth to the statement that the nation's sense of enhanced environmental awareness was the result of the actions of specific individuals. George Catlin, for example, first proposed the idea of a national park in 1832,[13] and Henry David Thoreau spoke poetically of his return to a natural world in 1858.[14] One of the individuals who had a tremendous impact during this period was Frederick Law Olmstead, one of the first professional landscape architects in the United States and the "father of Central Park." In 1864, Olmstead visited Yosemite and a year later received an appointment as a commissioner to help oversee management of the valley, making what were, at the time, novel suggestions on its preservation.[15] Olmstead's friend George E. Waring built the first separate sewer system in Lenox, Massachusetts, in 1876 and was a pioneer in the study of sanitary engineering. Waring became known as "the apostle of cleanliness" and was responsible for the beginnings of contemporary solid waste science, as well as pushing forward concerns about the public health impact of garbage.[16]

The concept of preserving natural areas came from a variety of sources. In 1870, a group of explorers recommended a portion of the upper Yellowstone River region be set aside to protect its geothermal features, wildlife, forests, and unique scenery, and the establishment of Yellowstone National Park in 1872 was the beginning of a pattern of preserving large undisturbed ecosystems. The public endorsed the idea, and Congress responded by creating Sequoia, Kings Canyon, and Yosemite National Parks in 1890, followed by Mount Rainier National Park in 1899. Interest in trees and forests was an important element of preservationism, perhaps best symbolized by the proclamation of the first Arbor Day on April 10, 1872. The event was the culmination of the work of J. Sterling Morton, editor of Nebraska's first newspaper, and Robert W. Furia, a prominent nurseryman who later became governor. The two men convinced the Nebraska state legislature to commemorate the day with tree plantings to make Nebraska "mentally and morally the best agricultural state in the Union." As a result, over one million trees were planted the first year, and Nebraska became known as the "Tree Planter's State" in 1895.

Not until 1892, with the founding of the Sierra Club by John Muir, was there any real interest in forming a more broadly based environmental organization.[17] Although the early organizations have been termed "pitifully weak" in membership and finances, these early groups had a sense of determination that was very strong. Most groups debated the scientific management of resources rather than organizing to protect them. But the idea of preserving natural resources and lands was germinating deep within American society.[18]

PROGRESSIVE REFORMS AND CONSERVATIONISM: 1900–1945

Despite these whispers of ideas and early efforts, the majority of environmental historians place the beginning of an actual "movement" at the turn of the century, when conservationism became a key element of the Progressive Era. In fact, the term *conservation* grew out of the efforts by pioneers like Frederick H. Newell, George Maxwell, and Francis G. Newlands to construct reservoirs to conserve spring flood waters for later use during the dry season. The concept behind conservation was "planned and efficient progress."[19]

In the United States, the infant environmental movement split into two camps: preservationists and conservationists. Under the leadership of Gifford Pinchot, the conservationists, influenced by forest management practices in Europe, believed sustainable exploitation of resources was possible. The preservationists, led by John Muir, sought to preserve wilderness areas from all but recreational and educational use. Pinchot, a Yale graduate who trained at the French Forest School and later received an appointment as forester on the seven-thousand-acre North Carolina estate of George W. Vanderbilt, became the nation's most publicized environmentalist. In 1898, he became chief of the Division of Forestry (later renamed the U.S. Forest Service) and, as a personal friend of Theodore Roosevelt, had tremendous influence over the development of conservation policy through his connections in Washington, DC. He personally convinced Roosevelt of the need to set aside forest preserves and to use techniques of scientific forestry to manage them.[20] In contrast, John Muir, who spent much of his life in California's Sierra Nevada, championed the protection of the Yosemite Valley and crusaded against the development of Yosemite's Hetch Hetchy reservoir, which he viewed as misuse of the region's natural resources.[21]

For the most part, the conservationists' position won out, at least at the national level. Prior to the turn of the century, there had been little federal consideration for conservation. The "zenith" can be traced to May 13–15, 1908, when a thousand national leaders met to attend a White House Conference on Resource Management, coordinated by Pinchot. This meeting was, in effect, one of the first official agenda-setting actions in environmental policy-making.[22] At the end of the conference, the leaders called upon the president to create a National Conservation Commission to develop an inventory of all natural resources. Roosevelt did so, appointing Pinchot as its chairman. By mid-1909, forty-one states had created similar organizations.[23] Pinchot also organized the Conservation Congresses, which included the familiar subjects of forests, soil and water, and eventually expanded to include issues such as the public control of railroads, the regulation of speculation and gambling in foodstuffs, the coordination of governmental agencies, and better rural schools.[24] The Congresses provided an opportunity for debate among federal, state, and local conservation leaders, but were heavily politicized. Bitterness and internal struggles brought an end to the annual events in 1917. Of prime importance to many conservation leaders was what came to be known as the "public land question." The possibilities of virtually unlimited economic growth in the West caused President Theodore Roosevelt to appoint a Public Lands Commission in 1903. While many hoped the commission would promote orderly growth, there was also concern the old practice of disposing nonagricultural lands to private owners would give way to public ownership and management.[25]

The Progressive Era is also noted for the birth of conservation organizations like the National Audubon Society in 1905, the National Parks Association in 1919 (on the heels of the creation of the National Park Service in 1916), and the Izaak Walton League in 1922. Pinchot organized the National Conservation Association in 1909, although the group's primary interests were limited to water power and mineral leasing—an extension of Roosevelt policy. The group disbanded in the 1920s. The Progressive reforms were focused on the term *efficiency*. There was a sense that it was possible to make better use of natural resources. The reformers were not radicals in the traditional political sense, and for the most part, Progressive conservation posed only a modest threat to the existing distribution of power in the United States.[26] As the term *conservation* broadened, it gradually lost its initial meaning. Roosevelt, for example, began to refer to the conservation of human health, and the National Conservation Congress devoted its entire 1912 session to "the conservation of human life." During the 1930s, the environmental movement again became a battle between conservation and preservation. As a result, environmental leaders redoubled their efforts to preserve scenic areas. In 1935, Aldo Leopold founded the Wilderness Society to protect public lands, and the National Wildlife Federation (1936) served as the first of the conservation education organizations, sponsoring National Wildlife Week in schools beginning in 1938. Conservation organizations were also closely allied with the four major engineering societies: the American Society of Civil Engineers, the American Society of Mechanical Engineers, the American Institute of Electrical Engineers, and the American Institute of Mining Engineers, which spearheaded the drive for efficiency. The Great Depression brought the federal government into new areas of responsibility, including environmental policy. Federal conservation interest intensified in the growth of agencies with specific resource responsibilities, beginning with the Tennessee Valley Authority in 1933, the Soil Conservation Service in 1935, and the Civilian Conservation Corps, which from 1933 to 1942 gave two million unemployed young men productive work.

RECREATION AND THE AGE OF ECOLOGY:
POST–WORLD WAR II TO 1969

After World War II, Americans' interest in the environment shifted to a new direction. Concern about the efficient scientific management of resources was replaced with desire to use the land for recreational purposes. Over thirty million Americans toured the national parks in 1950. The parks were, in the words of one observer, "in danger of being loved to death," since roads and services were still at prewar levels.[27] National Park Service Director Conrad Wirth presented Congress with a "wish list" of park needs that came to be known as Mission '66—a ten-year improvement program that would coincide with the fiftieth anniversary of the national park system. That plan served as the blueprint for massive growth in both national parks and recreational areas during the next twenty years.[28] Habitat protection became the focus of groups like the Defenders of Wildlife, founded in 1947 to preserve, enhance, and protect the diversity of wildlife and their habitats. In 1951, The Nature Conservancy began to acquire, through either purchase, gift, or exchange, ecologically significant tracts of land, many of which are habitats for endangered species.

The 1960s brought a battle between those who supported industrial growth and those who worried about the effects of pollution caused by growth. It was a decade when an author's prose or a single event could rouse the public's indignation. It also marked the beginning of legislative initiatives that would be fine-tuned over the next thirty years, and of tremendous growth in environmental organizations.

Two authors brought public attention to environmental problems during this decade. Rachel Carson's book *Silent Spring*[29] and Paul Ehrlich's *The Population Bomb*[30] warned the world of the dangers of pesticides and the exploding population. Several authors served up "doom-and-gloom" predictions of the problems facing the planet, and there was a real spirit of pessimism as to whether or not the environmental situation was hopeless. In January and February 1969, two oil spills five and a half miles off the coast of Santa Barbara, California, seemed to hit a public nerve like never before. Only eight days into his administration, President Richard Nixon was faced with an environmental crisis for which he was totally unprepared. The media captured the essence of the spills with images of birds soaked in gooey, black oil and pristine, white beaches soiled with globs of oil that washed up with each tide.[31]

Legislatively, the 1960s heralded a period of intense activity, as seen in Table 1.1. In a carryover of issues from the postwar period, parks and wilderness areas remained high on the public's, and on the legislature's, agenda. By 1960, the number of national park visitors had grown to seventy-two million, and Congress responded by creating the Land and Water Conservation Fund to add new wilderness areas and national parks. Congress also expanded recreational areas with the passage of the National Wilderness Act in 1964 and the Wild and Scenic Rivers and National Trails Acts in 1968. President Lyndon Johnson, as part of his environmental policy, which he called "the new conservation,"

Table 1.1 Major United States Environmental Legislation, 1947–1992

Year	Air Quality	Water Quality	Pesticides—Toxics	Solid Waste	Land	Other
1947 Truman			Federal Insecticide, Fungicide, and Rodenticide Act			
1956 Eisenhower		Water Pollution Control Act				
1963 Kennedy	Clean Air Act					
1964 Johnson					Land and Water Conservation Fund Act	
1965 Johnson		Water Quality Act				Highway Beautification Act
1966 Johnson						Endangered Species Conservation Act
1967 Johnson	Air Quality Act					
1968 Johnson					National Wild and Scenic River Act/ National Trails System Act	

Year / President				
1969 Nixon				National Environmental Policy Act/ Endangered Species Act Amendments
1970 Nixon	Clean Air Act Amendments	Water Quality Improvement Act	Resources Recovery Act	Environment Education Act
1971 Nixon		Alaska Native Claims Settlement Act		
1972 Nixon	Federal Water Pollution Control Act	Federal Environmental Pesticides Control Act	Coastal Zone Management Act	Marine Protection, Research, and Sanctuaries Act/ Noise Control Act
1973 Nixon				Endangered Species Act
1974 Nixon	Safe Drinking Water Act			

Continued

11

Table 1.1 *Continued*

Year	Air Quality	Water Quality	Pesticides—Toxics	Solid Waste	Land	Other
1976 Ford			Toxic Substances Control Act	Resource Recovery Act/ Solid Waste Act	Federal Land Policy and Management Act/National Forest Management Act	
1977 Carter	Clean Air Act Amendments	Clean Water Act Amendments			Surface Mining Control and Reclamation Act/Soil and Water Conservation Act	
1978 Carter						Public Utility Regulatory Policies Act
1980 Carter			Comprehensive Environmental Response, Compensation, and Liability Act (Superfund)		Alaska National Interest Lands Conservation Act	Fish and Wildlife Conservation Act
1982 Reagan						Nuclear Waste Policy Act
1984 Reagan				Resource Conservation and Recovery Act Amendments		

1985 Reagan					Food Security Act
1986 Reagan	Safe Drinking Water Act	Superfund Amendments			
1987 Reagan	Clean Water Act Amendments				
1988 Reagan			Federal Insecticide, Fungicide, and Rodenticide Act Amendments	Ocean Dumping Act	Nuclear Waste Policy Act Amendments/ Global Climate Protection Act
1990 Bush	Clean Air Act Amendments				
1992 Bush					Energy Policy Act

sought congressional support for urban parks to bring the land closer to the people.[32] Johnson's wife, Lady Bird, also spearheaded the drive to improve the nation's roadways through her highway beautification program and sought congressional support for the 1965 passage of the Highway Beautification Act.[33]

Although there were several legislative precursors during the 1940s and 1950s, many of the hallmark pieces of pollution legislation were enacted during this decade, with the signing of the first Clean Air Act in 1963 (amended as the Air Quality Act in 1967) and the Water Quality Act in 1965. The Endangered Species Conservation Act (1966) marked a return to federal interest in animal and plant habitat that had begun earlier in the century. The National Environmental Policy Act (NEPA), enacted in 1969, served as the foundation for policy initiatives that were to follow throughout the next twenty years.

Political leadership on environmental issues during the 1960s focused on a handful of individuals, and environmental organizations began to grow as well. Senator Edmund Muskie of Maine was among the most visible, but he also became the target of considerable criticism, especially when he became a leading contender for the Democratic presidential nomination. A 1969 report by the Ralph Nader organization gave Muskie credit for his early stewardship in the air pollution battle, but accused the senator of losing interest.[34] Other leaders, like Senator Henry Jackson of Washington (who chaired the Senate Interior and Insular Affairs Committee and was largely responsible for shepherding NEPA through Congress) and Representative John Dingell of Michigan, were primarily involved in the legislative arena. Not only did the number of environmental groups expand during the 1960s, but existing ones experienced tremendous growth. New organizations like the African Wildlife Foundation (1961), the World Wildlife Fund (1961), the Environmental Defense Fund (1967), and the Council on Economic Priorities (1969) broadened the spectrum of group concerns. Meanwhile, the Sierra Club's membership grew tenfold from 1952 to 1969, and the Wilderness Society went from twelve thousand members in 1960 to fifty-four thousand in 1970.[35] But one of the most compelling themes to emerge from the decade of the 1960s was that the federal government must take a more pervasive role in solving what was beginning to be called "the environmental crisis." The limited partnership between the federal government and the states was insufficient to solve what was already being spoken of in global terms.

EARTH DAYS AND DEREGULATION: 1970–1988

In August 1969, Wisconsin Senator Gaylord Nelson was on his way to Berkeley when he read an article in *Ramparts* magazine about the anti–Vietnam War teach-ins that were sweeping the country. Nelson, who was one of few members of Congress who had shown an interest in environmental issues, thought a similar approach might work to raise public awareness about the environment. In September, he proposed the idea during a speech in Seattle, and later that fall incorporated a nonprofit, nonpartisan organization called Environmental Teach-In, pledging $15,000 of his own funds to get it started.[36] In December 1969, he asked former Stanford student body president Denis Hayes to serve as national coordinator for what was to become Earth Day on April 22, 1970. Hayes, who postponed plans to enter Harvard Law School, worked with a $190,000 budget, purchasing a full-page ad in the *New York Times* to announce the teach-in. Not everyone was supportive. President Nixon, who had presented a thirty-seven-point environmental message to Congress a few months earlier, refused to issue a proclamation in support of Earth Day. Instead, the White House issued proclamations for National Archery Week and National Boating Week.[37]

Certainly 1970 marked a watershed year for new environmental organizations, with the founding of the Center for Science in the Public Interest, Citizens for a Better Environment, Environmental Action, Friends of the Earth, the League of Conservation Voters, Natural Resources Defense Council, and Save the Bay. Greenpeace and Public Citizen formed the following year. This period also marks the beginning of a turnaround in leverage as business and industry mobilized to slow the pace of environmental legislation, a topic discussed in Chapter 2. Environmental organizations were no longer able to monopolize the policy debate to serve their own interests. The range of environmental issues had become so extensive that organized environmental groups were unable to act effectively in all areas. Even more important, many issues had become matters not for public debate and legislative action but for administrative choice, an area in which politics was dominated by technical issues that placed a premium on the financial resources necessary to command expertise. This gave considerable political advantage to administrators and private corporate institutions that employed far more technical personnel than did environmentalists.[38]

The American public's attitude about the environment has never been very stable, and the decade of the 1970s is a perfect example. When George Gallup asked respondents in his national survey to identify the most important problem facing the nation in November 1967, the environment did not even make the list, nor did it appear when the question was asked in three surveys in 1968 or one in 1969. The Vietnam War and the economy overshadowed most Americans' lives during that period. Not until May 1970 (after Earth Day) did the topic appear as a concern, when it ranked second and was mentioned by 53 percent of those responding. By June 1970, the subject dropped off the list, replaced in the number one spot by the campus unrest caused by the Vietnam War that was sweeping the nation. Pollution and ecology returned to the list in March 1971 (ranked sixth with only 7 percent naming these as the most important problem) and by June 1971, the topics ranked tenth. Environmental issues reemerged as a topic of concern in August and October 1972 and in March 1973, when the subject ranked sixth. But in May 1973, although pollution was ranked as the fifth most important problem facing the nation, it began to be shadowed by another problem—the energy crisis, which ranked thirteenth. In January 1974, Gallup found the public considered the energy crisis to be its most important problem, named by 46 percent of the public, although by July that ranking dropped to number four, mentioned by 4 percent of those surveyed—a figure that stayed relatively constant throughout the rest of the decade.

President Nixon, who used the signing of the National Environmental Policy Act of 1969 to declare the next ten years as "the environmental decade," initially opposed the initiatives but eventually succumbed to increasing public pressure and instructed his staff to rush through new environmental legislation. With his creation of the Environmental Protection Agency (EPA) by Executive Order in 1970, Nixon moved ahead in the race to see whether the executive or legislative branch could move the most quickly to take advantage of the public's mood.

In the meantime, Congress was firmly on the environmental protection bandwagon, enacting more than twenty major pieces of legislation, many of which were refinements of earlier bills. Others, such as the Marine Mammal Protection Act (1972), the Federal Environmental Pesticides Control Act (1972), the Resource Conservation and Recovery Act (1976) and the Toxic Substances Control Act (1976) brought the federal government into new areas of environmental protection.

As had been the case in the 1960s, unexpected events periodically refocused attention on the environment. The 1973 Arab oil embargo, for example, pushed energy to the top of the policy agenda, although a succession of presidents had sought to make the United States "energy independent." President Jimmy Carter pushed through most of his energy conservation program while turning down the White House thermostat and wearing a sweater indoors. Nuclear power, which was being touted as a cleaner, more reliable alternative to foreign oil, suffered a major setback in 1979 when cooling water at the Three Mile Island nuclear power plant near Harrisburg, Pennsylvania, dipped below safe levels and triggered a meltdown. Although no radioactive fuel escaped and no one was injured, the accident cast a shadow of doubt over the entire nuclear energy program.

During the summer of 1978, media coverage of incidents near the Love Canal in Niagara Falls, New York, reawakened American concerns over toxic waste. The abandoned canal had been used as a dumping ground for waste during the 1940s by the Hooker Chemicals and Plastics Corporation, which filled in the site and sold it to the Niagara Falls Board of Education for $1. A school was built near the site in the midst of a residential area. When local health officials found higher-than-normal rates of birth defects, miscarriages, and other medical problems among Love Canal residents, President Carter ordered the federal government to purchase 240 homes nearest the site, eventually spending more than $30 million in relocation costs.[39]

Similar incidents occurred in 1979 in Kentucky, where seventeen thousand drums of leaking chemicals were discovered, and in 1983 in Times Beach, Missouri, where high levels of dioxin were thought to have contaminated the entire town. The Hudson River was found to be contaminated by more than a million pounds of PCBs (polychlorinated byphrenyls), and wells in the West were filled with cancer-causing carbon tetrachloride trichloroethylene (TCE). The impact of publicity surrounding Love Canal and similar disclosures can be seen in public opinion polls. In July 1978, Resources for the Future (RFF) surveyed Americans' attitude at a time when the inflation rate topped 10 percent and the tiny snail darter had stopped progress on the Tellico Dam. The RFF survey found environmental public support continued to hold firm with the number of people who felt "we are spending too little on environmental protection" increasing despite widespread economic problems.[40]

Just as the 1969 Santa Barbara oil spill had galvanized public opinion, the December 3, 1984, leak of deadly methyl isocyanate gas at a Union Carbide plant in Bhopal, India, reawakened interest in environmental disasters. The leak, which killed more than two thousand and injured two hundred thousand, was brought closer to home when it was revealed an identical Union Carbide plant was located in Institute, West Virginia. The public and governmental outcry resulted in a shutdown of the plant for several months for inspections and safety checks. These events also caused a shifting of legislative gears as interest changed to toxic and hazardous waste and the health impacts of pollution. With congressional enactment of the Resource Conservation and Recovery Act and the Toxic Substances Control Act in the 1970s, the foundation was laid for the Comprehensive Environmental Response, Compensation, and Liability Act ("Superfund") in 1980 (reauthorized in 1986), and the Hazardous and Solid Waste Amendments in 1984. Concerns about health found their way into the Safe Drinking Water Act Amendments of 1986 (an expansion of the 1974 law) and the Federal Insecticide, Fungicide, and Rodenticide Act Amendments of 1988.

But the 1980s brought an increase in the pessimistic attitudes Americans had toward the efforts that had been made in the previous decade. A Cambridge Reports survey from 1983 to 1989 found respondents felt that the overall quality of the environment was worse than it was five years before, with a sharp increase in pessimism beginning in 1987.[41] When the question of "most important problem" was asked again during the 1980s by the Gallup poll, energy often made the list of most important problems, although the environment did not. A separate Gallup survey conducted in September 1989 found 66 percent of the respondents said they were "extremely concerned" about the pollution of sea life and beaches from the dumping of garbage, medical wastes, and chemicals into the ocean, with the same percentage extremely concerned about the pollution of fresh-water rivers, lakes, and other sources of drinking water. Fifty percent of those surveyed said they were extremely concerned about air pollution, and 41 percent expressed concern over the disposal of household garbage and trash.[42]

Yet the 1980s environmental policy agenda was molded most by the administration of President Ronald Reagan, whose main concern was to reduce the amount of governmental regulation, a subject that will be discussed in Chapter 3. Reagan's budget cuts, personnel decisions, and a weakening of the previous decade's legislative efforts had a profound effect on the policy for the next ten years. Despite those changes, public concern over environmental degradation has risen substantially in recent years, commanding support from large majorities. What was less clear at the end of the 1980s was the strength of the public's commitment to environmental protection.[43]

GLOBAL AWARENESS AND THE NEW DEMOCRATS: THE 1990s

After declaring himself "the environmental president" during his 1988 campaign, George Bush was faced with not only the Reagan legacy of environmental slash and burn, but with a host of newly discovered environmental problems and crises as well, many with a global focus. In 1992, the Gallup International Institute's Health of the Planet Survey showed concern about the environment is not limited to wealthy industrialized nations of the Northern Hemisphere. Environmental problems were rated as one of the three most serious problems in half of the twenty-two nations surveyed, and only small percentages of people in any nation dismissed environmental issues as not serious. The survey found air and water pollution are perceived as the most serious environmental problems affecting nations, with the loss of natural resources mentioned most often by residents of other nations.[44]

Two major pieces of legislation enacted during the Bush administration were the Clean Air Act Amendments of 1990 and the 1992 Energy Policy Act, both of which represented a break in the legislative gridlock that characterized Congress under Republican administrations. Environmental organizations, many of which experienced a decline in membership growth after the initial burst of activity in the early 1970s, received a booster shot with Earth Day 1990. The Gallup organization classified about 20 percent of the American public as hardcore environmentalists—those who call themselves strong environmentalists and feel major disruptions are coming if we do not take drastic environmental actions even at the cost of economic growth.[45]

But perhaps the most noteworthy of the trends is the globalization of environmental protection. The Earth Summit refocused the need for environmental issues to be viewed globally, rather than locally. It also provided dramatic evidence of the need for international cooperation to solve the larger issues of global warming, transboundary pollution, biodiversity and the critical question of whether the industrialized world is willing to pay for environmental protection in developing countries. It also spotlighted the North/South split between industrialized and developing nations—a controversy not likely to be resolved by the end of this decade, and an issue discussed further in Part 6 of this book.

The inauguration of Bill Clinton and Al Gore marks yet another turning point in environmental politics. Although the environment never surfaced as a key issue in the 1992 presidential campaign, Clinton administration officials immediately called for peaceful coexistence between environmentalists and business as they prepared their legislative agenda.

Among the most noticeable changes was a sense that environmental policy will be written by the White House, not Congress, as had been the case during the previous twelve years. Clinton initially set the tone by eliminating the Council on Competitiveness and the White House Council on Environmental Quality, which both Bush and Reagan had used to sidestep EPA regulations. Clinton replaced the two bodies with a Council on Environmental Quality, naming Gore protege Kathleen McGinty as its chair. In a proactive move less than a month into his administration, Clinton also endorsed a Senate bill to create the Department of the Environment, elevating the EPA to cabinet-level status. Similar legislation had been introduced each session since 1989, but had never gained sufficient support.

Clinton's promise to accelerate and expand U.S. involvement in global environmental cooperative efforts will be shepherded through Congress by Gore and a new legion of activist members, many of whom ran on environmental platforms. Equally important are changes in Congressional leadership and an enhanced role for Republican moderates whose criticism of the administration's environmental policies was stifled under Bush. Four members in particular, Rep. Norman Y. Mineta, Rep. Gerry E. Studds, Sen. Max Baucus, and Sen. Daniel Patrick Moynihan, will chair committees and are closely allied with the environmental lobby.

Despite the changes in personnel, however, there is also a growing sense that environmental politics—especially during the past fifteen years—has been guided by popular opinion rather than by science. Critics point to sweeping government regulations enacted during the Reagan and Bush administrations to reduce concentrations of toxic compounds in water, air, and land even when there was little scientific evidence of risk to humans. Congress, responding to highly publicized concerns about the dangers of asbestos, radon, and toxic waste dumps, quickly wrote legislation that has ended up costing both the government and business an estimated $140 billion a year. Even William Reilly, the EPA Administrator under Bush, has said that in the past action was "based on responding to the nightly news. What we have had in the United States is environmental agenda-setting by episodic panic."[46]

When the American economy was relatively healthy, few bothered to question the cost/benefit ratio for such expenditures. But with resources growing more and more scarce, and with the federal government placing a new emphasis on domestic problems like health care, education, and the urban infrastructure, this questioning of environmental priorities seems long overdue.

SUMMARY

Historians and political scientists have identified five distinct periods in the development of American environmentalism, although 1970 is often viewed as the apex of the growth of the environmental movement. With the advent of the first Earth Day celebration, there is no doubt media and public attention focused on the environment. A number of crises, from the 1969 Santa Barbara oil spill to the energy crisis of the 1970s, have brought pressure to bear on policymakers who are charged with protecting the environment, and American political history is sprinkled with various legislative successes and failures as a result of those pressures. If there is a recognizable trend in environmental protection, it may be twofold: a fine-tuning of the legislation and a globalization of the issues.

NOTES

1. For a review of the philosophical underpinnings of the movement, see David Pepper, *The Roots of Modern Environmentalism* (London: Croom Helm, 1984).

2. Roderick Nash, *American Environmentalism* 3rd ed. (New York: McGraw-Hill, 1990), xi. Nash has published numerous works on American environmental history, including *The American Conservation Movement* (St. Charles, MO: Forum, 1974); *Wilderness and the American Mind* (New Haven: Yale University Press, 1982); and *The Rights of Nature: A History of Environmental Ethics* (Madison: University of Wisconsin Press, 1988).

3. The colonial period is also covered in David Cushan Coyle, *Conservation* (New Brunswick, NJ: Rutgers University Press, 1957).

4. Nash, *American Environmentalism*, xi.

5. Coyle, *Conservation*, 8–9, 21.

6. George Perkins Marsh, *Man and Nature; or Physical Geography as Modified by Human Action* (New York: Scribner, 1864). See also, David Lowenthal, *George Perkins Marsh: Versatile Vermonter* (New York: Columbia University Press, 1958).

7. Donald Worster, *American Environmentalism: The Formative Period 1860–1915* (New York: Wiley, 1973), 3.

8. One of the historians who has researched the sportsmen's movement is John F. Reiger, *American Sportsmen and the Origins of Conservation* (Norman: University of Oklahoma Press, 1986).

9. Ibid., 53.

10. The biographical materials on these early pioneers provide an excellent background into the formation of the early conservation movement. See, for example, George T. Morgan, Jr., *William B. Greeley, A Practical Forester* (St. Paul: Forest History Society, 1961), and Wallace Stegner, *Beyond the Hundredth Meridian: John Wesley Powell and the Second Coming of the West* (Boston: Houghton Mifflin, 1954).

11. Another one of the major contributors to the field of American environmental history is Joseph Petulla, *Environmental Protection in the United States* (San Francisco: San Francisco Study Center, 1987), 13–30.

12. Suellen Hoy, "Municipal Housekeeping: The Role of Women in Improving Urban Sanitation Practices," in *Pollution and Reform in American Cities 1870–1930*, ed. Martin Melosi (Austin: University of Texas Press, 1980), 173–98. See also the spring 1984 issue of *Environmental Review* for a summary of the contributions of women to the environmental movement.

13. See Harold McCracken, *George Catlin and the Old Frontier* (New York: Dial, 1959), for a biographical perspective on one of the frontier environmentalists.

14. There are two ways to gauge the impact of Thoreau on the development of the environmental movement, especially his sojourn at Walden Pond. One is to read his own words, such as *The Annotated Walden* (New York: Potter, 1970), and *Consciousness in Concord* (Boston: Houghton Mifflin, 1958). There have been numerous attempts to characterize this complex individual, including the following biographers: Milton Meltzer and Walter Harding, *A Thoreau Profile* (New York: Crowell, 1962); Sherman Paul, *The Shores of America: Thoreau's Inward Exploration* (Urbana: University of Illinois Press, 1959); and Robert Richardson, *Henry Thoreau: A Life of the Mind* (Berkeley: University of California Press, 1986).

15. Olmstead's contributions are many, not only his attempts to develop the urban landscape, but scenic preservation as well. Olmstead's accomplishments are chronicled in several biographies, including Albert Fein, *Frederick Law Olmstead and the American Environmental Tradition* (New York: Braziller, 1972); Charles C. McLaughlin, *The Formative Years* (Baltimore: Johns Hopkins University Press, 1977); Elizabeth Stevenson, *Flo: A Biography of Frederick Law Olmstead* (New York: Macmillan, 1977); and Cynthia Zaitzevsky, *Frederick Law Olmstead and the Boston Park System* (Cambridge, MA: Belknap Press, 1982).

16. The urban sanitation issue became one of the cornerstones of urban environmentalism. See George Rosen, *A History of Public Health* (New York: MD Publications, 1958).

17. There are few comprehensive studies of the early organizations, except for those produced by the groups themselves. See, for example, Michael Cohen, *The History of the Sierra Club* 1892–1970 (San Francisco: Sierra Club, 1988).

18. For more information on this early period, see Henry Clepper, *Origins of American Conservation* (New York: Ronald Press, 1966); and Peter Wild, *Pioneer Conservationists of Western America* (Missoula, MT: Mountain Press, 1979).

19. Samuel P. Hays, *Conservation and the Gospel of Efficiency* (Cambridge, MA: Harvard University Press. 1959), 5.

20. Pinchot writes of his efforts in *The Fight for Conservation* (New York: Harcourt Brace, 1910), and *Breaking New Ground* (New York: Harcourt Brace, 1947). Biographers who have identified his critical role in the Progressive movement include Martin Fausold, *Gifford Pinchot, Bull Moose Progressive* (Syracuse: Syracuse University Press, 1961); M. Nelson McGeary, *Gifford Pinchot: Forester-Politician* (Princeton: Princeton University Press, 1960); and Harold T. Pinkett, *Gifford Pinchot: Private and Public Forester* (Urbana: University of Illinois Press, 1970).

21. In contrast to Pinchot, Muir's views are found in his book, *Our National Parks* (Boston: Houghton Mifflin, 1901), and *The Yosemite* (New York: Century, 1912). One of the most widely researched environmental pioneers, Muir is the subject of dozens of biographers, including Michael P. Cohen, *The Pathless Way: John Muir and the American Wilderness* (Madison: University of Wisconsin Press, 1984); Stephen Fox, *John Muir and His Legacy* (Boston: Little, Brown, 1981); Frederick Turner, *Rediscovering America: John Muir in His Time and Ours* (New York: Viking, 1985); and Linnie M. Wolfe, *Son of the Wilderness: The Life of John Muir* (New York: Knopf, 1945).

22. Nash, *American Environmentalism*, 84.

23. Hays, *Conservatism and the Gospel of Efficiency*, 132.

24. The activities of the Conservation Congresses are outlined in Grant McConnell, "The Conservation Movement—Past and Present," *Western Political Quarterly* 7, no. 3 (September 1954): 463–78.

25. Hays, *Conservatism and the Gospel of Efficiency*, 69.

26. Many historians and analysts of the Progressive period have downgraded its importance to contemporary environmentalism. See Geoffrey Wandesforde-Smith, "Moral Outrage and the Progress of Environmental Policy: What Do We Tell the Next

Generation about How to Care for the Earth?" in *Environmental Policy in the 1990s*, ed. Norman J. Vig and Michael E. Kraft (Washington, DC: Congressional Quarterly Press, 1990), 334–35.

27. For a summary of the development of the parks and wilderness areas, see Dyan Zaslowsky and the Wilderness Society, *These American Lands* (New York: Henry Holt, 1986).

28. There is a wealth of historical information on the National Park Service and its programs, including William C. Everhart, *The National Park Service* (New York: Praeger, 1972); Ronald A. Foresta, *America's National Parks and Their Keepers* (Washington, DC: Resources for the Future, 1984); Alfred Runte, *National Parks: The American Experience* (Lincoln: University of Nebraska Press, 1982); David J. Simon, ed., *Our Common Lands* (Washington, DC: Island Press, 1988); and *Investing in Park Futures: A Blueprint for Tomorrow* (Washington, DC: National Parks and Conservation Association, 1988).

29. Rachel Carson, Silent Spring (Greenwich, CN: Fawcett, 1962). For biographical material on the woman who is largely credited with reviving the contemporary environmental movement, see Paul Brooks, *The House of Life: Rachel Carson at Work* (Boston: Houghton Mifflin, 1972); Carol Gartner, *Rachel Carson* (New York: Ungar 1983); H. Patricia Hynes, *The Recurring Silent Spring* (New York: Pergamon Press, 1989); and Philip Sterling, *Sea and Earth: The Life of Rachel Carson* (New York: Crowell, 1970).

30. Paul Ehrlich, *The Population Bomb* (New York: Ballentine, 1968).

31. For an account of this event, see Carol and John Steinhart, *Blowout: A Case Study of the Santa Barbara Oil Spill* (Belmont, CA: Wadsworth, 1972). An extensive bibliography on the spill was compiled by Kay Walstead, *Oil Pollution in the Santa Barbara Channel* (Santa Barbara: University of California, Santa Barbara Library, 1972).

32. Zaslowsky, *These American Lands*, 37.

33. See Lewis L. Gould, *Lady Bird Johnson and the Environment* (Lawrence: University of Kansas Press, 1988).

34. John C. Esposito, *Vanishing Air* (New York: Grossman, 1970), 292.

35. Samuel P. Hays, "From Conservation to Environment," *Environmental Review*, Fall 1982, 37.

36. Jack Lewis, "The Spirit of the First Earth Day," *EPA Journal* 16, no. 1 (January–February 1990): 9–10.

37. See John C. Whitaker, *Striking a Balance: Environment and Natural Resources Policy in the Nixon-Ford Years* (Washington, DC: American Enterprise Institute, 1976), 6.

38. Samuel P. Hays, *Beauty, Health and Permanence: Environmental Policy in the U.S. 1955–1985* (Cambridge, England, 1987), 61.

39. See Lois Gibbs, *Love Canal* (Albany: State University of New York Press, 1983); and Adeline Gordon Levine, *Love Canal: Science, Politics and People* (Lexington, MA: Heath, 1982).

40. Robert Cameron Mitchell, "The Public Speaks Again: A New Environmental Survey," *Resources* 60 (September–October 1978): 2.

41. David Rapp, "Special Report," *Congressional Quarterly*, January 20, 1990, 138.

42. "Household Waste Threatening Environment; Recycling Helps Ease Disposal Problem," *Gallup Report #280*, January 1990, 30–34.

43. See Riley E. Dunlap, "Public Opinion in the 1980s: Clear Consensus, Ambiguous Commitment," *Environment* 33, no. 8 (October 1991): 9–15, 32–37.

44. Press release, "Environment Given Priority Over Economic Growth in Both Rich and Poor Nations," Washington, DC, George H. Gallup International Institute, May 4, 1992. See also Riley E. Dunlap, George H. Gallup Jr., and Alec M. Gallup, *The*

Health of the Planet Survey (Washington, DC: George H. Gallup International Institute, May 1992).

45. George Gallup, Jr., and Frank Newport, "Americans Strongly in Tune with the Purpose of Earth Day 1990," *The Gallup Poll Monthly*, April 1990, 6.

46. Keith Schneider, "New View Calls Environmental Policy Misguided," *The New York Times*, March 21, 1993, 1.

FOR FURTHER READING

Riley E. Dunlap and Angela G. Mertig, eds. *American Environmentalism: The U.S. Environmental Movement 1970–1990*. Washington, DC: Taylor and Francis, 1992.

Samuel P. Hays. *Beauty, Health and Permanence: Environmental Politics in the US 1955–1985*. Cambridge, England: Cambridge University Press, 1987.

Samuel P. Hays. *Conservation and the Gospel of Efficiency*. Cambridge, MA: Harvard University Press, 1959.

Michael J. Lacey, ed. *Government and Environmental Politics: Essays on Historical Developments since World War II*. Washington, DC: Woodrow Wilson Center Press, 1991.

Roderick Nash. *American Environmentalism*, 3rd ed. New York: McGraw-Hill, 1990.

Robert C. Pahlke. *Environmentalism and the Future of Progressive Politics*. New Haven: Yale University Press, 1989.

David Pepper. *The Roots of Modern Environmentalism*. London: Croom Helm, 1984.

Joseph M. Petulla. *Environmental Protection in the United States*. San Francisco: San Francisco Study Center, 1987.

CHAPTER 2

Participants in the Environmental Debate

> Our goal is to destroy, to eradicate the environmental movement.
> —Ron Arnold, author, the *Wise Use Agenda*
>
> [Wise use] is the dark side of conservation, environmentalism's evil force.
> —*National Parks Magazine*[1]

There are various approaches to studying the policy process outlined in the preface, but one theory that appears to be especially applicable to environmental politics is group theory. Adherents to this approach believe that political decisions are the result of the struggles among competing interests who have access to the political process. Key to understanding group theory is the acceptance that some groups will have more access than others, whether due to superior financial resources, leadership, organization, or public support for their cause.[2]

Although this book does not attempt to delve into the theoretical debate over *how much* influence various groups have in the making of environmental policy or to apply the pluralist tradition of American politics to other countries to explain their environmental politics, it does describe their *role* in the political debate.[3] This chapter attempts to identify the key groups on both sides of the political debate in the United States and to provide an overview of international environmental parties and movements. It touches briefly on the groups' strategies, successes, and failures, and it provides a summary of their participation in the policymaking process.

ENVIRONMENTAL ORGANIZATIONS

In the one hundred years since the founding of the first American environmental associations, there has been a gradual evolution of the movement. Seven of the ten most powerful groups (known collectively as the "Group of Ten") were founded before 1960. Most have influential local or regional chapters and have broadened their interests from land and wildlife issues to broader "second-generation" issues that are not necessarily site or species specific.[4]

These mainstream organizations, identified in Table 2.1, have as a common strategy an emphasis on lobbying, although their specific focus often varies. The Sierra Club, the Wilderness Society, and the National Parks and Conservation Association, for example, have tended to emphasize the preservation of public lands for future generations, while groups such as the National Wildlife Federation and the Izaak Walton League, with a large percentage of sports enthusiasts and hunters within their constituency, are more involved with habitat preservation for wildlife.

When the Environmental Defense Fund (EDF) was founded in 1967, a new breed of organization joined these mainstream groups. EDF and later the Natural Resources Defense Council made environmental litigation an art form, moving group strategy from the legislative to the judicial arena. These groups have benefited from the citizen suit provisions in virtually every federal environmental statute since the 1970 Clean Air Act. The provisions allow "any person" to sue private parties for noncompliance with the law, and to sue not only for injunctive relief but also for civil penalties. This allows them to recover the cost of attorneys' fees and "mitigation fees" in lieu of, or in addition to, civil fines. The groups often receive from offending companies direct transfer payments, which help fund their operations and projects, making litigation an attractive group strategy.[5]

Other mainstream groups, although smaller in size and resources, conduct research or grass-roots campaigns. Two of the most prominent are Environmental Action and the League of Conservation Voters. Founded in 1970, Environ-

Table 2.1   Major U.S. Environmental Organizations

Group	Founded	Membership
Sierra Club	1892	540,000
National Audubon Society	1905	550,000
National Parks and Conservation Association	1919	200,000
Izaak Walton League	1922	53,000
Wilderness Society	1935	360,000
National Wildlife Federation	1936	5,800,000
Environmental Defense Fund	1967	150,000
Friends of the Earth*	1970	50,000
National Resources Defense Council	1970	170,000
Greenpeace (worldwide)	1971	4,000,000

* Friends of the Earth merged with the Environmental Policy Institute and the Oceanic Society.

Source: John Seredich, *Your Resource Guide to Environmental Organizations* (Irvine, CA: Smiling Dolphins Press, 1991), and data from individual organizations.

mental Action, which merged with the Environmental Task Force in 1988, has a membership of twenty thousand whose purpose is lobbying, research, education, and organizing. The group developed a "Dirty Dozen" campaign to spotlight the environmental records of members of Congress and has actively lobbied against utility companies and for bottle deposit legislation. Also founded in 1970, the League of Conservation Voters has two goals: to help elect pro-environment candidates and to monitor congressional performance. It is not the group's twenty-five thousand members that give it clout, but its annual report, the *National Environmental Scorecard*, which ranks the voting records of each member of Congress on environmental legislation. The league has also started a program to publicize what it calls "Greenscam," defined as members of Congress who portray themselves as environmentalists but consistently vote against antipollution bills.

Some environmental organizations are characterized by their emphasis on a single issue, as seen in the next three examples. These types of groups rarely shift from their area of concern to another issue, although with our understanding of cross-media pollution, some overlap is beginning to take place. With nearly a half-million members, Clean Water Action's main focus is on drinking water and groundwater resources. Founded in 1971, the organization also conducts research on toxic chemicals and waste sites. Recognizing the interrelatedness of pollution, Clean Water Action also became involved in the passage of the 1986 Superfund legislation and the 1990 Clean Air Act amendments. The Defenders of Wildlife work, as their group's name implies, to protect wildlife habitats through education and advocacy programs. Founded in 1947, the group is now working to strengthen the Endangered Species Act and funding for wildlife refuges. With a grass-roots membership of eighty thousand members, the Defenders of Wildlife has actively lobbied Congress to enact legislation protecting the grizzly bear, wolves, bald eagles, and mountain lions. The one hundred thousand members of the National Toxics Campaign, founded in 1984, have a broad issue agenda aimed at preventing pesticide pollution and reducing toxic waste. Their Consumer Pesticide Project, for example, is attempting to prohibit use of chemicals suspected of being carcinogenic that are used in food production, and urges the United States to stop selling pesticides banned in the United States to Third World countries. They also operate a Citizens' Environmental Laboratory at Boston University to provide low-cost testing for communities at risk from toxic contamination.

Among the more recently created environmental organizations are those seeking to preserve individual species, often with a purely regional base of operation. Many of these groups were organized in the 1980s after the initial burst of momentum in the environmental movement had passed. Although these groups limit their activities to individual species, they often form coalitions to preserve natural habitats and wildlife ranges. Their membership is typically smaller (ten thousand to forty thousand) and may include researchers dedicated to scientific study of the specie. Typical of such groups are Bat Conservation International, founded in 1982, and the Mountain Lion Preservation Foundation, founded in 1986. Both of these organizations emphasize education as well as research and habitat studies. The Mountain Lion Preservation Foundation, for example, has developed an aggressive media campaign in California to educate the public on the habitat needs of this animal, as well as working toward a permanent state ban on the hunting of the mountain lion, also known as the cougar, puma, and panther.

Property-oriented groups, like the Nature Conservancy and Ducks Unlimited, represent examples of two long-lived organizations that focus their efforts on management and preservation. Both groups have invested private funds in the purchase of lands that are set aside for wildlife habitats. One of the older environmental groups, Ducks Unlimited, was founded in 1937 by hunters seeking to preserve wetland habitats. The group has chapters throughout the United States. The Nature Conservancy was founded in 1951 and now has more than six hundred thousand members. Its accomplishments include the preservation of more than five million acres in fifty states plus global ecological preserves that are home to endangered species.

The international environmental movement is made up of two types of groups: Those that originated in the United States, have members throughout the world and have broadened their interests to more globalized concerns, and indigenous nongovernmental organizations. The largest international environmental organization, Greenpeace, now has over four million members worldwide. Founded in 1969 as the Don't Make a Wave Committee by a small group of Sierra Club members and peace activists, Greenpeace drew its name from a rented boat it used to protest nuclear weapons testing in the Aleutian Islands.[6] Its initial efforts were the Save the Whales campaign, later expanded to other sea animals such as the Steller sea lion and the dolphin, both of which are in conflict with commercial fishery interests. Since then, Greenpeace has extended its concerns to issues ranging from the use of chlorine bleach during paper processing, nuclear disarmament and weapons testing, toxic pollution, and nuclear power to drift nets and Antarctic protection. Regional offices throughout the world have more localized agendas.[7] Greenpeace activities have often bordered on the radical, as was the case in 1989 when a Greenpeace ship protested a Trident missile test and was rammed by a U.S. Navy vessel. The group is known, too, for its ability to use the media to its advantage, as it does when its activists are pictured in small boats placing themselves between whales and whaling ships.

Another large international organization, the World Wildlife Fund, has affiliate groups on five continents, sponsoring more than fourteen hundred conservation projects in one hundred countries. Many of the group's efforts focus on the protection and rescue of endangered species, such as the African elephant, Asian snow leopard, Bengal tiger, and peregrine falcon. It is perhaps best known for its research projects and resource management programs, including panda research and habitat protection at the Woolong Reserve in China and gorilla conservation in Rwanda.

One other type of group is also a participant in the environmental debate—radical environmentalists, many of whom shun the group label altogether. "A movement, not an organization," is how the members of Earth First! characterize themselves. Radical environmental organizations shun traditional organizational structure and administrative rules, preferring militant action termed "monkeywrenching," "ecotage," and "ecodefense." Dave Foreman, who co-founded Earth First! in 1980 with five others, has been called a terrorist by other environmental leaders, and there is no doubt the organization's tactics fit the label.[8] The group is best known for "spiking," the practice of putting large metal spikes in trees about to be cut by timber workers. The tactic poses a threat to workers when the spikes come into contact with saws either in the forest or at the mill. Foreman and other group members were arrested in 1989 for conspiring to sabotage three nuclear power facilities in Arizona, California, and Colorado, although he has now disavowed spiking and says he wants to work more with mainstream groups. Four members received prison terms in 1991 but Foreman pled guilty to conspiracy in a plea bargain that delayed his sentencing for five years. Other group members have blocked logging roads and threatened to sabotage utility power lines in forested areas.[9]

Although Earth First! is the most well known of the radical groups, there have been other flare-ups of radical environmental activity throughout the United States. During the 1970s, an individual calling himself "The Fox" targeted polluting industries in the Chicago area. The Billboard Bandits in Michigan and Bolt Weevils in Minnesota also operated sporadically in their regions. Another major radical group is the Sea Shepherd Conservation Society, founded by former Greenpeace director Paul Watson in 1977. The group has called itself "an independent policing body" whose purpose is to protect sea mammals and birds.[10] Watson, who was adopted into the Sioux nation after the 1973 Wounded Knee incident in South Dakota, has placed his body in front of whaler harpoons and seal hunters with the saying "We don't talk about problems; we act, we do, and we succeed."[11]

Those who have studied radical environmental organizations believe there are several factors that distinguish them from mainstream groups:

1. There is an emphasis on confronting problems through direct action, including breaking the law.
2. The main point of radical protests is the preservation of biological diversity.
3. Most radicals act on their own without direction from an organizational hierarchy.
4. Most radical environmentalists are destitute by choice.
5. These individuals usually have minimal hope they will be successful.[12]

Radical groups are driven by what has been termed *deep ecology*, a form of ecological consciousness founded on the idea man is no more important than any other species. Deep ecology has two philosophical underpinnings: self-realization and ecocentrism.[13] For the most part, radical groups are shunned by virtually all other environmental organizations, which often feel the movement's efforts are hampered by their emphasis on violence. But mainstream groups also use the radicals as a foil, realizing the posturing and activities of such groups cause their own agendas to be perceived as much more reasonable and acceptable.

Environmental organizations have periodically attempted to put aside their individual interests and have formed coalitions in an attempt to advance their collective interests. In 1946, the Natural Resources Council of America (NRCA) was formed to bring together conservation organizations, and the umbrella currently shields more than seventy groups, which are included by invitation only. The NRCA is primarily an information-sharing body, sponsoring policy briefings and surveys of public opinion on issues such as energy needs and conservation. Coalitions have also been formed to lobby specific pieces of legislation, such as the U.S. Forest Service 1978–79 wilderness designation, RARE II (Roadless Area Review and Evaluation), and the National Clean Air Coalition, which came together to fight for the 1977 and 1990 Clean Air Act amendments. Groups have also joined together to protest what they perceive as a lack of administrative leadership. For example, in 1981, several groups, led by the National Wildlife Federation, called upon President Reagan to fire Interior Secretary James Watt over his public land policies. More recently, informal coalitions have been formed, such as the Group of Ten (Environmental Defense Fund, Environmental Policy Institute, Friends of the Earth—the EPI and Friends of the Earth have now merged, Izaak Walton League, National Audubon Society, National Parks and Conservation Association, National Wildlife Federation, Natural Resources Defense Council, Sierra Club, and Wilderness Society). Consensus reports are becoming more commonplace, such as the 1985 publication of *An Environmental Agenda for the Future*[14] and *Blueprint for the Environment*,[15] which was prepared to assist the Bush administration in developing environmental policy. Such reports also give groups the appearance of more clout, since legislators perceive them as presenting a unified front.

With the flurry of environmental group activity in the late 1960s and early 1970s, the membership of the organizations grew enormously. When energy replaced the environment as a key issue during the Carter administration, the groups' direct-mail campaigns generally yielded just enough members to replace those who failed to renew. But two of Reagan's appointees, Secretary of the Interior James Watt and Environmental Protection Agency Administrator Anne Burford, were perceived as a threat to the movement, which resulted in a surge in membership as environmental organizations warned potential members of what might happen if they did not have the funds to closely monitor Reagan administration policies. The Wilderness Society's membership grew by 144 percent between 1980 and 1983, with the Sierra Club increasing by 90 percent and the Defenders of Wildlife and Friends of the Earth by 40 percent each. Another surge took place at the turn of the decade, when the national environmental lobby's U.S. membership exceeded three million.[16]

There have been two major criticisms relating to the membership of the environmental movement. One complaint is the movement's size has been grossly exaggerated and actually represents a small percentage of Americans. A second criticism is that the movement's leadership has failed to include members of ethnic and disadvantaged groups. Such criticisms appear to have been warranted. A study by Resources for the Future found that while support for environmental issues was strong, only 8 percent of those surveyed said they were members of a local or national environmental organization. The survey also found membership was drawn disproportionately from those who were from college-educated, higher-income segments of society. The survey showed 27 percent of those in the sample with incomes of $30,000 or more were members of an environmental group, more than six times the percentage of low-income persons who were members.[17] Other surveys have found environmentalists, when compared to the larger population, are considerably better educated, more likely to have white-collar jobs, and more likely to have high incomes.[18] Other critics argue the environmental movement has been largely based in the West, and does not represent the opinions and beliefs of the majority of Americans. They point to the fact the Sierra Club did not open its first chapter outside California until 1950—over fifty years after its founding.[19]

The second criticism—that people of color are noticeably absent from mainstream groups—is part of a perception by minority leaders that environmentalists do not share the same interests of the disadvantaged community. Those complaints were publicized in 1990 when two small but aggressive groups, the Gulf Coast Tenant Leadership Development Project in New Orleans and the Southwest Organizing Project in Albuquerque charged the country's biggest environmental groups with racism. One survey of African American leaders gave higher priority to issues like health care, jobs, and education, especially in urban areas.[20] As a result, most minority participation has been in localized grass-roots organizations like Mothers of East Los Angeles, Native Americans for a Clean Environment, Toxic Avengers of Brooklyn, and West Harlem Environmental Action.

Minority participation has been tied to what is often called the environmental justice movement, which focuses on the disproportionate environmental burden borne by disadvantaged neighborhoods, a topic discussed in more detail in Chapter 4. As a result, environmental organizations have often emerged from established social action groups, which have a broader base of interests. The efforts to forge such an alliance resulted in the First National People of Color Environmental Leadership Summit in October 1991, which drew delegates from every state and representatives of the mainstream environmental movement as well.[21]

It is important to note, however, that the same criticism could just as easily be made of the business/industry groups that have opposed the environmental movement. They, too, are made up of elites and wealthier interests than is true of the population as a whole, and could hardly be called representative of the American public. What is significant about environmental organizations generally, though, is what some observers call a "great schism" between grass-roots activists and the leadership of the large mainstream groups. Part of that perceived split is due to style. Where the national organizations like the Sierra Club and the National Wildlife Federation pay their executive officers high salaries and run massive fund-raising operations, most groups are strictly volunteer based and funded on minimal membership dues. A deeper conflict among the groups may be the substance of their interests. The Association of Sierra Club Members for Environmental Ethics, founded by dissident members in 1991, has accused the Sierra Club of compromising its principles in order to get legislation through Congress. Others have criticized groups like the National Audubon Society for bringing officials from industry onto their boards of directors.[22] While the disputes may not be enough to cause a real rift among groups, they are symptomatic of the fragmentation in the environmental movement that keeps it from speaking as one voice in the political arena.

ENVIRONMENTAL OPPOSITION IN THE UNITED STATES

The Progressive ideals of the conservation movement had almost universal support throughout the early twentieth century, although the early groups were still dominated by business organizations that were much more influential in the political arena. As the goals of the movement began to expand from conservation to environmentalism in the late 1960s and early 1970s, so too did the potential impact on business and industry, which had never really felt threatened before. The development of an organized environmental opposition involved three interests: farmers and ranchers, organized labor, and industry, and has recently coalesced in the "wise-use" movement.

The initial concern of farmers and ranchers was the tremendous influx of city dwellers who sought the tranquility of rural life after World War II. "Recreationists," as they were called, brought tourist dollars to rural economies badly in need of them, but they also brought with them litter, congestion, and noise. Urban visitors seldom paid much attention to property lines, and major battles developed over public access along the California coastline and through inland wetlands. Farmers who were used to controlling predators on their private property were suddenly facing raptor protection programs and angry wildlife enthusiasts who sought preservation of wolves and coyotes. Agricultural land use also came under fire, as environmentalists sought to legislate farm practices relating to pesticide use, soils, and irrigation. As development, including oil pipelines and utility transmission lines, began to intrude onto rural areas, farmers felt even more threatened. The two issues that have most galvanized farmers have been proposals to restrict the use of agricultural pesticides and herbicides and agricultural use of water, described in Chapter 7. In the case of pesticide use, rural interests have formed a coalition with chemical companies and their associations, bringing together members of the American Farm Bureau Federation and the National Agricultural Chemical Association, along with the National Association of State Departments of Agriculture, the Association of American Plant Food, Pesticide and Feed Control Officers, the National Association of County Agents, and the Christmas Tree Growers Association.[23] But the land-use issue has become even more controversial as a result of the Sagebrush Rebellion and the development of the wise-use movement, a topic discussed later in this chapter.

There are a number of environmental issues that have impacted workers, who have often been forced to take sides in the policy debate. On the one hand, organized labor has traditionally supported attempts to make for a safer workplace and working conditions. Most labor unions have also supported programs that involve occupational health issues, such as exposure to airborne particulates and toxic chemicals. The United Steelworkers of America, for example, have been longtime supporters of clean air legislation, an environmental problem caused to some extent by their industry.[24] Farmworkers in California have been active participants in federal pesticide legislation, and cotton dust exposure led the Amalgamated Clothing and Textile Workers Union to lobby the Occupational Safety and Health Administration to develop rules to protect workers in textile mills.

But at the same time, labor has often opposed pollution control efforts (and more recently, implementation of the Endangered Species Act) that affect job security. The United Auto Workers have consistently supported environmental regulations except when they affect the auto industry. The fear of loss of jobs due to environmental regulations has permeated many regions of the United States, often when the real reason for job loss is technological change and innovation. Environmentalists working within the energy industry unions have repeatedly argued that energy conservation has no negative impact on jobs, and is in fact beneficial to workers, a message that appears to be getting through.[25] It appears labor and environmental groups are forging an alliance on several issues, which may lessen labor's traditional role in opposition to policy initiatives, primarily workplace safety and indoor air quality.[26]

There is one primary segment of industry that has resisted environmental regulations and policies that threaten its bottom line—firms extracting natural resources like oil, gas, uranium, and timber, plus electric utilities, chemical manufacturers, and textile companies. But at the same time, industry leaders recognize they (and their employees and their families) breathe the same polluted air and face toxic contamination as does the rest of America. Industry's role has been described as "marked not by agreement on values but by tactics of containment, by a working philosophy of maximum feasible resistance and minimum feasible retreat."[27]

Businesses were initially slow to recognize the potential impact of the environmental movement on their operations, characterizing the activities of most groups as no more than a fad. But officials within the pulp and paper industry began in the late 1950s to understand how desires for more recreation land would likely mean a call for reduction in logging activities. Eventually, other industry leaders became alarmed at the rapid pace of environmental legislation, which accelerated during the late 1960s and into the 1970s. They countered by forming trade associations and nonprofit research groups to further their aims, pouring millions of dollars into education and public relations. The American Forest Institute, for example, was specifically created to justify the need for increased, rather than reduced, timber production. The oil industry has been especially hard hit as the environmental movement has gained more clout. In 1989, for example, the five top oil producers spent $3 billion in special charges—equal to 36 percent of their total profits—to pay for environmental problems. Mobil Oil Corporation spent $650,000 in 1990 to defeat a local election effort that would have banned the use of hydrogen fluoride at one of its refineries, and in Highlands, Texas, a state court ordered Exxon Corporation and a dump operator to pay nearly $1 million for putting hazardous waste in an unapproved dump site near the homes of three local residents.[28]

Today, industries affected by environmental regulations rely upon a threefold approach in their opposition to environmental groups. One, there is a continuation of the public relations campaigns that began in the early 1960s to paint industry with an environmental brush. Chevron Oil, for example, has run advertisements in national publications promoting its "People Do" projects to protect the habitat of endangered species in order to counter the public backlash that results after every oil spill, and Dow Chemical Company's efforts include sponsorship of the 1990 Earth Day activities in the company's hometown of Midland, Michigan.[29]

Two, virtually every sector of the economy relies upon a stable of federal and state lobbyists to review legislation that could potentially impact its operations. Southern California Edison, one of the nation's largest publicly owned utilities, hired Leon Billings, an influential former aide to Senator Edmund Muskie, to press its cause in Washington, and has other lobbyists monitoring the state capitol in Sacramento. Companies and trade associations also employ their own scientists, economists, and policy experts to refute the claims made by environmental groups. In March 1988, for example, the Business Roundtable, an industry coalition, produced its own economic analysis of the impact of proposed Clean Air Act amendments.[30]

Three, once programs reach the implementation stage, most industry interests regroup to press their case through the administrative maze. Since many of the implementation decisions are made by low-level administrators, or in a less public arena than Congress, industry has been much more successful in molding programs at this phase of the policy process. Typical of this strategy has been development of standards for assessing the risk of various substances. EPA rule development has frequently been hampered by companies that argued that information about various products and processes constituted trade secrets or were proprietary.

But perhaps the biggest change in industry's role in opposing environmental legislation is that these efforts have now shifted toward industry taking a proactive rather than reactive stance. During debate on the 1990 Clean Air Act Amendments, utility lobbyists brought with them to Washington dozens of amendments designed to reduce the cost of compliance with proposed acid rain legislation. The Clean Air Working Group, the major industry coalition, actively fought each amendment proposed by environmental groups.[31] Particular praise has been given to the chemical industry, which for years was accused of intransigence. Political leaders give the industry's lobbyists credit for drafting its own legislation rather than just opposing what was on the table. Monsanto Company's Charles Malloch told fellow industry representatives that such initiative was imperative at the rule-making phase of the Clean Air Act. "Anyone sitting on their hands waiting for the regs to come out is way behind the eightball."[32]

One reason why industry is taking a more activist role is the tremendous increase in environmental issues finding their way onto the ballot. From the early 1970s to 1986, citizens confirmed eighteen environmental measures placed on the ballot for popular approval. Yet in the single election of November 1988, American voters approved at least seventeen environmentally related propositions, including measures dealing with recycling, water quality, natural resources, and funding for environmental programs.[33] Faced with another round of ballot measures in November 1990, industry coalitions were up against their biggest fight in California with Proposition 128, known as "Big Green." A group of oil and chemical firms spent more than $6 million to oppose the measure, which would have banned pesticides, prohibited new offshore drilling, stopped the cutting of virgin redwood forests, and mandated major reductions in carbon dioxide emissions from utility plants. The voters defeated the ballot initiative nearly two to one.[34] Both the lumber industry and chemical industries decided to fight back by gathering signatures for their own ballot measures, the Global Warming and Clear-Cutting Reduction, Wildlife Protection and Reforestation Act of 1990, and the Consumer Pesticide Enforcement Act, termed by environmentalists as "Big Stump" and "Big Brown," respectively. Such measures are being called "trojan horse initiatives" because they are perceived as disarming the initiative process, one of the most effective tools for environmental protection in California.[35] Subsequent elections have seen the defeat of recycling and nuclear power measures in Oregon, growth control initiatives in Washington State, stream protection laws in Missouri, and environmental bond issues in New York.[36]

Several industry strategists have attempted to work more closely with environmental groups, leading to charges some organizations have been captured by Big Business. Companies like Apple Computer and Hewlett-Packard were heavily criticized when they donated equipment for Earth Day 1990, as did Shaklee, the first official sponsor with its $50,000 donation. Businesses have made major financial contributions to organizations that previously would never even speak to them.[37] Environmental organizations have also extended their hands in peace as well. In 1983, the National Wildlife Federation proposed the creation of a Corporate Conservation Council of invited companies, which would each contribute $15,000 in support of an effort toward meaningful dialogue. Intended as a way of ending the angry confrontational relationship between business and environmentalists, the group includes among its corporate members Pennzoil Company, Weyerhauser, Dow Chemical, Exxon, and Consolidated Edison.[38] While it is unlikely the two sides' interests will ever coalesce completely, there is a growing sense that business, at least, has more to gain from cooperation than from confrontation. For companies continually under the regulatory hammer, such cooperative efforts may become the rule rather than the exception.

In 1988, a different type of environmental opposition surfaced as an outgrowth of a meeting of 250 groups at the Multiple Use Strategy Conference sponsored by the Center for Defense of Free Enterprise. One of the group's leaders, Ron Arnold, coined the phrase "wise use" in describing twenty-five goals to reform the country's environmental policies, including opening up national parks and wilderness areas to mineral exploration, expanding visitor facilities in the parks, and restricting application of the Endangered Species Act. Today, the wise use movement is a loosely organized coalition of hundreds of groups led by three umbrella organizations: the Alliance for America, the National Inholders Association, and the Western States Public Lands Coalition. The groups share a deep antigovernment feeling and opposition to efforts by environmentalists to close off use of federal lands. Their efforts are supported by legal assistance from the Mountain States Legal Foundation, agricultural groups, and oil, timber, and mining companies. Although there are similarities between the wise use movement and the Sagebrush Rebellion, one difference between the two is that the current efforts are marked by efforts to broaden the base of support beyond purely western issues.

The annual September "Fly in for Freedom" lobbying effort in Washington, DC, brings in representatives from a diverse range of groups who are urged to wear work clothes with special attention to gloves, boots, hard hats, and bandannas. In addition to cattlemen opposing higher grazing fees, the grass-roots efforts tap into gulf shrimpers opposing the use of turtle-excluding devices, Alaskans seeking oil drilling, and private property owners from eastern states battling the National Park Service. What seems to bother environmentalists most is the fact the wise use movement's leaders are using the same tactics they themselves have used successfully for more than two decades. They appear to be well organized, well funded, and ready to even out the political seesaw that has characterized the policy process thus far.[39]

INTERNATIONAL ENVIRONMENTAL PARTIES AND MOVEMENTS

While this chapter has thus far reviewed the environmental movement in the United States, environmental politics in other parts of the world is less a "movement" and more dependent upon the activities of nongovernmental organizations (NGOs). The term is used to describe all organizations that are neither governmental nor for profit, and may include groups ranging from rural people's leagues and tribal unions to private relief associations, irrigation user groups, and local development associations.[40] NGOs can be classified as grass-roots organizations (membership oriented, often in developing nations), service NGOs (supporting the development of grass-roots groups), or policy specific (environment, human rights, family planning).[41] One characteristic the groups have in common is they are much more parochial—concerned almost exclusively about environmental issues in their region. Only a handful have begun to address the global issues of concern to many of the mainstream organizations in the United States, such as global warming and stratospheric ozone depletion. Cultural differences are the major factor behind the variations in the formation of environmental interest groups from one nation to another. In democratic nations, the pluralist system legitimizes interest group membership. But what are acceptable tactics in one nation may be considered unacceptable or even criminal in others. Why, for example, are there few groups demanding better air quality in Mexico, despite the capital city's pollution problems? One study of Mexican political beliefs and values concluded that Mexicans generally do not relate easily to abstract or impersonal organizations but only to the individual who leads the movement. Mexicans' *personalismo* makes it difficult to start and sustain groups that lack such high-profile figures.[42]

Similarly, interest groups are not a part of the political culture of France, but are a key element of political life in Sweden, which also has the advantage of a small population and open lines of communication for environmental messages. With the exception of the Green Parties of Europe, most environmental organizations have minimal popular support and virtually no financial base. Their protests often become heard only when they are picked up by the American press or when their cause is taken up by U.S. groups like Greenpeace. In nondemocratic countries such as China, the government has cracked down on Western influences altogether, making it difficult for groups like the World Wildlife Fund to have much of an impact, leaving little room for environmental groups, domestic or foreign.[43]

Still, NGOs are growing in both number and influence, particularly in developing nations. Unlike their counterparts in Northern Hemisphere countries, NGOs in the south perform somewhat different functions. They often fill a vacuum left by ineffective or nonexistent government programs, or extend the reach of resource-poor national governments. They may also forge links with NGOs whose issues are decidedly nonenvironmental, such as the networking that is beginning to occur with human rights and economic development NGOs. They also tend to be new; only about 30 percent of all development NGOs in the south are more than fifteen years old, and only 50 percent are more than ten. Lastly, NGOs in developing countries may serve as an independent voice for public participation, either in opposition to a government program or by placing pressures on government to create new programs.[44]

Unlike the environmental movement in the United States, which has failed to capture (or be captured by) one of the two major political parties, nearly twenty Green Parties exist worldwide, as seen in Table 2.2. Although they vary considerably in strength and impact on their respective political systems, they are growing in membership and in the percentage of the electorate they represent.

The first Green Party was the United Tasmania Group, which contested the April 21, 1972, local elections in the Tasmanian region of Australia. Although the party was unsuccessful in the ten elections it contested prior to its dissolution in 1976, it was instrumental in placing the environment at the top of the Australian political agenda.[45] A month later, New Zealand's Values party was formed, based on a concern about the nation's rapid urbanization and a campaign to save Manapouri Lake from a hydroelectric project. The party also drew support from those who protested French nuclear weapons testing in the Pacific and felt the National and Labour parties were not attentive to environmental issues. The party's name was changed in 1986 to the Values, Green Party of Aotearoa.[46]

The major wave of Green party activity has been in Europe, primarily because the structure of European political systems allows political parties, even small ones, a major role in policy-making. During the 1970s, one of the first to

Table 2.2 Green Political Parties

Nation	Political Party	Year Founded
Australia	United Tasmania Group	1972
	Nuclear Disarmament Party	1984
	Rainbow Alliance	1988
Austria	Die Grune Alternative	1982
Belgium	Agalev	1982
	Ecolo	1980
Canada	Green Party of Canada	1984
Denmark	DeGronne	1983
Finland	Vihrea Liitto	1987
France	Les Verts	1982
	Generation Ecologie	1990
Germany	Die Grunen	1980
Ireland	Comhaontas Glas	1981
Italy	Federazione delle Liste Verdi	1986
Luxembourg	Die Greng Alternativ	1983
Mexico	Partido Ecologista de Mexico	1984
Netherlands	De Groenen	1983
New Zealand	Values, Green Party of Aotearoa	1972
Sweden	Miljopartiet de Grona	1981
Switzerland	Le Parti Ecologiste/De Grune Partei	1983
United Kingdom	People/Green Party	1973
United States	Green Party USA	1984

form was in Germany, where a loose coalition of groups, the Bund Burgerini-tiativen Umweltschutz (BBU) organized massive demonstrations opposing nu-clear energy but had little political power. Since the German political structure discriminates against groups that receive less than 5 percent of the vote, the Greens formed an electoral alliance and have seen considerable success, forming the country's fourth political party, Die Grunen, in 1980.[47] East Germany formed its own Green Party in late 1989 just prior to reunification. Its members were critical of the growing emphasis on material goods, but what made the party unique in environmental circles was its support of nuclear power, in large part due to a lack of energy alternatives.[48] Despite the diverse character of its membership, by 1983 the German Greens had entered both state and federal parliaments. Their current support level is still well below that of the 1980s, even though they managed to receive about 6 percent of voter support in the 1991 elections.[49]

There are several characteristics common to the Green party movements. First, their successes thus far seem to be limited to getting their members elected at the local and regional levels, and they have not been nationally successful. One of Europe's strongest Green parties, Les Verts of France, is typical of this phenomenon. France's electoral system, which works against small political groups, may make large-scale electoral achievement virtually impossible. Even so, Rene Dumont ran as an ecological candidate for president in 1974, long before the Green party became active, and captured enough media attention to serve as an encouragement for the formation of a political party six years later.[50] In 1989, the Verts captured nearly 11 percent of the national vote for seats in the European Parliament, and a second Green party, Generation Ecologie, has overtaken the Verts and is expected to do well in municipal elections.[51] Second, countries using a system of majority voting often preclude electoral success. Even though the British Green party polled nearly 15 percent of the vote in the 1989 European elections, the Greens were shut out of the European Parliament because Britain does not use proportional representation.[52] The Swedish Greens must pass a 4 percent vote hurdle to win parliamentary seats in national elections.

Third, even in those countries with proportional representation, some Green parties have had little success, as in Norway and in Denmark. Instead of seeking elected office, some parties prefer to affect legislation. In the Nether-lands, the Christian Democratic party has successfully won public support for its green policies, including a twenty-year National Environmental Plan, which includes taxing gasoline and levies on polluting industries.[53] Several other na-tions, including Greece, Canada, Iceland, Mexico, Norway, Portugal, and Spain, have attempted to form Green parties, although none has been firmly enough established to make an electoral challenge.[54]

Despite the prevalence of Green parties throughout Western Europe, a broad spectrum of interest groups and other organizations have formed. One of the oldest environmental movements outside the United States took place in Britain, beginning with the founding of the Commons, Open Spaces and Footpaths

Preservation Society in 1865. Many of Britain's groups have been local or regional, emphasizing aesthetics and later, what was called the "open air movement." England's Great Depression of 1880 brought with it a spirit of pessimism and disillusionment with progress, which resulted in a call for the preservation of monuments and relics.[55] The British environmental movement has also been tied to business cycles; it has been strongest toward the end of periods of sustained economic expansion. With greater economic prosperity, people shift their interest from immediate material needs to the nonmaterial aspects of their lives. As a result, economic advances in the late 1960s and early 1970s led to a tremendous growth spurt in the membership of existing nature groups and an expansion in new groups, paralleling activity in the United States during that same period. For example, from 1968 to 1972, the membership of the Society for the Promotion of Nature Conservation grew from 35,000 to 75,000 and the membership of the Royal Society for the Protection of Birds increased from 41,000 to 108,000.[56] One unique aspect of Britain's environmental movement is the fact that its leadership has come largely from the landed aristocracy, including members of the royal family like Prince Charles. Today, nearly three million Britons are members of environmental groups.[57]

The first Italian environmental groups were also nature lovers' associations, followed by local and national action groups. Italia Nostra, founded in 1955 to preserve the nation's historical, artistic and natural heritage, was followed by Pro Natura Italica in 1959, dedicated to endangered species (and renamed Federnatura). But the largest nature group is the Italian branch of the World Wildlife Fund, which has more than sixty thousand members throughout Italy.[58] The leftist movement of the 1960s and the antinuclear protests of the late 1970s led to the founding of the League for the Environment in 1980. The group focuses on hunting, nuclear power, agrochemicals, and urban and marine pollution. It sponsors Green Train in cooperation with the Italian railway system to monitor atmospheric pollution and Green Schooner, which targets marine pollution. Greenpeace has also recently established an Italian affiliate, as has Friends of the Earth, which is affiliated with the Radical party.[59]

During the 1970s, other Western European nations formed traditional environmental groups, such as Luxembourg's Organization for the Protection of Birds and Nature, and Natura, which acted as an umbrella organization for local groups. Luxembourg also hosts a small antinuclear power movement and the Mouvement Ecologique, a youth group.[60] Most of the other European groups are localized with few members, such as Greece's Ecological Initiative, and Portugal's Grupo de Estudos de Ordenamento Terratorio e Ambienta (Study Group for the Planning of Land and Environment) and Liga Para a Porteccao de Natureza (League for the Protection of Nature). Officials estimate fifteen thousand Portuguese belong to nearly three hundred locally based organizations. Nature conservancy has been the theme of the more than three hundred groups organized in Spain since the Spanish Association for Planning of Land and Environment was founded in 1970.[61]

Despite some of the worst pollution and environmental problems in the world, the environment has been neglected as a political issue in most of the nations of Eastern Europe. Most groups have been informal and disorganized, although they have become increasingly active in Poland and the Baltic states. With political freedom has come popular demands the government attend to the massive pollution problems facing the region. The fledgling environmental movement was strong enough in Hungary to force the government to cancel its participation in a massive hydropower project with Czechoslovakia.[62] Another local group forced the closure of a bauxite mine that caused damage to a lake near Heviz.[63] In Bulgaria, the formation of a small group called Ecoglasnost is the beginning of a fledgling protest movement as old barriers begin to fall. The group has concentrated its efforts on limiting hydroengineering projects within the country, such as the diversion of the Mesta River, which is projected to destroy lands designated as biosphere reserve. Ecoglasnost has also researched contamination of the Black Sea and has campaigned against a pharmaceutical plant in a Sofia suburb that emits noxious fumes over nearby housing, schools, and a cancer hospital.[64]

A mass environmental movement in the republics of the former Soviet Union is only beginning to emerge, as evidenced by the recent founding of a Russian division of Greenpeace. But most of the groups are independent and have not yet begun to form coalitions on key issues.[65] There are five major groups that have formed during the past five years, the largest of which is the Social-Ecological Union (SEU), an umbrella group with two hundred branches, mostly in the Russian Republic. In 1988, the Ecological Union broke off from the SEU seeking more limited change. The Ecological Foundation seeks to set up a trust fund with payments from polluters that would pay for toxic waste cleanup and research into alternative energy, while the Ecological Society of the Soviet Union is associated with an extreme Russian nationalist group. Prior to the August 1991 coup attempt, the All-Union Movement of Greens was supported by the Communist youth organization Komsomol.[66] Another feature of Soviet environmentalism is that many leaders of the popular political fronts started their careers as leaders of the environmental movement. The movement has become, in one sense, a political training group.[67] Funding for environmental initiatives and networking assistance comes from the Association for the Support of Ecological Initiatives, a support group established in 1989 by the Soviet Foundation for Social Inventions.[68]

In Asia, environmental organizations are contrasted between those operating in industrialized regions like Japan and Hong Kong, and those of the developing states. Throughout the vast continent of Asia, the majority of environmental organizations have formed to protest logging and deforestation. In India, massive destruction of forest resources prior to independence in 1947 has been called "the most complex system of resource extraction which any European empire ever established in the developing world."[69] One of the first Indian environmental groups, Dasohli Gram Swarajya Mandal, began a logging public awareness campaign in 1964 that led to the Chipko Andalan movement. Chipko, which means "to cling to," is literally India's tree huggers, Himalayan Indians who have launched protests over logging. The country is losing 1.3 million hectares of forest every year, and the "social forestry" programs launched during the 1970s have failed to halt massive deforestation, a topic outlined in more detail in Chapter 14.[70] Indian environmentalists have fast developed political clout over the issue of proposed dams and hydroelectric projects, which are estimated to disrupt the lives of 1.2 million people and would flood archaeological sites. In September 1989, party officials brought the foreign press and Bombay film stars to Harsud, one of the towns scheduled to be submerged by one dam, picking up tremendous media coverage.[71] One of the largest grassroots NGOs in the region is the Bangladesh Rural Advancement Committee, which started as a relief agency and has now expanded its concerns to help its members organize and obtain bank credit.

One of the few native groups to organize in Asia, the Penan people of Sarawak, Malaysia, have loosely formed protest groups to protest timber practices in that region. The ten thousand members of the nomadic tribe have joined with the Kenyaks and Kelabits to stage antilogging demonstrations, and most have been arrested and jailed because their activities have taken place on private lands. Other resistance has come from organizations outside Malaysia, like the Japan Tropical Forest Action Network, the National Wildlife Federation, and Greenpeace.[72] But such external group pressures have recently come under fire from the Malaysian government, which arrested eight Europeans in 1991 who entered Sarawak posing as tourists. They were charged with distributing antilogging literature and trespass after chaining themselves to log barges and cranes. The Malaysian prime minister urged the demonstrators to pressure their own Western governments to pay more for tropical timber so the country would need fewer trees to maintain its current level of earnings. But there is no doubt the government wants Western environmentalists to stay out of Malaysia.[73] Beginning in the 1980s, Indonesian politics saw the emergence of nongovernmental organizations that have been heavily regulated by the government. The NGOs have nevertheless attracted attention for their efforts to litigate on behalf of residents seeking compensation for pollution. They have also formed a loose association for about four hundred smaller environmental groups, the Indonesian Environmental Forum.[74]

The issues of developed countries in Asia are quite different. Considered an "eco-outlaw" because of its continued policy of support for whaling and timber imports (and its recently amended policy on driftnets), Japanese culture places a unique burden on environmental organizations, which have difficulty in becoming established. There is a strong link between government and industry, both of which see economic growth as their primary goal, and an unwillingness of the courts to check the power of the administration. As a result, economic interests have generally prevailed over the efforts of environmental groups seeking tighter regulatory control. Neither the media nor academia has played much of a role in the development of environmental policy, much of which was enacted after World War II. There are three types of interest groups concerned about environmental issues in Japan today: traditional pressure groups with a limited interest in environmental issues, conservation groups emphasizing wildlife and habitat protection, and ad hoc militant groups focused on injury compensation or anti-development.[75] There is also some Western influence from groups like the Sierra Club and Friends of the Earth, but it is minimal.[76] The Japanese coordinator of Greenpeace estimates the group's membership at only about three hundred, and since donations are not tax deductible under Japanese law, the organization is dependent upon its Amsterdam headquarters for its budget. To the Japanese, grass-roots activism is largely unknown.[77] Some observers predict, however, that the next five to ten years could represent a major transition period for Japanese environmentalism due to the weakening of the ruling party and its link to industry, and the growing international awareness of environmental policy. Japan's leadership role at the Earth Summit is indicative of this new trend.

As one of the most polluted and heavily populated nations in the world, Taiwan's growing grass-roots movement has been compared to Japan in the late 1960s and early 1970s. The movement is primarily made up of middle-class Taiwanese, although it has also gained the support of the intelligentsia. Most of the opposition has been focused on oil-refining facilities at Houchin, although in 1984 protestors sacked the offices of the San Huang Pesticide Company and have protested pollution traced to Du Pont and the Lee Chang Yung Chemical Company.[78] One of the most recent developments in the environmental movement in Taiwan has been demonstrations against the Taiwan Power Company's plans to build its first nuclear power plants since 1981. Nuclear power currently provides nearly 40 percent of the nation's energy needs, but protestors have accused the company of criminal malpractice and disregarding safety and environmental concerns.[79]

Somewhat surprisingly, Hong Kong, although one of the most industrialized nations in Asia, has only a limited number of environmental groups, including local branches of Friends of the Earth and the World Wildlife Fund. Their efforts, along with local organizations like the Conservancy Association and Green Power, have led to increased environmental awareness throughout the territory, especially in schools. But overall, there has been no widespread mobilization of public opinion on issues of territorywide importance. The region's political and economic future seems to preoccupy the minds of Hong Kong residents.[80] What makes the situation even more surprising is nearly a quarter of Hong Kong's residents breathe polluted air, and the Ho Chung River is referred to by locals as the "black river" because of pollution caused by bleaching and dyeing factories.[81]

Despite the magnitude of its environmental problems, virtually nothing is known about environmental movements in China, if they do, in fact, exist at all. Although Western researchers have identified environmental statutes, little is known about how they came about and what their impact has been, due to the "unpredictable" nature of the Chinese legal system. Environmental protest appears to be almost unknown.[82] Thus, it is not possible to characterize the involvement of China's NGOs in environmental protection as most like those of developing or industrialized nations, although it is unlikely that there are sufficient organizations to characterize China as having an "environmental movement" at all.

Prior to the mid-1960s, the Catholic Church and other NGOs in Latin America coalesced around the issues of charitable work and relief efforts, but that emphasis shifted in the late 1960s to one of social justice. Priests and nuns actively recruited their parishioners to form grass-roots NGOs, which worked with poor people to improve their quality of life. As the countries became more democratized in the 1980s, other types of NGOs, including a few devoted to the environment, began to form. Environmental NGOs in Latin America are limited by three factors: elitism, secrecy, and authoritarianism. Interest groups have historically been very weak, and most nations lack any institutionalized channels for citizen participation—essential for the growth of an indigenous environmental movement. Policy decisions are usually made by whatever private interests have captured the area, and in most Latin American nations, these interests are timber and landowners. The few environmental groups in Latin America that do exist have coalesced around the issue of tropical forest deforestation, especially in Brazil, as will be discussed in Chapter 14. Most of the protests, however, have been spearheaded by nonnative groups like the World Rainforest Movement. There are exceptions, however. A group of Brazilian scientists and industrialists have joined together to promote the Floram project (*florestas pasa o ambiente*—forests for the environment), the planting of ten billion trees.[83] Two Brazilian researchers, Jose Goldemberg and Jose Lutzenberger, have become outspoken environmentalists and work closely with Western organizations.[84] The one nation in Latin America where environmentalism has become more politicized is Mexico. The Party of the Democratic Revolution, a left of center group, has become identified with environmental issues and has defeated the ruling Institutional Revolutionary party in Mexico City, the world's largest and one of the smoggiest cities.[85]

Environmental activity has been slow to evolve in Africa and the Middle East, the exception being organizations founded for wildlife preservation. As is the case in Asia and Latin America, some groups are beginning to protest logging and hydroelectric projects. In Botswana, for example, the Kalahari Conservation Society has joined with Greenpeace in opposing the creation of new reservoirs and dredging of the Boro River. The primary issue, however, involves the activities of the Debswana Diamond Mining Company, a joint partnership between the government of Botswana and the DeBeers Diamond Company. Conservationists question whether the new water sources are really needed by the native population or if they are an attempt by the mining company to expand its operations further in the environmentally sensitive region.[86] An emerging issue, which will be discussed in more depth in Chapter 5, is the dumping of nuclear and industrial wastes from richer nations into poor African states. But the issue has been politicized not by Africans themselves, but by representatives of the Green party in the European Parliament.[87] One of the few groups that has formed is Kenya's Green Belt movement, founded in 1977 to raise environmental awareness and encourage soil protection. Led by Wangari Maathai, an individual becomes a member simply by planting a tree. The movement hopes to encourage women to start tree nurseries as an income-producing activity.[88] But critics of the government's environmental policy, like Maathai, believe that the government discourages groups like Green Belt from forming. In her words, "African governments . . . have not yet accepted the fact that people can direct their own destiny. They want to guide them and they want to be followed blindly. They do not want their people informed or organized because organized groups threaten their position."[89] Most of the continent is like Ethiopia, where the Peasant Associations (PAs) established after the 1975 revolution are the only associational groups allowed. The PAs are responsible for local efforts to preserve the land and its natural resources, but for the most part, implementation of such programs has been slow, at best.[90] As a whole, however, the NGOs of Africa are among the most fragile in the world, often dependent upon the resources of Northern Hemisphere groups for survival.

The Persian Gulf War highlighted the environmental problems facing the Middle East, which is almost devoid of internally based environmental organizations. Although groups like Greenpeace have attempted to organize throughout the region, they have been, for the most part, unsuccessful. There has been little development of an "environmental consciousness" and a lack of the kinds of pollution problems facing most developing nations has allowed governments the luxury of focusing on economic growth instead. The one regional exception is Israel. In 1953, the Society for the Protection of Nature in Israel was founded, and the nature conservation movement preceded any other organized environmental activity by twenty years. With more than forty-five thousand members, five hundred employees, and a $10 million annual budget, the society has been successful in designating more than three hundred nature reserves throughout Israel.[91] But like most of the rest of the continent, environmental groups are just beginning to form, and cannot begin to match the number or scope of those in the United States or Europe. They also are largely dependent upon outside assistance, both in terms of funding and organizational structure, rather than internal support for their efforts.

Studies of NGOs indicate they are evolving in three directions: The southern NGOs are seeking greater autonomy from those in the north; they are forming international networks and coalitions to keep abreast of issues; and they are performing new roles in legal defense and policy research. The first trend appears to be the most critical as Southern Hemisphere NGOs seek to distance themselves from their dependence upon their northern partners. Long dependent for financial support from their northern donors, these groups now seek the transfer of the technical expertise they need to gain independence. They hope to set their own environmental protection agendas rather than have the terms of their activities dictated by outside sources they perceive to be less familiar with local problems. Technological advances like facsimile machines and computer-linked networks have allowed groups to coordinate their efforts on a global scale, and they have steadily increased their presence in the diplomatic world as well. NGOs held a parallel conference at both the 1972 and 1992 United Nations environmental meetings, and several organizations were accredited by the UN to participate in the preparatory meetings leading up to the Earth Summit. Although these trends indicate that NGOs are growing in both numbers and importance, their influence on global environmental protection is still limited by a lack of stable funding sources and political sophistication.[92]

SUMMARY

The debate over how best to protect the environment has involved a wide spectrum of environmental organizations, from mainstream groups that operate out of Washington, DC, and utilize traditional interest group strategies like lobbying, to organizations focused on a single issue and radical groups. Although attempts have been made to form coalitions, the environmental movement remains fragmented. While these groups support an enhanced governmental role in environmental protection, the United States has also experienced waves of environmental opposition, most notably in the late 1960s and early 1970s, led by industries facing government regulation of their business practices. As a result, industry has more recently taken a proactive approach to legislation, and some efforts at cooperation with environmental organizations are beginning to take place. On an international level, the debate over protection focuses on the Green parties, which began to develop in the 1970s and which have become most visible in Europe. Although other nongovernmental organizations have also formed, they are not nearly as organized or as large as their American counterparts and are often dependent upon U.S. financial assistance for their survival.

NOTES

1. Richard M. Stapleton, "Greed vs. Green," *National Parks* 66, nos. 11–12 (November–December 1992): 32.

2. For more on group theory, see David Truman, *The Governmental Process* (New York: Knopf, 1951); Earl Latham, *The Group Basis of Politics* (New York: Octagon Books, 1965), and Jeffrey M. Berry, *The Interest Group Society*, 2nd ed. (Boston: Little, Brown, 1989).

3. For another view of the role of groups, see Michael S. Greve and Fred L. Smith, Jr., eds., *Environmental Politics: Public Costs, Private Rewards* (New York: Praeger, 1992).

4. Riley E. Dunlap and Angela G. Mertig, "The Evolution of the U.S. Environmental Movement from 1970 to 1990: An Overview," in *American Environmentalism: The U.S. Environmental Movement 1970–1990*, ed. Riley E. Dunlap

and Angela G. Mertig, (Washington, DC: Taylor and Francis, 1992), 14.

5. See Michael S. Greve, "Private Enforcement, Private Rewards: How Environmental Suits Became an Entitlement Program," in *Environmental Politics: Public Costs, Private Rewards*, ed. Michael S. Greve and Fred L. Smith, Jr. (New York: Praeger, 1992), 105–109.

6. Rik Scarce, *Eco-Warriors: Understanding the Radical Environmental Movement* (Chicago: Noble Press, 1990), 47.

7. See Robert Hunter, *Warriors of the Rainbow: A Chronicle of the Greenpeace Movement* (New York: Holt, Rinehart and Winston, 1979).

8. Foreman outlines his involvement in his book *Confessions of an Eco-Warrior*. New York: Harmony Books, 1991.

9. Douglas S. Looney, "Protector or Provocateur?" *Sports Illustrated*, May 27, 1991, 54–57.

10. See Paul Watson, *Sea Shepherd* (New York: Norton, 1982).

11. John Seredich, *Your Resource Guide to Environmental Organizations* (Irvine, CA: Smiling Dolphins Press, 1991).

12. Scarce, *Eco-Warriors*, 4–7.

13. See Bill Devall and George Sessions, *Deep Ecology* (Salt Lake City: Gibbs Smith, 1985).

14. Robert Cahn, ed., *An Environmental Agenda for the Future* (Washington, DC: Island Press, 1985).

15. T. Allan Comp, ed., *Blueprint for the Future: A Plan for Federal Action* (Salt Lake City: Howe Brothers, 1989).

16. Robert Cameron Mitchell, Angela G. Mertig, and Riley E. Dunlap, "Twenty Years of Environmental Mobilization: Trends among National Environmental Organizations," in *American Environmentalism: The U.S. Environmental Movement 1970–1990*, eds. Riley E. Dunlap and Angela G. Mertig (Washington, DC: Taylor and Francis, 1992), 15; Robert Cameron Mitchell, "Public Opinion and the Green Lobby: Poised for the 1990s?" in *Environmental Policy in the 1990s*, eds. Norman J. Vig and Michael E. Kraft, (Washington, DC: Congressional Quarterly Press, 1990), 90–91.

17. Robert Cameron Mitchell, "The Public Speaks Again: A New Environmental Survey," *Resources* 60 (September–November 1978): 4.

18. Craig R. Humphrey and Frederick H. Buttel, *Environment, Energy and Society* (Belmont, CA: Wadsworth, 1982).

19. Stephen Fox, *The American Conservation Movement* (Madison: University of Wisconsin Press, 1985), 279.

20. See John M. Ostheimer and Leonard G. Ritt, *Environment, Energy, and Black Americans* (Beverly Hills, CA: Sage, 1976). See also Hawley Truax, "Beyond White Environmentalism: Minorities and the Environment," *Environmental Action* 21 (1990): 19–30.

21. See Robert D. Bullard and Beverly H. Wright, "The Quest for Environmental Equity: Mobilizing the African-American Community for Social Change," in *American Environmentalism: The U.S. Environmental Movement 1970–1990*, ed. Riley E. Dunlap and Angela G. Mertig (Washington, DC: Taylor and Francis, 1992), 39–49; Marcia Coyle, "When Movements Coalesce," *National Law Journal*, September 21, 1992, S-10; and Donald Snow, *Inside the Environmental Movement* (Washington, DC: Island Press, 1992).

22. See Sharon Begley and Patricia King, "The War among the Greens," *Newsweek*, May 4, 1992, 78.

23. Samuel P. Hays, *Beauty, Health and Permanence: Environmental Politics in the United States 1955–1985* (Cambridge: Cambridge University Press, 1987), 295.

24. See United Steelworkers of America, *Poison in Our Air* (Washington, DC: United Steelworkers of America, 1969).

25. See Frederick H. Buttel, Charles C. Geisler and Irving W. Wiswall, eds., *Labor and the Environment* (Westport, CT: Greenwood Press, 1984), 1–2.

26. For a discussion of these changes, see John Heritage, "Labor's Stake in Steel Cleanup," *EPA Journal*, March, 1979, 32–33; Rebecca Logan and Dorothy Nelkin, "Labor and Nuclear Power," *Environment* 22, no. 2 (March 1980): 6–13, 34; and Alan S. Miller, "Towards an Environment/Labor Coalition," *Environment* 22, no. 5 (June 1980): 3–39.

27. Hays, *Beauty, Health and Permanence*, 308.

28. Mark Ivey, "The Oil Industry Races to Refine Its Image," *Business Week*, April 23, 1990, 98.

29. See Art Kleiner, "The Three Faces of Dow," *Garbage*, July–August 1991, 52–58.

30. D. Kirk Davidson, "Straws in the Wind: The Nature of Corporate Commitment to Environmental Issues," in *The Corporation, Ethics and the Environment*, ed. W. Mitchell Hoffman (New York: Quorum Books, 1990).

31. The battle among the groups is outlined in George Hager, "For Industry and Opponents, a Showdown Is in the Air," *Environment '90* (Washington, DC: Congressional Quarterly Press, 1990), 10.

32. Bryan Lee, "Washington Report," *Journal of the Air and Waste Management Association* 41, no. 8 (August 1991): 1022.

33. John Mark Johnson, "Citizens Initiate Ballot Measures," *Environment* 32, no. 7 (September 1990): 4–5, 43–45.

34. Several authors have analyzed the initiative, one of the most highly publicized in U.S. electoral history. See Bradley Johnson, "Big Business Attacks Big Green," *Advertising Age* 61 (October 22, 1990): 4; "Black Day for California's 'Big Green,'" *New Scientist*, November 17, 1990, 20; Richard Lacayo, "No Lack of Initiatives," *Time*, September 3, 1990, 52; and Elizabeth Schaefer, "A Daunting Proposition," *Nature* 347 (September 27, 1990): 323.

35. Seth Zuckerman, "Flying False Colors," *Sierra* 75, no. 5 (September–October 1990): 20–24.

36. See Richard Lacayo, "Green Ballots vs. Greenbacks," *Time*, November 19, 1990, 44.

37. Eve Pell, "Buying In," *Mother Jones*, April–May 1990, 23–27.

38. For a summary of the proposal, see "Wildlife's 'Corporate Detente,'" *Environmental Forum* 1, no. 10 (February 1983): 41–43.

39. For different views of the movement, see Roberta Ulrich, "Multiple Use Groups Alarm 'Green' Forces," *The Oregonian*, December 6, 1992, A-1, and Stapleton, "Greed vs. Green," 32–37.

40. See Lester D. Brown, *Understanding World Organizations: Guidelines for Donors* (Washington, DC: World Bank, Country Economics Department, 1989).

41. Robert Livernash, "The Growing Influence of NGOs in the Developing World," *Environment* 34, no. 5 (June 1992): 12–20, 41–43.

42. Cynthia Enloe, *The Politics of Pollution in a Comparative Perspective* (New York: David McKay, 1975): 54.

43. For a review of this phenomenon, see Lester Ross, *Environmental Policy in China* (Bloomington: University of Indiana Press, 1988).

44. Livernash, "Growing Influence of NGOs," 12–13.

45. Sara Parkin, *Green Parties: An International Guide* (London: Heretic Books, 1989), 80.

46. Parkin, *Green Parties*, 267.

47. Konrad von Moltke, "The Greens of Europe: A New Environmentalism," *EPA Journal* 16, no. 1 (January–February 1990): 46–47. See also E. Gene Frankland, "Parliamentary Politics and the Development of the Green Party in West Germany," *The*

Review of Politics 51, no. 3 (Summer 1989): 386–412, and Thomas Poguntke, "Unconventional Participation in Party Politics: The Experience of the German Greens," *Political Studies* 40, no. 2 (June 1992): 239–54.

48. Steven Dickman, "Grappling with a Dirty Past," *Nature* 342, December 7, 1989, 606.

49. See Wolfgang Rudig, "Green Party Politics around the World," *Environment* 33, no. 8 (October 1991): 7–9, 25–31.

50. Diana Johnstone, "Europe's Green Light," *The Progressive* 53 (July 1989): 12. See also John McCormick, *The Global Environmental Movement* (London: Belhaven Press, 1989).

51. "Going Green," *The Economist*, February 29, 1992, 52.

52. Wolfgang Rudig, "Green Politics in Britain," *Environment* 33, no. 8 (October 1991): 27.

53. "Dutch Voters Land Lubbers Back in Power on Strength of Green Ticket," *New Scientist*, September 16, 1989, 24.

54. Parkin, *Green Parties*, 234–248. This volume is one of the most complete references on the Green party movements internationally, especially its coverage of emerging parties. The American counterpart is the Green Party USA, which was originally formed in 1984 as the Green Committees of Correspondence. Like the European Greens, their efforts have been focused at the local level rather than national politics, and have secured ballot access as major parties in a handful of states.

55. Philip Lowe and Jane Goyder, *Environmental Groups in Politics* (London: George Allen and Unwin, 1983), 20.

56. David Vogel, "Environmental Policy in Europe and Japan," in *Environmental Policy in the 1990s*, eds. Norman J. Vig and Michael E. Kraft (Washington, DC: Congressional Quarterly Press, 1990), 262.

57. McCormick, *Global Environmental Movement*, viii.

58. Angela Liberatore and Rudolf Lewanski, "The Evolution of Italian Environmental Policy," *Environment* 32, no. 5 (June 1990): 14.

59. Liberatore and Lewanski, "Evolution of Italian Environmental Policy," 14.

60. Parkin, *Green Parties*, 169–170.

61. Ibid., 241, 246.

62. Debora MacKenzie, "The Green Wave Heads East," *New Scientist*, June 16, 1990, 2.

63. See "Pyrrhic Victory," *The Economist*, May 27, 1989, 73.

64. See Vera Rich, "Bulgaria on a Learning Curve," *Nature* 342 (November 9, 1989); 108, and Denise Searle and Mike Power, "Bulgarian Authorities Close the Door on Green Activists," *New Scientist*, September 16, 1989, 25.

65. Alexi Yablokov, "A Perspective from Another Country: The Soviet Task," *EPA Journal* 16, no. 1 (January–February 1990): 50–52.

66. "The Poisoned Giant Wakes Up," *The Economist*, November 4, 1989, 23–26.

67. "Environmentalism in the Soviet Union," *Environment* 32, no. 2 (March 1990): 5–9, 26–30.

68. "Ecological Initiatives in the USSR," *Environment* 31, no. 6 (July–August 1989): 21.

69. Richard P. Tucker, "The Depletion of India's Forests under British Imperialism," in *The Ends of the Earth*, ed. Donald Worster, (Cambridge: Cambridge University Press, 1988), 140.

70. See James Clad, "Greens Find Voice: Environmental Lobby Campaigns against Dams," *Far Eastern Economic Review*, October 19, 1989, 25; and Douglas Stevens, "The Forest and the Trees," *Commonweal* 115 (October 7, 1988): 526–30.

71. Clad, "Greens Find Voice," 24.

72. For an explanation of the issues, see Michael Cross, "Logging Agreement Fails to Protect Sarawak," *New Scientist*, December 1, 1990, 23.

73. Suhaini Aznam, "Timber and Tribes," *Far Eastern Economic Review*, August 1, 1991, 19–20.

74. Robert Cribb, "The Politics of Pollution Control in Indonesia," *Asian Survey* 30, no. 12 (December 1990): 1123–35.

75. Brendan F. D. Barrett and Riki Therivel, *Environmental Policy and Impact Assessment in Japan* (London: Routledge, 1991), 8–9.

76. See Richard Forrest, "Japan: The Dependent Eco-Outlaw," *New Perspectives Quarterly* (Fall 1990): 68; and Paul Blustein, "Environmental Excess Wrapped with a Ribbon," *Washington Post Weekly*, May 6, 1991, 22.

77. Richard Read, "Greenpeace Pioneers Struggle to Get Japan's Attention," *The Oregonian*, May 19, 1991, A-9. See also Michael Cross, "Japan Nods Its Head towards the Environment," *New Scientist*, September 16, 1989, 24.

78. Jonathan Moore, "Protests in this Green and Poisoned Land," *Far Eastern Economic Review*, February 25, 1989, 45.

79. See Carl Goldstein, "Nuclear Qualms," *Far Eastern Economic Review*, July 4, 1991, 39–40.

80. See Peter Hills and William Barron, "Hong Kong: Can the Dragon Clean Its Nest?" *Environment* 32, no. 8 (October 1990): 17–45.

81. Emily Lau, "A License to Pollute," *Far Eastern Economic Review*, May 10, 1990, 23.

82. The compilation of statutes was prepared by Lester Ross and Mitchell A. Silk, *Environmental Law and Policy in the People's Republic of China* (New York: Quorum Books, 1987). For a further discussion of environmental issues in China, see Bernhard Glaeser, *Learning from China? Development and Environment in Third World Countries* (London: George Allen and Unwin, 1987).

83. Brian Homewood, "Brazilians Launch Plan to Bring Back the Trees," *New Scientist*, September 6, 1990, 32.

84. Fred Pearce, "Saviours of the Amazon," *New Scientist*, October 6, 1990, 62.

85. See "Smog City," *The Economist*, May 18, 1991, 50.

86. See Sue Armstrong, "Botswana's Water Plan Hits the Rocks," *New Scientist*, January 19, 1991, 23.

87. Debora MacKenzie and James Mpinga, "Africa Wages War on Dumpers of Poisonous Waste," *New Scientist*, June 23, 1988, 30–31.

88. A profile of the African leader is presented in Daphne Topouzis, "Wangari Maathai: Empowering the Grassroots," *Africa Report* 35, no. 5 (November–December 1990): 30–32.

89. Topouzis, "Wangari Maathai," 31.

90. See John Campbell, "Land of Peasants: The Dilemma Confronting Ethiopian Resource Conservation," *African Affairs* 90, no. 358 (January 1991): 5–21.

91. Uri Marinav and Shoshana Gabbay, "Israel," in *International Public Policy Sourcebook* ed. Fredric N. Bolotin, (New York: Greenwood Press, 1989), 257–73.

92. See also William B. Wood, George B. Demko, and Phyllis Mofson, "Ecopolitics in the Global Greenhouse," *Environment* 31, no. 7 (September 1989): 12–17, 32–34.

FOR FURTHER READING

Robert D. Bullard. *Confronting Environmental Racism*. Boston: South End Press, 1993.
Bill Devall and George Sessions. *Deep Ecology*. Salt Lake City: Gibbs Smith, 1985.
John McCormick. *Reclaiming Paradise: The Global Environmental Movement*. Bloomington: Indiana University Press, 1989.

Sara Parkin. *Green Parties: An International Guide*. London: Heretic Books, 1989.

Rik Scarce. *Eco-Warriors: Understanding the Radical Environmental Movement*. Chicago: Noble Press, 1990.

James A. Tober. *Wildlife and the Public Interest*. New York: Praeger, 1989.

Leslie McSpadden Wenner. *Energy and Environmental Interest Groups*. New York: Greenwood Press, 1990.

CHAPTER 3

The Political Process

Once you've seen one redwood, you've seen them all.
—Ronald Reagan, 1976[1]

Environmentalists cheered the election of Bill Clinton and Al Gore in 1992, believing that "the new Democrats" would bring to Washington a renewed interest in environmental issues that had been absent for the previous twelve years. With the appointment of Carol Browner as administrator of the Environmental Protection Agency, Bruce Babbitt as secretary of the interior, and Hazel O'Leary as secretary of energy, Clinton made clear his campaign pledge to bring those with a commitment to environmental protection into his administration. The politics of environmental deregulation and budget and staff cuts, which were a hallmark of the Reagan and Bush administrations, may be in for a dramatic turnaround.

This chapter identifies the institutions and actors (more commonly referred to as "official policymakers") who possess the legal authority to engage in the formation of environmental policy. Some, such as members of Congress or state legislators, have primary policymaking authority that stems from a constitutional source. Others, such as agency administrators, are termed supplementary policymakers because they gain their authority to act from others or from legislation.[2]

This institutional overview begins with an analysis of the two agencies with the principal responsibilities for stewardship of the environment in the United States, the Department of the Interior and the Environmental Protection Agency, and the role of the presidential leadership. The chapter goes on to discuss the role of Congress and key legislative committees, and the function of the courts in reviewing and enforcing environmental policy. Agencies with more narrow environmental jurisdiction, such as the U.S. Forest Service, the Bureau of Land Management, and the National Park Service, will be discussed more fully in subsequent chapters relating to their functions. The chapter concludes with a brief overview of the role of state and local governments and the fragmentation of environmental policy.

THE EXECUTIVE BRANCH AGENCIES

Despite the prolonged public interest in conservation and environmental protection outlined in Chapter 1, the federal government's involvement is actually relatively recent. During the first one hundred years after the nation's founding, both the president and Congress were much more deeply involved with foreign affairs, paying little attention to internal domestic problems until the growth of the country literally demanded it. The creation of a federal environmental policy was sporadic and unfocused, with responsibility for the environment scattered among a host of agencies.[3] Today, the Department of the Interior, established by congressional legislation in 1849, and the Environmental Protection Agency, created by executive order in 1970, have jurisdiction over the implementation of most of the nation's environmental policies.

Under its first secretary, Thomas Ewing, the Department of the Interior was given domestic housekeeping responsibilities quite different from today's cabinet-level department. Initially, the Department controlled the General Land Office, Office of Indian Affairs, the Pension Office and Patent Office, as well as supervision over the commissioner of public buildings, Board of Inspectors, the warden of the District of Columbia Penitentiary, the census, mines, and accounts of marshals of the U.S. courts. Gradually, a shift began to occur as the agency's responsibilities were transferred to other agencies within the executive branch. Eventually, the need to manage newly discovered public resources, especially land and mineral rights, led to the development of several agencies that later came under the Department of the Interior's umbrella, as seen in Table 3.1. The secretary of the interior is nominated by the president and confirmed by the Senate, as are the agency directors.

Table 3.1 Agencies of the U.S. Department of the Interior

Agency	Established
Bureau of Indian Affairs	1824[a]
Bureau of Land Management	1946[b]
Bureau of Mines	1910
Bureau of Reclamation	1902
Minerals Management Service	1982
National Park Service	1916
Office of Surface Mining Reclamation and Enforcement	1977
U.S. Geological Survey	1879
U.S. Fish and Wildlife Service	1940[c]

[a]Originally in War Department; transferred to Interior in 1849.
[b]Combined the responsibilities of the General Land Office, created in 1812, and the Grazing Service, established in 1934.
[c]Combined responsibilities of the Bureau of Fisheries, established in 1871, and the Bureau of Biological Survey, created in 1885.

The EPA, in contrast, is an independent agency in the executive branch, headed by an administrator, a deputy, and nine assistant administrators, all nominated by the president and confirmed by the Senate. The EPA has responsibility for administering a broad spectrum of environmental laws, as seen in the organizational chart in Figure 3.1. In one sense, it is a regulatory agency, issuing permits, setting and monitoring standards, and enforcing federal laws.

Prior to the Clinton administration, the president also received policy advice on environmental matters from the Council on Environmental Quality (CEQ), created as part of the National Environmental Policy Act of 1969. Its members recommended policy to the president and to some degree evaluated environmental protection programs within the executive branch. The CEQ did not have any

Figure 3.1   The Structure of the Environmental Protection Agency

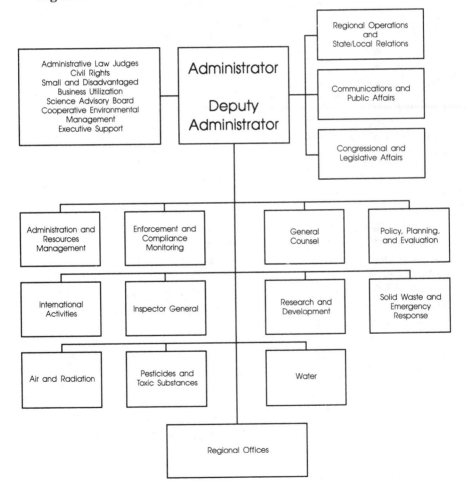

Table 3.2   Other Federal Agencies and Commissions with Environmental Policy Jurisdiction

Department	Agency/Commission
Agriculture	Agriculture Stabilization and Conservation Service
	Soil Conservation Service
Commerce	National Bureau of Standards
	National Oceanic and Atmospheric Administration
Defense	Army Corps of Engineers
Energy	Federal Energy Regulatory Commission
	Office of Conservation and Renewable Energy
Health and	
Human Services	Food and Drug Administration
	National Institute for Occupational Safety and Health
Labor	Mine Safety and Health Administration
Transportation	Federal Aviation Administration
	Federal Highway Administration
	Materials Transportation Bureau
	National Transportation Safety Board
	U.S. Coast Guard

Commissions/Regulatory Agencies

Consumer Product Safety Commission
Federal Maritime Commission
Federal Trade Commission
Nuclear Regulatory Commission

regulatory authority, and its recommendations were purely advisory. Clinton replaced the CEQ with the White House Office of Environmental Policy, elevating the status of the body within the administration's hierarchy.

Sometimes, the agency may have powers and an interest level comparable to that of the Department of the Interior or EPA, as is the case with the Nuclear Regulatory Commission, which authorizes the construction of nuclear power plants and supervises their operation. Other agencies, like the Federal Aviation Administration, may not have environmental concerns as their primary mission, but may be affected by regulations or legislation implemented by other agencies. Thus, the FAA was consulted in 1990 when air-quality officials within the EPA began to consider legislation that would govern the amount of particulates released in aircraft exhaust emissions.

The process of implementing environmental policy is complicated by interest groups, which are playing an increasingly significant role at this stage of policy development. Industry, especially, has made great strides in crafting policies that parallel its needs. Industry groups have often appeared to "give up" their interests at the policy adoption stage, only to come back stronger than ever during the implementation phase. For the most part, this strategy has been successful in influencing environmental legislation. Industry, ever mindful of its public image, has often accepted or provided only token resistance to proposed legislation that would negatively affect it during the policy formulation and adoption phase, which is highly visible and public. Instead, industry has done its best to circumvent costly or logistically difficult environmental regulations when they reach the implementation stage—the responsibility of bureaucratic organizations and agencies like the EPA.

One way in which environmental groups have been kept out of the implementation process is through industry efforts to remove rule making from the public domain. The kinds of complex, time-consuming procedures that are typical of the rule-making process provide a shield against external intervention and a legitimate basis for resisting external demands for information exchanges. The rule-making process involved with the implementation of the seven-hundred-page 1990 Clean Air Amendments is exemplary of this problem. The EPA must complete 150 regulatory activities, including one hundred rule makings, in only two years—an unheard of time frame. To put the process in perspective, consider the fact that in the past EPA has issued seven or eight major regulations *per year* on all phases of environmental law—from pesticides to solid waste to air and water pollution. While the issue of nitrogen oxide emissions (one of two acid-rain-causing chemicals) took only two pages of the act itself, the regulations crafted by the EPA are expected to take up two hundred or more pages.

Participation by interest groups is made even more difficult by the short comment periods necessitated by the scheduling. From the perspective of those interested in influencing the rule, the tight deadlines mean that the agency has likely already made up its mind and that comments will not bring about many changes in direction.[4] Implementation is also hampered by the complexity of the rule-making process itself. Although the Resource Conservation and Recovery Act (RCRA) was enacted in 1976, it took the EPA four years to implement the first rules under the act. In the meantime, state governments held their own agonizingly slow rule makings or waited until federal funds were made available, giving industry more time to muster its defenses.[5]

The responsibility for implementing policy has often been left to agencies and commissions ill equipped for the task. In 1979, for example, when RCRA rule making was finally under way, the process was considered so technical and complex that both the EPA and the environmental community suffered from a lack of expertise. Most of the comments that were received on the individual rules were from companies subject to them.[6] And during the implementation of the 1990 Clean Air Act, the EPA was forced to hire outside consultants, many of them drawn from industry, to draft preliminary rules, especially those dealing with air toxics, where the EPA's expertise is notoriously lacking.

Finally, policy implementation is an incremental process. It is made in a series of small steps, each one dependent on the previous one. The process is time-consuming and seldom results in any major legislative or policy advances. The history of water quality legislation, for example, is one of fine-tuning rather than abrupt or dramatic change. Congress has been unwilling to orchestrate a complete revamping of the legislation initially passed in 1965, and as a result, agencies like the EPA have followed suit. There have been no major advances in water quality issues, and none are expected until the legislation is reauthorized.

PRESIDENTIAL LEADERSHIP

Historically, the president has had a limited role in environmental politics, with much of the power delegated to the executive branch agencies. Not until Richard Nixon's tenure began in 1969 did the environment become a presidential priority, and even then, he was reluctant to act. After years of study and staff negotiations, President Nixon agreed to a federal reorganization plan calling for an independent pollution control agency which later became the EPA.

The agency opened its doors under the stewardship of William Ruckelshaus, a graduate of Harvard Law School and former Indiana assistant attorney general. Although he had virtually no background in environmental issues, Ruckelshaus had the support of Nixon's attorney general, John Mitchell, and was confirmed after only two days of hearings. On the day of his selection as administrator, Ruckelshaus was briefed by Nixon, who gave him the impression that he considered the environmental problem "faddish."[7] Ruckelshaus came to the EPA with three priorities: to create a well-defined enforcement image for the agency, to carry out the provisions of the newly amended Clean Air Act, and to gain control over the costs of regulatory decision making.[8] In setting up the agency, Ruckelshaus decided each regional organization within the EPA should mirror the full agency's structure, with staff capabilities in every program area and delegation of responsibility to regional offices, creating an organizational structure that gave the agency a rare capability to make decisions, move programs ahead, and motivate people to produce high volumes of work.[9] Inside the EPA, morale was high, due in large part to Ruckelshaus's accessibility to his staff. Outside, he became a forceful spokesperson for the public interest and was well respected by both sides in the environmental debate. Early on, Ruckelshaus concentrated on air and water pollution, assigning three-quarters of his staff to that task. As a result, there was an improvement in noncompliance with air quality standards in most cities, and the agency affected a change from aesthetic concerns about the recreational uses of water to health concerns.[10]

Nixon's efforts to give credibility to the Department of the Interior were not nearly as successful. It appears that the creation of the EPA relegated the department to backseat status as far as environmental issues were concerned. A succession of secretaries came and went (see Table 3.3) while the EPA administrators garnered publicity and notoriety. Despite these efforts, there is some doubt as to how much Nixon really cared about the environment as an issue. Some staff members believed the Nixon reorganization experts were neither proponents nor opponents of environmental reform; their specialty was management and organization. They focused on the environment because that was the area in which political pressures were creating a demand for action.

Typical is the case of Walter Hickel, who Nixon chose in late 1968 as the new interior secretary, setting off a storm of protest. Hickel, who had grown up in Kansas and lived on a tenant farm during the depression, was a Golden Gloves boxer who loved to fight. As governor of Alaska, he was accused of being a pawn of the U.S. Chamber of Commerce and of the oil industry. After four days of defensive hearings, his nomination was confirmed. Hickel's bold style was his undoing; he offended the president in a rambling letter about Nixon's policies (eventually leaked to the press) after the Kent State shootings. The gaffe came at a time when the president's staff was considering the reorganization proposal, which would have elevated Hickel to head the new Department of Natural Resources. He was fired Thanksgiving Day, 1970.[11]

To his credit, it should be noted that it was under Nixon that the United States first began to take a more global approach to environmental protection. Ruckelshaus was successful in convincing Nixon of the important role the United States could play at the United Nations Conference on the Human Environment in June 1972 in Stockholm. Although the United States was not totally in agreement with the priorities of the United Nations Environment Programme, which grew out of the Stockholm conference, Nixon persuaded Congress to pay the largest share (36 percent) of the new secretariat's budget.[12]

When Gerald Ford took over as president upon Nixon's resignation, he made few changes in the way environmental policy was being conducted. Russell Train remained head of the EPA under President Ford and served in that

Table 3.3   Environmental Agency Leadership, 1970–1993

President	Secretary of the Interior	EPA Administrator
Nixon	Rogers Morton (1971–74)	William Ruckelshaus (1970–73)
Ford	Rogers Morton (1974–75)	Russell Train (1973–77)
	Stanley Hathaway (1975)	
	Thomas Kleppe (1975–77)	
Carter	Cecil Andrus	Douglas Costle (1977–1981)
Reagan	James Watt (1981–83)	Anne Burford (1981–83)
	William Clark (1983–85)	William Ruckelshaus (1983–85)
	Donald Hodel (1985–89)	Lee Thomas (1985–89)
Bush	Manuel Lujan (1989–92)	William Reilly (1989–92)
Clinton	Bruce Babbitt (1993–)	Carol Browner (1993–)

position until Ford was defeated by Jimmy Carter in 1976. He kept most of Nixon's other environmental appointees, including Interior Secretary Rogers Morton. For the most part, the crush of environmental programs that marked the Nixon years slowed considerably under Ford for three reasons. One, the energy shortage created by the 1973 Arab oil embargo pushed pollution off the legislative agenda for several years, a topic that will be discussed in Chapter 6. Two, there was a growing concern that the cost to industry to comply with EPA standards was slowing the economy at a time when expansion was needed. Lastly, the environmental momentum of the early 1970s faded by 1976, and Ford did little to refuel it. Congressional initiatives expanded the EPA's authorities with the Safe Drinking Water Act of 1974, the Toxic Substances Control Act of 1976, and the Resource Conservation and Recovery Act of 1976 (legislation discussed in later chapters), but Ford's unsuccessful presidential campaign made him an observer, rather than a participant, in the policymaking process. The environmental slate for Gerald Ford is a clean, albeit empty one.

In 1976, groups like the League of Conservation Voters gave presidential candidate Jimmy Carter very high grades for his environmental record as governor of Georgia, although his campaign focused more on other issues like human rights and the economy. President Carter openly courted environmental groups during his single-term administration, and he counted on their support to carry him through to reelection in 1980, which he lost to Ronald Reagan. He received high marks from environmental groups that believed he would emphasize environmental issues in his administration, but he initially offended one of the environmental movement's heroes Senator Edmund Muskie, of Maine. Carter began by choosing Douglas Costle to head the EPA over Muskie's objections. Costle, a Seattle native, attended Harvard and the University of Chicago Law School, and had worked at the Office of Management and Budget under Nixon. His main environmental credential was a stint as commissioner for environmental affairs in Connecticut, but he had a strong financial management background from working at the Congressional Budget Office.

Under Costle, the EPA became the first federal agency to adopt Carter's plan of zero-based budgeting. Costle's main aim in taking over the agency was "to convince the public that EPA was first and foremost a public health agency, not a guardian of birds and bunnies."[13] Taking Costle's lead, Congress responded by passing the Superfund authorization in late 1980, establishing a $1.6 billion emergency fund to clean up toxic contaminants spilled or dumped into the environment. The result was a major shift in the agency's regulatory focus from conventional pollutants to toxics. This allowed the agency room to grow and justification for a 25 percent budget increase at a time when the president was preaching strict austerity.

Carter had a number of environmental achievements during his term, including passage of the landmark Alaska Land Bill in 1980, which added millions of acres of pristine wilderness under federal protection. As part of his attempt to gain group support, he convinced Congress to consider a windfall profits tax on oil to fund solar research, and pushed stronger energy conservation measures.[14] But the inability of Congress to develop a comprehensive energy policy under his administration has led most observers to conclude that Carter was not an especially effective leader in environmental policy or in protecting the environment.

The eight years of Ronald Reagan's administration mark a stormy chapter in environmental politics. Critics believe that he almost singlehandedly destroyed the progress that had been made in the area of pollution control. Supporters point to his legislative achievements and say the picture was not so bleak after all, but critics argue those successes came as a result of congressional initiative, not from Reagan. During his stint as governor of California and as president, Reagan was heavily influenced by probusiness interests like Colorado brewer Joseph Coors, who urged him to take a more conservative approach to environmental regulation. Coors and his allies were represented in Reagan's inner circle by Senator Paul Laxalt of Nevada, and they focused their attention on the appointment of a conservative secretary of the interior who would show prudent respect for development interests, especially in the West.[15]

Their candidate was James Watt, a Wyoming native who had served as a legislative aide to Senator Milward Simpson. He had served as a member of the Nixon transition team in 1968 to help Walter Hickel through his confirmation hearings as secretary of the interior, and was then appointed deputy secretary for water and power. In 1977, he founded the Mountain States Legal Foundation, a conservative anti-environmental law firm, and was later connected to the leadership of the Sagebrush Rebellion, which will be discussed in Chapter 4. Although some of Reagan's advisors preferred Clifford P. Hansen, former governor and senator from Wyoming, for the Interior slot, Watt's rhetorical style and ability to bring in dollars as a conservative fund-raiser for Reagan gave him a decided edge. He was a spokesperson for the New Right among those who believed Reagan was drifting too close to the political center.[16]

Watt divided people into two categories—liberals and Americans—and called the Audubon Society "a chanting mob."[17] He perceived environmentalists as "dangerous and subversive, suggesting they sought to weaken America and to undermine freedom. He called them extremists and likened them to Nazis."[18] More telling, however, was the comparison of Watt to his predecessor, Cecil Andrus, who had said, "I am part of the environmental movement and I intend to make the Interior Department responsive to the movement's needs."[19] Watt discovered he had great independence in molding the agency to conform to his policy interests. Among his first directives, he ordered a moratorium on any further National Park acquisitions and announced his intention to open up federal lands to mining and logging. He proposed to permit leasing of 1.3 million acres off the California coast for offshore oil and gas exploration, and auctioned off 1.1 billion tons of coal in the Powder River Basin of Montana and Wyoming, actions that infuriated environmentalists. By summer 1981, Watt had made enough enemies that the Sierra Club, the National Wildlife Federation, and the Audubon Society gathered more than one million signatures seeking Watt's ouster. Together, ten organizations urged President Reagan to fire Watt in a stinging indictment that purported to show how he had subverted environmental policy.

His supporters, however, point to the fact that under Watt, the federal government did spend more than $1 billion to restore and improve the existing national parks, and 1.8 million acres were added to the nation's wilderness system. His vision was to develop America's energy resources and to remove what many perceived as excessive regulation of business, efforts at which he was successful.[20] But by late 1982, Watt was under heavy criticism for his actions, although he was blunt enough to say out loud what many in the Reagan administration were thinking. Reagan called Watt's record "darn good"[21] but urged him to reconcile with environmental groups, to whom he had stopped speaking just six weeks into his job. They continued to criticize him for refusing to touch more than $1 billion in the Land and Water Conservation Fund that had been set aside for national park acquisition, and for spending only about half of the amount of funds for land acquisition appropriated by Congress.[22]

Watt's bluntness turned out to haunt him after he banned the Beach Boys from performing on the Capitol Mall, embarrassing the president and the First Lady (a great admirer of the group), who rescheduled the concert. Then, in a speech before Chamber of Commerce lobbyists, he recalled that an Interior Department coal advisory panel was comprised of "a black, a woman, two Jews and a cripple," a remark widely criticized in the press, making Watt a true liability to Reagan, who sought his resignation. Shortly thereafter, Reagan appointed William Clark to head the Department of the Interior—a man whose term was as undistinguished as Watt's had been tumultuous. Clark served less than a year and a half and was replaced by Donald Hodel, another moderate.

Reagan's appointment of Anne Gorsuch as administrator of the Environmental Protection Agency proved to be even more of an embarrassment than Watt. Gorsuch, a former member of the Colorado legislature, became one of the youngest of Reagan's appointees despite her lack of administrative experience. She began her term as administrator by reorganizing the agency, abolishing divisions only to reestablish them later. The EPA's highly politicized staff members demoralized careerists, and the agency was constantly under siege from both environmental groups (who believed Gorsuch's appointment signaled Reagan's support for industry interests) and from members of Congress. More telling, perhaps, was the loss of a fifth of the EPA's personnel and major cuts in the agency's budget beginning in 1980.[23]

Under Gorsuch, (who later married Robert Burford) the Office of Enforcement was dismantled, and personnel within the agency found their positions downgraded. Environmental professionals were often passed over for promotion by political appointees, and neither of the two original associate administrators served more than one hundred days.[24] The Reagan administration became embroiled in further controversy when several top EPA administrators, including the agency's general counsel, were investigated or accused of conflict of interest, perjury, and other misdeeds. By the end of his third year in office, more than twenty senior EPA employees had been removed from office, and several key agency officials had resigned under pressure.[25]

The biggest fall was Burford's. In fall 1982, John Dingell, chair of the House Committee on Energy and Commerce, initiated an investigation of alleged abuses in Superfund enforcement and sought EPA documents as a part of the case. Dingell subpoenaed Burford to appear to provide the committee with the documents, but on the basis of Justice Department advice, she declined to do so, citing the doctrine of executive privilege. In December 1982, the House voted to declare her in contempt of Congress. Eventually a compromise was struck that allowed the committee to examine nearly all the documents they sought, and the contempt citation was dropped.

The contempt charge was coupled with charges of EPA mismanagement of cleanup operations after discovery of the toxic chemical dioxin in roadways at Times Beach, Missouri. The project had been handled by the EPA assistant administrator for hazardous waste, Rita Lavelle, who was eventually fired by Reagan. Lavelle was the only EPA official to face criminal charges and was convicted of perjury and obstructing a congressional investigation. She was sentenced to six months in prison and fined $10,000. The incident cast further doubt on Burford's ability to manage the agency, and she resigned March 9, 1983. At a press conference two days later, Reagan said he believed that it was he, not Burford, who was the real target of Congress's action. He said that he never would have asked for her resignation.[26] Congress did not let up even after Burford resigned. At the end of August 1984, a House Energy and Commerce Oversight Committee concluded that from 1981 to 1983 "top level officials of the EPA violated their public trust by disregarding the public health and environment, manipulating the Superfund program for political purposes, engaging in unethical conduct, and participating in other abuses."[27]

To return the agency to some semblance of credibility, Reagan called upon the EPA's first administrator, William Ruckelshaus, who returned to coordinate salvage operations. Ruckelshaus restored morale to the middle-level EPA staff, reversed the adversarial posture of the EPA toward Congress and the media, and brought in new and experienced administrators to replace political appointees.[28] During his second stint as administrator, Ruckelshaus revised the standards for the lead content in gasoline and declared an emergency ban on ethylene dibromide (EDP), a pesticide widely used in grain and food production. Ruckelshaus served until after Reagan's reelection, when the president appointed his third EPA administrator, Lee Thomas.

Thomas, a South Carolina native, became the first nonlawyer to head the agency. He had previously worked in the Federal Emergency Management Administration, and headed the Times Beach Task Force that led to Rita Lavelle's firing. When she left, he took over her position as coordinator of hazardous waste, Superfund, and RCRA programs. Seen as a career EPA employee, he redefined the agency's mission. On the one hand, he focused attention on localized concern like medical waste and the garbage crisis, that were threatening urban areas. At the same time, he brought attention to global concerns like the weakening of the ozone layer and chlorofluorocarbons (CFCs). Thomas made sure that the EPA became an active participant in international forums and returned the environment to the policy agenda.[29] Another major achievement was the full restoration of the EPA's reputation for strong enforcement, especially after the agency reached a 1985 agreement with Westinghouse Corporation to spend $100 million to clean up toxic waste at its Indiana facilities. This was followed in 1986 by an agreement with Aerojet General to clean up a toxic dump near Sacramento (estimated to cost the company $82 million) and in 1988 by a $1 billion cleanup agreement with Shell Oil and the U.S. Army at the Rocky Mountain arsenal near Denver.

Many environmentalists believed George Bush's campaign promise to be "the environmental president" when he appointed William Reilly to head the EPA in 1989. Reilly, who had previously served as head of the U.S. branch of the World Wildlife Fund, was the first environmental professional to serve as administrator. He had also established a reputation as a moderate while serving with the Washington, DC-based Conservation Foundation. The Sierra Club took a wait-and-see attitude, declaring that Reilly was "clearly tagged to be the administration's good guy in a very tough job."[30] Reilly's agenda was clearly different from those of the Reagan appointees. In several early speeches and articles, he reiterated the need for pollution prevention as "a fundamental part of all our activities, all our initiatives, and all our economic growth," making it the theme of the EPA's Earth Day celebrations in April 1990.[31] He also pointed to science and risk assessment "to help the Agency put together a much more coherent agenda than has characterized the past 20 years."[32] Reilly and Bush were jointly praised for having broken the legislative gridlock that characterized clean air legislation since the amendments had last been revised in 1977, a topic discussed further in Chapter 9.

Some observers believe, however, that Reilly's efforts were often derailed by members of the White House staff, especially by former chief of staff John Sununu, who toned down EPA pronouncements on global warming and wetlands preservation, and by budget director Richard Darman, who once called Reilly "a global rock star."[33] Sununu was also criticized by environmentalists who believe he blocked serious international negotiations on global warming. Reilly was caught up in White House politics again in June 1992 when a memo to President Bush on negotiations at the Earth Summit were leaked to the press; some insiders believe that Vice President Dan Quayle's office was responsible.

Bush's other appointees were given mixed reviews, from Michael Deland, head of CEQ and an ardent environmentalist, to James Watkins, Bush's secretary of energy, who won praise for his commitment to alternative energy and energy conservation policy, although critics of the administration feel his comments have not been translated into substantive policy change. The appointment of Manuel Lujan, Jr., a former member of Congress from New Mexico, as secretary of the interior, was criticized by environmental groups that felt he favored the logging and mining interests of the West. Lujan's critics became even more alarmed when Lujan agreed in October 1991 to convene the so-called Endangered Species God Squad to review the denial of timber permits on Bureau of Land Management property because they threatened the habitat of the northern spotted owl, a species that had been declared threatened the previous year (an issue that will be discussed in Chapter 4). But the secretary's supporters argued that he was taking a more reasonable approach to the Endangered Species Act and simply invoking a mechanism provided for under law. Equally controversial was the president's wetlands policy, which will also be discussed further in Chapter 4. By redefining what constitutes a wetland, the administration has exempted thousands of acres of land from federal protection—a move that pleased the business community and angered environmentalists, who took the matter to court.

Did Bush live up to his claims as "the environmental president"? In his 1991 message on environmental quality, Bush pointed to adoption of an international agreement on CFCs, enactment of the Oil Pollution Act of 1990, enactment of an environmentally progressive farm bill, and his commitment to environmental stewardship. He noted that in 1990, the EPA's enforcement staff had a record of felony indictments that was 33 percent higher than in 1989. His America the Beautiful tree-planting initiative hoped to add one billion new trees annually over the next ten years.[34] In December 1990, for example, he established the President's Commission on Environmental Quality to build public/private partnerships to achieve concrete results in the area of pollution prevention, conservation, education, and international cooperation. Critics counter that under Vice President Quayle, the Council on Competitiveness thwarted congressional intent, with House Subcommittee on Health and the Environment Chair Henry Waxman accusing the council of "helping polluters block EPA's efforts."[35] Proving that almost everything he does offends someone, Bush was criticized by both environmentalists and conservatives.

Voters had a clear choice on environmental issues in the 1992 presidential election. While Bush proposed giving greater consideration to protecting jobs in enforcing the Endangered Species Act, Bill Clinton ran on an environmentalist's dream platform. One of the key provisions of the Clinton campaign was a promise to limit U.S. carbon dioxide emissions to 1990 levels by the year 2000 to halt global warming—an issue for which Bush was soundly criticized for not supporting at the Earth Summit. Clinton also pledged to create recycling and energy conservation incentives, to set national water pollution runoff standards, and to support a forty-mile-per-gallon fuel standard. In direct contrast to Bush, Clinton promised to restore to the United Nations Population Fund monies that had previously been cut off (an issue discussed further in Chapter 17) and to oppose drilling in the Arctic National Wildlife Refuge. These viewpoints, along with his appointments to executive branch agencies, gave environmentalists room for hope and a sense of renewed executive branch leadership.

CONGRESSIONAL POLICYMAKING

Although Congress has primary responsibility for policy formulation and adoption, the nature of the institution has hampered that role.[36] Congress's current inability to develop an overall national environmental policy has been termed "environmental gridlock"[37] referring to the contrast between the institution's rapid pace and initiative during the 1960s and 1970s in comparison to the body's current inability to move forward with a legislative agenda. There are a number of reasons to explain current congressional inaction:

1. The fragmentation of the committee system decentralizes both power and the decision-making process. Environmental issues do not "belong" to any one committee within Congress. Eleven of the Senate's standing committees and fourteen of those in the House claim some environmental jurisdiction. Depending upon the title of a particular piece of legislation, and the subject matter, there is a great deal of latitude in deciding which committee(s) should have jurisdiction. For example, a bill dealing with global warming could be heard by the Senate's Agriculture, Appropriations, Commerce, Science and Transportation, Energy and Natural Resources, or Environment and Public Works committees, since each claims some degree of jurisdiction over that subject. Similarly, in the House, the same bill might be heard by either the Agriculture, Appropriations, Foreign Affairs Committee, or Science, Space and Technology Committee. When environmental issues are "hot," a certain rivalry causes competition among committees as to which one will have the greatest chance of influencing the bill's content.

2. The pressures of an increasing number of "green" groups and industry interests have made it more difficult to build congressional consensus. The same committee fragmentation that is a characteristic of the modern Congress also gives interest groups more access to the legislative process. If a group feels one committee is less accommodating to its interests, it may seek a more favorable venue before another committee or subcommittee. At any one point in the legislative process, there may be dozens of groups vying for members' attention, and environmental groups have lost the power advantage they once enjoyed at the problem identification stage of the policy process.

3. Members of Congress often lack the time and expertise needed to produce sophisticated legislation. One of the more recent criticisms of Congress is that it is "an assembly of scientific amateurs enacting programs of great technical complexity to ameliorate scientifically complicated environmental ills most legislators but dimly understand."[38] Nowhere is this incapacitation better viewed but in the congressional hearings on the 1990 Clean Air Act amendments. Many of the more technical aspects of the legislation, such as those applicable only to utility oil-fired boilers, were so obtuse that several members left it up to their staff to dicker with industry lobbyists over the feasibility of proposed controls. Similarly, when debate on highly sophisticated bills dealing with stratospheric ozone depletion becomes a battle of one expert's research against another, many members of Congress are simply at a loss as to whom to believe. The result is often legislation that is watered down or intentionally vague. Time and the hectic pace of lawmaking also have an impact on congressional policymaking. Staff members taking notes on the 1990 Clean Air Act amendments hurriedly jotted down proposed amendments, the authors of which were often unsure exactly where they would fit in the mammoth bill. Lobbyists, watching the markup process, found their notes of committee sessions often differed from those of staff, and it was not unusual to see the two groups huddling over pages of red-lined, handwritten legislation.
4. Localized reelection concerns override a "national" view of environmental policymaking. It is difficult for a member of Congress from northern California to convince a colleague from an urban district in New York of the relative importance of a bill barring timber exports to Japan. As reelection pressures mount (especially in the House, where the fever strikes every two years), bargaining becomes an essential style of policymaking. Members with little personal interest in an issue could often care less about the legislative outcome, and only by bargaining for something of value to their own district do they have a reason to become involved. Votes on pork barrel projects like dams and parklands, for example, are often based on the "you-scratch-my-back-I'll-scratch-yours" principle, with virtually no thought to consistency or even the regional impact of the decision. Local concerns determine which grants get funded and which do not, and legislators in positions of seniority, especially members of the powerful Appropriations committees, are particularly adept at bringing projects and facilities "back home."

COURTS AND ENVIRONMENTAL POLITICS

The courts have two primary functions in the making of environmental policy: to exercise their authority for judicial review and to interpret statutes through cases brought to them. In doing so, they use the Constitution to determine the legality of actions of the executive and legislative branches, and to define the meaning of laws, which are often open to differing interpretations.

Often courts have authority to determine who has access to the judicial process and may play an activist role in policymaking through their decisions.

Prior to the passage of NEPA in 1970, most courts' involvement in environmental issues was limited to the adjudication of disputes between polluting industries and citizens affected by pollution. The result in most cases was a cease and desist order and perhaps a fine. But the administrative requirements under NEPA, the need for agency compliance, and Congress's failure to spell out legislative intent in several sections of the act opened up a whole new era of judicial activism. Studies of NEPA litigation show that the willingness of the courts to review agency decisions, especially in the early 1970s, was due to a number of factors, including public support for the environment, a tendency toward strict enforcement of statutory procedural requirements, and most importantly, timing. NEPA was enacted when the courts were generally tightening their review of agency decision making.[39]

Several important environmental decisions came about during this period of judicial activism. Interpreting congressional intent in the opening words of the 1970 Clean Air Act, the U.S. Supreme Court upheld a district court order that instructed the EPA to prevent the "significant deterioration" of air quality in regions that had already met federal standards.[40] A 1973 decision by the District of Columbia Circuit forced the EPA to prepare plans to reduce ozone and carbon monoxide (key components of smog) for cities using transportation control measures.[41] The legal concept of "standing"—the right of an individual or group to bring an issue before a court—was greatly expanded as well. The constitutional basis for standing is found in Article III, which gives courts the authority to decide "cases and controversies," which has been historically interpreted to mean an individual had the right to bring a suit only when there was a clear showing that the person had been harmed, either in terms of personal injury or loss of property. Thus, most suits against polluting industries could be brought only by citizens actually affected by the pollution. Environmental groups found it difficult to qualify as litigants in most suits because environmental harm was not considered by most courts to be personal in nature, so litigation was infrequent.[42] Gradually, however, the courts began to allow members of environmental groups to sue on behalf of the public interest, increasing the number of lawsuits against industries and, later, against agencies that failed to comply with environmental laws and regulations.[43]

There is a great deal of evidence to conclude the courts are now becoming the arena of choice for resolving all types of environmental disputes. Lawsuits have been filed in 80 percent of the EPA's rule makings to date.[44] On the one hand, environmental groups have been particularly successful in using the courts to force enforcement of environmental regulations. A suit by the Coalition for Clean Air against the South Coast Air Quality Management District, the agency responsible for controlling stationary sources of air pollution in the Los Angeles Basin, compelled the agency to move forward on preparing a State Implementation Plan (SIP) to meet federal air quality standards. Coalition members criticized the agency for stalling on the preparation of the EPA-mandated plan, and only legal action got the plan moving forward.

It is to industry's advantage to litigate environmental regulations because the process has the net effect of stalling the implementation of rules. Industry can demur during the policy formation and adoption stage, thereby avoiding the bad press that comes from such activity, in hopes of moving the courts closer to their position.[45]

STATE AND LOCAL POLICYMAKING

Most analysts give the federal government low marks to date, and as one observer notes, fragmentation has been the prevailing pattern in the formation and implementation of federal environmental policy. Efforts to integrate the federal role in environmental management have been sporadic and have had minimal impact.[46] State and local attempts to deal with environmental problems have been similarly fragmented. Although most states developed resource management agencies by 1950 (especially to deal with forests or mines), there was little interest in environmental protection. In the early 1950s, local health departments were given authority over air quality as scientists began monitoring the negative health effects of air pollution. In contrast, jurisdiction over water pollution was taken away from health officials and made a separate agency in most cities.[47]

State agencies expanded in response to federal mandates in the late 1960s and early 1970s, initially creating environmental agencies on a single-media basis, such as state air quality boards or water commissions. The federal statutes relied upon state agencies for implementation, providing funds for planning, monitoring, management, and technical studies.[48] Gradually, two patterns of state initiative emerged. Some states, such as New York and Washington, created "superagencies" or "little EPAs" for purposes of administrative efficiency. In some cases, this was done for political acceptability, rather than to integrate an entire program of environmental management.[49] Minnesota, for example, created its Pollution Control Agency in 1967 by shifting responsibility for water pollution control out of the state health department and giving it air and solid waste authority as well. Most of these consolidated programs have a part-time citizen board, which is often subject to attack because members lack sufficient technical expertise. A second pattern was to create a totally new environmental agency focusing on pollution control. Illinois, for example, created a powerful, full-time, five-member Pollution Control Board with a full research staff, the Institute for Environmental Quality.[50]

As the technical competence of state government grew, so too did an "environmental presence," which business and industry interests found unacceptable. They turned to the federal government for regulatory relief and federal preemption of state authority.[51] The New Federalism, which actually began with the State and Local Fiscal Assistance Act of 1972, is exemplified by the Reagan administration's philosophy of "getting government off the backs of the people."[52] His belief in a reduction in the scope of federal activity, privatization, and the devolution of policy and fiscal responsibility to the states resulted in an EPA unwilling to serve as policy initiator or congressional advocate. To fill that void, state officials began to band together to lobby collectively. In the area of air quality, for example, eight states formed the Northeast States for Coordinated Air Use Management (NESCAUM) to actively lobby for reauthorization of the Clean Air Act in 1987 when the EPA was no longer its congressional policy advocate. The group prepared legislative proposals, technical support and documentation for its position, termed "a complete role reversal, with states serving as policy initiators."[53]

However, states have not generally been willing to take a position of leadership. A study of the implementation of the 1986 Superfund amendments found that few states had complied with a requirement that governors designate a state official to serve as a trustee for the state's natural resources. The trustee has the authority to bring natural resource damage claims in federal court. By April 1988, eighteen months after enactment of the Superfund provisions, only one-third of the states had designated a trustee, and by April 1989, only thirty-nine states had complied. The survey found that several states were in complete ignorance of the requirement, while others had complied even before the implementing regulations were drafted.[54]

Policy analyst James Lester has sought to explain why there is such a variation in the way in which states respond to environmental problems. One reason is the "severity argument"—that those states with the most concentrated population growth and urbanization (and therefore the most severe pollution problems) take the most active role in dealing with them. A second reason, the "wealth argument," states that there is a direct relationship between the state's resource base and its commitment to environmental protection. Third, the "partisanship argument" is that states with a Democratically leaning legislature are more likely to work toward environmental protection than are Republican-controlled states. Lastly, there is the "organizational capacity argument," which states that administrative and organizational reforms are the best predictors of environmental policy outputs, so that professional legislatures are more likely to enact environmental legislation than those that are part time, unprofessional ones.[55] Since most federal statutes require state implementation, local governments have played relatively subordinate roles to that of the state. The exceptions have been in those states where the environmental movement has been very strong and have pressured local officials to enact environmental regulations more stringent than those of the federal or state government, as is the case in several western states.

Several studies have found that there is a much stronger level of environmental interest in the West in comparison with other regions.[56] That interest is found in both public opinion polls and legislative voting records, as well as in measures of the use of wilderness areas and in legislation. To some extent, statewide groups like the Colorado Environmental Council and regional branches of national organizations like the Sierra Club and Audubon Society have found a sympathetic audience at the state level. Pioneering legislation like Oregon's bottle bill and California's recycling programs are due in large part to an effective environmental lobby. Since political values are often based on a specific place where citizens live, work, and play, it is not surprising that local governments are beginning to play a larger role in policy formation. Local initiatives may be the result of a smoke plume from a local factory or of an attempt to make the town more aesthetically pleasing to residents or tourists. But local officials must also balance those concerns with the historic tradition and prevailing mood of business toward development and growth, combined with a steadily decreasing revenue base that precludes many otherwise desirable environmental projects from being funded.[57]

SUMMARY

Even though Congress holds the constitutional responsibility for enacting legislation to protect the environment, the Department of the Interior and the Environmental Protection Agency are the two leading agencies in the development of environmental policy. Their ability to protect the environment is affected, to a large extent, by their resources. The level of presidential support has been among the most important factors that determines how effective environmental agencies will be. This phenomenon was especially apparent during the eight years of the Reagan administration, when the EPA's budget was slashed and the agency underwent a traumatic reorganization and made personnel changes. The protection of the environment has been a priority when it has been a focus of the president and his staff and has slipped when other interests have come first. Many observers believe the judicial arena is taking on new importance in the settling of environmental disputes, especially by environmental organizations and individuals frustrated by the slow pace of administrative rule-making.

NOTES

1. The remark was quoted in Ted Morgan, "The Good Life," *New York Times Magazine*, July 4, 1976, 71.

2. James E. Anderson, *Public Policymaking: An Introduction* (Boston: Houghton Mifflin, 1990), 51.

3. For the historical background of the nation's earliest attempts at environmental protection, see U.S. Department of the Interior, *Creation of the Department of the Interior* (Washington, DC: U.S. Department of the Interior, 1976); and Donald C. Swain, "Conservation in the 1920s," in *American Environmentalism*, 3rd ed., ed. Roderick Nash (New York: McGraw-Hill, 1990), 117–25.

4. Henry V. Nickel, "Now, the Rush to Regulate," *The Environmental Forum* 8, no. 1 (January–February 1991): 19.

5. See Joseph Petulla, *Environmental Protection in the United States* (San Francisco: San Francisco Study Center, 1987), 98–99.

6. Marc K. Landy, Marc J. Roberts, and Stephen R. Thomas, *The EPA: Asking the Wrong Questions* (New York: Oxford University Press, 1990), 117.

7. Alfred A. Marcus, *Promise and Performance: Choosing and Implementing an Environmental Policy* (Westport, CT: Greenwood Press, 1980), 87.

8. Ibid., 85.

9. John Quarles, *Cleaning Up America: An Insider's View of the EPA* (Boston: Houghton Mifflin, 1976), 34.

10. Steven A. Cohen, "EPA: A Qualified Success," in *Controversies in Environmental Policy*, ed. Sheldon Kamieniecki et al. (Albany: State University of New York Press, 1986).

11. Quarles, *Cleaning Up America*, 17–19.

12. John McCormick, *Reclaiming Paradise: The Global Environmental Movement* (Bloomington: Indiana University Press, 1989), 110.

13. Landy, Roberts, and Thomas, *EPA*, 41.

14. See C. Brant Short, *Ronald Reagan and the Public Lands* (College Station: Texas A & M University Press, 1989), 47.

15. Lou Cannon, *President Reagan: The Role of a Lifetime* (New York: Simon & Schuster, 1991), 530–31. Cannon has spent much of his life as a Reagan biographer, chronicling both his terms as governor and as president.

16. Short, *Ronald Reagan and the Public Lands*, 57.

17. Cannon, *President Reagan*, 531.

18. Jonathan Lash, Katherine Gillman, and David Sheridan, *A Season of Spoils: The Reagan Administration's Attack on the Environment* (New York: Pantheon Books, 1984), 231.

19. Ron Arnold, *At the Eye of the Storm: James Watt and the Environmentalists* (Chicago: Regency Gateway, 1982), 94.

20. Ibid., 93.

21. Cannon, *President Reagan*, 532.

22. Lash, Gillman, and Sheridan, *Season of Spoils*, 287–97.

23. Needless to say, Burford's account of the personnel loss and her subsequent fall from grace is somewhat different. She attributes the changes to natural attrition within the agency. See Anne Burford, with John Greenya, *Are You Tough Enough?* (New York: McGraw-Hill, 1986).

24. See Richard E. Cohen, "The Gorsuch Affair," *National Journal*, January 8, 1983, 80.

25. Haynes Johnson, *Sleepwalking through History: America in the Reagan Years* (New York: Norton, 1991), 170.

26. *Public Papers of the President of the United States: Ronald Reagan, 1983* (Washington, DC: Government Printing Office, 1984), 388–89.

27. Johnson, *Sleepwalking through History*, 171.

28. Landy, Roberts, and Thomas, *EPA*, 251–52.

29. Ibid., 256.

30. Tom Turner, "Changing the Guards," *Mother Earth News*, May–June 1989, 56.

31. William K. Reilly, "Pollution Prevention: An Environmental Goal for the '90s," *EPA Journal* 16, no. 1 (January–February 1990): 5.

32. "A Vision for EPA's Future," *EPA Journal* 16, no. 6 (September–October 1990): 5.

33. "William Reilly's Green Precision Weapons," *The Economist*, March 30, 1991, 28.

34. Executive Office of the President, Council on Environmental Quality, *The 21st Annual Report of the Council on Environmental Quality* (Washington, DC: U.S. Government Printing Office, 1991).

35. "Quailing over Clean Air," *Environment* 33, no. 6 (July–August 1991): 24.

36. For a general discussion of Congress and environmental policy-making, see Richard A. Cooley and Geoffrey Wandesforde-Smith, *Congress and the Environment* (Seattle: University of Washington Press, 1970). A less contemporary but still accurate view is provided by Henry M. Jackson, "Environmental Policy and the Congress," *Public Administration Review* 28, no. 4 (July–August 1968): 303–05.

37. Michael E. Kraft, "Environmental Gridlock: Searching for Consensus in Congress," in *Environmental Policy in the 1990s*, ed. Norman J. Vig and Michael E. Kraft (Washington, DC: Congressional Quarterly Press, 1990), 103–24.

38. Walter A. Rosenbaum, *Environmental Politics and Policy*, 2nd ed. (Washington, DC: Congressional Quarterly Press, 1991), 83.

39. Frederick R. Anderson, *NEPA in the Courts* (Baltimore: Johns Hopkins University Press, 1973), 17.

40. *Sierra Club v. Ruckelshaus*, 344 F.Supp. 2253 (1972).

41. *Natural Resources Defense Council v. EPA*, 475 F.2nd 968 (1973). For a thorough analysis of the courts' review of the Clean Air Act, see R. Shep Melnick, *Regulation and the Courts: The Case of the Clean Air Act* (Washington, DC: Brookings Institution, 1983).

42. Werner F. Grunbaum, *Judicial Policymaking: The Supreme Court and Environmental Quality* (Morristown, NJ: General Learning Press, 1976), 4.

43. The case that is generally regarded as opening the door to environmental group litigation is *Scenic Hudson Preservation Conference v. Federal Power Commission*, 453 F.2d 463 (2nd Cir., 1971). The local conservation group challenged the application of New York Edison Company to build a power plant on Storm King Mountain in the Hudson River Valley, and was granted standing by the Second Circuit Court under the Federal Power Act, which directs the Federal Power Commission to consider the impact of proposed projects.

44. Marianne Lavelle, "Talking about Air," *The National Law Journal*, June 10, 1991, 30.

45. See Lettie M. Wenner, *The Environmental Decade in Court* (Bloomington: Indiana University Press, 1982).

46. Barry G. Rabe, *Fragmentation and Integration in State Environmental Management* (Washington, DC: Conservation Foundation, 1986), 17.

47. J. Clarence Davies, *The Politics of Pollution* (New York: Pegasus, 1970), 128.

48. See Samuel P. Hays, *Beauty, Health and Permanence: Environmental Politics in the United States 1955–1985* (Cambridge, England: Cambridge University Press, 1987), 441.

49. Rabe, *Fragmentation and Integration*, 31.

50. See Elizabeth Haskell, "State Governments Tackle Pollution," in *Managing the Environment*, United States Environmental Protection Agency, Document EPA/600/5-73-010 (Washington, DC: U.S. Environmental Protection Agency, 1973), 135, 138.

51. Hays, *Beauty, Health, and Permanence*, 443.

52. For an explanation of the emerging trends of state innovation, see James P. Lester, "A New Federalism?" in *Environmental Policy in the 1990s*, ed. Norman J. Vig and Michael E. Kraft (Washington, DC: Congressional Quarterly Press, 1990), 59–79.

53. Edward Laverty, "Legacy of the 1980s in State Environmental Administration," in *Regulatory Federalism, Natural Resources, and Environmental Management*, ed. Michael S. Hamilton (Washington, DC: American Society for Public Administration, 1990), 68–70.

54. Susan J. Buck and Edward M. Hathway, "Designating State Natural Resource Trustees under the Superfund Amendments," in *Regulatory Federalism*, ed. Hamilton, 83–94.

55. Lester, "A New Federalism?" 70–71.

56. See, for example, Samuel P. Hays, "The New Environmental West," *Journal of Policy History* 3, no. 3 (1991): 223–48; and Continental Group, *Toward Responsible Growth: Economic and Environmental Concern in the Balance* (Stamford, CT: Continental Group, 1982).

57. To understand how states organize their programs, see Deborah Hitchcock Jessup, *Guide to State Environmental Programs* (Washington, DC: Bureau of National Affairs, 1990).

FOR FURTHER READING

Anne Burford, with John Greenya. *Are You Tough Enough?* New York: McGraw-Hill, 1986.

Marc K. Landy, Marc J. Roberts, and Stephen R. Thomas. *The EPA: Asking the Wrong Questions.* New York: Oxford University Press, 1990.

Jonathan Lash, Katherine Gillman, and David Sheridan. *A Season of Spoils: The Reagan Administration's Attack on the Environment.* New York: Pantheon Books, 1984.

Alfred A. Marcus. *Promise and Performance: Choosing and Implementing an Environmental Policy.* Westport, CT: Greenwood Press, 1980.

Barry G. Rabe. *Fragmentation and Integration in State Environmental Management.* Washington, DC: Conservation Foundation, 1986.

Robert A. Shanley. *Presidential Influence and Environmental Policy.* Westport, CT: Greenwood Press, 1992.

John C. Whitaker. *Striking a Balance: Environment and Natural Resources Policy in the Nixon–Ford Years.* Washington, D.C.: American Enterprise Institute, 1976.

PART 2

The Land

CHAPTER 4

Stewardship and Protection: Public and Private Lands

What you're seeing is people all over the country that are reaching the point of desperation. The Government issues more and more regulations, and we're losing local control over our land.

—David Howard, chairman of Alliance for America, a national coalition of property owner groups[1]

When the United States was in its infancy, "public lands" referred to the entire area west of the thirteen original colonies. The government, however, was not interested in being in the land business and began selling millions of acres to private owners as quickly as possible. The disposal process started with the Ordinance of 1785, which allowed the sale of parcels of land to the highest bidder at a minimum price of $1 per acre, with a 640-acre minimum. The disposal process did not end until 1934, when President Franklin Roosevelt signed the Taylor Grazing Act, which ended private settlement and established grazing districts on the remaining federal lands. By then more than one billion acres of public land had been brought under private ownership, with 170 million acres remaining under public domain.

The federal government slowed its marketing approach to public land in 1872 when it established Yellowstone National Park. This shift in both attitude and policy—from selling land to preserving it—was due in large part to the Progressive Era and the pleas of Thoreau and Emerson for government intervention to protect natural areas. Under growing pressure from the conservation movement, Congress began to tighten up the government's somewhat cavalier attitude toward land in the public domain. With passage of the 1891 Forest Reserve Act (repealed in 1907) the federal government began to set aside forest land to protect future timber supplies. Subsequent legislation in 1906 gave the president authority to withdraw federal lands from settlement and development if they had national or historic interest, and the 1920 Mineral Leasing Act authorized leases, rather than outright sales, of public lands for extraction of oil, gas, coal, and other minerals.

Congress has designated five major uses for public lands under its control: wilderness (lands set aside as undeveloped areas), national forests (areas reserved to ensure a continuous supply of timber, not exclusive of other uses), national parks (which are open to the public for recreational use and closed, for the most part, to economic use), national wildlife refuges (which provide a permanent habitat for migratory birds and animals); and rangelands (open for livestock grazing on a permit basis).

Today, five agencies hold responsibility for managing over 650 million acres of public lands: the Bureau of Land Management (270 million acres), the U.S. Forest Service (191 million acres), the U.S. Fish and Wildlife Service (92 million acres), the National Park Service (80 million acres), and the Department of Defense (25 million acres). Each agency has its own clientele, some of which overlap, and its own agenda in how it implements federal law. The conflicts created by shared jurisdiction are epitomized by the term *multiple use*, which refers to those federal lands that have been designated for a variety of purposes, ranging from grazing to recreational use. By its very name, multiple-use designation means that groups compete for the permitted right to use the land. A second component of the multiple-use policy is sustained yield, which means that no more forage or timber may be harvested than can be produced.

Several legislative efforts demonstrate the government's continued commitment to the multiple-use concept. In 1960, Congress enacted the Multiple Use Sustained Yield Act of 1960, and four years later, the Classification and Multiple Use Act. These two pieces of legislation recognized that land held within the public domain might be used for activities other than logging and grazing, although the laws were minimally successful in changing patterns of use that had existed for decades. When the Federal Land Policy and Management Act was enacted in 1976, it reiterated the government's position on multiple use. The legislation required full public participation in land management decisions and specified that all public lands under federal management were to continue under federal ownership unless their sale was in the national interest. Critics of multiple use, however, call the policy a charade, arguing that it is a smokescreen used by the federal government to justify the exploitation of public lands and resources by favored commodity interests.[2]

This chapter outlines the challenges now facing the federal government as it seeks to manage its public lands. There are several continuing debates that will be explored, including the perspectives of the stakeholders involved with each issue. The chapter continues with an overview of contemporary land-use issues and how environmental politics affects management decisions dealing with both public and private lands.

GRAZING RIGHTS AND WRONGS

In 1934, the Taylor Grazing Act established a federal Division of Grazing to work with the General Land Office to establish grazing districts, set fees, and grant permits for use. The two agencies later merged to become the Bureau of

Land Management (BLM). Fees are calculated on the basis of an Animal Unit Month (AUM)—the amount of forage required to feed a cow and her calf, a horse, or five goats or sheep for a month. Access to federal lands is fixed to base property ownership, so that those who own the greatest amount of property get priority for federal grazing privileges. A great deal of public land is involved—grazing is now permitted on 89 percent of all BLM land and 69 percent of all Forest Service lands, totaling more than 256 million acres.[3] Grazing is also permitted on many national wildlife refuges and within some national parks. When the Taylor Act went into effect in 1936, the fee was five cents per AUM, although the U.S. Forest Service and BLM have often differed in the rates they charged. Congress passed legislation in 1978 to require a uniform grazing fee, which reached a high of $2.36 per AUM in 1980. Shortly thereafter, the Public Rangelands Improvement Act required fees to be set by a formula which took into account production costs and beef prices; in 1993 the fees were set at $1.86 per AUM.[4]

Environmental organizations want the federal government to bring the charges more in line with what it costs to graze animals on the private market, which currently averages $9.22 per AUM, rather than subsidizing ranchers. Ranchers rely upon the subsidies as a way of providing their industry with a stable source of forage for their livestock. They also believe that public subsidies keep the cost of meat at a reasonable level for consumers and help to sustain the economic base for the rural West. So far, efforts to raise grazing fees (with increases pegged at anywhere from $2.56 to $8.70 per AUM) have been unsuccessful.[5]

In addition to the financial subsidies provided by the federal grazing program, critics point to the ecological damage caused by livestock. Overgrazing is claimed to have led to erosion and stream sedimentation in riparian habitats, and to have devastated populations of game birds, song birds, and fish. In one study, the General Accounting Office (GAO) found that more U.S. plant species are wiped out or endangered by livestock grazing than by any other single factor. Livestock are also major consumers of one of the West's most precious resources—water—which is needed to irrigate hay and other crops. Grazing also forces out populations of wildlife that cannot compete for forage and water.[6]

Besides fee increases, several solutions have been proposed to deal with the grazing issue. Using the slogan "Cattle Free by '93," some environmental groups are lobbying for a complete prohibition against grazing on federal lands. Others believe that agencies like the BLM simply need more funds to repair overgrazing damage and to monitor land use. A third option, proposed by the Sierra Club, would be to allow grazing on those lands that have not been abused, but to ban the practice on those that are already in unsatisfactory condition. That option is viewed as an acknowledgment that conservationists' achievements are not keeping up with chronic abuse of public lands.[7]

But most observers feel that the powerful livestock lobby will continue to control the outcome of the grazing issue.[8] The number of grazing permittees— about twenty-three thousand—is actually quite small, but their influence is not.

One 1988 GAO report found that "the BLM is not managing the permittees, rather, permittees are managing the BLM."[9] Occasionally, environmental groups have been successful in forcing the federal government to analyze the impact of grazing, as was the case in 1974 when the Natural Resources Defense Council won a landmark suit that forced the BLM to develop 144 environmental impact statements on grazing. But in response, ranchers fought back in a Rocky Mountain West movement during the late 1970s, which environmentalists called "The Great Terrain Robbery," better known as "The Sagebrush Rebellion."

During the late 1970s, several western groups were formed by conservatives and ranchers dissatisfied with the policies of the Bureau of Land Management. The movement had three objectives: to convince state legislatures to pass resolutions demanding that Bureau of Land Management and Forest Service lands be transferred from the federal government to individual states, to create a financial war chest for legal challenges in the federal courts, and to develop a broad public education campaign to get western voters to support the movement. The rebellion was portrayed as a "states' rights" issue, although it became obvious that what the organizers really wanted was to eliminate the federal government from having any say in how ranchers used the land. The Sagebrush Rebellion was the first organized and politically viable challenge to the environmental movement since the early 1950s. One observer, however, believes that although there was a rebellion for a time, only one side showed up to fight.[10]

The movement was successful in gaining favorable legislation in Arizona, New Mexico, Utah, and Wyoming, but by 1982 it had fizzled as a significant factor in western politics, especially in urban areas. Efforts to join the rebellion failed in Idaho, Montana, Oregon, South Dakota, and Washington State and were ended by gubernatorial veto in California and Colorado. Supporters believed that the election of Ronald Reagan in 1980, and his subsequent appointment of James Watt as secretary of the interior, would enhance their efforts, and there was certainly a more conservative approach to land policy taken during his administration. In 1982, Watt ordered his staff to investigate the disposal of federal lands, and Congress introduced bills to sell public lands as a way of reducing the federal deficit.

By late 1982, the Sagebrush Rebellion came under siege from those who believed the states were ill equipped to manage public lands properly. Government officials like former interior secretary Cecil Andrus and Arizona governor Bruce Babbitt, members of the hunting and fishing lobby, and organized environmental organizations like the Sierra Club and Audubon Society all criticized the movement as insensitive to the preservation of public lands. Under an umbrella group called Save Our Public Lands, the preservation lobbyists targeted Watt until he became a major liability to Reagan and was forced to resign in late 1983. Eventually, legal funds dried up, congressional legislation withered, and Reagan backed away from the cause. The movement disintegrated as it lost its leadership, but was successful in sensitizing federal agencies to the concerns of local users; however it was never effective in its primary goal of establishing a legal claim by western states to federal lands.

FORESTS AND TIMBER MANAGEMENT

About one-third, or approximately 730 million acres, of the U.S. land area is forested, two-thirds of which (about 480 million acres) is considered timberland, capable of growing commercial crops of trees. The federal government owns about 20 percent of those lands, with 7 percent owned by state and local governments, 1 percent by Indian tribes, 58 percent by private nonindustrial owners, and 14 percent by the forest industry. The battle over forest resources is complex, expanding to include concerns about jobs, economic diversity, endangered species, and global warming. At opposite ends in this conflict are timber companies and environmental groups, with federal agencies caught squarely in the middle.[11]

While the Bureau of Land Management has been the primary target of those who are dissatisfied with federal land policy, the U.S. Forest Service and the National Park Service have been criticized by environmental organizations for their stewardship of the nation's forests. That criticism goes back to the origin of the Forest Service in 1873, when the American Association for the Advancement of Science petitioned Congress to enact legislation to protect and properly manage U.S. forests. Despite the creation of a special bureau, the Division of Forestry, timber management practices were rife with scandal and exploitation. From 1910 to 1928, the agency concerned itself primarily with fire prevention and control, and Congress failed to gain control over forests on private lands.

It was not until the Forest Service gradually began increasing the harvest of national forest land after World War II that the agency became the focus of environmentalists. The need for timber that resulted from postwar economic growth was in conflict with public demand for recreational use of the nation's forests, and political battles erupted between the Forest Service and the National Park Service.[12] Environmental organizations have criticized the Forest Service on several fronts. First, they believe that the agency has placed timber considerations above all other uses and that it has been captured by the lumber lobby. Their criticism is based on the fact that unlike most federal agencies, which receive their entire budgets in the form of congressional appropriations, the Forest Service is allowed to keep almost all the money it earns from timber sales, which amounted to more than $629 million in 1990. Supporters counter that the timber sale program is one of the few national forest activities that earns a profit. In 1990, the program returned $327 million to states for county schools and roads.[13] The agency has now become the largest branch of the Department of Agriculture, with almost thirty-five thousand employees. It has also become the nation's largest road-building organization, with a network of timber roads eight times the size of the interstate highway system. The larger the sales, the larger the agency (and its clout).

In contrast, timber industry officials point to the battle over the northern spotted owl (discussed in Chapter 15) as evidence that environmentalists will do anything to shut down logging. Relying upon scientific studies to augment legal methods to preserve old growth, groups like the Oregon Natural Resources

Council and the Sierra Club fought for years to have the owl designated "threatened" under the Endangered Species Act. The designation forced the federal government to develop a recovery plan that set aside millions of acres of forest, previously scheduled for logging, as owl habitat.[14]

In addition to pressures from the outside, the Forest Service has been criticized by its own staff in several highly publicized media accounts of internal agency struggles. One of the employees' primary criticisms has been that decisions on how much timber to cut (termed the "allowable sale quantity") are being made without comprehensive forest planning, a requirement of the 1976 National Forest Management Act.[15] The legislation was designed to halt clear-cutting—the logging of all trees within a given stand—a practice that, in addition to being aesthetically unpleasing, often leads to erosion. Employee allegations that the Forest Service has set timber harvests on the basis of political considerations, rather than scientific analysis, are becoming commonplace.[16] One former staffer founded a group called the Association of Forest Service Employees for Environmental Ethics, which now has more than two thousand members. The group advises its members on their First Amendment rights to speak out against agency policies, but most remain silent for fear of losing their jobs.

There is considerable disagreement among forestry professionals and others over what the term *old growth* means, but it has become a rallying point in the timber management debate. One definition is that trees between one hundred fifty and two thousand years old make up "ancient forests," most of them in a corridor along the coast of California, Oregon, and Washington State. Although such trees make up less than 5 percent of the nation's entire forested acreage, environmentalists believe that logging within public lands has become excessive. Environmental groups seek to preserve ancient forests for a number of reasons, ranging from their place in the forest ecosystem and as habitat for endangered species to their spiritual value and place in native American religious practices.

Why are these magnificent trees being logged? The Forest Service has three classifications of forest management: preservation (in which no trees are logged), intensive (in which all trees are cut), and nonintensive (in which not every tree is cut). Some old-growth forests have been placed in the nonintensive category because decades of fire suppression policies let ground cover build up, stifling growth of new trees. Environmental groups counter that the Forest Service policy is simply an excuse for logging, and that little care is given to preserving old growth. From its perspective, the timber industry argues that America's working forests are being locked up by "no-use" advocates even though modern management makes forests an endlessly renewable resource. They point to the fact that America has nearly double the volume in its forests that it had half a century ago, and that new seedlings are being planted at a rate that far exceeds the number of trees being logged. More than six million seedlings are being planted every day,[17] although survival rates have recently come into question.

Economics has become a key issue in the battle over forest use. Environmentalists and timber workers share a common frustration over the destination of the trees once they are logged. Logs harvested from privately held lands may be exported to Japan, for example, which pays prices a third higher than U.S. market value. This results in the export of the highest-quality logs, costing thousands of jobs in the American wood-processing industry. Many communities in the Pacific Northwest are dependent on timber sales from public lands, since federal law requires that 25 percent of those National Forest timber revenues be returned to county government. In some counties, timber sale revenues from federal land totals nearly half of the county's overall budget. When timber sales are reduced, counties are forced to cut services, with the resulting impact felt throughout the region. Some communities are attempting to diversify their economic base into other types of industry and jobs, but such changes will not come overnight, and not without affecting local economies. In balancing the equation, timber companies point to the fact that nearly 1.2 million workers earn their living from forestry—growing, managing and harvesting trees, and producing products from them. The paper products manufacturing industry employs seven hundred thousand workers, generating sales of more than $100 billion a year.

The Forest Service also has been criticized for timber management policies that are characterized as being inefficient. One study by the environmental organization Resources for the Future, found Forest Service timber management expenditures are only minimally related to timber production potential, as measured by actual receipts from timber sales.[18] One congressional committee study found that 110 of the nation's 120 national forests are losing money, since trees are being sold to timber companies at a price lower than what it costs to prepare a site for logging and manage the sales. The loss to taxpayers over the past decade is estimated at $5.6 billion.[19] And a 1992 study by the congressional Office of Technology Assessment criticized the agency for favoring timber interests over protecting and preserving undeveloped land. The study said the agency's budgets, planning process, and historical perspective favor physical production over the forests' other values. Industry sources agree that costs exceed revenues in some cases, but point out that the Forest Service has a mandate to improve the forest and manage resources for the greatest net benefit, not the greatest dollar return. They agree that sales that fail to provide benefits to the public, multiple-use values, or the health of the forest should be eliminated.[20] Sweeping reforms, including a total restructuring of the agency and new budgetary incentives, have been proposed as the criticism continues.[21]

A number of proposals have been developed to preserve ancient forests while allowing for "wise use" of existing forest resources. One policy being proposed to counter the criticism has been termed "new forestry," whose principles include leaving live trees and dead snags for wildlife, and allowing dead logs and debris to remain to replenish the soil.[22] Other proposals include cutting less frequently (at intervals of three hundred fifty years rather than the current sixty to eighty years), leaving wider buffer zones along streams to protect habitats, and clustering clear-cuts instead of dispersing them evenly throughout the forests.[23]

Other efforts are aimed at preserving the remaining stands of old growth scattered throughout the Pacific Northwest. Several stands of redwoods are federally protected in areas like California's Redwoods National Park, but redwoods growing on private lands and in state preserves are subject to sale and logging. Groups like the Save-the-Redwoods League and the Nature Conservancy have raised funds to purchase property slated for logging, but millions of acres of trees of all species are still held privately and subject to future sale. The Sierra Club has proposed California's sequoia groves be declared a World Heritage Site, a designation adopted by the United Nations in 1972 to preserve great landmarks around the Earth. The designation already has been applied to more than three hundred sites, including the Taj Mahal, St. Peter's in Rome, Yellowstone National Park, and the Grand Canyon. The designation would provide protection under international treaties in which the United States is already a partner.

No matter what the outcome of the federal litigation, there is no doubt the battle over America's forests is becoming more politicized. While environmentalists are relying upon the courts to protect the forests, timber workers have dug in their heels and have threatened to fight to save their way of life through the ballot box, giving their support to public officials who side with loggers over preservationists. There is evidence the public's concern for the environment is strongly linked to economics, as evidenced by two examples. First, an initiative to protect old-growth forests in California was turned down by voters in 1990, and second, Oregon Governor Barbara Roberts became the target of three statewide recall efforts after comments she made were interpreted as antitimber. One analyst summed up the problem as follows: "Voters want clean air, clean water and unspoiled landscapes. What they don't want just now is the bill."[24] Or as one Oregonian's bumper sticker succinctly put it, "Loggers pay taxes—owls don't."

Another aspect of the policy issue is the fact consumers continue to demand products made from trees. Forest lands are harvested because each American uses the equivalent of a one-hundred-foot tree every year. Each new house requires an average thirteen thousand board feet of lumber and up to ten thousand square feet of panels. Americans use over seven hundred pounds of paper each year for books, toilet paper, packaging, and newspapers. As long as the demand for timber products continues, the debate over how to manage forests will continue as well.

"THE BEST IDEA AMERICA EVER HAD": THE NATIONAL PARKS

When President Woodrow Wilson signed the National Park Service Act in 1916, he brought thirty-six national parks under a single federal agency in what was termed by former British ambassador to the United States James Bryce as "the best idea America ever had." The concept of a national park has now been copied by more than one hundred twenty other nations around the world. Since it was created, the U.S. system has been enlarged to nearly three hundred sixty sites containing eighty million acres,[25] and with such growth has come a wealth of management and policy problems. On the occasion of the National Park Service's (NPS) seventy-fifth anniversary in 1991, the question of the role of the national park system in protecting the public lands once again gained a place on the policy agenda.

The debate on the future of the NPS focuses on four primary issues, best outlined in a three-year study by the National Parks and Conservation Association (NPCA), an independent organization whose purpose is to support the national parks. The study outlines the group's concerns on how best to operate the system into the next century.[26] First, despite the rapid growth of the number of sites within the system, there is concern over attempts to include virtually every site within the nation's borders that needs protection as a national park. Some authorities believe that not every monument, site, or region needs federal protection, but in fact would be better served by state or local government, or even by private groups. Some efforts have been made, for example, to establish joint responsibility, such as the Lyndon B. Johnson National Historical Park in Texas, and groups such as the Nature Conservancy have privately purchased lands not yet protected by other jurisdictions.

However, the NPCA noted that continued expansion of the park system is necessary to keep pace with the influx of visitors, which is expected to rise from an estimated 275 million in 1992 to 500 million by 2010. The group recommended the NPS begin acquiring the two million acres of private land located within the parks (with an estimated value of $2 billion), and enhance its mapping capability to make whatever boundary adjustments are necessary to include sensitive or valuable sites currently outside park borders. Concerns have also been raised about the encroachment of commercial development along park boundaries and into wildlife habitats. Boundaries for the parks have typically been segments of latitude and longitude, thereby threatening fragile ecosystems by bisecting them. Other concerns are more aesthetic and visual. For example, a cable television tower tops Red Hill, a ridge overlooking Antietam National Battlefield in Maryland, and new homes and a shopping mall are planned for Grove Farm, where President Abraham Lincoln and General George McClellan met following the Antietam battle. When historians and conservationists fought proposed development on a part of Virginia's Manassas battlefield in 1988, they relied upon computer simulations to convince members of Congress to purchase adjacent property, evidence that as population grows, the battle to preserve scenic and historic sites is heating up.[27] Controversies like these are proof the "battle over the battlefield" is still going on.

Based on a 1972 NPS study recommending the addition of a minimum of 196 areas, the NPCA identified forty-six natural areas, forty sites of historical significance, and ecological reserves, marine and estuarine ecosystems that should be added to the system. Congressional legislation has already been proposed to expand Death Valley and Joshua Tree national monuments (making them national parks) and a new unit, Mojave National Monument.

Critics of the proposed expansion question whether such growth is warranted when many existing parks are in need of infrastructure improvement and are suffering from personnel shortages. The NPCA estimates that the parks are already suffering from a $2 billion backlog in maintenance needs. A typical example is the proposed Hells Canyon National Park, a parcel of about one hundred fifty thousand acres along the Idaho and Oregon border that includes the nation's deepest gorge. Supporters, such as the Alliance for the Wild Rockies, argue that the designation is the only way to preserve the region, which would include the Snake River Breaks National Recreation Area and the Chief Joseph National Preserve. The federal government has begun the management effort by creating the Hells Canyon National Recreation Area, but environmentalists believe the region needs further protection and have called for a ban on timber harvesting and grazing in the proposed national park. But local public officials, including the two members of Congress who represent the area, have urged Congress to abandon the idea, reasoning that new units should not be added when there is already a backlog of repairs at existing parks.[28]

Second, the parks are walking what has been called "a tightrope between preservation and enjoyment."[29] Studies have already shown that many of the parks, such as Yosemite, have exceeded their carrying capacity for automobiles. Conflicts have arisen among users, such as those who want to ban scenic helicopter flights over the Grand Canyon or restrict mountain bikes or horses and pack animals on park trails. The NPCA has urged Congress to develop an independent research arm and a consistent, long-term visitor management policy, including designations of some uses as inappropriate in a park setting. Those concerns were underscored by another study released in August 1992 by the prestigious National Research Council. The group's report, which was requested by park service director James Ridenour, noted that NPS officials are called upon to make far-reaching choices between preserving natural treasures and providing service to mounting numbers of campers and sightseers without having an adequate science capability for those decisions.

Third, the activities of concessionaires and those with leases inside the parks have been the target of considerable legislative and public criticism. In 1965, Congress enacted the Concessions Policy Act, which was designed to limit concessions to those "necessary and appropriate" to the parks' purposes. The vagueness of the legislation has brought beauty parlors, banks, and video arcades to the parks along with more compatible enterprises like lodging and restaurants. The 560 concession operations, which range from family-run companies to large corporations, pay the U.S. Treasury a franchise fee based on their annual gross receipts, which in 1991 amounted to about $12.5 million for $500 million in sales, and prompting critics like Arkansas senator Dale Bumpers to argue the fees are too low and result in a virtual giveaway at public expense.[30]

The battle has centered on Yosemite National Park, whose twenty-year concessionaire franchise was purchased in 1973 by a subsidiary of MCA, Yosemite Park and Curry Company. Members of the Yosemite Restoration Trust, an environmentally oriented nonprofit organization seeking to reduce commercial activities within the park, have continually criticized the Curry Company's plans, which at one time included a tramway from the valley floor to the top of Half Dome.[31] A month before Bill Clinton was inaugurated, the NPS announced it was awarding a fifteen-year contract to Delaware North Company, a decision criticized by environmentalists who felt the choice should be postponed until after the new president took office. Under the terms of the contract, which must be approved by Congress, the firm will pay a franchise fee of 20.2 percent of gross revenue to the government (compared to three-quarters of 1 percent under the previous agreement). In addition, the new concessionaire committed to spending $6 million on repairs during the first year of the contract, and will put nearly $5 million into a capital improvement fund run by the NPS.[32]

Another controversy involves mining within the national parks. Most Americans are unaware there are several thousand mining claims and six million acres of mineral rights within NPS boundaries, and that a section of the agency, the Mining and Minerals Branch, oversees mineral development within the parks. Some mineral rights were established before the areas became national parks, while others stem from the 1872 General Mining Law, which granted almost limitless rights to extract ore from public lands. An individual who discovers mineral ore may stake a claim on federal land and simply pay a $2.50-per-acre fee to establish a patent, which transfers ownership from public to private hands—a provision that has been called "the law with no brain."[33] The landowner also receives the right to develop the property, even for nonmining purposes. New mining claims were terminated with passage of the Mining in the Parks Act in 1976, but abandoned mines and shafts still pose a formidable health and safety hazard. A 1989 NPS study found mining debris including barrels of fuel, solvents, and dynamite at Wrangell-St. Elias National Park, and dangerous radiation leaks just off the footpath off the West Rim Drive in Grand Canyon National Park. Groups like the Western States Public Lands Coalition believe the right to mine should transcend all public lands, including national parks, but environmental organizations feel the original intent of the law is now obsolete.[34]

Fourth, a study commissioned to examine the NPS on its seventy-fifth anniversary concluded that the agency is so weakened by internal problems and is so overwhelmed by outside pressures that it is on the verge of being unable to perform its job. A fourteen-member committee of park service officials, conservationists, and academics produced the report, known as the "Vail Agenda," in 1992. The document is highly critical of the way the agency treats its employees, and portrays an agency hobbled by budgetary problems, and poor pay, morale, and training. It cites examples where the park service is not living up to its mandate of educating the public and interpreting its sites, and recommends that the NPS be more aggressive in defending its properties against threats from activities outside park boundaries, especially in the Rocky Mountain West.[35]

Several groups believe the National Park Service should be removed from the Department of the Interior and made an independent agency. Critics point to staffing problems (the average entry level salary is only $15,000, and there is little career mobility within the agency), interference by the department in congressional hearings, staff shortages (NPCA recommends the immediate hiring of twelve hundred new rangers), and a lack of recruitment and training programs. Others point to the NPS's handling of the 1988 summer fire in Yellowstone National Park as an example of mismanagement and confusion over how the parks should be run. The agency's "let burn" policy was perceived as indifference by much of the public, when in fact it was part of a deliberate fire-suppression policy.[36] There is no doubt the management record of the NPS has been tumultuous—three of its directors were fired in five years—but the problems of the national parks go far beyond directors and staff. The unanswered question, as former NPS director George B. Hartzog, Jr., puts it, is, Whose parks are these, and for what purposes?[37]

WETLANDS

At the height of his campaign for president in 1988, George Bush announced on the shores of Boston Harbor there would be "no net loss" of the nation's remaining wetlands—a concept that was the brainchild of then-Conservation Foundation president William K. Reilly (later Bush's nominee to become administrator of the Environmental Protection Agency). During the 1992 presidential campaign, the term came back to haunt Bush as one of the major failures of his administration, eliciting criticism from both environmentalists and property owners.[38]

The Clean Water Act of 1972 included provisions that required anyone seeking to build or otherwise conduct business that would alter the landscape of wetlands to first obtain a permit from the Army Corps of Engineers. The policy was originally devised to protect sensitive ecological areas that serve as breeding grounds for migratory birds, plant habitats, and natural flood and storm control systems. A 1991 study by the Department of the Interior found that out of an original 221 million acres of wetland in the lower forty-eight states, only 103.3 million acres of wetland remain intact, with losses continuing at the rate of about two hundred to three hundred thousand acres each year, with the greatest acreage losses in Florida, Louisiana, Texas, Arkansas, Minnesota, and Illinois.[39] About 75 percent, or seventy-seven million acres, are privately owned. There is little disagreement over the importance of these areas—a 1987 National Wildlife Federation study reported that 45 percent of endangered animals and 26 percent of endangered plants depend directly or indirectly on wetlands.

Of particular interest in the act is Section 404, which makes it unlawful to put dredged or fill material into navigable waters—the term *wetlands* was never mentioned in the legislation. In 1975, a D.C. Court of Appeals decision held that the Clean Water Act applied not only to rivers but also to wetlands that drain into rivers, and eventually the statute was applied to isolated wetlands with no connection to rivers or waterways. Four agencies—the Department of Agriculture, the EPA, the Department of the Interior, and the Army Corps of Engineers—have developed regulations to implement the law and to designate about fifty million acres of land as wetlands. Each agency, however, had its own interpretation of the wetlands definition, so in 1989, regulations were tightened and made more consistent. Business interests and property owners soon found that land at least appearing to be dry most of the year was protected under the Clean Water Act. Oil companies feared that millions of acres of Alaskan tundra—which is classified as wetlands because water is frozen underneath— would be closed to development.

Farmers have been among the most vocal critics of federal wetlands policies. As a part of the 1985 food security bill, "Swampbuster" legislation made farmers ineligible for federal loans, price supports, and disaster payments if they drained existing wetlands on their property and converted them to cultivation.[40] One EPA study found that the law virtually eliminated wetland conversions, but a year later political pressure from a Republican facing a tough reelection battle brought about a suspension of the Swampbuster provisions in North Dakota, and penalties nationwide were reduced in 1990. The concerns were brought to the attention of the president by a group called the National Wetlands Coalition led by oil and gas, farming, and housing industry representatives, who had formed in 1989 to oppose sections of the wetlands program implementation. The organization asked the White House Council on Competitiveness, chaired by Vice President Dan Quayle, to develop a less restrictive wetlands definition.[41] The result was the release of the *Federal Manual for Identifying and Delineating Jurisdictional Wetlands* in August 1991. Under the new manual, the definition of wetlands was expanded to include areas that had mucky or peat-based soil, were havens to specific plants that thrived in moist areas or had water within eighteen inches of the surface for at least seven days during the growing season, and an additional fifty million acres came under federal protection. Two sections of the manual proved to be particularly controversial: first, a criterion of fifteen consecutive days of flooding or twenty-one days of saturation to the surface during the growing season as a wetlands designation, and second, the establishing of various types of evidence and procedures for deciding whether or not an area is a wetland.

More than eighty thousand formal comments, most of them highly critical of the proposal manual, were sent to the EPA. Critics of the proposed rules change argued that millions of acres of previously protected land would be opened to development. A National Wildlife Federation study maintained that the revised definition would exclude seasonal wetlands like prairie potholes (depressions in the Plains states left by glacial retreat that are filled by spring snowmelt), vernal pools (shallow depressions found in Oregon and California that flood during rainy season), and bottomland hardwood forested floodplains, which are a valuable agent of flood control and groundwater cleansing. A group of wetland scientists and environmental organizations, arguing that there was no scientific basis for the redefinition, called upon Congress to study the problem further.[42] They also feared the fourteen states that have adopted their own wetland protection programs would be pressured to make them consistent with federal law. In contrast to the president's policy, a December 1991 report by the National Research Council recommended the United States embark upon a policy of wetlands restoration, with a goal of a net gain of ten million acres of wetlands by 2010, a program that would go far beyond the Bush administration's policy of "no net loss." Failure to implement such a policy, the report warned, would lead to permanent ecological damage that would reduce the quality of American life.[43]

While the congressional hearings over the wetlands designations continued, the agencies charged with implementing the Clean Water Act have each interpreted the President Bush's mandate in different ways. The Army Corps of Engineers used a 1987 version of a wetlands manual, the EPA and the Fish and Wildlife Service used another developed in 1989, the Soil Conservation Service had its own slightly different criteria, and some federal agencies adopted the 1991 manual's proposed rules.[44]

Two developments forced the Clinton administration to reexamine its wetlands policies almost immediately. In April 1992 the Court of Appeals for the Seventh Circuit ruled in favor of a developer who was fined fifty-five thousand dollars by the EPA because he failed to obtain a permit from the Army Corps of Engineers to fill a small pond. The court ruled that EPA did not have the authority to impose the fine under the provisions of the Clean Water Act because the pond was an isolated wetland with no relationship or interdependence with any other body of water, nor was it part of an aquatic ecosystem.

The EPA had relied upon the commerce clause for its regulatory authority, arguing before the court that migratory birds might potentially use the pond. The court, however, in a footnote, noted that birds might also drink from a puddle in the median of a highway, potentially placing regulation of puddles under the agency's broad reading of the commerce clause.

This new judicial interpretation of wetlands caused both the EPA and the Army Corps of Engineers in 1993 to revert to the use of the 1987 manual, abandoning the proposed rewriting of federal wetlands regulations spearheaded by President Bush. The move by the two agencies represents a compromise between the stricter 1989 manual opposed by property owners and the more liberal 1991 regulations, but also put pressure on the Clinton administration to confront the problem without delay.[45]

While environmental organizations say the loopholes in the new policy could lead to the loss of designation of half of the nation's remaining wetlands,[46] other groups believe wetlands protection is best accomplished by private organizations and conservation foundations. Ducks Unlimited, for example, has raised over $400 million to purchase and protect about four million acres of wetlands and constructed over three thousand wetlands projects. Corporate interests, like the Louisiana Land and Exploration Company, have also undertaken marsh management programs.[47] Wetlands already receive adequate protection from existing state laws and federal endangered species legislation, many property owners feel, and the Clean Water Act definitions take away their ability to control the use of their land.[48]

One of the most interesting aspects of the wetlands controversy, however, is the politicization of the entire designation process. Early on during the Bush administration, it became clear to most observers that the development of a new wetlands criteria would deteriorate to a battle between developers and property rights advocates against environmentalists. The scientific community, with years of detailed reports and field testing, was gradually squeezed out of the process, with the result being a document that satisfied neither side.[49] The Bush administration politicized the problem even more on the eve of the November 1992 election by proposing to exempt the entire state of Alaska from a key federal restriction on the commercial development of wetlands. If accepted by Congress and the Clinton administration, the proposal, called the "Alaska rule," would ease permit requirements for oil and gas exploration, construction, timber harvesting and mining in a group of arctic ecosystems nearly twice as large in acreage as all of the remaining wetlands in the continental United States.

PRIVATE LAND-USE ISSUES

The battle over land has not been confined to the public domain, but in recent years has spilled over to include the environmental impact of private land use as well. Although the United States was founded on a principle of individualism that allowed each property owner to use his land as he saw fit, that concept is increasingly being tested in the courts. Environmentalists argue that property owners' rights may be limited when the inappropriate use of that land threatens the public good. Property owners just as vociferously argue that they have an unrestricted right to use their land for whatever purpose they choose.

The controversy has mushroomed with the onset of urban sprawl. Owners of facilities that handle the burdens of modern living, such as utility power plants, nuclear waste sites, landfills, and sewage treatment plants have traditionally been sited in remote or rural settings far from the customers they serve. Now they are being told they must move or shut down operation as residential areas encroach upon their previously distant locations. Neighbors argue that property values plummet and their children's health is threatened when their homes are close to power lines or dump sites. Suddenly no community wants them nearby.

NIMBYism

NIMBYs are noisy. NIMBYs are powerful. NIMBYs are everywhere. NIM-BYs are people who live near enough to corporate or government projects—and are upset enough about them—to work to stop, stall or shrink them. NIMBYs organize, march, sue and petition to block the developers they think are threatening them. They twist the arms of politicians and they learn how to influence regulators. They fight fiercely and then, win or lose, they vanish.[50]

This succinct definition identifies one of the most formidable of current land-use issues—NIMBY—an acronym for "Not in my backyard." NIMBYism has been described as a new force in American business life and is largely the result of efforts by state and local governments to increase public participation—a process that began in the late 1960s and early 1970s. Environmental legislation that mushroomed during this period often had mechanisms built in that provided the public with an opportunity to have input into the policymaking process, ranging from open public hearings and lengthy comment periods to full disclosure and rights to petition against a project. The assumption was such procedures would prevent projects from being sited in "bad" locations where the public did not want them to be built. As a result, citizens who oppose a project can use these tools to halt corporate and government projects they don't like or want "in their backyard." NIMBYism has most often been used to oppose projects termed LULUs—locally unwanted land uses. The term is often applied to major industrial plants, utility operations, and toxic or hazardous waste facilities, but NIMBYism also has been used against drug and alcohol rehabilitation centers, halfway houses, and group homes for mentally or physically challenged individuals. All of these projects or facilities are perceived by their neighbors as being harmful in some way, whether they produce smoke, dust, or noise, or lower property values. Some LULUs are government sponsored, like landfills or airports, while others are privately developed.

Increasingly, NIMBYism has taken on racial overtones, especially among minority group leaders who argue there is a tremendous racial disparity in the siting of LULUs, the cleanup of toxic waste sites, and penalties for polluting ethnic neighborhoods. The protests began in 1982 in Warren County, North Carolina, when the residents, most of whom were black, discovered their community had been selected as the location of a landfill for soil contaminated with highly toxic polychlorinated biphenyls (PCBs). Hundreds of demonstrators were jailed in an unsuccessful attempt to stop construction.

That incident was followed by a landmark 1987 study by the United Church of Christ's Commission on Racial Justice, which found that three of every five black and Hispanic Americans live in a community with uncontrolled toxic waste sites.[51] The commission's executive director, the Rev. Benjamin Chavis, coined the term *environmental racism* to describe the need for a movement combining the civil rights movement of the 1960s and the environmental movement of the 1970s. The study led the Rev. Jesse Jackson to launch a "toxics tour" of African-American communities coinciding with Earth Day in April 1990. The media attention for the tour led Jackson to bring five hundred demonstrators to protest plans for California's first toxic waste incinerator at Kettleman City, a predominantly Hispanic community.

The EPA has responded that the charges are unfounded and that poverty, low property values, and a lack of political power invite polluters, not racism.[52] But a 1992 study indicates the federal government gives a preference to white communities in cleaning up toxic waste sites. According to the report, the average penalties imposed in court for violations of all federal environmental laws were 46 percent higher in white communities, and 500 percent higher penalties were imposed under hazardous waste laws. The study also found it took longer for abandoned hazardous waste sites in minority areas to be cleaned up, and that more intensive treatment takes place at locations in white communities.[53]

Who are the NIMBYs? One survey found that demographic characteristics can be used to identify those most, and least, likely to oppose a project. NIMBYs tend to be located in the Northeast and West, particularly in California; they live in large (over two hundred fifty thousand population) urban communities, are liberal, young or middle-aged, college-educated Democrats of middle to high incomes, and may be housewives or professionals. In contrast, the least resistant, from a demographic standpoint, are conservative residents of small communities (under twenty-five thousand) in the rural South and in states like Michigan, Catholics, and low-income ranchers or farmers with a high school education or less.[54] Critics of NIMBYs argue that they enjoy the fruits of technological progress (like electricity or sanitation) but don't want to pay the price (like a utility substation or landfill).

Why is NIMBYism so pervasive?[55] Some attribute the concept to widespread distrust of corporations following major environmental crises like the leakage of poison gas in Bhopal, India, the toxic pollution of Love Canal, the radiation leak at Three Mile Island, or the Santa Barbara and Exxon Valdez oil spills. There is often a public perception that corporate executives are not being totally truthful about such incidents and, therefore, cannot be trusted when they tell local residents that a proposed facility is totally safe. Coupled with those concerns may be a generalized fear about anything chemical, a "chemophobia" about substances that are complex and often unknown. For example, in Rialto, California, sponsors of a proposed facility that would have used tires as fuel to burn nonhazardous waste provided residents with extensive information on the safety of the incineration process. Despite their claims, they had to dodge rumors that the plant was actually going to be burning drums of toxic chemicals and syringes from AIDS patients at a local hospital. The more bizarre and outlandish the rumors became, the more vocal the opposition became as well. The company planning to build the facility eventually abandoned the idea after several years of lawsuits and millions of dollars in legal fees.

NIMBYism is also a related to a property owner's fears that property values will plummet if a home or business is located near an undesirable facility. Even the most beautiful pastoral view can be spoiled by smokestacks reaching to the sky or the smell of noxious (even if perfectly safe) odors from a project. Combined with that view may be limited information about the project. Some researchers believe there is a relationship between the level of knowledge residents have about a project and their perception of risk, especially when there is scientific ambiguity or contradictions about the risk. Skepticism about the nature of risk is not limited to the public, either. A survey of one hundred seventy toxicologists found that more than 57 percent disagreed or strongly disagreed with the following statement; "If a scientific study produced evidence that a chemical causes cancer in animals, then we can be reasonably sure that the chemical will cause cancer in humans."[56] If the scientific community is faced with such uncertainty, who can the public believe?

In order to avert NIMBYism, companies are taking a variety of steps to protect their investment and reduce litigation. Community groups and homeowners are often brought in at the earliest stages of the planning process so that they are involved and consulted from the very beginning, rather than reading about the project in their local newspaper. This strategy helps to cut down on the rumors that often accompany a project that is not fully publicized. Another political option to NIMBYism is environmental dispute resolution, or EDR, in which the parties use informal, face-to-face negotiations to settle their differences rather than costly and time-consuming litigation. Some states have now built in EDR as a part of the process of approving solid or hazardous waste disposal sites, and the EPA regularly uses the technique when drafting environmental regulations.

Those who support EDR argue that it is less costly and less time-consuming than taking a developer or government agency to court. Homeowners, for example, may be reluctant to file suit against a corporate giant and may lack the legal expertise and resources to oppose a project. Civil cases may take years to wend their way through the legal system, resulting in costly delays for project sponsors and uncertainty for citizens. Courts by their very nature are adversarial proceedings, meaning that one party must "win" while the other must "lose," even though the differences between them may be negotiable. EDR can also help the parties to resolve issues that have no legal basis but where there is opposition nonetheless. Unless the parties can deal with the substantive issues of a dispute, the controversy is never really resolved.[57]

Critics of EDR, however, argue that there is little real evidence that environmental litigation is actually as time-consuming as proponents of EDR claim. It may not be cheaper, since mediators must still be paid and the process often takes place in addition to litigation. It may not be an especially democratic process, since mediators often choose whom to invite to the negotiating table, and there may be disparities in power between the two sides. "Repeat players" like corporations may enjoy a decided advantage over the novice "one shotters" or individual citizens who are unfamiliar with the legal system or lack negotiating expertise. Critics point to the fact that the business community is much more supportive of EDR than environmental groups as evidence that the process serves one side more than the other.[58]

Occasionally, a community will openly court a facility that has been shunned by other regions. A number of isolated rural California cities, for example, have competed to have state prisons located in their area, using the economic benefits of new jobs as a trade-off against any negative impact. But many of the kinds of land uses that are partners to progress, such as medical waste depositories, landfills, and utility power plants and transmission lines, face an uphill battle for anybody's backyard. Some environmental disputes may not be negotiable under any circumstances, as the clash of values between certain types of land use and individual citizens becomes even more incompatible. The political gridlock that develops has been characterized as a breakdown in the political process rather than an example of greedy entrepreneurs or corrupt politicians reacting to selfish citizen activists, a pejorative definition of NIMBYism that may not always be accurate.[59]

SLAPPs and SLAPP Backs

Sociology professor Penelope Canan and law professor George W. Pring of the University of Denver coined the acronym SLAPP (Strategic Lawsuits against Public Participation) in their 1988 study that described the proliferation of legal actions brought in an attempt to stifle political expression.[60] The authors found that many property owners were using civil actions against environmentalists and citizens' groups to intimidate or harass them into silence. The SLAPP suits, it is argued, make it prohibitively expensive for opponents of controversial projects to exercise their First Amendment rights and participate in public debates over land-use decisions.

In a typical SLAPP suit, a property owner would claim injury (such as defamation, damage to a business, or conspiracy) when a group or individual circulated a petition, appeared at a public hearing, or wrote a letter to an editor of a newspaper in opposition to a proposed project. An estimated four hundred cases nationwide have already been filed, most of them in wealthy urban areas. The cases last an average of three years, with the plaintiffs seeking damages of $9 million. SLAPPs are seldom successful; over 80 percent of the SLAPPs studied were dropped or won by the targeted defendant, but they are nevertheless intimidating. The SLAPP strategy has become so common that one organization, the Citizens' Clearinghouse on Hazardous Wastes, has formed "Project SLAPP Back" to help environmental groups threatened by such suits. Defendants have involved a range of groups from the Beverly Hills chapter of the League of Women Voters to a Colorado community group seeking to protect an elk meadow.[61]

Private developers are not the only ones filing suit. In New York, the state's Industrial Development Agency sued 328 opponents of a proposed trash incinerator for $1.5 million, alleging that the citizens were impeding a $74 million bond issue to finance the incinerator. The unique aspect of the SLAPP was that three previous suits attempting to stop the incinerator project had already been defeated, and the opponents had filed their lawsuit just one day before the bonds were to be delivered on Wall Street. The suit unnerved potential bond purchasers, and the underwriter was forced to discount the bond issue, which cost the development agency $1.5 million. Hence, the SLAPP for $1.5 million against the project's opponents.[62]

Sometimes SLAPPs are filed by small developers as a way of recouping legal fees and financial losses from projects that are stalled by environmental groups. For example, the owner of a proposed condominium project in Dillon, Colorado, filed a SLAPP suit for $1.6 million against residents on adjacent land who opposed the development, claiming abuse of process, interference with business opportunity, private nuisance, and trespass. In an interview, the developer admitted that the SLAPP had been filed because he had been forced to spend a considerable amount of money on legal fees, which he hoped to recover in the suit. Although the court dismissed the SLAPP suit, the developer incurred additional legal fees and eventually declared bankruptcy.[63]

SLAPPs not only intimidate those who are sued—they can also prove costly in terms of time and money. As a result, some groups and individuals are countering with SLAPP-backs. Victor Monia, head of a Saratoga, California group, West Valley Taxpayers and Environmentalists Association, was SLAPPed for $40 million by a developer who claimed he had been defamed in a flier circulated by the group prior to a development moratorium election. After the developer's suit was later dropped, Monia SLAPPed back with a malicious prosecution suit, and won. Three Kern County, California, farmers who placed a newspaper advertisement supporting the controversial Peripheral Canal water project were SLAPPed by a grower who opposed them, and won a $13.5 million jury verdict when they SLAPPed back. But even with the relatively high success rate of SLAPP backs, most of those involved admit that the cost and anxiety of facing a multimillion dollar lawsuit can make even the most ardent environmentalist or community activist think twice. Even supporters who sign petitions or are members of organizations are potentially liable—a factor that might intimidate them from participation.

Developers counter that SLAPPs make up only a tiny portion of the legal cases in American courts, and actually reflect builders' frustrations with no-growth crusades. They point out that several property owners who have gone through all the legal permits and processes have their projects held up by environmental groups who sue them without real justification, as was the case with the New York incineration project. There is, in fact, some truth to developers' claims that many legal actions are simply nuisance suits designed to stall projects which are a part of urban growth.[64] Others dispute the typical "David vs. Goliath" stereotype of SLAPPs. Often, the disputes involve small developers rather than huge corporations, since their economic and financial well-being may be tied to the success of a single project.[65]

Recently, however, anti-SLAPP legislation has been enacted in New York, California, and Washington State, and other states are considering similar mea-

What the Government Taketh Away . . .

One of the most potentially significant land-use cases to date was decided by the U.S. Supreme Court in 1992. David Lucas, a South Carolina developer, had been prohibited from developing two seaside lots on land he owned. A lower court had awarded Lucas $1.2 million in damages when he successfully argued that whose was to protect sensitive beaches on barrier islands, the building ban was unfair because his lots were already surrounded by other homes. Local officials and environmentalists, appealed the award to the U.S. Supreme Court. In a landmark decision favoring property owners, the Court ruled that the builder may seek compensation for the "taking" of his property if the government can prove that the development would cause environmental damage and must be restricted.

Compensation is not automatic; owners must still make the difficult case that they have lost their lands' "economically viable use"—a phrase that remains vague. The decision is likely to open a Pandora's box of future litigation as individual property owners seek to gain compensation for regulatory decision making. The Lucas decision means that local governments must show their decisions are based on "background principles of nuisance and property law" that would have prohibited what the landowner wanted to do, not just a change in attitude about land use. Still unresolved are questions of how much compensation is due when zoning affects only part of an owner's property, or when historic preservation is involved.[69]

sures. The legislation places new burdens of proof on the filer of the lawsuit, and some states require monetary sanctions for groundless or frivolous SLAPPs. The attorneys general of five states have intervened in SLAPPs to protect their citizens, and nationwide passage of a model anti-SLAPP bill is likely.[66]

In addition to SLAPPs, another new legal strategy has surfaced. Some landowners are turning to the courts to challenge environmental laws that they believe are restricting their rights to use their own property and that amount to a "taking." They believe that under the Fifth Amendment to the Constitution, they should be compensated for whatever losses they incur as a result of the government's action. University of Chicago law professor Richard A. Epstein, who was among the first to develop the concept,[67] notes that Congress has considered legislation to compensate owners prevented from using their lands. In 1991, fifty-two such claims—the most cases filed in at least a decade—were filed in the U.S. Claims Court, which was set up specifically to hear property cases not involving injury.

The Claims Court judges, mostly conservative Reagan appointees, have sided in favor of landowners in numerous cases, including a 1991 ruling in which the federal government was directed to pay a Wyoming coal company more than $150 million after the Department of the Interior barred mining on its land. The government appealed, and the U.S. Supreme Court upheld the lower court's ruling. The Appeals Court for the Federal Circuit is also considering two other appeals. In one case, a New Jersey housing developer was awarded $2.68 million in compensation after the Army Corps of Engineers barred construction on wetlands on a parcel the company had purchased. In the second case, a mining firm was awarded $1 million after the corps halted mining on land west of Miami due to concerns that the project would pollute local groundwater.[68]

TRENDS IN LAND USE AND MANAGEMENT

Given these examples of current land-use controversies, what does this tell us about trends in how America's land-use policies have developed?

First, attitudes about the management of public lands have evolved slowly in the United States, from a policy of divestiture and conservation to one of preservation. Those attitudes reflect the changing consciousness about the environment, which has had its peaks and valleys throughout U.S. history. When citizens are concerned about land use, they demand to be involved and participate fully. When they are apathetic, decisions get made without them.

Second, land-use policies are tempered by politics. Frustrated by their attempts to influence presidential policymaking, environmental groups have often turned to Congress or the president in hopes of exploiting regional and partisan rivalries. Many of the legislative mandates given to the agencies responsible for land management are vague and often contradictory, and Congress has seldom seemed eager to be more explicit in its direction. This is due, in part, to congressional sidestepping of many of the more controversial conflicts in resource use. Should deserts be opened up to all-terrain vehicles, or left in a pristine condition where no one can enjoy them? Should the national parks be made more accessible so that they can accommodate more visitors, or should traffic be limited so as not to destroy their scenic beauty through overuse? Should private property owners be told by governmental regulatory agencies how their land can be used? The answers to those questions depend, in large part, on which member of Congress, in what region of the country, is answering them.

Third, the future of public lands appears to have a price tag attached. Although there is a general sense that Americans want to preserve wilderness areas, scenic wonders, and some historic sites, they become less willing to do so when the decisions directly affect their pocketbooks. They may be willing to pay slightly higher fees to use state or national parks, but they rebel when the choice is between preservation of a single species and putting food on their family's table. As a result, land-use policies are more likely to take into account the economic impact of decisions rather than purely scientific ones.

Fourth, decisions about land-use policies are often made in the cloistered setting of administrative hearing rooms, poorly attended by those affected by the decision-making process, and only marginally publicized. The language of re-source management is esoteric, and the science often unsubstantiated. Thus, the debate over the future of public lands has historically been dominated by re-source users, such as timber and mining companies. More recently, however, environmental groups have "learned the language" of land and forest manage-ment, often hiring former industry experts. Still, most Americans know little about what is happening to the millions of acres still under federal control, and only well-organized groups that closely monitor regulatory actions (most of them based in the West) are in a position to speak for the public interest.[70]

Lastly, there is evidence of a growing rebellion against government intru-sion, especially among small property owners who are fighting land-use restric-tions, and by members of the wise-use movement discussed previously. Sometimes the protesters can convince officials to soften their rules. Elmyra Taylor's modern home in Hanover, Virginia, was lumped into a historic district in 1988 without her consent, limiting her ability to make any changes without approval from a local architectural board. In response, she and her neighbors decorated their homes with Christmas lights and pink flamingos. The board of supervisors later eased its restrictions.[71]

SUMMARY

The stewardship of America's public lands is exemplary of major policy shifts in the federal government's attitudes toward environmental protection. Initially, the government sought to dispose of millions of acres by selling them to homesteaders, a process that began in 1785. This policy not only encouraged expansion into the western frontier but also brought hard currency into the growing nation's coffers. During the Progressive Era and the blossoming of the conservation movement, the policy changed as attempts were made to preserve natural areas, especially during the development of the national park system. Today, the public lands debate flourishes on several fronts: Angry environmen-talists believe western lands are being exploited by ranchers who graze their cattle on subsidized federal land (and a reaction by ranchers during the late 1970s called the Sagebrush Rebellion). Another battle pits timber companies and their workers against those who feel agencies like the U.S. Forest Service are no longer protecting either trees or the public interest; the National Park System has come under fire by organizations who believe the program has expanded unnecessarily, and by those who feel the parks' infrastructure and staffing levels are deteriorating because of overuse and budget cuts. Among the most contro-versial of the environmental protection issues is preservation of wetlands; envi-ronmentalists believe President Bush reneged on his promise of "no net loss" and landowners who feel federal regulations unnecessarily restrict their rights to use their land as they see fit. In the 1980s and early 1990s, state and local governments began to play a more important role in land management as urban sprawl and population growth threatens the quality of life for many Americans.

As a result, public officials are being forced to make difficult (and often unpopular) decisions about the siting of facilities like sanitary landfills, electric utility substations, and transmission lines. Those decisions are resulting in a new wave of citizen participation in land-use decision making, creating a list of alphabet soup problems—NIMBYs, LULUs, and SLAPPs—and enhancing the role of the courts in an attempt to determine how the land is best used.

NOTES

1. Keith Schneider, "Environment Laws Face a Stiff Test from Landowners," *New York Times*, January 20, 1992, A-1.

2. Denzel and Nancy Ferguson, *Sacred Cows at the Public Trough* (Bend, OR: Maverick Publications, 1983), 171–72.

3. George Wuerthner, "How the West Was Eaten," *Wilderness* 54, no. 192 (Spring 1991): 28–37.

4. See Wesley Calef, *Private Grazing and Public Lands* (Chicago: University of Chicago Press, 1960); Phillip O. Foss, *Politics and Grass* (Seattle: University of Washington Press, 1960); and Gary D. Libecap, *Locking Up the Range* (Cambridge, MA: Ballinger, 1981).

5. See Phillip A. Davis, "Grazing Fee Increase OK'd by Interior Subcommittee," *Congressional Quarterly Weekly Report*, June 8, 1991, 1497.

6. George Wuerthner, "The Price Is Wrong," *Sierra* 75, no. 5 (September–October 1990): 38–43.

7. Rose Strickland, "Taking the Bull by the Horns," *Sierra* 75, no. 5 (September–October 1990): 46–48.

8. See William Voigt, *Public Grazing Lands* (New Brunswick, NJ: Rutgers University Press, 1976).

9. Wuerthner, "How the West Was Eaten," 36.

10. William L. Graf, *Wilderness Preservation and the Sagebrush Rebellions* (Savage, MD: Rowman and Littlefield, 1990), 229.

11. For an explanation of the influence of the various groups, see Paul Culhane, *Public Lands Politics* (Baltimore: Johns Hopkins University Press, 1981).

12. Ibid., 41–55.

13. For an industry view of these issues, see *Forest Resource Fact Book*, 2nd ed. (Memphis, TN: National Hardwood Lumber Association, 1991).

14. See U.S. Department of the Interior, Bureau of Land Management, *Management Guidelines for the Conservation of the Northern Spotted Owl* (Washington, DC: U.S. Government Printing Office, September 24, 1991).

15. See Charles F. Wilkinson and H. Michael Anderson, *Land and Resource Planning in the National Forests* (Washington, DC: Island Press, 1987).

16. See, for example, Paul Schneider, "When a Whistle Blows in the Forest," *Audubon* 7 (July 1990); 42–49; and Jim Stiak, "Memos to the Chief," *Sierra* 75, no. 4 (July–August 1990): 26–29.

17. For the industry perspective, see the publications of the American Forest Council, American Forest Resource Alliance, the California Redwood Association, and the Timber Association of California.

18. Marion Clawson, "The National Forests," *Science* 191, February 20, 1976: 762–67.

19. Schneider, "When a Whistle Blows in the Forest," 46.

20. *Forest Resource Fact Book*, 14.

21. See Randal O'Toole, *Reforming the Forest Service* (Washington, DC: Island Press, 1988).

22. See Jerry Franklin, "Toward a New Forestry," *American Forests* (November–December 1989): 37–44.

23. Stiak, 28.

24. Richard Lacayo, "Green Ballots vs. Greenbacks," *Time*, November 19, 1990, 44.

25. For a map and listing of the NPS sites, see Paul Pritchard, "The Best Idea America Ever Had," *National Geographic* 80, no. 2, (August 1991): 36–59.

26. National Parks and Conservation Association, *Investing in Park Futures, The National Park System Plan: A Blueprint for Tomorrow* (Washington, DC: 1988). The nine-volume study includes an executive summary of the organization's recommendations.

27. Randolph Harrison, "Protecting U.S. National Parks," *Environment* 32, no. 1 (January–February 1990): 18–19.

28. For an assessment of the Bush administration's policies, see Bruce Craig, "Promises to Keep," *National Parks* 65, nos. 11–12 (November–December 1991): 18–19. Eight park experts give the president a grade of "D" for his stand on new parks and operational initiatives, and a similar grade on park protection and commitment to Alaska's national parks.

29. *Investing in Park Futures*, 11.

30. Dale Bumpers, "Profit from the Parks," *National Parks* 65, nos. 3–4 (March–April 1991): 16–17.

31. Paul Rauber, "Yosemite: Paradise Regained?" *Sierra* 76, no. 2 (March–April 1991): 24–27.

32. Carl Nolte, "Government Selects Operator for Yosemite," *San Francisco Chronicle*, December 18, 1992, A-1.

33. Todd Wilkinson, "Undermining the Parks", *National Parks* 65, nos. 1–2 (January–February 1991): 28–31.

34. Ibid., 31.

35. Tom Kenworth, "It's No Day at the Beach for the National Park Service," *Washington Post National Weekly Edition*, April 13–19, 1992, 34.

36. For opposing views on the NPS management of the fire, see Paul Schullery, "Yellowstone: The Smoke Clears," *National Parks* 63, nos. 3–4 (March–April 1989): 18–21; Michael Rogers, "Once Burned, Twice Careful," *Newsweek*, August 27, 1990, 50–52; Thomas Hackett, "Fire," *The New Yorker*, October 2, 1989, 50–69; "Senate Holds Hearing on NPS Fire Policy," *National Parks* 63, nos. 1–2 (January–February 1989): 10–11; George Wuerthner, Larry Mehlhaff, and Geoffrey O'Gara, "Beyond the Burn," *Sierra* 74, no. 1 (January–February 1989): 40–51.

37. George P. Hartzog, Jr., *Battling for the National Parks* (Mt. Kisco, NY: Moyer Bell Limited, 1988). Hartzog served as director of the National Park Service from 1963 to 1972.

38. See Frank Graham, Jr., "Of Broccoli and Marshes," *Audubon* 7 (July 1990): 102.

39. U.S. Department of the Interior, U.S. Fish and Wildlife Service, *Wetlands Status and Trends* (Washington, DC: U.S. Government Printing Office, 1991). See also Michael Williams, ed., *Wetlands: A Threatened Landscape* (New York: Basil Blackwell, 1991).

40. See Curtis Bohlen, "Controversy over Federal Definition of Wetlands," *BioScience*, (March 1991); 139. See also Paul F. Scodari, *Wetlands Protection* (Washington, DC: Environmental Law Institute, 1990).

41. Keith Schneider, "Administration Proposes Opening Vast Protected Areas to Builders," *New York Times*, August 3, 1991, 1.

42. Warren E. Leary, "In Wetlands Debate, Acres and Dollars Hinge on Definitions," *New York Times*, October 15, 1991, C-4.

43. William K. Stevens, "Panel Urges Big Wetlands Restoration Project," *New York Times*, December 12, 1991, A-16.

44. Jon Kusler, "Wetlands Delineation: An Issue of Science or Politics?" *Environment* 34, no. 2 (March 1992): 7–11, 29–37.

45. Stephen M. Johnson, "Federal Regulation of Isolated Wetlands," *Environmental Law* 23, No. 1 (1993): 1.

46. Led by the Environmental Defense Fund, numerous mainstream groups have testified in opposition to the policy. See Marguerite Holloway, "High and Dry," *Scientific American* 265 (December 1991): 16–17.

47. There is considerable concern as to whether or not critical coastal marshes in Louisiana are being protected. See Donald G. Schueler, "Losing Louisiana," *Audubon* 7 (March 1990): 78.

48. John G. Miniter, "Muddy Waters: The Quagmire of Wetlands Regulation," *Policy Review* 56 (Spring 1991): 75–76.

49. Kusler, "Wetlands Delineation," 8.

50. William Glaberson, "Coping in the Age of 'Nimby,'" *New York Times*, June 19, 1988, Section 3, 1.

51. Commission for Racial Justice, *Toxic Waste and Race: A National Report on the Racial and Socioeconomic Characteristics of Communities with Toxic Waste Sites* (New York: United Church of Christ, 1987).

52. Michael Satchell, "A Whiff of Discrimination?" *U.S. News & World Report*, May 4, 1992, 34–45.

53. Marianne Lavelle and Marcia Coyle, "Unequal Protection: The Racial Divide in Environmental Law," *National Law Journal*, September 21, 1992, S-2.

54. Glaberson, "Coping in the New Age of 'Nimby,'" 25.

55. There is a tremendous amount of research into the concerns raised by residents in typical NIMBY settings. See, for example, Michael E. Kraft and Bruce B. Clary, "Citizen Participation and the NIMBY Syndrome: Public Response to Radioactive Waste Disposal," *Western Political Quarterly* 44 (June 1991): 299–329; Daniel Mazmanian and David Morell, "The 'NIMBY' Syndrome: Facility Siting and the Failure of Democratic Discourse," in *Environmental Policy in the 1990s*, ed. Norman J. Vig and Michael E. Kraft (Washington, DC: Congressional Quarterly Press, 1990), 125–43; David Morell and Christopher Magorian, *Siting Hazardous Waste Facilities: Local Opposition and the Myth of Preemption* (Cambridge, MA: Ballinger, 1982).

56. Howard Kunreuther and Ruth Patrick, "Managing the Risks of Hazardous Waste," *Environment* 33, no. 3 (April 1991): 15.

57. See James E. Crowfoot and Julia M. Wondolleck, *Environmental Disputes: Community Involvement in Conflict Resolution* (Washington, DC: Island Press, 1990).

58. Douglas J. Amy, "Environmental Dispute Resolution: The Promise and the Pitfalls," in *Environmental Policy in the 1990s*, ed. Norman J. Vig and Michael E. Kraft (Washington, DC: Congressional Quarterly Press, 1990), 211–34. A more expansive explanation of EDR is found in Amy's *The Politics of Environmental Mediation* (New York: Columbia University Press, 1987). See also Gerald Cormick, "Mediating Environmental Controversies: Perspectives and First Experiences," *Earth Law Journal* 2 (1976): 215; and J. Walton Blackburn, "Environmental Mediation as an Alternative to Litigation," *Policy Studies Journal* 16, no. 3 (Spring 1988): 563; James E. Crowfoot and Julia M. Wondolleck, *Community Involvement in Conflict Resolution* (Washington, DC: Island Press, 1990).

59. See Denis J. Brion, *Essential Industry and the NIMBY Phenomenon* (New York: Quorum Books, 1991). The author uses the siting of hazardous waste treatment facilities in Massachusetts as a case study for his view of NIMBYism.

60. Penelope Canan and George W. Pring, "Strategic Lawsuits against Public Participation," *Social Problems* 35, no. 5 (December 1988): 506–19. See also Penelope

Canan and George W. Pring, "Studying Strategic Lawsuits against Public Participation: Mixing Quantitative and Qualitative Approaches," *Law and Society Review* 22, no. 2 (1988): 385–95.

61. See Robert H. Boyle, "Activists at Risk of Being SLAPPed," *Sports Illustrated*, March 25, 1991, 20–23.

62. Jason Zweig, "A SLAPP in the Face," *Forbes*, May 29, 1989, 106.

63. The case is cited in Penelope Canan, Gloria Satterfield, Laurie Larson, and Martin Kretzmann, "Political Claims, Legal Derailment, and the Context of Disputes," *Law and Society Review* 24, no. 4 (1990): 923–52.

64. See David Rosenberg and S. Shavell, "A Model in Which Suits Are Brought for Their Nuisance Value," *International Review of Law and Economics* 5 (1985): 3–13.

65. For the building industry's view, see Katherine Bishop, "New Tool of Developers and Others Quells Private Opposition to Projects," *New York Times*, April 26, 1991, B-9.

66. George W. Pring and Penelope Canan, "Striking Back at the Dreaded SLAPP," *National Law Journal* October 12, 1992, 13–14.

67. Richard A. Epstein, *Takings, Private Property and the Power of Eminent Domain* (Cambridge, MA: Harvard University Press, 1985).

68. Schneider, "Environment Laws Face a Stiff Test," A-8.

69. See Ted Gest and Lisa J. Moore, "The Tide Turns for Property Owners," *U.S. News & World Report*, July 13, 1992, 57.

70. See Walter Rosenbaum, *Environmental Politics and Policy* (Washington, DC: Congressional Quarterly, 1991), 279–98.

71. Lisa J. Moore, "When Landowners Clash with the Law," *U.S. News & World Report*, April 6, 1992, 80–81.

FOR FURTHER READING

Denis J. Brion. *Essential Industry and the NIMBY Phenomenon.* New York: Quorum Books, 1991.

Paul J. Culhane. *Public Lands Politics.* Baltimore: Johns Hopkins University Press, 1981.

Phillip O. Foss, ed. *Federal Lands Policy.* New York: Greenwood Press, 1987.

John C. Freemuth. *Islands under Siege: National Parks and the Politics of External Threats.* Lawrence: University of Kansas Press, 1991.

William L. Graf. *Wilderness Preservation and the Sagebrush Rebellions.* Savage, MD: Rowman and Littlefield, 1990.

George B. Hartzog, Jr. *Battling for the National Parks.* Mt. Kisco, NY: Moyer Bell, 1988.

Jon A. Kusler and Mary E. Kentula. *Wetland Creation and Restoration.* Washington, DC: Island Press, 1990.

CHAPTER 5

Waste Not, Want Not

We can spend every tax dollar we have to find a home for our garbage in the Midwest at the expense of police, teachers, and hospitals if that's what we really want. It isn't a question of recycle or burn. We have to do both.
—Steven Polan, former New York City Sanitation commissioner[1]

In 1986, Islip, a community on New York's Long Island, closed its landfill to school and commercial trash. The local hauler, Waste Alternatives, was paying $86 a ton to cart the city's trash upstate, so when United Marine Transport Services offered to charge only $50 a ton to bale, load, and barge the trash and ship it "somewhere down South," the company readily agreed. In March 1987, the barge Mobro 4000 attempted to tie up at the dock in Morehead City, North Carolina. Officials there refused to allow the barge to unload, and the trash odyssey began. For the next six thousand miles and 164 days, the barge tried to dock in Louisiana, Florida, New York, Mexico, Belize, and the Bahamas in an attempt to find someone, somewhere, willing to accept the city's trash. Mexico and Cuba even sent gunboats to make sure the barge stayed away from their shores as well. Turned away from ports along the eastern and southern seaboard, the trash was eventually burned in Brooklyn, with the ashes buried where the journey had begun—back in Islip.[2]

The tale of the garbage barge symbolizes one of the environmental protection problems often considered the most neglected issue of the decade— managing waste. Historically, man has simply covered up the refuse of life with dirt or dumped it where it was out of sight and out of mind. Now, old habits are coming back to haunt us as we (a) produce more waste than ever before and (b) run out of places to put it. This chapter explores the management of waste and the strategies that are being developed to try to deal with this ongoing and highly politicized problem. The discussion begins with an overview of the problems of solid and hazardous waste generation and disposal. The main focus of the chapter, however, is an analysis of the regulatory framework of waste management, with particular emphasis on international regimes to control the hazardous waste trade.

THE NATURE OF WASTE: GENERATION AND DISPOSAL

Historians who have studied man's development note there has not always been a refuse problem, at least of the magnitude of modern times. Refuse is primarily an urban problem, exacerbated by limited space and dense populations. It must also be perceived to be a problem—understood to have a negative effect on human life—or else it will be viewed as an annoyance rather than as a health or environmental problem. That transition occurred in the United States between 1880 and 1920, when the "garbage nuisance" was first recognized. City dwellers could no longer ignore the piles of garbage and manure from horsecars that covered sidewalks and streets or polluted local waterways, and a sense of community responsibility evolved as citizens developed an awareness of doing something about the problem. Garbage was seen as not only a health issue, but also an aesthetic one—detracting from the overall attractiveness of city living. Gradually, municipal governments developed street-cleaning and disposal programs (controlled by health officials and representatives of civic organizations) to begin to grapple with the massive wastes generated by a growing industrial society.[3]

Just before the turn of the century, Americans imported one of the most common European methods of waste disposal—the "destructor," or garbage furnace. The British, with insufficient cheap land or water as dumping areas, had turned to incineration, which was hailed as a waste panacea. Cities throughout the United States quickly installed incinerators, while researchers continued to experiment with other European technologies such as extracting oil and other byproducts through the compression of city garbage. During the first quarter of the twentieth century, the emphasis was on waste elimination, with little thought given to controlling the generation of waste. After World War I, however, the growth of the American economy changed the refuse situation with a dramatic increase in packaging materials—plastics, paper goods, and synthetics—which became a part of the waste stream. This not only increased the amount of waste, but posed new collection and disposal problems for local governments to contend with. One researcher estimates solid waste increased about five times as rapidly as population after World War I. The most dramatic change in the composition of waste was the massive increase in the proportion of paper, which by 1975 accounted for nearly half of all municipal refuse. This increase is attributed to rampant consumerism during the 1970s, which fostered a boom in the packaging industry.[4]

Researchers estimate the annual U.S. trash output at between 180 and 250 million tons, or four pounds per person per day, with the remainder from agricultural and mining activities. Figure 5.1 shows the components of today's municipal waste—most of which is made up of paper and cardboard products. Americans deserve their reputation for being a "throw-away society," since they produce more than twice the consumer trash of any other industrialized nation. Much of our waste comes from the packaging of products we use daily— aluminum cans, cardboard boxes, cellophane, plastic jugs, and glass bottles, but

Figure 5.1 Municipal Solid Waste Generation

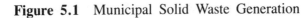
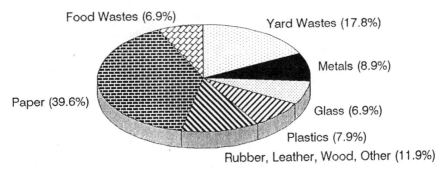

Food Wastes (6.9%)

Yard Wastes (17.8%)

Metals (8.9%)

Paper (39.6%)

Glass (6.9%)

Plastics (7.9%)

Rubber, Leather, Wood, Other (11.9%)

it also includes less obvious waste like abandoned appliances, junked automobiles, and used tires.

The Environmental Protection Agency estimates of the amount of municipal solid waste (MSW) likely to be generated in the future are staggering. Without source reduction (reducing the volume of waste material before it enters the waste stream initially) the amount of waste generated in 1995 is expected to reach 200 million tons, or 4.2 pounds per person per day, and by 2000, 216 million tons, or 4.4 pounds per person per day. The per capita figure for the year 2000 is a 10 percent increase over 1988 levels. By 2010, the figure jumps to 250 million tons, or 4.9 pounds per person per day.[5]

Hazardous waste, another critical element of the disposal issue, consists of substances (liquid, solid, or sludges) considered flammable, corrosive, reactive, explosive, or toxic (defined as containing one or more of thirty-nine specific compounds at levels that exceed established limits). Federal regulations also classify as hazardous any other wastes mixed with hazardous waste, as well as byproducts of the treatment of hazardous waste. Hazardous waste may be a byproduct of manufacturing processes or commercial and consumer products—like cleaning fluid or battery acid—that have been discarded, and may include heavy metals from electroplating operations, solvents, and degreasing agents. Hazardous waste also poses problems when used by consumers and farms, which must find appropriate methods of disposal. Revelations in the early 1990s about massive hazardous waste dumps at U.S. military bases have spotlighted a whole new set of cleanup problems.[6]

The problem is acute because in the past, waste generators were often unaware or unconcerned about the potential toxic effects of hazardous waste. Dangerous chemicals may percolate from holding ponds into underlying ground water, or wash over the ground into surface water and wetlands. Some hazardous waste evaporates into the air, or explodes, while other types soak into the soil and contaminate the ground. Still other forms bioaccumulate in plants and animals, which are later consumed by human beings as food. Typical hazardous wastes include dioxin, petroleum, lead, asbestos, and PCBs. As researchers discovered the potential consequences of mishandling, they raised questions about what to do with it and, eventually, how to regulate hazardous waste.

Primitive cultures had an easy answer to disposal—they simply left it where they created it. Leftover or spoiled food and excrement were allowed to rot on the ground where they naturally decomposed and returned to the earth as fertilizing compost, completing the naturally occurring ecological cycle. Aside from odors and foraging wildlife, waste did not pose much of a problem until it got in the way of other human activities. As the population grew, people began to burn their waste or bury it in the ground—practices that have remained unchanged throughout most of our history. In its most recent survey of what happens to municipal waste, the EPA reported 73 percent is landfilled, 14 percent is burned, and the remaining 13 percent is recovered, or removed from the waste stream through recycling or composting.[7] But the issue has become complex and politicized, as a survey of disposal methods shows.

Burial and Landfills

Dumping and burial have been among the most common ways of disposing of municipal waste, although communities have developed sanitary landfills as a way of avoiding the environmental problems caused by burial. In the late 1970s, the United States had nearly twenty thousand landfills; at present, there are about six thousand facilities in operation. Eight states—Connecticut, Kentucky, Massachusetts, New Jersey, Ohio, Pennsylvania, Virginia, and West Virginia—face an acute shortage of landfill space and are expected to reach full capacity by 1995. The number of landfills declined as the federal government began regulating waste disposal in the 1960s. One of the biggest concerns over landfill operation has been pollution; since most landfills accept whatever household garbage is collected by waste haulers, there is often little screening of what gets dumped. As a result, landfills may contain a variety of substances, ranging from paints and solvents to toxic chemicals, which residents routinely put into their curbside trash. In older landfills, leachate (formed when water from rain or the waste itself percolates through the landfill) sometimes seeps into the ground, polluting the surrounding groundwater. Today's sanitary landfills, in contrast, are located on land where the risk of seepage is minimal, and most facilities are lined with layers of clay and plastic. A complex series of pipes and pumping equipment collects and distills the leachate and vents flammable methane gas, which is formed by the decomposition of waste. Many landfills now recover the gas and distribute it to customers, or use it to generate electricity.

The amount of MSW landfilled in the United States each year varies considerably depending, in large part, on political and public acceptance of various disposal methods. In 1960, for example, approximately 62 percent of MSW was sent to landfills, but the figure increased to 81 percent in 1980, and decreased to 73 percent in 1988. When the use of incineration for MSW declines and recovery rates are low, the MSW percentage sent to landfills increases. Similarly, when recovery and combustion of MSW increase, the percentage of MSW discarded to landfills declines.[8] The most critical political problem facing policymakers is the shortage of landfill space available in the United States. Only 20 percent of the landfills in operation in 1986 are expected to be open in the year 2008, despite increasing amounts of waste. As a result of this shortage of landfill space, the cost of disposal has risen astronomically. In Philadelphia, for example, the city's disposal costs have risen from $20 to $90 per ton since 1980.[9]

Why has the shortage occurred? The criteria for what becomes an acceptable disposal site have changed, making it difficult to increase either the number or capacity of burial facilities. Historically, the key criterion for landfill operation was accessibility, but that gradually changed to a goal of minimizing health risks. By the 1930s, the United States switched from open dumping to sanitary landfills, which involves the compaction and burying of waste. Most cities established their landfills on the most inexpensive and accessible land available, which typically was a gravel pit, quarry, or wetland, with little attention given to environmental considerations. With the advent of the environmental movement in the 1960s and 1970s, planners began to consider whether a proposed site was near a residential area, susceptible to natural phenomena like earthquakes or flooding, a potential threat to water quality, and the hauling distance from where the refuse was collected. Disposal costs today increase by as much as $1 per ton for every mile the garbage is transported. Today's landfill operations are tightly regulated by federal restrictions, which govern the location, design, operating, and closure requirements, as well as cleanup standards for existing contamination.

Incineration

Many European nations have been successful at instituting waste incineration programs to deal with municipal waste. Their modern facilities produce minimal levels of visible emissions and have the added advantage of generating electricity as a byproduct. The United States, in contrast, has been unsuccessful in convincing either policymakers or its citizens of the acceptability of incineration as a disposal method since the first garbage furnace was installed in 1885 on Governor's Island, New York.

Incineration was initially accepted as a disposal method because it was considered the most sanitary and economical method available. Modifications of the European technology proved ineffective, however, for U.S. needs. Sanitation engineers became critical of the facilities, which often produced gas and smoke emissions because the waste was not completely burned when furnace temperatures were lowered to save on fuel consumption. Beyond design and operational problems, many of the incinerators were built by unscrupulous or inexperienced companies, and by 1909, 102 of the 180 furnaces erected between 1885 and

1908 had been abandoned or dismantled. Later adaptations of English technology produced a second generation of incinerators, and the facilities flourished until the 1960s. At that point, concerns about air pollution surfaced, and cities like Los Angeles began to legislate against incinerators, setting standards so high they virtually outlawed the plants. Although the technology was available to increase their efficiency and reduce polluting emissions, the cost of upgrading equipment was high in comparison to disposal in sanitary landfills.[10]

Although there is still some support for burning waste, especially among those who note the advantage of reducing the volume of waste or who view the capacity of the incinerator as an energy generator, critics of the method have brought a virtual end to new facility development in the United States. Even with improved technology, many facilities have suffered from mechanical breakdowns and costly repairs, and attempts to transfer European incineration technology to the United States have often been unsuccessful because American trash contains considerably more plastic that, when burned, produces toxic gases and leads to corrosion of equipment. Even those plants that run efficiently are being closely scrutinized for adverse health effects. Environmental groups have raised questions about the toxicity of both the gases and the ash produced by the combustion process.

Despite these objections and problems, over one hundred waste-to-energy plants are now in operation nationwide. Most of the plants are called "mass-burn" facilities because they use unsegregated waste as a fuel, producing electricity that can then be sold to customers. Refuse-derived fuel plants, in contrast, remove materials that can be recycled from the waste stream, such as plastics and glass, and shred the remaining components, which are then burned in boilers. They have several advantages over other municipal disposal options because they require no change in waste collection patterns, their management can be turned over to a private owner if desired, low-cost financing mechanisms are available, and the market for the electricity they produce is guaranteed under the 1978 Public Utilities Regulatory Policies Act. Incineration is also considered one of the most effective ways of dealing with hazardous wastes.[11] Still, only about 14 percent of U.S. municipal waste is incinerated today, compared to countries like Denmark, Japan, Sweden, and Switzerland, which burn more than half their waste.[12] The EPA projects combustion will increase significantly as a waste management strategy between 1995 and 2000, accounting for over half of the disposal of the MSW by 2000.[13]

Public opposition to incineration has proved to be the most formidable barrier to siting any new facilities,[14] ending projects throughout the United States, from the LANCER facility in Los Angeles to the Brooklyn Navy Yard, where opponents promised to block a proposed incinerator with their bodies. New Jersey residents even rejected a referendum on the state's ballot over an incinerator that had been planned and approved for a decade. Political leaders have found the topic so volatile that it has created an acronym of its own—NIMTOO—for "Not in My Term of Office." The phrase refers to the virtual

Lancer: The L.A. Experience

Termed "the Twenty-first Century Solid Waste Management Solution," the City of Los Angeles proposed three mass-burn incineration projects during the late 1970s in hopes of solving the massive garbage disposal problems faced by the growing metropolis. The Los Angeles City Energy Recovery Project, known by its acronym LANCER, was designed to burn as much as 70 percent of the city's municipal solid waste and at the same time, generate electric power for Los Angeles. LANCER was developed at a time when the city was recognizing both the severity of its air quality problem and the need to move from its traditional disposal practices, which included open dumps, backyard incineration, and feeding organic wastes to swine.

After the city's senior sanitation engineer returned from a tour of facilities in Europe and Japan, Los Angeles officials jumped on the incineration bandwagon, choosing as a site for their facility a parcel in a deteriorating residential area that had once been a thriving industrial and commercial section. The community was young, poor, and 96 percent minorities. By the time the city began holding informational workshops for residents in late 1985, Los Angeles was firmly committed to the project, with the local councilman using his office as command center. Community opposition was slow to emerge, due perhaps to a lack of information about what the project really was. One elderly resident thought LANCER was a shopping center, and most of the workshops were sparsely attended.

The political battles waged on two fronts: the financing of the project and the selection of a vendor. Brokerage firms, which stood to gain huge commissions and fees if chosen, heavily lobbied the council for the right to sell the bonds for the project. Meanwhile, a group of residents near the proposed site formed Concerned Citizens of South Central Los Angeles to oppose the project. The group's members were politically unsophisticated in dealing with environmental issues, but they successfully formed a coalition with other opposition groups like Not Yet New York and the California Alliance in Defense of Residential Environments, headed by veteran environmental activists who lent credibility and expertise to the effort.

The city responded with a public relations campaign, which included a $250,000 LANCER information center, complete with a video, fliers, and a paid staff of eight community representatives. Fearing the involvement of the outside groups and their membership, most of whom were upper-class whites, the city handed out leaflets that warned, "Don't let people who live outside your community tell you what to think." That approach backfired, and the environmental groups capitalized on documents warning about the potential health risks of the facility to nearby residents. Opponents also raised the issue of financial risk and further flexed their political muscle in the June 1987 election by defeating two city council incumbents, including the council president, who had supported the project.

The LANCER project died in mid-1987 after supporters had spent $12 million in their ten-year effort to bring incineration to Los Angeles. The cause of death was due a number of factors, including organized community opposition, which grew stronger as the health risk estimates were challenged, the economic uncertainties of the project, and a flawed decision-making process that turned the project into a political liability for those who had originally supported it. With two new anti-LANCER city council members on board, the mayor announced at a news conference he was withdrawing his support, and despite attempts by lobbyists to salvage the project by perhaps moving it to another site, the LANCER chapter ended.[16]

paralysis over solid waste that keeps municipal officials from approving incineration projects in favor of more expensive disposal solutions.[15] The situation is quite different from that of Europe, where incineration has been more widely accepted. The difference lies perhaps in the contrast of political systems, since nations like Denmark and Germany have a strong history of centralized decision making. This precludes the kinds of public participation and access to the legal system that allows citizens in the United States to have such an impact on decisions like siting.

Ocean Dumping

The dumping of wastes into the ocean is one of the few disposal methods that has received almost universal condemnation. The initial objections to the practice were not necessarily environmental—too much of the garbage dumped off the New York coast in the early 1900s floated back to shore. The practice was also considered too costly, since barges had to tow the garbage to deep water to keep it from floating back to the surface and washing up on local beaches. The legal ramifications of dumping municipal waste into waterways— as downstream cities filed lawsuits against upstream cities—limited the practice as well. Besides, burial of waste seemed much more attractive and inexpensive to early sanitation engineers by the 1920s. In 1933, New Jersey coastal cities went to court to force New York City to halt ocean dumping, a ruling affirmed by the U.S. Supreme Court in 1934, when the practice ceased as a major means of disposal.

The Supreme Court ruling applied only to municipal waste, however, and the ocean dumping of industrial and commercial waste continued unabated. By the end of the 1960s, an estimated fifty million tons of waste were dumped into the ocean, most of it in the East, where the rate doubled between 1959 and 1968. In the mid-1970s, there were nearly 120 ocean sites for waste disposal supervised by the U.S. Coast Guard. Of particular concern has been the use of ocean dumping for toxic wastes.[17] Not until passage of the Marine Protection, Research, and Sanctuaries Act in 1972 was there a federal effort to stop the practice, followed by the Ocean Dumping Ban Act in 1988, which restricted offshore dumping of sewage sludge and other wastes.

In 1992, attempts were made to circumvent the ban by allowing the Defense Department to test a new technology called deep ocean isolation. The process involves the use of submersibles to deposit waste directly on the ocean floor, thus avoiding the ocean currents that can allow waste to migrate. Despite legislative efforts to thwart any attempt at renewed ocean dumping, some believe it is foolish to close off 70 percent of the world's surface to waste disposal without even allowing tests to proceed.[18]

Recycling

The terms *recycling* and *recovery* refer to the reuse of materials, and most waste management analysts believe recycling represents one of the most underused yet promising strategies for waste disposal.[19] There are two aspects of recycling: primary recycling, in which the original material is made back into the same material and is also recyclable (such as newspapers back into newspapers), and secondary recycling, in which products are made into other products that may or may not be recyclable (such as cereal boxes made out of waste paper). Recycling gained acceptance in the early 1970s as the public became more aware of the garbage crisis, the need to conserve natural resources, and the shortage of landfill space. About 7 percent of the MSW was recovered in the 1960s and 1970s, then increased gradually during the 1980s to about 13 percent today.

Recycling is actually less an environmental issue than it is an economic supply-and-demand issue. A shortage of markets for recycled goods represents the biggest obstacle to this waste management approach. During the early 1970s, recycling gained acceptance not only in the public's mind but economically as well. Rising costs of land disposal and incineration made recycling a booming business. Junked autos, worthless a few years before, were bringing up to $50 each, and prices for copper scrap rose 100 percent. Lead batteries became profitable recycling targets when the price of battery lead rose fourfold. Under President Richard Nixon, the federal government considered providing tax credits and direct cash subsidies to encourage the sale of recycled materials, but a 1974 EPA report called such incentives unnecessary because demand for recycling was high and prices were rising. Some states sought their own forms of monetary incentives, such as Oregon's pioneering bottle-deposit law in 1972. The federal subsidy and incentive concepts never gained acceptance in Congress, however, and were not revived by President Gerald Ford when he assumed office after Nixon's resignation. Unfortunately for the future of recycling, prices collapsed in 1974 as quickly as they had risen, with waste paper prices dropping from $60 per ton in March 1974 to $5 by mid-1975.[20]

During the late 1980s, supplies of newspapers, cans, plastic, and glass began to pile up when communities and individuals believed they might be able to squeeze cash from trash, even when there were few markets for recycled goods. The problem was compounded further by consumer reluctance to absorb the higher cost of recycled materials and by a slumping economy, which reduced paper sales and made manufacturers reluctant to build new mills capable of processing used paper and cardboard. That reluctance appears to have been overcome at the beginning of the 1990s. American Paper Institute officials report that the United States is on track to achieve the industry's 1995 goal of recovering 40 percent of all the paper Americans use. Nearly one hundred new paper recycling projects have recently been initiated or announced, with thirty-one million tons of paper and paperboard recovered in 1991, a 6 percent increase over the previous year.[21]

There are several ways in which recycling can be made more attractive to both consumers and recyclers. The most obvious is to boost the demand side to create an appetite for the swollen supply of materials, or apply sanctions against those who use virgin material. In 1992, for example, the Bush administration took the incentive route by directing all federal agencies to purchase environmentally sound supplies, including those made of recycled materials, and several states, including California, have enacted similar legislation for their state agencies. Other approaches have included providing tax incentives for new recycling operations, mandating commercial recycling, inverting rate structures for residential waste collection (with the price increasing with the number of trash cans collected at curbside), and organic waste recycling.[22]

Is recycling a viable waste disposal alternative in the United States? The American experience has not been nearly so successful as programs in other parts of the world. Even though other countries do not produce nearly the amounts of waste as the United States, recycling is much more commonly used elsewhere. Deposits on beverage containers are almost universally used, and more reverse vending machines (where returned containers are accepted) are common in Europe. Source separation programs are in place throughout Western Europe and Japan, and even in developing nations like Egypt and Thailand, institutionalized scavenging and recycling programs are fully operational.[23] The effectiveness of recycling in the United States appears to be largely dependent upon the way in which the programs are implemented. A national survey of 450 municipal recycling programs found several characteristics common to successful recycling efforts. The most successful voluntary efforts were in cities with clear, challenging goals for recycling a specific proportion of their waste stream, curbside pickup, free bins, private collection services, and compost programs. Mandatory recycling programs were most successful when they included the ability to issue sanctions or warnings for improper separation. In both types of programs, the highest participation was in cities that employed experienced recycling coordinators.[24] What all this means is there are still a number of obstacles to be overcome before recycling—despite its inherent attractiveness—can be considered more than a supplemental answer to the solid waste dilemma. Based on current trends and information, the EPA projects 20 to 28 percent of MSW will be recovered annually by 1995, but this increase will require fundamental changes in government programs, technology, and corporate and consumer behavior.

Source Reduction

The reduction of the amount of toxicity of garbage, more commonly known as source reduction, is now viewed as the most likely contribution to the global waste problem. Its benefits are twofold—source reduction not only decreases the amount of waste that must be managed but also preserves natural resources and reduces pollution generated during the manufacturing and packaging process. Despite those benefits only a handful of states have adopted source reduction goals, while almost all have recycling goals.

Source reduction relies largely on behavioral changes, for the most part, and some corporations have begun to reduce the amount of waste they generate as models for residential consumers. AT&T, for example, reduces office paper waste by promoting double-sided copying; the Seattle-based Rainier Brewing Company began buying back and refilling its beer bottles in 1990; Toyota Motor Manufacturing switched to standardized reusable shipping containers, which save the company millions of dollars each year.[25] While business works actively to promote source reduction, consumers are gradually showing retailers that they are interested in purchasing products with reduced packaging. From compact disc long boxes to laundry detergent, the public is accepting less packaging as an acceptable way of reducing refuse in the municipal waste stream.

THE POLITICAL RESPONSE

Unlike some environmental protection issues for which the federal government has assumed primary responsibility, waste management regulations are usually locally enacted and implemented. There are three major pieces of federal legislation that underscore the government's "hands-off" policy toward waste. In 1965, Congress passed the Solid Waste Disposal Act, but it was designed to offer financial and technical assistance rather than for regulatory purposes. The federal Bureau of Solid Waste Management, housed in the Department of Health, Education, and Welfare, had jurisdiction over solid waste, but shared responsibility with the Bureau of Mines in the Interior Department. The agencies were underfunded and suffered from heavy personnel turnover, with the Bureau of Solid Waste Management moving its headquarters three times in five years. Creation of the EPA led to a consolidation of agency responsibilities, coinciding with the passage of the Resource Recovery Act of 1970. The 1970 legislation authorized a fourteenfold increase in funding—from $17 million to $239 million—for demonstration grants for recycling systems and for studies of methods to encourage resource recovery. The 1970 legislation also provided the foundation for the development of state waste management programs, and by 1975, forty-eight states had developed some form of program, with budgets ranging from zero to $1.2 million. Most of the state waste management programs were minimal, structuring themselves around the federal support programs rather than using federal assistance to help them develop a more comprehensive effort.[26]

Not until the passage of the Resource Conservation and Recovery Act of 1976 (RCRA) did Congress intrude into what had been essentially local and state jurisdiction.[27] The RCRA required states to develop solid waste management plans and also mandated the closing of all open dumps. The only disposal methods allowed under the legislation were sanitary landfills or recycling, with little attention paid to other potentially effective options such as a bottle deposit or waste recovery facilities. Despite the RCRA legislation, many states were slow to develop alternatives and turned to exporting their waste to other states whose landfills had not yet reached capacity. In a 1978 case involving Philadelphia and New Jersey, the U.S. Supreme Court ruled attempts by states to restrict interstate transfers of waste violated the Commerce Clause of the Constitution.[28] The Supreme Court reiterated that position in two 1992 cases, and as a result there is little that states with plenty of landfill space—like Indiana and New Mexico—can do to stop other states' dumping. The RCRA expired in 1988, with several states still unable to complete the solid waste management plans required by the 1976 law.

Congressional attempts to pass a sweeping reauthorization of the RCRA have been unsuccessful as the legislative gridlock over solid waste continues.[29] Congress has repeatedly rejected a national bottle-deposit system, avoided the issue of industrial wastes from manufacturing and mining, and rolled back industrywide recycling rates for paper and plastic. Both business and environmental groups have opposed most reauthorization efforts thus far because proposed legislation neither promotes enough recycling nor creates markets for recycled materials. A complete overhaul of the RCRA—sought by both industry and environmentalists—is unlikely as Congress continues its incremental and piecemeal approach to waste legislation.

During the past fifteen years, both Congress and the EPA have done an environmental about-face by shifting their attention from solid to hazardous and toxic waste. Shortly after the RCRA's passage in 1976, the EPA's Office of Solid Waste, facing political pressures from citizens' groups and public concerns for immediate action, abruptly changed focus, and with the election of Ronald Reagan, the federal solid waste effort was completely eclipsed by hazardous waste concerns. The agency's solid waste budget was reduced from $29 million in 1979 to $16 million in 1981 to $320,000 in 1982, while staff was reduced from 128 to 74 in 1981, with 73 of those 74 positions eliminated in 1982.[30] The RCRA's hazardous waste provisions require permits for companies storing, treating, or disposing of hazardous waste, and give the EPA the authority to levy fines or hold individuals criminally liable for improperly disposed waste. This created a "cradle to grave" program by which the EPA regulates hazardous wastes from the time they are generated to the time of disposal.

Congress followed the RCRA provisions with the Comprehensive Environmental Response, Compensation and Liability Act (CERCLA), more commonly known as Superfund, enacted in 1980. The CERCLA legislation initially included a $1.6 billion appropriation to clean up abandoned toxic and hazardous waste sites throughout the United States.[31] But further research indicated the

number and magnitude of site cleanups was much larger than originally estimated. Realizing the long-term nature of waste cleanup, Congress reauthorized
the program in 1986 for another five years, adding $8.6 billion to the fund, and
in 1990, continued the program an additional five years with another $5.1
billion. Under Superfund, the EPA established a National Priorities List (NPL)
of targeted sites, a relatively small subset of a larger inventory of about thirty-
four thousand potential hazardous waste sites. There are currently about twelve
hundred sites on the NPL, based on the quantity and toxicity of the wastes
involved, the number of people potentially or actually exposed, the likely path-
ways of exposure, and the importance and vulnerability of the underlying supply
of groundwater. About one hundred sites are added to the NPL each year.
Cleanup projects vary considerably from site to site, ranging from an abandoned
steel mill to small parcels of land where toxic waste was once stored and leaked
into the ground. Currently, landfills account for 41 percent of the sites, followed
by industrial lagoons (37 percent) and manufacturing sites (33 percent). The
EPA estimates generators already treat or dispose of about 98 percent of the
nation's hazardous waste on-site, with about four million tons per year transported off site for treatment, storage, or disposal. Initially, most wastes at NPL
sites were moved off site, but now over 70 percent of the projects also involve
treatment at the site itself. This avoids the problems associated with transporting
waste and trying to find a place to take it once it has been removed. Congress
also dealt with the cleanup problem under the corrective action program of the
RCRA amendments. The legislation requires companies who are permitted to
operate a hazardous waste treatment, storage, or disposal facility also be responsible for the cleanup of that facility. Unlike Superfund, where the federal government must find the responsible party, RCRA permittees must themselves
submit a cleanup plan, with a potential thirty-six hundred to four thousand sites
involved.

Of more recent regulatory concern are underground storage tanks, the majority of which may leak and contaminate drinking water supplies. The United
States is estimated to have over two million underground tanks that store petroleum and other chemicals, and the EPA estimates 20 percent of the regulated
tanks are leaking or have the potential to leak. Many of the tanks were installed
during the 1950s, and the average lifetime use is only fifteen to twenty years.
The EPA began regulating the tanks in 1984 under the RCRA amendments,
requiring owners and operators to meet strict requirements for design, construction, and installation, including repair or closure of systems that do not meet
federal guidelines. Calling it the "sleeping giant," the EPA estimates $50 billion
will be spent on underground storage tank cleanup by the end of the decade—
far more than the cost of cleaning up Superfund sites.[32] In 1986, Congress
established a $500 million Leaking Underground Storage Tank Trust Fund to be
used by states for cleanup costs. The fund is supported by a one-tenth of a cent
federal tax on certain petroleum products, primarily motor fuels. The trust fund
was reauthorized by Congress in 1990 for another five years.[33]

Critics like the nonprofit group Clean Sites charge that the EPA has been unsuccessful in its cleanup efforts, completing work at only sixty-four Super-fund sites by the end of 1991 at an average cost of $25 million each. Although cleanup plans were under way or had been developed at an additional six hundred sites, the remainder were at the "investigation step," where the nature of the contamination is under evaluation. The group estimates fewer than five hundred sites will be deleted from the existing NPL by the year 2000, with an additional seven hundred new sites added to the list over the same period. As a result, there will still be fifteen hundred dangerous hazardous waste sites to clean up, or two hundred more than we now have.[34] The cost of cleanup for all the sites currently on the NPL is $27 billion—far more than the $15.3 billion authorized by Congress to date. Even more serious is the fact that by the end of 1992, only 10 percent of the country's hazardous waste sites will have been eliminated. The total cost of cleaning up U.S. hazardous waste sites will reach more than $750 billion, researchers estimate.[35] Of particular concern are military bases, which had often disposed of solvents, dead batteries, dirty oil, unex-ploded shells and bombs, and other wastes by dumping them on-site. Eleven of the bases slated to be closed by the Department of Defense by 1997 are on the Superfund priority list, and cleanup is estimated to cost billions of dollars.

Residents near toxic waste sites sometimes resort to the legal system when they feel the political process has failed to adequately deal with the cleanup issue and protect public health. Proving that a site caused health problems leads to a complex legal maze from which few plaintiffs successfully emerge. A number of obstacles face those victims seeking compensation from toxic waste, including the fact that many chemical-caused illness have a long latency period (perhaps twenty to thirty years) and the difficulty of assessing the effects of exposure. Some state laws provide that the statute of limitations begins with the first date of exposure, limiting claims by those exposed over the long term. In addition, hazardous waste injuries require potential claimants to submit to (and pay for) sophisticated and expensive medical and toxicological testing, and to pay legal fees that may extend for years. Class-action suits are difficult to pursue because even if a group of workers were exposed to a chemical hazard, the effects on one worker, a forty-year-old male, is likely to be considerably different from the effect on a twenty-four-year-old female of childbearing age. Not surprisingly, potential industrial defendants have opposed attempts to legis-late ways of easing the compensation process.[36]

In their defense, EPA officials point to a number of successes and innova-tive efforts. For example, the agency makes every effort possible to find the companies or individuals responsible for originally creating or dumping the waste, and now close to two-thirds of the cleanup costs are being paid for by those parties. The net result of Superfund cleanup work at NPL sites has been to reduce potential risks from exposure to hazardous waste to more than 23.5 million of the 41 million people who live within four miles of the sites.[37]

There is a clear-cut difference between the government response to solid and hazardous waste. Although Congress has been more successful at develop-ing a consensus on the regulation of hazardous waste than solid waste, the EPA has had little success in implementing those regulations because of congressional failure to provide sufficient funds for cleanup. While the battle over disposal methods flares up and RCRA reauthorization looks doubtful, state and local governments are stalling on alternative waste management solutions, preferring inaction over potentially controversial strategies. Meanwhile, the garbage piles up at a rate of 180 million tons a year, and if that trend continues, Americans will generate 216 million tons of trash annually by the year 2000.

RADIOACTIVE AND HAZARDOUS WASTE DISPOSAL

Among the more politicized waste management problems is the "back end" of the nuclear fuel cycle—the storage and disposal of radioactive waste. Nuclear power facilities produce a variety of substances—solids, liquids, gases, and sludges—which must be treated to remove contaminants or diluted to reduce their toxicity and then stored. More than twenty thousand metric tons of highly radioactive used fuel are stored in pools of water at nuclear power plants in thirty states. In addition, the country must find a way to dispose of four decades of waste produced by the country's seventeen principal and one hundred secondary weapons factories left over from the nuclear arms race. Cleanup is estimated at $200 billion over the next thirty years, far exceeding the amount estimated for the government bailout of the savings and loan industry.[38]

Radioactive waste decays at varying rates, so different types of disposal are needed for different types of waste. Some waste materials may need to be stored for as long as a thousand years, and there is considerable disagreement as to whether or not safe storage for that long a period is technologically feasible. While low-level solid waste can be safely stored in containers that are buried in shallow trenches, researchers have looked at several alternatives for high-level radioactive waste, including reprocessing, deep injection of level wastes, sea dumping, and deep burial in natural or man-made mines. The latter alternative seems to have gained the most acceptance, although few long-term repositories have actually been built. Scientists are also exploring more radical alternatives such as nuclear incineration, extraterrestrial disposal, and burial in Antarctic ice sheets.[39]

One of the unresolved issues is the question of who is responsible for storing spent nuclear materials. With the passage of the Nuclear Waste Policy Act in 1982, the Energy Department is required to assume ownership of the material in 1998 and store it in a permanent underground repository or in a temporary, aboveground site to be used only until the permanent one is ready. Congress initially authorized construction of two long-term storage facilities, one in the West and the other in the eastern United States, and in 1986 the Energy Department announced the selection of three proposed western sites in Nevada, Texas, and Washington State, but postponed further screening of an eastern location. States became embroiled in the controversy when governors of all three states, who have a major role in the selection of a site under the 1982 legislation, announced their opposition to construction. Policies changed during the Reagan administration when the government announced that storage was no longer a federal responsibility but one for the utilities themselves to handle. State and local government opposition to the siting of a facility began to surface in response to citizens who felt nuclear storage of any kind was unacceptable— the NIMBY syndrome discussed in Chapter 4. The 175-square-kilometer Nevada site—Yucca Mountain—was eventually selected in 1987 over the protests of the Nevada legislature, which vowed to fight at every juncture. State officials have been joined by a number of groups including the Natural Resources Defense Council, the National Audubon Society, and the Sierra Club. Opponents argue that Congress is preempting a state's authority to protect its citizens, and cite scientific evidence (disputed by the U.S. Geological Survey) that the Yucca Mountain location is unsafe. Overwhelming opposition (including passage of a 1989 bill by the Nevada legislature forbidding any government agency from storing high-level radioactive waste anywhere in the state) is coupled with a 1992 Energy Department report that Yucca Mountain's facility cannot be ready before 2010.[40] A 1993 study determined the strategy would be $10–50 billion more costly than other alternatives and recommended the project be shelved and reconsidered. For the short term, utility companies are storing spent fuel at existing nuclear power plant sites (which are nearing capacity) while the Energy Department looks for military bases, Indian reservations, and nuclear weapons factories for temporary storage to comply with the law.

It appeared the federal government had solved part of the storage problem in 1991 when the Energy Department announced it would open an experimental facility, the Waste Isolation Pilot Plant (WIPP), a huge network of rock salt caverns near Carlsbad, New Mexico. The department notified the governor's office it was preparing to ship the first drums of radioactive waste from Idaho to the facility, and a resolution to the radioactive waste problem seemed close at hand. But in 1992, a federal judge ruled it was illegal for the Energy Department to take over the sixteen-square-mile site from the Interior Department without congressional approval, refusing to allow the Energy Department to ship any waste to WIPP without a state hazardous waste permit. The result: Congress has not acted to give its approval to the land transfer; New Mexico's Environmental Department says it will take a minimum of two years to process the hazardous waste application; and the court ruling will be appealed, which could take months. The WIPP facility was ten years in planning, cost $1.35 billion to build, and $14 million a month to maintain.

Environmentalists argue that the United States has failed to come up with a reliable nuclear waste strategy, and the problem is getting worse. Typical of the problem is the situation at the Rocky Flats, Colorado, plutonium plant, which makes triggers for nuclear warheads. The plant gained public attention in December 1989 when its plutonium operations were suspended. Former employees have filed suit against the plant operators, alleging major violations of federal safety rules. One worker reported that radiation decontamination teams slept on the job or played cards, and that company radiation inspectors dismissed contamination incidents as statistical errors. The facility is running out of storage space, but Energy Department officials admit the issue no longer has a sense of urgency as the United States phases out its nuclear weapons program. Although the Energy Department maintains its commitment to underground storage, legal challenges and political disputes over siting and security are likely to hold up the process for years to come. In the meantime, above-ground storage of radioactive waste continues at sites across the United States.

KEEPING OUR WASTES AT HOME

While most nations have dealt with their waste management problems independent of one another, there is a common international thread that now binds them together—the importing and exporting of wastes from one country to another. The issue gained prominence in 1988 when three thousand tons of a flaky black material were dumped on a Haitian beach. A barge carrying the substance had entered the port with a permit to unload "fertilizer," which later turned out to be municipal incinerator ash from Philadelphia laced with toxic residue. Investigations into who was responsible for dumping the ash (some of which still sits in uncovered barrels on the beach) are continuing, as is litigation over the incident. Most of the trade is between industrialized nations with restrictive (and costly) regulations on hazardous waste disposal, and developing cash-poor countries in the Pacific, Latin America, the Caribbean and Africa. Although they often lack adequate facilities or technology for accepting or disposing of hazardous waste, the financial incentives (often extralegal) are often too tempting to pass up. The EPA estimates the cost of disposing of a ton of hazardous wastes in the United States at $250 to $300 per ton; some developing countries will charge as little as $40 to accept waste. There is also an extensive and growing waste trade among the members of the European Community (EC), and some experts believe as much as 10 percent of the thirty million tons of hazardous waste generated each year passes between European countries, with a smaller amount of domestic refuse and recyclable materials traded.[41]

At the 1972 UN Conference on the Human Environment, delegates made a commitment to regulate waste trading, although it was not until 1984–85 that a UN Environment Programme committee developed the Cairo Guidelines implementing that pledge. The guidelines included notification procedures, prior consent by receiving nations, and verification the receiving nation has requirements for disposal at least as stringent as those of the exporter. Despite those restrictions, a coalition of African nations argued the agreement was tantamount to exploitation or "waste colonialism." In 1987, the United Nations attempted to devise an agreement that would satisfy the African nations (which sought an outright ban on exports) and exporters (still seeking inexpensive ways of disposing of their wastes). In 1989, two attempts were made to further restrict the international trade in wastes. A group of sixty-eight less-industrialized nations from Africa, the Caribbean, and the Pacific, collectively known as the ACP countries, joined with EC officials in signing the Lome Convention, which bans all radioactive and hazardous waste shipments from the EC to ACP countries. A second agreement, the Basel Convention on the Control of Transboundary Movements of Hazardous Wastes and Their Disposal, which took effect in 1992, does not ban waste trade but allows hazardous wastes to be exported as long as there is "informed consent" or full notification and acceptance of any shipments. Even though members of the European Economic Community and other nations have pledged not to export their hazardous wastes regardless of the Basel Convention, twelve African states subsequently signed the Bamako Convention in 1991 banning the import of hazardous wastes from any country—a move that further emphasized their determination not to become a dumping ground for other countries.[42] The U.S. position in the debate has been to support ratification of the Basel Convention, even though the shipping of hazardous wastes is not a commonly accepted practice in the United States. The EPA estimates only about 1 percent (approximately 139,000 tons in 1990) of U.S. hazardous wastes are exported, with the bulk shipped to Canada and Mexico, and the rest to six other nations, primarily for recycling. Imports to the United States from those nations were estimated at about 110,000 tons that same year.

Despite the acceptance of these international regimes and a ban by ninety nations thus far, environmental groups like Greenpeace feel that the agreements do not go far enough. They believe each country should be responsible for disposing of its own waste, rather than shipping it off to other nations, and have called for a total international ban.[43] Some groups have focused on transboundary pollution, arguing that U.S-owned companies in Mexico—*maquiladoras*—should be held responsible for shipping their waste back to the United States, as should U.S. military bases on foreign soil. The *maquiladoras* issue is a particularly controversial problem. An estimated two thousand plants (many of them owned by corporations like IBM, Chrysler, and General Electric) line the border between the United States and Mexico, importing raw materials from the United States and shipping their products back import-duty free. Lower labor costs and less restrictive environmental regulations make the *maquiladoras* attractive to American investors while providing Mexico's second-largest source of foreign currency, behind petroleum.[44] Despite a 1987 agreement requiring the *maquiladoras* and their subsidiaries to ship their waste back to the United States, the program has not been enforced and environmentalists argue the agreement is full of loopholes. Representatives of the Border Ecology Project, a nonprofit group monitoring the issue, point out that corporations can "donate" their waste to Mexican charities, which then sell them to unlicensed recycling plants with little understanding of the waste they are handling. Other concerns have been raised over the dumping of waste into streams and rivers along the border, causing health problems as the contamination flows downstream and back into the

United States. The National Toxics campaign has warned that without strict regulation, we could be "turning the border into a two thousand mile-long Love Canal."[45]

POLICY STALLED: TOO LITTLE TOO LATE

Various agencies and analysts are exploring a number of waste management strategies, from technological solutions like soil washing, chemical dechlorination, underground vacuum extraction, and bioremediation—the use of microbes to break down organic contaminants—to the use of price incentives. Critics of existing waste management practices have endorsed the concept of a cost-based disposal fee, and use of the "polluter pays" principle.[46] Despite these proposals, political scientist Zachary Smith has referred to the waste management issue as an environmental policy paradox. Even though officials have been aware of the shortage of landfill space for decades, and could have anticipated the need for alternatives, they have been unable to develop a viable long-term policy to deal with the problem. Why? Smith points to the lack of a publicly perceived crisis, the incentives that have caused policymakers to choose short-term, low-cost options, and the incremental nature of the policy process. He notes with regard to hazardous waste that officials at the federal level have failed to follow through on policy development with an appropriate level of resources to clean up the thousands of identified sites in the United States. In addition, the involvement of organized crime in the disposal industry has been connected to illegal disposal, or "midnight dumping" of hazardous wastes—a problem not yet solved by government officials at any level.[47]

It is equally accurate to characterize America's waste management practices as the policy of deferral. The inability of policymakers now to plan for future disposal needs (whether the waste be solid, hazardous, or radioactive) simply means they are putting off until tomorrow an inevitable, and growing, environmental protection problem. Future generations will be forced to deal with the mounting heaps of trash, barrels of toxic waste, and radioactive refuse that is already piling up in our cities, chemical companies, and at utilities all around the country. Other analysts note there is a lack of information about the full costs of various disposal alternatives. Without sufficient research into the "true" costs of waste management strategies, it is impossible for the most efficient systems to be developed.[48] Meanwhile, it appears as if the future of American waste management will involve a combination of disposal methods, rather than any single strategy. Technological strategies and price incentives are of little value, however, until the legislative gridlock is broken and policymakers get serious about finding a solution, rather than just passing stopgap measures for short-term fixes. We know the problem is there, but no one seems willing to get down and dirty to tackle it.

SUMMARY

From the turn of the century, when Americans, especially city dwellers, first recognized the "garbage nuisance," public officials have been attempting to find ways to deal with the mountains of waste that have built up. Strategies ranging from burial to incineration to ocean dumping to recycling have been attempted, each with its own set of costs and benefits. The impetus for decision making is the fact that America's landfills are rapidly reaching capacity or are being closed to comply with environmental regulations. Cities are simply running out of room for their trash and have turned to exporting their trash to other states whose landfills are not yet full. The federal government has generally had a "hands-off" policy, leaving the problem to be solved by state and local officials. But neither the public nor politicians seem willing to make a decision to deal with solid waste—a policy-making process that has stalled while the problem continues to grow. Meanwhile, the issues of radioactive waste disposal and toxic waste have eclipsed the solid waste problem and have become the focus of legislative interests. There is an international component as well now that some industrialized nations have begun shipping their hazardous waste to developing countries. Despite attempts by the United Nations to develop a convention to deal with the problem, the export trade continues because there is a lack of a consensus on how to deal with such wastes. The primary policy issue is whether or not communities (and their leaders) will respond to the waste problem in a timely fashion.

NOTES

1. Quoted in Michael Specter, "Incinerators: Unwanted and Politically Dangerous," *New York Times*, December 12, 1991, B-1.

2. Shirley E. Perlman, "In the Barge's Wake," in Newsday, *Rush to Burn: Solving America's Garbage Crisis?* (Washington, DC: Island Press, 1989), 243–48. In 1986, a similar odyssey involved a cargo ship called the Khian Sea, which took ash from Philadelphia's incinerators on a twenty-six-month journey before its cargo was mysteriously dumped somewhere in the ocean. Captain Arturo Fuentes told reporters, "I do not know what they did with the ash."

3. Martin V. Melosi, *Garbage in the Cities: Refuse, Reform and the Environment, 1880–1980* (College Station: Texas A & M University Press, 1981), 3.

4. Ibid., 189–92. In fairness to the industry, however, it should be noted that the development of packaging has some beneficial consequences. Packaging has extended the shelf life of many goods (especially produce and dairy products) that otherwise might have rotted or spoiled. Packaging also allows products to be stored and shipped in bulk, and often results in lower pricing of goods.

5. U.S. Environmental Protection Agency, *Characterization of Municipal Solid Waste in the United States: 1990 Update*, EPA/530-SW-90-042 (Washington, DC: U.S. Government Printing Office, June 1990), ES-3.

6. See Seth Shulman, *The Threat at Home: Confronting the Toxic Legacy of the U.S. Military* (Boston: Beacon Press, 1992).

7. *Characterization of Municipal Solid Waste*, ES-6.

8. Ibid., ES-13.

9. Cynthia Pollock, *Mining Urban Wastes: The Potential for Recycling* (Washington, DC: Worldwatch Institute, April 1987), 15. There are some analysts, however, who believe the United States is not running out of landfill space. See A. Clark Wiseman, "Impediments to Economically Efficient Solid Waste Management," *Resources* (Fall 1991): 9–11.

10. Melosi, *Garbage in the Cities*, 171–76, 217–18.

11. See Howard E. Hesketh, *Incineration for Site Cleanup and Destruction of Hazardous Wastes* (Lancaster, PA: Technomic Publishing Company, 1990).

12. Pollock, *Mining Urban Wastes*, 16–17.

13. *Characterization of Municipal Solid Waste*, 75.

14. See, for example, Jon R. Luoma, "Trash Can Realities," *Audubon* 7 (March 1990): 86–97; and Neil Seldman, "Waste Management: Mass Burn Is Dying," *Environment* 31, no. 7 (September 1989): 42–44.

15. Specter, "Incinerators," B-11.

16. This synopsis of the LANCER controversy is drawn from Louis Blumberg and Robert Gottlieb, *War on Waste: Can America Win Its Battle with Garbage?* (Washington, DC: Island Press, 1989).

17. See Bruce Piasecki, ed., *Beyond Dumping: New Strategies for Controlling Toxic Waste* (Westport, CT: Quorum Books, 1984).

18. J. Scott Orr, "Pressure Applied on Dumping Ban," *The Oregonian*, November 29, 1992, A-19.

19. See Richard A. Denison, ed., *Recycling and Incineration: Evaluating the Choices* (Washington, DC: Island Press, 1990).

20. John C. Whitaker, *Striking a Balance: Environment and Natural Resources Policy in the Nixon–Ford Years* (Washington, DC: American Enterprise Institute, 1976), 113–16.

21. "Paper Recycling Growth Shows Solid Progress toward 1995 Goal," *Journal of the Air Waste Management Association* 42, no. 6 (June 1992): 758.

22. Whitaker, *Striking a Balance*, 199–201. See also U.S. Council of Mayors, *Recycling America* (Washington, DC: June 1991); and Anna Maria Gillis, "Shrinking the Trash Heap," *Bioscience* 42, no. 2 (February 1992): 90–93.

23. Pollock, *Mining Urban Wastes*, 32–41.

24. David H. Folz and Joseph M. Hazlett, "Public Participation and Recycling Performance: Explaining Program Success," *Public Administration Review* 51, no. 6 (November–December 1991): 526–32. See also David H. Folz, "Recyclng Program Design, Management and Participation: A National Survey of Municipal Expertise," *Public Administration Review* 51, no. 3 (May–June 1991): 222–31.

25. Bette Fishbein and David Saphire, "Slowing the Waste Behemoth," *EPA Journal* 16, no. 3 (July–August 1992): 46–49.

26. Blumberg and Gottleib, *War on Waste*, 63.

27. See William L. Kovacs and John F. Klucsik, "The New Federal Role in Solid Waste Management: The Resource Conservation and Recovery Act of 1976," *Columbia Journal of Environmental Law* 3 (March 1977): 205.

28. *City of Philadelphia v. New Jersey*, 437 U.S. 617 (1978).

29. See, for example, U.S. Congress, Senate, Committee on Environment and Public Works, Subcommittee on Environmental Protection, *RCRA Amendments of 1991*, hearing, 102nd Cong., 1st sess., June 5, 6, 18; July 24, 25, 1991 (Washington, DC: U.S. Government Printing Office, 1991).

30. Blumberg and Gottleib, *War on Waste*, 66–67.

31. See Richard C. Fortuna and David J. Lennett, *Hazardous Waste Regulation, The New Era: An Analysis and Guide to RCRA and the 1984 Amendments* (New York: McGraw-Hill, 1987). See also William Harris Frank and Timothy B. Atkeson, *Superfund, Litigation and Cleanup* (Washington, DC: Bureau of National Affairs, 1985);

and Mary Devine Worobec, *Toxic Substances Controls Guide* (Washington, DC: Bureau of National Affairs, 1989).

32. "Questions the Public Is Asking: An Interview with Don Clay," *EPA Journal* 17, no. 3 (July–August 1991): 18.

33. See Geoffrey Commons, "Plugging the Leak in Underground Storage Tanks: The 1984 RCRA Amendments," *Vermont Law Review* 11 (Spring 1986): 267. See also Jack Lewis, "Superfund, RCRA, and UST: The Clean-up Threesome," *EPA Journal* 17, no. 3 (July–August 1991): 14.

34. Thomas P. Grumbly, "Superfund: Candidly Speaking," *EPA Journal* 17, no. 3 (July–August 1991): 20.

35. Milton Russell, E. William Colglazier, and Bruce E. Tonn, "The U.S. Hazardous Waste Legacy," *Environment* 34, no. 6 (July–August 1992): 12–15.

36. Frank P. Grad, "Compensating Toxic-Waste Victims," *Technology Review*, October 1985, 48–50.

37. Lewis, "Superfund, RCRA, and UST," 7–14.

38. Douglas Pasternak, with Peter Cary, "A $200 Billion Scandal," *U.S. News & World Report*, December 14, 1992, 34–47.

39. See Peter R. Mounfield, *World Nuclear Power* (New York: Routledge, 1991), 329–82. See also John L. Campbell, "The State and the Nuclear Waste Crisis: An Institutional Analysis of Policy Constraints," *Social Problems* 34, no. 1 (February 1987): 7–22.

40. See Paul Slovic, Mark Layman, and James H. Flynn, "Risk Perception, Trust, and Nuclear Waste: Lessons from Yucca Mountain," *Environment* 33, no. 3 (April 1991): 6–7; William J. Broad, "Experts Clash on Risk of Nuclear Waste Site," *New York Times*, December 3, 1991, B-10; Charles R. Malone, "National Energy Strategy and High-Level Nuclear Waste," *Bioscience* 41, no. 11 (December 1991): 759; and Eliot Marshall, "The Geopolitics of Nuclear Waste," *Science*, February 22, 1991, 864–67.

41. Duncan Lawrence and Brian Wynne, "Transporting Waste in the European Community: A Free Market?" *Environment* 31, no. 6 (July–August 1989): 14.

42. Gareth Porter and Janet Welsh Brown, *Global Environmental Politics* (Boulder, CO: Westview Press, 1991), 86. See also C. Russell H. Shearer, "Comparative Analysis of the Basel and Bamako Conventions on Hazardous Waste," *Environmental Law* 23, no. 1 (1993): 141.

43. For a summary of the Greenpeace view, see the statement of James Vallette, coordinator of the Greenpeace International Hazardous Exports-Imports Prevention Project in U.S. Congress, House, Committee on Energy and Commerce, Subcommittee on Transportation and Hazardous Materials, *Basel Convention on the Export of Waste*, hearing, 102nd Cong., 1st sess., October 10, 1991 (Washington, DC: U.S. Government Printing Office, 1991), 185–98. See also the Greenpeace Publication *Toxic Trade*, no. 5.2 (Washington, DC, 1992).

44. See Joseph Grunwald, "Opportunity Missed: Mexico and Maquiladoras," *Brookings Review* 9, no. 1 (Winter 1990): 44–48; Tom Dworetsky, "Trashing Mexico: Free Trade or Free Ride?" *Omni* 14, no. 6 (March 1992): 22.

45. "Mexico's Maquiladoras—Free Trade, or Foul Play?" *E Magazine* 11, no. 4 (July–August 1991): 31–37.

46. See Congressional Budget Office, *Federal Options for Reducing Waste Disposal* (Washington, DC: U.S. Government Printing Office, October 1991); and Frank Ackerman, "Taxing the Trash Away," *Environment* 34, no. 5 (June 1992): 2–5.

47. Zachary A. Smith, *The Environmental Policy Paradox* (Englewood Cliffs, NJ: Prentice-Hall, 1992), 164–91.

48. See Wiseman, "Impediments to Economically Efficient Solid Waste Management," 11.

FOR FURTHER READING

Louis Blumberg and Robert Gottlieb, War on Waste: *Can America Win Its Battle with Garbage?* Washington, DC: Island Press, 1989.

Center for Investigative Reporting and Bill Moyers. *Global Dumping Ground: The International Traffic in Hazardous Waste.* Cabin John, MD: Seven Locks Press, 1990.

Richard A. Denison, ed. *Recycling and Incineration: Evaluating the Choices.* Washington, DC: Island Press, 1990.

David Mazmanian and David Morrell. *Beyond Superfailure: America's Toxics Policy for the 1990s.* Boulder, CO: Westview Press, 1992.

Martin V. Melosi. *Garbage in the Cities: Refuse, Reform and the Environment, 1880–1980.* College Station: Texas A & M University Press, 1981.

Newsday. *Rush to Burn: Solving America's Garbage Crisis?* Washington, DC: Island Press, 1989.

Cynthia Pollock. *Mining Urban Wastes: The Potential for Recycling.* Washington, DC: Worldwatch Institute, 1987.

William D. Robinson, ed. *The Solid Waste Handbook.* New York: Wiley, 1986.

CHAPTER 6

The Politics of Energy: Old Debates and New Sources

> The hard fact is that we now have no effective energy policy. We have a choice between the many reasons to do nothing and looking for ways to get the job done.
>
> —former President Jimmy Carter, commenting on U.S. energy vulnerability after the Persian Gulf Crisis[1]

In October 1973, media headlines trumpeted the fact that America was in the throes of an "energy crisis" when the nations of the Organization of Petroleum Exporting Countries (OPEC) announced increases in the price of a barrel of oil. The price of oil jumped from $3 a barrel to $11.65 in three months in 1973.[2] Suddenly the United States, which for years had been a major importer of foreign oil, found itself lining up at the world pump like other nations that had become dependent upon Middle Eastern resources. Political officials and consumers alike, who had previously filled their tanks with little thought of where the oil was coming from, were suddenly forced to take a long, hard look at our energy resources, both foreign and domestic. Automobile owners found they could buy gas only every other day of the week when the government instituted an "odd/even" purchasing system, officials ordered the thermostats to be turned down in public buildings and schools, and some communities even outlawed Christmas light displays as an excessive use of energy. But as quickly as it had surfaced, concern about the country's energy policies faded, and even a second energy crisis in 1979–80 failed to ignite public interest. Americans assumed that there was a virtually unlimited supply of fuel available—it was simply a matter of turning on the spigot. In August 1990, when Iraq's Saddam Hussein ordered his troops into Kuwait, once again threatening the world's oil supplies, few Americans showed much evidence of concern about whether or not their local gasoline pumps would go dry. When President Bush signed the Energy Policy Act of 1992—the first major legislative attempt to curb U.S. oil dependence in more than a decade—his action failed to generate more than a single day's media headlines.

While it may be difficult to get as emotionally involved in energy policy as compared to the destruction of the rain forest or the protection of the blue whale, it nevertheless has produced strong feelings on both sides. Anti-nuclear-power activists have been arrested as they protested the siting of nuclear waste facilities, and opponents of a geothermal project in Hawaii have been equally vociferous in their state. Representatives of electric utilities are just as adamant about the safety record of nuclear plants, and farmers have a hard time understanding why their state's hydroelectric facilities are unable to provide them with the water they need in deference to a fish. Energy has also been called a "transparent" sector of society because no one buys or uses energy as an end in itself. All demand for energy is indirect and derived only from the benefits it provides. People do not buy gasoline because they *want* gasoline, but because they need it for their cars to take them where they want to go. Similarly, a manufacturing plant has a need for electricity only to run the machines that make the products the company sells.[3]

Our growing electricity needs make the debate both timely and controversial. Although energy is an issue of global concern, a stable, affordable supply is acutely important to the United States, which has just 5 percent of the world's population, but consumes 26 percent of the world's energy. During the past two decades, U.S. electricity consumption has increased by 92 percent and is estimated to increase by about 2.5 percent per year during the 1990s. At that rate, the United States could require within the next twenty years an additional 270,000 megawatts—the equivalent of 270 large coal or nuclear power plants. This demand comes when the nation is responding to environmental regulations that call for reducing power plant emissions from fossil-fueled plants, a virtual halt to building any new facilities, and political controversy over siting and the perceived dangers of nuclear power. Coupled with that opposition is the fact the average lead time for building new power plants is ten years. If consumption continues to increase at current rates, the United States could be facing an energy shortage as early as the end of this decade.

This chapter examines the politics of energy, focusing on the United States. It reviews the various energy sources and the problems associated with them, and chronicles the technological changes that are reducing our current dependence upon fossil fuels, revisiting the nuclear power debate. The next section of the chapter looks at the political environment and actors by examining events that led to the 1973 oil crisis, and the subsequent regulatory aspects of energy policy. Lastly, the chapter concludes with an overview of future trends and projections for changes in energy use and conservation.

THE ENERGY PIE

Energy is needed to produce goods and services in four basic economic sectors: residential (heat for rooms and hot water, appliances), commercial (including air conditioners in commercial buildings), industry (especially steel, paper, and chemicals), and transportation (of both people and goods). The crux of the energy debate has been to find efficient, environmentally safe, economical and stable sources of supply to meet those needs. Historically speaking, the United States has endured three global energy transitions, each separated by a sixty-year interval. In 1850, the United States derived nearly 90 percent of its energy needs from wood, and it remained the dominant fuel into the late nineteenth century. In 1910, coal replaced wood as the dominant fuel, capturing 70 percent of all energy produced and consumed. Along with the transition from wood to coal came the migration from rural areas to the cities, the development of an industrial base, and the railroad era. In 1970, the third phase began when oil and gas reached the 70 percent level. Although there is no evidence that oil production will follow the same pattern as wood and coal, it is likely that there will be more changes in the relative percentages of each energy source.[4]

Edward Teller, the "father" of the atomic bomb, once commented, "No single prescription exists for a solution to the energy problem. Energy conservation is not enough. Petroleum is not enough. Nuclear energy is not enough. Solar energy and geothermal energy are not enough. New ideas and developments will not be enough. Only the proper combination of all these will suffice."[5] Like a recipe for an "energy pie," which is essentially the situation in the United States today (see fig. 6.1), Teller suggests that the answer to our global energy needs must be found in a blend of energy sources and strategies, rather than a single fuel. This concept seems relatively reasonable were the costs and benefits of various forms of energy equal, but that is far from the case. Some forms of energy are relatively inexpensive to produce but are not in abundant supply. Other sources are expensive but less polluting. Still others are

Figure 6.1   U.S. Energy Production by Source, 1990 (in quadrillion BTU)

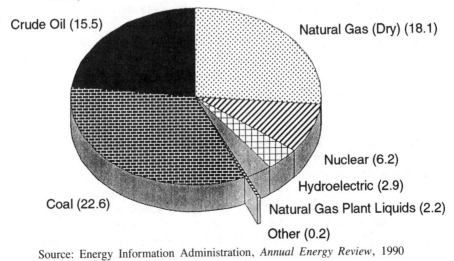

Crude Oil (15.5)

Natural Gas (Dry) (18.1)

Nuclear (6.2)

Hydroelectric (2.9)

Coal (22.6)

Natural Gas Plant Liquids (2.2)

Other (0.2)

Source: Energy Information Administration, *Annual Energy Review*, 1990

considered unsafe but could be made available to consumers around the world for pennies a day, improving the standard of living for millions of people in developing nations. A brief survey of fuel types follows.

FOSSIL FUELS

Petroleum

In the two decades following World War II, the American life-style changed dramatically. In the postwar boom, Americans fell in love with the automobile, with the number of motor vehicles doubling between 1952 and 1972. Most cars were heavier and less mileage efficient than earlier models, further increasing the demand for petroleum. At the same time, new household appliances appeared—electric dishwashers, clothes driers, washing machines—that further expanded the demand for electricity. By the time the 1973 oil crisis hit, Americans had been repeatedly told that the global petroleum reserves were about to be depleted and that, as the supply dwindled, the cost of a barrel of oil would skyrocket. Both halves of that prediction were faulty. Prices did go up but then fell. The current world oil reserves are twice as large as they were in 1970, and in 1990, Saudi Arabia announced the discovery of new reserves that would allow the country to continue pumping oil at the current rate for at least another century. Why, then, is there still a perception of an oil crisis? The answer to that question is twofold. One, the United States is increasingly reliant upon imported oil, and 70 percent of known world oil reserves available for export come from the nations of the Persian Gulf, one of the most politically explosive regions in the world. Since crude oil provides 23 percent of America's energy pie and more than 90 percent of the fuel used in transportation, the country is literally at the mercy of foreign nations as long as we continue to rely upon them for our energy needs. Two, the burning of fossil fuels like petroleum contributes to poor air quality, acid rain, and greenhouse warming. As a result, the petroleum industry is being heavily regulated to reduce emissions into the air, water, and soil.

Coal

One of the ways in which the United States could reduce its dependence upon imported oil would be to use the fossil fuel in its own backyard—coal—which is found in thirty-eight of the fifty states. The United States is home to about one-quarter of the world's known coal supplies, and even exports more than one hundred million tons per year. There are a number of factors that have led to a reduction in coal's slice of the energy pie, which is now about one-third. One, new requirements under the 1990 Clean Air Act amendments (explained further in Chapter 10) are forcing coal-burning plants to reduce their emissions of sulfur dioxide, which contributes to acid rain, by installing costly technology or to use more expensive but less polluting low-sulfur fuels. Two, the average age of coal-burning plants in the United States is twenty-five years, and many facilities are outdated. Utility firms and potential investors are often hesitant to finance repairs or new controls on a facility that is ready for retirement. Still, the idea that coal will be the fuel of the future still exists, bound closely to the future of the electric utility industry and the possibility of political disruption of Middle Eastern oil supplies.[6]

Natural Gas

Another readily available source of energy is natural gas, which makes up about 30 percent of the energy pie in dry and plant liquid form. Domestic supplies are estimated at ten times the current annual production, with more reserves being discovered each year. The barrier to increased use of natural gas, which is a clean, virtually pollution-free source of energy, involves public opposition to new pipelines and offshore drilling. A proposed pipeline from Wyoming to California was derailed when researchers found the proposed route passed through habitats of the endangered desert tortoise. An offshore drilling moratorium has brought an end to new exploration, even though two-thirds of the energy from offshore is natural gas. In February 1991, the Department of the Interior proposed opening up thousands of miles of the outer continental shelf for oil and gas exploration, including areas off the East Coast from central New Jersey to southern Georgia, along the eastern part of the Gulf of Mexico, and the California coast near Santa Barbara, which is believed to be the last large concentration of untapped oil and gas in the continental United States. The most controversial proposal involved the opening up of 1.5 million acres in the Arctic National Wildlife Refuge—an issue discussed further in Chapter 16. Intense opposition by groups like the Natural Resources Defense Council and the Sierra Club led to a pullback of the plan, but there is little doubt that the areas are still open to exploration and drilling at some point in the future.

RENEWABLE ENERGY SOURCES

When the 1973 oil crisis hit, the world turned to various forms of alternative, renewable energy as a potential replacement for fossil fuels. Although some of these sources have been used extensively in other countries, with the exception of hydroelectric power, the United States has only recently begun experimenting with them. Supporters of renewable energy point out that they produce no waste to be disposed of and no greenhouse gases. They generally do not deplete limited supplies of fuel, are safe for workers, and can be constructed more quickly than facilities using fossil fuels or nuclear power. Currently, these sources make up about 5 percent of the U.S. energy pie, although that figure is growing as the fossil fuel dependency is reduced. Their biggest drawbacks are their unreliability as a fuel source and the higher cost of producing and distributing electricity from them. The political process has greatly affected U.S. attention to alternative fuel sources, and the federal government's support for renewable energy research can be tied to both electoral cycles and to the cost of oil. Passage of the 1978 Public Utilities Regulatory Policies Act (PURPA), for example, required utilities to purchase power from nonutilities at an "avoided cost" rate (the rate of expense the utility would have incurred if it generated the energy itself). PURPA became an incentive for alternative sources like cogenerators (large industrial power users who produce steam and electricity for their own needs and sell the excess to local utilities) and small hydroelectric plants that were guaranteed a market for the electricity they generated. In the wake of PURPA, the number of license applications for small hydropower projects soared from one hundred applications from 1976 to 1979 to forty-five hundred between 1980 and 1983. Passage of the Crude Oil Windfall Profits Tax in 1981, which provided an 11 percent investment tax credit for small hydropower facilities, also served as an important development incentive.[7] Funds for renewable fuel research reached $720 million at the end of the Carter administration in 1980, and dropped to $115 million during the Bush administration in fiscal 1989.

Critics of renewable energy point out that few places enjoy the right geography to make use of solar, wind, and geothermal energy, and as a result, these three types of energy sources make up less than 1 percent of the energy pie today. California is one of the few states with the right combination of geography and weather, but coal still remains the primary fuel for electricity in thirty-three states, with six eastern states depending mainly on nuclear power, five northeastern states on fuel oil, four West Coast states on hydroelectric power, and two on natural gas. This brief survey of alternative energy shows that some sources are more likely to be developed than others, and why.

Hydroelectric Power

As one of the world's oldest sources of renewable energy, the United States has maintained some reliance upon electricity produced from turbines at dams and other water sources for over a century. Hydroelectric power accounted for about 4 percent of the energy pie in 1990—a level that has changed only slightly since 1970, even with an increase in small hydro operations. Hydroelectric power is among the cheapest sources of energy available, although its use is becoming more limited as environmental groups have lobbied Congress in opposition to the siting of new dams along scenic waterways. In October 1986, passage of the Electric Consumer Protection Act required that environmental concerns be given "equitable treatment" with the development purposes of the Federal Water Power Act, and provided protection for recreational value, water quality, and fish and wildlife.[8] There is also a limited growth potential to hydroelectric power, since most bodies of water that can be profitably dammed and developed are already in use. Still, hydropower remains a reliable, cost-effective source of electricity.[9]

Solar Power

Solar power is generally divided into two types: passive (such as siting a house on a lot to take advantage of the sun's natural warming effect) and active (which uses some kind of man-made device to collect and store heat). Passive solar heating is usually built into the design of a home or office building, while active solar heating has the advantage of being retrofitted onto existing structures. Active solar devices have been used most often for small applications, such as heating swimming pools or heating hot water. Solar power was initially hailed as a prime alternative energy source because the sun's rays touch every portion of the planet (some areas more than others, of course) and the resource is free (although collecting it is not!). The technology is already available to provide between 20 and 25 percent of our energy needs from the sunshine, which naturally reaches the Earth.

Solar power got a big push from the Carter administration in the late 1970s when the federal government provided funds for private research and development and tax credits for individuals installing solar equipment in their homes. Under the Reagan administration, however, the federal research subsidies were drastically cut, and Congress voted to end the tax incentives in 1985. Since the federal grant dollars have been cut back, most of the solar power research has been conducted by western utility companies, most of whom are under pressure to fund less polluting energy sources. Research has been focused in two areas: large facilities producing electricity for commercial and residential customers, and smaller applications for home use. Thus far, large projects have not been especially successful, with the parent company of one of the world's largest facilities, Luz International, declaring bankruptcy in 1991.[10] In 1991, three California utilities announced they were planning to build an experimental solar energy plant in the Mojave desert—a prototype using giant mirrors to melt nitrate salt, which would be used to convert water to steam to drive a turbine generator. The facility, expected to be completed by late 1994, is anticipated to be more cost-effective than earlier smaller plants, and nonpolluting, since it does not rely upon fossil fuels.[11] In the smaller application category, Texas Instruments and Southern California Edison have teamed up in another venture to produce a solar panel that could be mounted on south-facing rooftops. The new technology uses photovoltaic cells produced from an impure form of silicon at a cost less than a fifth of those now on the market. The cells, wrapped in aluminum sheeting, would replace shingles on new housing at a cost of about $3,000 and would produce about one-third of the electricity used by an average household. The Solar Energy Research Institute projects that by the year 2030, photovoltaics could supply half of America's electrical power. The technology works best in those areas with uniform sunshine, and in regions where residents will not reject the building of solar facilities. Even in the Southwest, which receives more sunlight than any other region, about three square miles of land are required to collect from solar radiation the energy produced by a standard power station. Despite these innovations, solar power alone cannot meet all of the world's energy needs.

Wind Power

The U.S. government hailed wind as a promising energy source during the 1970s, since it has several characteristics that make it comparable to solar power. The wind is free, and can be harnessed relatively easily and turned into electricity. Currently, about seventeen thousand wind turbines are in operation in the United States, most of them in California, where development was encouraged through generous tax incentives. One difference is that wind power is more geographically limited, with certain areas more likely to be used as collection points than others. But the biggest problem is the fickle nature of the wind—people cannot control when and where it will blow. In California, for example, the thousands of wind turbines at the Altamont Pass fifty miles east of the San Francisco Bay region deliver only one-quarter of the power they could theoretically generate. The cost of producing a kilowatt-hour of electricity of wind power has steadily dropped to about seven cents per hour, just slightly more than the cost of production from coal-burning facilities and less than nuclear plants.

Wind power has won acceptance in areas suffering from poor air quality like Sacramento, California. There, the local utility has accepted a private firm's bid to build a wind farm, which will provide electricity at a cost of only 4.5 cents per kilowatt hour to replace capacity once provided by the Rancho Seco nuclear plant, which was closed down in a referendum. The overall goal is for the utility to receive 75 percent of its total energy needs from renewables and conservation by the year 2000.[12] Still, opposition to the sight of thousands of large metal structures on the landscape has limited wind power application to just a few sites in the United States, and it will require major attitudinal changes before such projects are widespread.

Geothermal Power

Tapping the reservoirs of energy under the Earth's surface is one of the unexplored sources of potential energy, advocates believe. Geothermal energy is produced when hot, dry rocks and water generate steam for electric power.

Geothermal projects have been proposed at a number of locations, including northern California, home of the nation's largest geothermal field, and along the national park boundaries at Oregon's Crater Lake.[13] But support for geothermal power has diminished considerably due to a blowout at the drilling site on the Big Island of Hawaii in 1991, and extended controversy over threats to endangered species and the Hawaii rain forest.[14] Expansion of geothermal projects will require massive amounts of research and development dollars, which to date have not materialized.

Biomass Conversion/Synfuels

The burning of wood and other plant matter to produce electricity or fuel (such as ethanol and methanol) is referred to as biomass conversion, and it now accounts of about 4 percent of U.S. energy production. The transportation energy problem is an important aspect of the U.S. energy pie, since Americans are so reliant upon their automobiles. As a result, attempts to concoct nonpetroleum-based fuels (liquids and gases from coal, biomass and peat, oil shale and "unconventional" natural gas) were at one time an important element of U.S. strategy and seen as an alternative when oil reserves ran dry.[15] The technology has been available for decades, and Congress began subsidizing synthetic fuel development in 1944. The White House did not catch "synfuel fever" until late 1979 and the passage of the $20 billion Energy Security Act and creation of the U.S. Synthetic Fuels Corporation. Environmental groups have opposed synfuel production for a number of reasons, including concerns about possible violation of clean air laws, carcinogenic and toxic contamination, and land disruption and water pollution from synfuels plants. Funding for synfuels research ended in 1986, and this alternative energy source has had little federal support since that time.[16] Still, industry is pressing forward with attempts to find an environmentally safe method of biofuel production. In 1992, two U.S. firms announced plans to build a facility to produce ethanol from pulp and paper mill sludge. The plant is expected to initially produce ten million gallons of fuel per year, with a boost to one hundred million gallons annually within five years.[17]

Despite the fact that a considerable amount of federal and private funds have been spent on researching and developing alternative energy sources, there are a number of factors that have made these technologies less attractive than they initially appeared in the 1970s. When oil prices stabilized during the 1980s, the rush to develop alternatives to foreign imports slowed down. The price of crude oil fell to $13 a barrel in 1986, and plentiful supplies of cheap, imported oil reduced pump prices even more. The virtual panic that had driven the search for alternatives after the Arab oil embargo subsided, and most policymakers returned to their love affair with oil and gas. Second, the public interest in new gadgets and gizmos also faded as the nation became indifferent to energy issues generally. Many potential customers decided to wait until the new solar panels

Is There an Electric Car in Your Future?

If you live in California, the answer soon may be yes. Electric cars, once thought of as a staple element of futuristic films, are not likely to replace the 150 million vehicles currently being driven in the United States. But as states adopt legislation to curb automotive emissions to help clean up the air, electric vehicles are more likely to be used for deliveries and other stop-and-go commutes. Part of the reason for the surge in development is a mandate from the California legislature that any automaker with in-state sales of more than five thousand cars a year be required to sell at least 2 percent of its fleet in zero-emission vehicles, starting in 1998. That deadline places electric cars ahead of other fuels, such as hydrogen, which are at least a decade away from full production, or methanol or compressed natural gas-fueled vehicles, which although low emission, do not meet the zero-emission standard. An estimated forty thousand electric vehicles are expected to be sold in California the first year.

Although electric vehicles have been available in Europe as conversions of conventional cars, Japanese and American automakers have concentrated on producing vans that can go up to 120 miles on a single charge. The big hurdle to development thus far has been the battery pack. Chrysler, Ford, and General Motors jointly operate the U.S. Advanced Battery Consortium to pool their knowledge, and have been experimenting with nickel-cadmium, sodium-sulfur, and nickel-iron batteries to replace the lead-acid batteries used in traditional cars. As currently designed, the batteries take about six to eight hours to recharge, although no specialized equipment is necessary. The car could be parked in the owner's garage, plugged in, and allowed to recharge overnight. The downside is that the battery packs are costly—from $3,000 to $5,000—and must be replaced every two to four years. Top speed for Chrysler's TEVan, already in production, is about sixty-five miles per hour, making it best suited for in-town driving rather than long freeway trips.

The electric vehicles being driven today have a number of advantages over their gasoline-powered counterparts. The most obvious difference is that each vehicle represents a possible savings of ten to twenty barrels of oil each year, so that extensive replacement could reduce American dependence on foreign oil. Electric cars are quiet and nonpolluting, and technology-forcing legislation like California's mandate will serve as an incentive for automakers to expedite their research into even more efficient vehicles by the end of this decade. General Motors's experimental electric car, the Impact, will soon be joined by Mercedes, Mitsubishi, and BMW vehicles as other nations get on the electric vehicle bandwagon.

and home wind turbines were fine-tuned and the technology further refined. Alternative sources never gained public acceptance among mainstream America. And finally, pocketbook issues, as they often do, altered behavior. When the federal government offered tax incentives, companies and products flourished; when the incentives were removed, interest waned.

REVISITING NUCLEAR POWER

Unlike many environmental problems, it is possible to identify the exact place and moment in time when nuclear power became a political issue. That moment was 3:25 P.M. on December 2, 1942, and the place was a former squash court beneath the West Stands of Stagg Field in Chicago. A group of scientists under the direction of Enrico Fermi created the first man-made self-sustaining nuclear reaction, followed two and a half years later by the explosion of a nuclear weapon beneath the sands of New Mexico. It became a political issue because the United States was in the midst of World War II, and nuclear weapons were considered the only way to bring about a swift conclusion to the war. Thus, nuclear power was first thought of not as an energy source but as a military weapon. Advances in technology were pushed through government agencies not to provide electricity but for their destructive capabilities. But the most important element of nuclear power development from the splitting of the atom through the first weapons testing and into the late 1960s was secrecy—a factor that slowed the evolution of the technology and limited its spread to just a handful of nations.[18]

Although the United States and the Soviet Union produced small amounts of electricity from experimental reactors in the early 1950s, the first full-scale commercial applications were at Calder Hall in the United Kingdom in 1956 and in France in 1962. But the English efforts were rapidly overtaken by the United States, then by France, then by Japan and Germany. The United States did not seriously consider sharing its fuel-enrichment technology with other nations until late 1970, leaving a major gap in global development. After the end of World War II, the federal government took several steps that bolstered nuclear power as a source of energy. In 1954, Congress enacted the Atomic Energy Act, which permitted private ownership of nuclear reactors and private use of nuclear fuels under lease arrangements. For the first time, an emerging private sector nuclear power industry could gain access to classified government information on nuclear fuels. The legislation was followed by the Power Demonstration Reactor Programs from 1955 to 1963 through which the federal government encouraged the construction of prototype nuclear power stations throughout the United States. By 1960, the Atomic Energy Commission (AEC), the federal agency charged with regulating the new facilities, announced its objective of making nuclear power economically competitive by 1968 in those parts of the country dependent on high-cost fossil fuels.[19]

The result of the government's policy was a massive expansion of nuclear-generating facilities, beginning with an announcement in 1960 by Southern California Edison of its plan to build a huge facility at San Onofre, California, and a similar announcement by Pacific Gas and Electric to build a privately funded plant at Bodega Bay, California.[20] In 1962, as an incentive to encourage the building of large-capacity nuclear plants, the AEC offered to pay part of the design costs, and the rush to build began. Nine nuclear power plants were ordered by American utility companies during 1965, twenty-two in 1966, and twenty-four in 1967. With the passage of the Air Quality Act in 1967 and its crackdown on polluting coal and oil-fired plants in urban areas, utility companies were convinced that nuclear power was the energy source of the future. Environmentalists had already begun to complain about the damage done by coal mining, and as one analyst puts it, coal's days seemed to be numbered. Orders for new nuclear plants continued: seventeen in 1970, twenty-eight in 1971, forty-two in 1973, and twenty-four in 1974. Yet all of the nuclear power plants ordered since 1974 have either been canceled or placed on an indefinite construction schedule.[21]

What happened to shorten the promising beginnings of nuclear power? There are several explanations as to why more than one hundred reactor projects since 1972 have been canceled or stopped in mid-completion. First, the growth of the environmental movement in the early 1970s, combined with zealous antiwar sentiment, led to a strong sense of public opposition to anything associated with nuclear weapons, including nuclear power as an energy source. Second, that same public pressure led to increased government sensitivity about the impacts of new projects, as seen in the history of legislation outlined in Chapter 1. In 1971, the U.S. Court of Appeals ruled that the AEC had failed to follow the provisions of the National Environmental Policy Act in licensing the Calvert Cliffs facility near Baltimore, Maryland, followed by a similar ruling on the Quad Cities nuclear power station on the Mississippi River in Illinois. Both decisions focused attention on the environmental impacts of nuclear facilities and led to increased scrutiny of license applications.

Third, media coverage of a malfunctioning cooling system at Three Mile Island in 1979 and the explosion of a nuclear reactor at Chernobyl in 1986 made utilities still considering nuclear power think twice about the effects of widespread public opposition to such projects. These attitudes are still prevalent today and account for the general reluctance of policymakers to even consider this power source as an option.[22] Fourth, economics played a key role in scuttling the building of new facilities. Government estimates on the growth in demand for electricity in the 1970s turned out to be overly optimistic, and as demand for energy decreased, the cost of building new plants went up, making them non–cost-effective. In 1971, the estimated cost of building a typical facility was $345 million, but by 1980 the figure had climbed to $3.2 billion. The federal government had spent nearly $18 billion in subsidizing the commercial development of nuclear power by 1980, and smaller utilities could not afford to build on their own.

In addition, construction and licensing of new plants were taking as long as ten years—delaying the point at which utilities could begin passing the costs on to consumers and recouping their investments. Financial horror stories began to proliferate. Of five nuclear reactors started in the 1970s by the Washington Public Power Supply System, only one has been completed, and the utility ultimately defaulted on $2.25 billion in bonds in 1983. When the Long Island Lighting Company began building its Shoreham plant in April 1973, the cost was estimated at $300 million. Delayed by protests from nearby residents and federally mandated design changes, the cost escalated to $5.5 billion by the time it was completed in December 1984. Suddenly plans for *all* types of power plants—not just nuclear—were being shelved as they became too costly.

Despite the fact that the United States has come to a virtual halt in its construction of nuclear power plants, four other nations have pushed forward, with more than two-thirds of the world's facilities operating in France, Japan, the United Kingdom, and in the republics of the former Soviet Union. Some regions have become almost totally dependent upon nuclear power, while others have been untouched by nuclear technology, including Australasia, Africa (except for South Africa), the Arab states of the Middle East, Southeast Asia, and most of Latin America (except Mexico, Argentina, and Brazil). For the most part, these nations have only traditional "poor country" energy sources— fuelwood, charcoal, and forage for animals, and there is almost a complete absence of nuclear power. Although the United States began to provide fissile material and millions of dollars in grants for research reactors in 1953, very few Third World countries have reached the point of having commercial nuclear power plants connected to their electricity supply networks.

There are several reasons why nuclear power has been limited to the most-industrialized nations. Prior to 1973, world oil prices were low enough to make nuclear power seem less attractive as an energy source than fossil fuels. In addition, most developing nations were too poor or too much in debt to develop nuclear plants, which are extremely capital-intensive. To do so would have meant sacrificing other priorities that were deemed more important. Lastly, concerns about the proliferation of nuclear weapons preoccupied those nations with the capacity for producing plutonium and uranium, limiting their desires to share the necessary raw materials. Despite international agreements, at least seven countries are believed to have developed nuclear weapons capabilities outside the safeguards of the International Atomic Energy Agency: Argentina, Colombia, India, North Korea, Pakistan, Israel, and South Africa.[23]

Will nuclear power ever be reconsidered as a major source of energy? The answer to that question has little to do with science or technology and much to do with politics. Some industry officials believe such a change can take place only if the regulatory framework for licensing facilities is streamlined by Congress. Other analysts feel that utilities would be more likely to gain public acceptance for new nuclear facilities if they were sited or expanded near existing plants rather than in new areas. Public opposition to nuclear facilities, although still strong, appears to have leveled off. Attempts to close down facilities or ban nuclear power altogether have not been successful in a number of states, suggesting that Americans may not be so disenchanted with nuclear power to close down the industry completely. But most observers believe that unless Congress moves forward with a plan to store nuclear waste (an issue discussed in the previous chapter), and dismantles aging reactors,[24] the nuclear energy debate will remain at a standstill, with 113 nuclear reactors now in operation in the United States and none under construction.

THE HISTORY OF POLICY PARALYSIS

Historically, U.S. energy policy has been separated by fuel, with different institutional associations and interests for each type and few attempts at coalition building. Coal interests from the Northeast have dealt with the Bureau of Mines, while states with uranium were more likely to converse with the Atomic Energy committees in Congress and the Nuclear Regulatory Commission. Seldom did jurisdictional boundaries cross over from one fuel to another, and as a result, terms like *disarray, turmoil,* and *inertia* are often used to describe U.S. energy policy. Those terms are in part applicable because of the maze of legislative and regulatory obstacles that have developed, along with a profusion of competing interests. The result is an energy policy that is highly segmented and neither comprehensive nor effective. While many analysts have attempted to explain why U.S. energy policy has been so ineffective, the consensus appears to be that the government has intervened unnecessarily rather than allowing market forces to allocate scarce energy resources.[25] How did such a policy develop?

Before 1900, the U.S. government had an ad hoc approach to what was perceived to be an unlimited supply of energy resources. A sense of abundance and virtual giveaways of public lands resulted in many valuable resources coming under private ownership. Although there were early rumblings of competition among interests representing the various fuels, it was not until after the turn of the century that the government began to intervene. In order to assure a stable and competitive oil market, the government relied upon the Sherman Anti-Trust Act in 1911 to break up the Standard Oil monopoly, and during World War I, President Woodrow Wilson established the Petroleum Advisory Committee to allocate American supplies. After the 1921 Teapot Dome scandal, in which officials were convicted of leasing federal lands to oil companies in exchange for bribes, the Federal Oil Conservation Board was created to oversee the oil industry. By the 1930s, the federal government's role had changed to one of consumer protection, expanding its jurisdiction with the Natural Gas Act of 1938 and the creation of the Tennessee Valley Authority. There was never an attempt made to coordinate policy across fuel and use areas. Each area of energy supply—coal, gas, hydropower, oil, and nuclear power—was handled separately, as was each consumption sector—utilities, transportation, industrial, and residential. During the 1950s, as Congress approved a massive interstate highway system and transportation network, the Supreme Court ratified the Federal Power Commission's power to regulate natural gas prices, which held prices artificially low as gas consumption skyrocketed.[26]

As the environmental movement developed in the late 1960s and early 1970s, the process of developing energy policy became increasingly complex as more interests demanded to be included in the decision-making process. At the same time, the importance of energy as a political issue brought in congressional leaders who sought to respond to their constituents' demands that something be done about the long lines at the gas pumps and rising prices for fuels. One study of energy policy found eight distinct groups active in national energy politics.[27]

Between 1969 and 1973, a confluence of negative factors and events changed the history of American energy policy forever. First, predictions by a few officials about a dependence upon foreign oil came true. Although the United States first began importing oil as early as 1947, oil from Arab sources reached over a million barrels a day by 1973, more than double the amount imported eighteen months earlier and 30 percent of total U.S. demand. Second, domestic oil production decreased because of price disparities over foreign oil and increasing costs for exploration and recovery. Third, new environmental legislation discouraged production of coal and nuclear power, and brought a delay in completion of the trans-Alaska pipeline at the same time Americans were driving more miles than ever before. Finally, the highly publicized Santa Barbara oil spill in 1969 had led to a five-year moratorium on offshore drilling, further restricting American oil production. The result was a nation made vulnerable to the vagaries of Middle Eastern politics.

The Nixon administration's approach to energy policy in the 1970s was marked by a series of failed attempts to do something about the impending crisis. Initially, the government imposed an Economic Stabilization Program, which froze prices on crude oil and petroleum products for ninety days, and froze wages and prices nationwide. In early 1973, Nixon restructured the country's mandatory oil import quota plan, which had limited foreign oil imports and allowed an unlimited purchase of home heating oil and diesel oil for a four-month period. This action was followed by the creation of a hand-picked Special Committee on Energy made up of key Nixon advisers, who recommended steps be taken to cope with price increase and fuel shortages. The strategy was to increase energy supplies, with little concern for modifying demand or conserving energy. By midyear, the administration's mandatory fuel allocation program had led to the closure of hundreds of independent gasoline stations. Then the administration shifted its policies once again by proposing $100 million be spent on research and development for new energy technology, and creation of a Federal Energy Administration to coordinate policy.

In October 1973, OPEC members, resentful of U.S. aid to Israel, voted to cut their oil production and to end all petroleum exports to the United States, resulting in a sharp increase in world oil prices, and forcing the Nixon administration to drastically revise its approach. Nixon responded with Project Independence to eliminate foreign oil imports by 1980, and Congress enacted the Emergency Petroleum Allocation Act to distribute fuel supplies evenly. But Congress failed to agree on the provisions of the National Energy Emergency Act, the cornerstone of the administration's programs, and as the Watergate scandal unfolded, U.S. policies became less and less focused.

Analyses of the politics of energy during this period point out a number of lessons learned from the 1973 crisis. For example, a "cry-wolf syndrome" arose when the first warnings appeared about dependence upon foreign oil. One survey had even found that the majority of Americans were unaware that the United States imported any oil and were unable to understand how the most technically advanced nation in the world simply couldn't produce enough oil to meet demand. As a result, the concerns were often ignored or disbelieved. Decisions were often based on poor quality or misleading information, and confused and often contradictory policies resulted. A turnover in leadership (four different people held the position of White House energy policy coordinator in 1973) exacerbated the problem. The role of "energy czar" passed through the hands of seven men from 1971 to 1973, each of whom had a different concept of what U.S. energy policy should look like. Some, like Secretary of Agriculture Earl Butz, were given new titles and responsibilities, while others, like George Lincoln, were made head of agencies that were then abruptly abolished (Office of Emergency Planning).[28] Lastly, by treating each fuel source separately and allowing the disparate interest groups to be so deeply involved in the decision-making process, the government never really took control of the crisis.[29]

As a result of the 1973 crisis, a host of agencies took turns formulating energy policy. The Federal Energy Administration was created in May 1974, but the agency lacked direction and suffered from a lack of a clear sense of mission. It was designed to bring together smaller agencies that had historically been in conflict with one another, and was caught between the competing objectives of regulating prices and expediting domestic resource development. After Nixon's resignation, Congress attempted to pick up the pieces by enacting the Energy Policy and Conservation Act of 1975, which levied a windfall profits tax on oil to control imports and gave the president the power to ration gas in an emergency. Other provisions included appliance standards, improved auto mileage standards, and authorized petroleum stockpiling.

The politics of energy took a different turn during the administration of President Jimmy Carter. The creation of a separate Cabinet-level Department of Energy in 1977 underscored the nation's crisis mentality and Carter's campaign promise to reorganize government. The agency was charged with regulating fuel consumption, providing incentives for energy conservation, and research and development into alternative energy sources. Congressional support for the Energy Department came on the heels of a public mood that demanded change and an administration determined to avoid a replay of the 1973 crisis. In 1977, an acute natural gas shortage led Carter to propose his National Energy Plan (NEP) as he characterized the energy situation as "the moral equivalent of war." The NEP differed from the Nixon administration's strategies because it called for greater fuel efficiency and conservation rather than increased production. In 1977, Congress also replaced the Federal Power Commission, which had been created in 1920, with the Federal Energy Regulatory Commission (FERC), giving the agency responsibility for oversight of the electric power and natural gas industries.

By the time Congress passed the National Energy Act in October 1978, Carter's NEP had been gutted. In retrospect, it has been argued that the Carter proposal was doomed from the beginning. Members of Congress found that their constituents were unwilling to make sacrifices (like reducing the number of miles they drove yearly) because they didn't feel there really was an energy shortage. Voters made it clear they believed the entire energy crisis was concocted by the big oil companies to force prices upward and generate bigger profits. In addition, the Carter administration was guilty of taking its case directly to the people, rather than developing a program in consultation with Congress. The legislative package that was drafted by the White House was hastily written, filled with technical errors, and so unwieldy (530 pages covering 113 provisions) that it was difficult for Congress to grapple with it in committee hearings. Carter also alienated both environmentalists and the energy industry with his proposals, especially the Energy Mobilization Board and a windfall tax on oil. Although Carter succeeded in enunciating an integrated, comprehensive national energy plan, he failed to have it fully implemented.[30]

The Reagan administration, in contrast, marks an eight-year period of amicable cooperation between the petroleum and coal industries and the administration, and a dramatic shift in energy research and development.[31] Reagan's strategy, outlined in his 1981 National Energy Plan, was to limit governmental intervention as much as possible, especially with regard to regulatory agencies, while supporting nuclear power and cutting research funds for alternative energy sources. Renouncing the Carter administration's goal of meeting 20 percent of the nation's energy needs through solar power by the year 2000, Reagan even symbolically had his staff remove the solar panels Carter had installed at the White House. He was unsuccessful in dissolving the Department of Energy, which he viewed as indicative of Carter's "big government" approach, although his appointment of former South Carolina governor James Edwards signaled his intentions. In a 1982 speech, Edwards announced he wanted "to close down the [Department of Energy], bury it once and for all, and salt the earth over it so it won't spring up again." Edwards was later replaced by Donald Hodel, who shared Edwards's goal.[32] The Reagan presidency was marked by a return to the strategies of the 1960s—including reliance on the free market to control prices, dependence on fossil fuels, tax benefits for oil producers, and little support for conservation.

George Bush continued the policies initiated by his predecessor. His 1991 national energy strategy sought to achieve roughly equal measures of new energy production and conservation. One of the cornerstones of that policy was to open up 1.5 million acres of the nineteen-million acre Arctic National Wildlife Refuge in northeast Alaska for oil and gas exploration (discussed in Chapter 16). After the Persian Gulf Crisis in 1991, Congress seemed more inclined to move forward on energy policy, finally enacting the comprehensive Energy Policy Act of 1992 just prior to the November election. The new law restructures the electric utility industry to promote more competition, provides tax relief to independent oil and gas drillers, encourages energy conservation and efficiency, promotes renewable energy and cars that run on alternative fuels, makes it easier to build nuclear power plants, authorizes billions of dollars for energy-related research and development, and creates a climate protection office within the Energy Department. Critics point out that the bill does not address the issue of automobile fuel efficiency (one of the planks in Bill Clinton's environmental platform) and does not significantly reduce U.S. dependence on foreign oil, but rather caps existing levels of use. Still, it marks the first time in a decade that Congress has been able to compromise on the most contentious provisions—those dealing with alternative fuels and energy-related tax provisions.[33]

It is important to consider U.S. energy policy in light of a global perspective, although this section provides only a snapshot view of what the future holds for the United States, rather than a region-by-region overview of what the energy picture looks like in other nations. Energy is considered to be a global issue for a number of reasons. It transcends the traditional boundaries of the nation-state and cannot be resolved by a single country. It is an issue that possesses a present imperative which forces nations to press for resolution (i.e., oil is a finite commodity and thus it is crucial that alternative sources be found). The resolution of the issue requires policy action—it will not resolve itself. Finally, energy is a global issue because of its persistence on the policy agenda—there is no consensus about how to solve the problems that have been identified.[34]

Energy consumption is closely tied to economic development, and future projections of energy use show a changing profile of fuels as we approach the next century, as seen in Figure 6.2. Total world consumption is projected to grow steadily well into the next decade, on average about half as fast as world economic growth as measured by gross domestic product. Oil will continue to be the most important source of energy, but the growth in oil consumption is the slowest of all the major energy sources. The fastest-growing fuel is natural gas, which will grow over one and one-half times as fast as oil. The most noteworthy projection, however, is that energy consumption in the developing countries will grow about twice as fast as industrial countries. The growth of urban areas

Figure 6.2 World Energy Consumption, by Type, 1990–2010 (in quadrillion BTU)

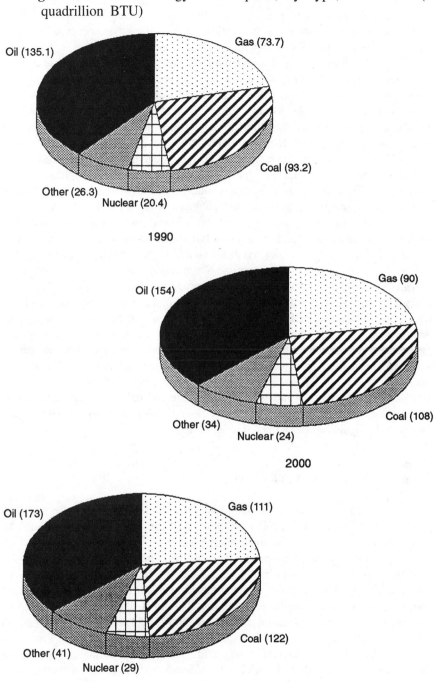

1990

2000

2010

and industrial activities that accompany development bring with them increased demands for transportation, electrification, and all the other energy-using appliances and amenities associated with modernization.

The U.S. energy pie looks somewhat different from the energy use of other countries. Western Europe, for example, has become heavily dependent upon imported energy since World War II and the switch from native coal resources to oil imported from the Middle East. A vocal anti–nuclear power lobby in several European nations has limited the development of facilities in parts of France and in the United Kingdom, Germany, and Sweden. In Eastern Europe and the republics of the former Soviet Union, coal has been the predominant energy source, although nuclear energy has been used in those regions far from coal reserves. Japan, with virtually no indigenous fossil fuels, has become a leader in both energy conservation and nuclear power, but still imports nearly 90 percent of its energy in the form of oil. China, in contrast, has sufficient hydroelectric power and coal reserves to last well into the twenty-second century at current levels of output, but has been unable to develop an adequate distribution system to get power to consumers. South Korea and Taiwan have been able to vigorously develop their nuclear power programs with little public opposition and significant government support. Most developing nations are heavily dependent upon traditional fuels (coal, timber) and must import oil, although Latin American countries are now expanding their hydroelectric power. The sources of energy vary throughout the globe, depending upon a nation's resources and, to some extent at least, political forces. In absolute terms, the United States, the republics of the former Soviet Union, and China consumed the most energy in 1990 and will remain the largest consumers through 2010, although total energy consumption in the states of the former Soviet Union declined in 1990 and is likely to be lower in 1995 than it was in 1990.

FUTURE ENERGY TRENDS

If the past is indicative of the future, the American energy pie may look quite different by the year 2000. Over the past forty years, the U.S. outlook has changed somewhat as new sources have become more competitively priced and traditional sources of fuel—primarily crude oil and coal—have become less reliable or polluting, as seen in Figure 6.3. As the figure indicates, coal production has increased since 1960, while production of oil has been reduced following the Arab oil crisis in the early 1970s. The most dramatic change has been the increase in the production of energy from nuclear sources, despite the political barriers and a virtual end to construction of new facilities. Projections for the future indicate nuclear power will be surpassed by natural gas as the second largest source of U.S. electricity generation. Similarly, renewable energy use is expected to increase sharply by 2010 as new technologies are developed and the prices of other energy sources increase. The most significant market

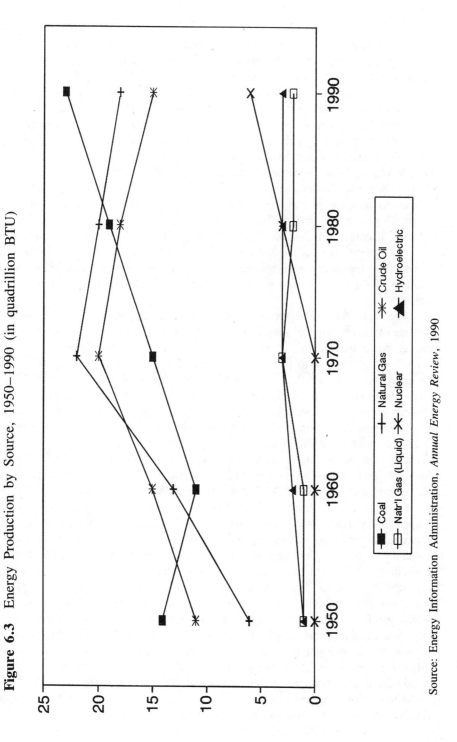

Figure 6.3 Energy Production by Source, 1950–1990 (in quadrillion BTU)

Coal ■ — Natural Gas + — Crude Oil ✳
Natr'l Gas (Liquid) □ — Nuclear ✳ — Hydroelectric ▲

Source: Energy Information Administration, *Annual Energy Review*, 1990

145

penetration is expected from geothermal installations, the use of municipal solid waste as fuel, and various biomass applications, with nonhydropower sources increasing to as much as 39 percent of the energy pie near 2010.[35]

But it is the consumption side of the equation that raises concern among many decision makers. Although total energy use has shown little increase since 1990, the resumption of normal economic growth (at a rate of 2–3 percent per year) and the prospect of relatively low energy prices (compared to the peaks of the 1970s) are projected to raise total energy use in all sectors in the next twenty years. Where will the additional energy come from? Domestic oil production is gradually decreasing, while the demand for petroleum is increasing, leading to projections that the amount of imported petroleum will jump from about 42 percent in 1990 to between 53 and 69 percent by 2010. The United States will continue its reliance upon Middle Eastern oil (source of the majority of proven reserves) as will other producing nations whose supplies are beginning to be exhausted. Some analysts believe this will lead to a competition for Saudi Arabian oil at a time when political pressures in the Gulf region continue to simmer.

There are two basic scenarios of what the next decade will bring to the politics of energy. One of the most prevalent views is that we must dramatically change our consumption patterns—the so-called conservation alternative. Proponents believe the way to satisfy the world's energy appetite is simply to go on an energy diet; rather than looking for new sources of power, we should be conserving what is available and getting more out of it. Advocates of this strategy point to the fact that Western Europeans use only half as much energy as Americans to maintain their life-style—evidence that energy conservation does not mean a starvation diet.

Can Americans simply agree to use less energy in order to reduce the need for new power plants? That question has already been answered as a result of the oil crises of the 1970s. Despite the fact that the American economy grew by more than 40 percent from 1973 to 1986, the amount of power consumed by the United States during that same period remained stable. Residential fuel use, for example, dropped appreciably after the 1979–80 crisis when thermostats were voluntarily lowered. One way in which we could make a serious impact on our dependence on foreign oil would be to require that automobiles be more energy efficient. The federal government took the initial steps in this direction in 1975 when Congress enacted Corporate Average Fuel Economy (CAFE) standards, which specified targets for miles per gallon. Although the Reagan administration later weakened those standards, the average new car in the United States today is rated at twenty-eight miles per gallon, twice as high as the 1974 average—a difference that saves four million barrels of oil per day. Increasing CAFE standards, and encouraging Americans to cut down their driving by 25 percent, could reduce oil consumption for cars by half and eliminate the need for Middle Eastern oil imports. Other researchers have pointed out that only economic incentives for public utilities will provide the impetus the country needs to develop a full conservation effort.[36]

Although representatives of both political parties have given their support for energy conservation as a key element in future energy planning, their rhetoric has failed to result thus far in any substantial conservation legislation. Four explanations for this gap between appearance and substance have been offered. First, despite the prevailing myth that predatory oil and gas producers have blocked or resisted price controls (the most effective conservation incentive), there is evidence that public interest groups have failed to exert much influence in protecting consumer interests. The kinds of consumer advocates who pressed states for electric rate reform during the 1970s have been largely silent since that time. Second, public opinion, often said to be the driving force behind legislative decision making, has not reached consensus on energy issues. The public appears caught between a desire to avoid energy rip-offs while at the same time showing little willingness to support federal control of industry. Third, energy policies have been filtered through localized interests and congressional blocs (Western-Eastern, oil vs. gas, Democrats-Republicans, etc.) making it difficult for Congress to come up with a national sentiment on energy conservation. Lastly, energy policy is but one example of several policy issues symptomatic of a larger pathology—periodic institutional immobilism, or, as it is more commonly known, policy paralysis. Like civil rights legislation in the 1960s, or budget debates in the 1980s, energy has bogged down in a complex political system that is short on leadership and long on intense political convictions.[37]

A second, more controversial scenario for the future begins with the premise the events of 1973–74 were not an energy crisis, but rather the beginning of a New Energy Era—a time of uncertainty and volatility, which decision makers must learn to face, and with which they must struggle over the coming decades. That view believes energy decisions are made in the private sector rather than by the government, since governments are neither producers nor consumers of energy. Advocates of this view believe that the United States has blundered in its approach to energy policy in the past by relying upon outdated and inappropriate ideas about the role of the public and private sectors. They support an Integrated Energy System (IES) approach, which involves fuel sources that are clean, secure and reliable, safe, economic, and robust. More simply, IES would involve using existing renewable fuel sources but take advantage of improvements in technology and better ways to put the pieces together to improve system efficiency and social acceptability. For example, IES might involve greater reliance upon cogeneration and combined cycle systems, as well as newer technologies like carbon dioxide recovery from combustion processes.[38] Are the kinds of legal and institutional barriers that exist to implementing IES surmountable? Supporters of IES believe that the public (and public officials) will accept a fine-tuning of the energy pie recipe rather than a complete change in its ingredients. So far, however, there has been little incentive for decision makers to even look at the menu, and they are unlikely to do so until the next energy crisis intrudes.

SUMMARY

Political events like the 1973 Arab oil embargo, the passage of the 1990 Clean Air Act, and the 1991 Gulf War, and the 1992 Energy Policy Act have been milestones in the development of U.S. energy policy, since they forced policymakers to confront U.S. dependence upon foreign oil. After the 1973 oil crisis, for example, research and federal support for alternative energy sources flourished, and serious energy conservation measures were enacted. But during the 1980s, as the price of oil dropped and supplies stabilized, Americans began using more oil than ever before. Recent air quality legislation is now beginning to force technological advances, and is likely to lead to a gradual decrease in the use of fossil fuels to produce electricity. In the regulatory arena, energy policy has been characterized as the politics of disarray, focused upon only in times of crisis. There are two ways of looking at the world's energy future. One view is that rather than looking toward new sources we must go on an energy diet and conserve existing resources. A second scenario assumes the world entered a New Energy Era in the early 1970s and argues that most decisions about energy will not be made in the political arena but in the marketplace. Supporters of this view recommend that the world continue its reliance upon fossil fuels but implement an Integrated Energy System based on evolving technology to better use those resources. Given the historical record, however, it is unlikely that there will be great strides made in global energy policy until another crisis is upon us.

NOTES

1. Quoted in Keith Melville, ed., *Energy Options: Finding a Solution to the Power Predicament* (New York: McGraw-Hill, 1992), 4.

2. To put those figures in perspective, the reader should keep in mind that the price rose from $13 to $34 per barrel following the cutoff of Iranian oil in 1979. The price in 1992 had declined to $21 per barrel.

3. This view of energy is presented in Thomas H. Lee, Ben C. Bell, Jr., and Richard D. Tabors, *Energy Aftermath* (Boston: Harvard Business School Press, 1990), 1.

4. Barry B. Hughes et al., *Energy in the Global Arena: Actors, Values, Policies and Futures* (Durham, NC: Duke University Press, 1985), 10–11.

5. Edward Teller, *Energy from Heaven and Earth* (San Francisco: W.H. Freeman, 1979), 2.

6. For an analysis of coal policies, see Walter Rosenbaum, *Energy Politics and Public Policy*, 2nd ed. (Washington, DC: Congressional Quarterly Press, 1987), 161–87.

7. Constance Elizabeth Hunt, *Down by the River* (Washington, DC: Island Press, 1988), 200–201.

8. Ibid., 215–43.

9. See John D. Echeverria, Pope Barrow, and Richard Roos-Collins, *Rivers at Risk: The Citizen's Guide To Hydropower* (Washington, DC: Island Press, 1989).

10. See Christopher Anderson, "The Future Is Now (Again)," *Nature* 354 (December 5, 1991): 344–45.

11. Michael Lev, "California Utilities Plan New Solar Energy Plant," *New York Times*, August 29, 1991, D-5.

12. Peter Asmus, "A Fresh Breeze: New Technologies Revitalize Wind Power," *California Journal* 23, no. 8 (August 1992): 413–15.

13. See Richard A. Kerr, "Geothermal Tragedy of the Commons," *Science* 253, no. 5016 (July 12, 1991): 134–35; and "Developer Drills at Crater Lake Border," *National Parks* 64, nos. 1–2 (January–February 1990): 9–10.

14. See Ian Anderson, "Blowout Blights Future of Hawaii's Geothermal Power," *New Scientist*, July 20, 1991, 17; and Mark Mardon, "Steamed Up over Rainforests," *Sierra* 75, no. 3 (May–June 1990): 80–82.

15. See Daniel Sperling, *New Transportation Fuels: A Strategic Approach to Technological Change* (Berkeley: University of California Press, 1988).

16. See Daniel Sperling, ed., *Alternative Transportation Fuels: An Environmental and Energy Solution* (Westport, CT: Quorum Books, 1989).

17. Otis Port, "Turning Paper-Mill Sludge into Clean Burning Fuel," *Business Week*, October 19, 1992, 61.

18. For a comprehensive history of the development of atomic power, see Margaret Gowing, *Reflections on Atomic Energy History* (Cambridge: Cambridge University Press, 1978).

19. See Peter R. Mounfield, *World Nuclear Power* (New York: Routledge, 1991).

20. That project was later canceled by the company.

21. Mounfield, *World Nuclear Power*, 73.

22. See Paul Slovic, Mark Layman, and James H. Flynn, "Risk Perception, Trust, and Nuclear Waste: Lessons from Yucca Mountain," *Environment* 33, no. 32 (April 1991): 6.

23. Mounfield, *World Nuclear Power*, 48.

24. See Bill Breen, "Dismantling Nuclear Reactors," *Garbage* 4, no. 2 (March–April 1992): 40–47.

25. See, for example, Walter J. Mead, *Energy and the Environment: Conflict in Public Policy* (Washington, DC: American Enterprise Institute, 1978).

26. James Everett Katz, *Congress and National Energy Policy* (New Brunswick, NJ: Transaction Books, 1984), 5–7.

27. John E. Chubb, *Interest Groups and the Bureaucracy: The Politics of Energy* (Stanford: Stanford University Press, 1983), 14–15.

28. See John C. Whitaker, *Striking a Balance: Environment and Natural Resources Policy in the Nixon–Ford Years* (Washington, DC: American Enterprise Institute, 1976), 66–68.

29. There are a number of highly readable accounts of this period, including Lester A. Sobel, ed., *Energy Crisis, Vol. 1, 1969–1973* (New York: Facts on File, 1974); and Robert J. Kalter and William A. Vogely, eds., *Energy Supply and Government Policy* (Ithaca: Cornell University Press, 1976).

30. Katz, *Congress and National Energy Policy*, 70–132.

31. See Claude E. Barfield, *Science Policy from Ford To Reagan: Change and Continuity* (Washington, DC: American Enterprise Institute, 1982); and Don E. Kash and Robert W. Rycroft, *U.S. Energy Policy: Crisis and Complacency* (Norman: University of Oklahoma Press, 1984.

32. Katz, *Congress and National Energy Policy*, 165.

33. Holly Idelson, "National Energy Strategy Provisions," *Congressional Quarterly*, November 28, 1992, 3722–30.

34. For an comprehensive explanation of this approach, see Hughes et al., *Energy in the Global Arena*, xii–xviii.

35. Energy Information Administration, *Annual Energy Outlook 1992* (Washington, DC: U.S. Government Printing Office, January, 1992), viii–ix.

36. See, for example, Peter N. Nemetz, *Economic Incentives for Energy Conservation* (New York: Wiley, 1984); and John C. Sawhill and Richard Cotton, eds., *Energy Conservation: Successes and Failures* (Washington, DC: Brookings Institution, 1986).

37. These four explanations were developed by Pietro S. Nivola, *The Politics of Energy Conservation* (Washington, DC: Brookings Institution, 1986), 252–85.

38. A summary of the IES approach is found in Lee, Bell, and Tabors, *Energy Aftermath*, 219–50.

FOR FURTHER READING

David Howard Davis. *Energy Politics*, 4th ed. New York: St. Martin's Press, 1993.

Kenneth D. Frederick and Roger A. Sedjo, eds. *America's Renewable Resources*. Washington, DC: Resources for the Future, 1991.

Richard J. Gilbert, ed. *Regulatory Choices: A Perspective on Developments in Energy Policy*. Berkeley: University of California Press, 1991.

Barry B. Hughes et al. *Energy in the Global Arena: Actors, Values, Policies and Futures*. Durham, NC: Duke University Press, 1985.

James Everett Katz. *Congress and National Energy Policy*. New Brunswick, NJ: Transaction Books, 1984.

Thomas H. Lee, Ben C. Ball, Jr., and Richard D. Tabors. *Energy Aftermath*. Boston: Harvard Business School Press, 1990.

Pietro S. Nivola. *The Politics of Energy Conservation*. Washington, DC: Brookings Institution, 1986.

Walter A. Rosenbaum. *Energy, Politics, and Public Policy*, 2nd ed. Washington, DC: Congressional Quarterly Press, 1987.

PART 3

The Water

CHAPTER 7

Managing Resources:
The Water Wars

The drought in California has escalated to a full-scale crisis. The tap
has run dry—and there is no relief in sight. The reservoirs are at all
time lows. There is virtually no snowpack. We are halfway through
the season when we normally get our rains and we aren't getting any.
We have compounded the problem over the last four years of the
drought by using up most of our reserves. It is a bleak picture—for
cities and towns, for fish and wildlife, for our forests and parks, and
for agriculture. The losses are enormous. We may never fully recover.
  —Congressman George Miller, testifying on the California drought in
1991[1]

The scarcity and availability of water, and the ways in which it is being used,
are at issue not only in the United States but by governments in virtually every
region of the globe. What makes water management interesting from a political
perspective is that the officials and agencies that make water policy often labor
in relatively obscure agencies, and speak a language all their own. The terms to
measure water, the science of keeping it clean, and the economics over who
controls water resources are not the sort of thing most of us think about or talk
about in our everyday conversation. "Waterspeak" includes references to acre
feet, maximum contaminant level goals, interflow zones, calichefication, and
NAWAPA. And yet the prize of the "water wars" that this chapter chronicles is
absolutely critical to our existence. Without water, we cannot live.

The basic political issue is that there is a continual shortage of fresh water
for 40 percent of the world's population, with only one-half of 1 percent of the
world's total water supply easily and economically available for human use. The
rest is in effect "locked up" in oceans, polar ice caps, surface collectors like
lakes and rivers, in clouds, or under Earth's surface yet too deep to be drilled in
wells. Coupled with the problem of supply is the planet's expanding population
and the basic human need for water, along with increased agricultural and
industrial demand. In some areas of the world, natural causes like climate
change and drought have led to shortages.

This chapter examines the world's management of its water resources, beginning with an overview of the reasons behind Earth's water shortages. The chapter then goes on to look at the results of those shortages from a global perspective, and concludes with a survey of the proposed solutions and their successes and failures.

WHY DON'T WE HAVE ENOUGH WATER?

Human use of water has increased more than thirty-five-fold over the past three centuries, with most of the increase in the developing nations of the world. There are three basic reasons why, despite significant outlays of funds, there is a shortage of fresh water for almost half of the world's population. The first reason deals with personal water use and an increasing global population. Each individual consumes only about two quarts of water per day, but there are dozens of other daily uses, such as washing clothing, taking baths or showers, cooking meals, flushing toilets, and watering lawns, as seen in Table 7.1. For example, the average American's personal water use averages ninety gallons per day, and another six hundred gallons a day are used in the manufacturing, chemical, and industrial processes that create the goods and services we take for granted as a part of modern life. That includes water used, for example, by utility power plants, breweries, steel makers, and mining operations. Agricultural use accounts for an additional eight hundred gallons per person per day, for a total close to fifteen hundred gallons per person per day.[2]

How much water do we need, and how much do we have? That question is at the heart of the water management debate. Unfortunately, the United States does not have an up-to-date assessment of its existing water supply, so many of the political decisions that are being made are based largely on speculation rather than on science. A similar problem exists internationally. As a result, political decisions about water management are often made in a scientific vacuum, based largely on the claims of competing interest groups and users.

But personal water consumption is just part of the water management problem. The world's population is growing at such an alarming rate (an issue that

Table 7.1   How Much Water Does It Take . . . ?

To brush your teeth?	2 gallons
To flush a toilet?	5–7 gallons
To shave with water running?	10–15 gallons
To run a dishwasher?	12 gallons
To wash dishes by hand?	20 gallons
To take a shower?	25–50 gallons
To wash a load of clothes?	59 gallons
To wash a car with a hose?	150 gallons

will be discussed in Chapter 17) that existing sources of fresh water are insufficient to meet the human demand. Researchers know that Earth's population doubled between 1950 and 1987, and expect that it will reach 6.25 billion by the year 2000. In a worst-case scenario, the population could reach fourteen billion by 2050. The factor that exacerbates the sheer number of people living on the planet is *where* they live. By 2000, one-half of the world's population will live in cities, placing increased demand on infrastructures that are already stretched thin and in need of massive repair. Many of those cities are in areas with minimal rainfall or severe water shortages already, like Los Angeles, New York, Mexico City, and Calcutta. China, for example, has over half of the world's population but only 8 percent of the world's renewable fresh water sources, placing the entire nation in a state of water peril. Already, more than two hundred cities, most of them located in the North China Plain, lack sufficient water and a quarter of those face acute shortages, especially near Beijing. If present trends continue, the region will have 6 percent less water than needed by the end of this century.[3] In contrast, Latin America has abundant supplies of water, but there, too, the water is unevenly distributed. While Brazil has an oversupply, Peru is chronically short of water. The climate of the country varies considerably, and the government has attempted to regulate supplies by massive dam and reservoir projects.

A second cause of water scarcity is the increased demand for industrial, commercial, and agricultural use of water. Almost every industrialized nation is relying more and more on water for manufacturing, oil refineries, and utility power plants. There is also a considerable amount of water used in commercial settings, like office air-conditioning systems, which use water to cool air for employee and customer comfort. These industrial and commercial needs are greatest in urban areas, where the population base already places its own demands on the water system.

Agricultural water use is also behind the scarcity issue. Irrigation is the answer to how to grow crops in areas where there is insufficient natural rainfall. Piping systems and wells transfer water from natural sources (lakes, streams, or aquifers) to fields, basically altering the natural hydrological cycle. It takes nearly one thousand gallons of water to grow each pound of food we consume, making agricultural irrigation a major water consumer, although consumption varies considerably from one country to another. In the Middle East, where high birthrates combine with a lack of rainfall, irrigation is a massive undertaking. Egypt, for example, irrigates 100 percent of its cropland, while Israel irrigates almost two-thirds. Jordan anticipates a 50 percent increase in its water needs by 2005, and several nations are considering the need to shift water usage away from agriculture in order to satisfy demands for drinking water.[4] In the years after World War II, especially the 1960s and 1970s, irrigated land tripled worldwide to 160 million hectares, mostly in China, India, and Pakistan. Currently, 250 million hectares of land are being irrigated. The least-irrigated acreage (less than five million hectares) is in the sub-Saharan region of Africa. Most of this increase came largely at the urging of international donors hoping to increase food production—a generally accepted justification. The United Nations Food and Agriculture Organization estimates irrigation will have to increase by 40 percent over the next twenty years to meet expected food supply demands. The largest planned increase in irrigated acreage will come in India, Pakistan, China, Mexico, and Brazil.[5]

The pressure to grow more and more food to meet the needs of the growing population is faced globally. The republics of the former Soviet Union have slowly drained the Aral Sea by diverting water for crop irrigation. The Aral Sea, located in central Asia, was once the fourth-largest lake on Earth, but has now shrunk to two-thirds its original size.[6] In the United States, there are signs that too many farms are trying to irrigate too much land with too little water. Of the 165 billion gallons of water used in states west of the one-hundredth meridian (a line stretching north to south from North Dakota through Texas), 145 billion gallons, or 88 percent, will go to irrigation. Areas to the west of the meridian generally receive less than twenty inches of rain per year, while those to the east have a problem of too much water in some states.[7] Despite the political costs of doing so, a shift in water priorities from agriculture to other uses would help to alleviate the scarcity problem in this country.[8]

There are, however, many political considerations that make irrigation controversial throughout much of the developing world. Critics of massive irrigation projects point out that such schemes often involve massive relocation efforts as new dams and reservoirs are built. The building of the Aswan Dam in Egypt, for example, involved the relocation of over one hundred thousand people,[9] and between 1979 and 1985, the World Bank approved financing for forty hydropower projects that resulted in the resettlement of at least six hundred thousand people in twenty-seven countries.[10] Critics of massive irrigation projects also argue that they benefit only wealthy farmers, not the population as a whole, and may lead to public health problems from water-borne diseases and parasites.[11]

Lastly, natural causes are also responsible for water shortages. The United States has had several recent periods of severe drought that have made water management a critical political issue in almost every state. In 1977, Californians began using "gray water"—kitchen sink and bathtub drainage—on their lawns when a severe drought hit the state. Signs were posted in college and university bathrooms urging conservation ("Is this trip necessary?"), and one of the most popular bumper stickers seen throughout the state reminded drivers, "Save Water: Shower with a Friend." Severe drought conditions in New York in 1985 led to a ban on watering lawns, and in 1986, drought in the southeastern United States led to massive crop and livestock losses. California, Oregon, and Washington State declared drought conditions from 1986 to 1992, with the impact of water shortages affecting everything from ski resorts to forest fire conditions. Several of California's endangered bird populations are considered at risk from the drought, as are winter-run Chinook salmon due to diversion of water for human use.[12] The severe drought in western states has had additional environmental impacts. Hydroelectric capacity in these regions has been greatly reduced, causing California utilities to rely more upon fossil fuels, which have increased emissions of carbon dioxide by more than 25 percent. These increased emissions affect air quality in urban areas where pollution is already severe.

The same situation is true internationally. Drought in north-central and western Africa from 1968 to 1973 had devastating consequences for a region that already suffered from growing population and diminishing resources. India faced a massive drought in the mid-1980s, even though the nation's monsoon rains produce significant amounts of water. The Indian government has attempted to capture the runoff in large dams, but deforestation has led to massive flooding, and some streams and rivers now dry up for parts of the year.

THE AMERICAN WATER WARS

American water policy is among the most politicized in the world, colored by political appointments and powerful industry lobbies, as this overview will indicate. It is a policy that has recently changed as political clout has shifted from the farm and agricultural lobby, which controlled policy at the turn of the century, to urban interests who now dominate Congress. Water management in the United States has primarily been the responsibility of two federal agencies, although that responsibility is shared with a large number of public and private entities ranging from local sewage companies and irrigation districts to state water boards. The Corps of Engineers was originally created in 1802 under the Department of the Army and became the main construction arm of the federal government. In 1824, Congress gave the corps authority over navigational operations, and the agency gained additional jurisdiction through the Flood Control Act of 1936. Just four years after Franklin Roosevelt brought his New Deal to Washington, the corps was embarking upon a reservoir construction program that erected ten large dams a year, on average, for fifty years. The authority was expanded further in 1972 with passage of the Clean Water Act, which brought its jurisdiction into wetlands permits.

The Reclamation Service (later renamed the Bureau of Reclamation) was authorized by Congress in 1902 with responsibility for aiding western settlement in a seventeen-state area.[13] One of the factors that made the bureau popular among western farmers is that it was chartered with a limitation that it serve only those landowners who held title to 160 acres or less, and thus the agency rapidly came to be influenced by local interests. During its early years, the bureau constructed massive water development projects, canals, and public works programs, such as Washington's Grand Coulee Dam (the largest-single purpose peacetime appropriation in U.S. history) and California's Central Valley Project. Between them, the two federal agencies quickly established a reputation as the home of the pork barrel—congressionally approved water projects that benefited a single district. Projects like dams and flood control channels brought a visible product (and jobs) to the home base of a member of Congress, paid for by liberal cost-sharing formulas and substantial federal financing. In 1920, the Federal Water Power Act created the Federal Power Commission, which was replaced in 1977 by the Federal Energy Regulatory Commission. The commission was initially responsible for regulating the nation's water resources, but its charter was eventually redirected to oversee the electric power and natural gas industries.

There has always been a closely knit relationship between the congressional committees that had oversight responsibility for the agencies, the two agencies, and local water interest lobbies. Decisions on which projects to fund, and at what level, were frequently made by those leaders with the most political clout, or because of pressure from campaign contributors, rather than on the merits of good water management. Around 1900, for example, the National Rivers Congress, made up of powerful business figures, contractors, and members of Congress (who were honorary members of the group) began monitoring Corps of Engineers projects. They were extremely successful at convincing Congress to continue authorizing funds for projects that had long since been completed. The water lobby became so powerful that in its heyday in the early 1960s, the chair of the House Appropriations Committee would boast that "practically every Congressional district" was included in the omnibus public works bills, and that "there is something here for everybody."[14]

For the most part, America's growth spurt continued unabated after World War II, and few questioned the advisability of the corps and bureau's massive undertakings. New water technology, modern farming and cropping techniques, and widespread pesticide use made agricultural expansion a key element of the postwar boom, with cheap, government-subsidized water the key. Land irrigated with government-financed water grew from 2.7 million acres in 1930 to more than 4 million acres after the war and nearly 7 million acres by 1960. But during the late 1950s and mid-1960s, water resource planning changed from an emphasis on economic development to municipal, industrial, and recreational purposes. The water lobby was forced to make some concessions to environmental groups, outraged when projects began to infringe upon scenic or preserved areas, such as a proposal to build Echo Park Dam in Dinosaur National Monument.[15] The Sierra Club mobilized its members when a plan to build a hydroelectric plant in the Grand Canyon surfaced, and in so doing, lost its federal tax-exempt status. The bureau "compromised" by agreeing instead to expand the coal-fired power plant at Mojave, near the four corners area, and environmentalists believed they had saved the Grand Canyon. In an ironic twist, the Mojave facility later became the center of a totally different environmental issue when its emissions were thought to be the source of air pollution and haze over the Grand Canyon.

There is another clear pattern to U.S. water policy: the regional nature of the dispute. Growing urban development in California once led to a call by some members of Congress for the state to import water from its water-rich neighbors in the Pacific Northwest. Frostbelt state representatives bristled at the idea that all the federal money was going to their sunbelt colleagues. And although the tug of war over rights to the Colorado River between Arizona and California is essentially over, the dispute created more legal documents (by weight) than any other in the history of U.S. litigation, on any subject.

By the mid-1970s, environmental groups turned their attention to water issues, becoming a potent force in policymaking. Groups like the Sierra Club, the American Rivers Conservation Council, the National Wildlife Federation, and the Natural Resources Defense Council pressured Congress to follow the requirements of the National Environmental Policy Act and used litigation as a tool of forcing compliance with new legislative initiatives. Bolstered by environmental support during his campaign, President Jimmy Carter began his administration in 1977 by developing a "hit list" of nineteen water projects that were to be deleted from the federal budget, including the Central Arizona Project. Carter underestimated the powerful water industry lobby, however, which was able to convince Congress to restore all nineteen appropriations.

Water industry officials cheered the 1980 election of Ronald Reagan, believing his appointment of Robert Broadbent, a Nevada legislator, as head of the Bureau of Reclamation was a positive omen. It turned out to be a conflicting sign, however, as Reagan continued Carter's cost-sharing requirements on water projects (the portion of a water project to be borne by the federal government). As states and local governments began to realize they might have to pay a larger share of the cost for many of the projects, they became less attractive, and in some cases, financially burdensome. Part of the shift in policy can be traced to the growing clout of urban political interests over those of agriculture, as city politicians began to question why farmers were getting all the cheap water.[16]

Equally important was the discovery of dead waterfowl at the Kesterson National Wildlife Refuge in California's San Joaquin Valley. Ducks and geese were dying of a mysterious sickness that not only killed them, but resulted in birth deformities in their chicks. The eventual cause was found to be selenium, a trace element that can be toxic in high concentrations. The selenium was carried by the San Luis Drain from the politically powerful Westlands Water District in Fresno and Tulare counties. In 1985, Interior Secretary Donald Hodel called for a halt in the drainage by June 30, 1986, but the public had by then had just about enough of the Bureau of Reclamation's projects and its negligence.[17] By 1987, the policy change became clear when James Zigler, the Interior Department's assistant secretary for water and science, announced that the bureau was changing its mission from an agency based on federally supported construction to one based on resource management. The empire-building days of the corps and the bureau were over, replaced by an administration that was paying more attention to urban needs for a stable water supply than to agricultural interests seeking cheap water for their fields.

Pricing inequities continue to be at the heart of the battle over water management in the United States. The "real" cost of providing and distributing water is often impossible to determine, and historically, municipalities have been reluctant to try to pass those costs on to developers and commercial interests. City leaders often avoided charging a new business the true cost of water delivery for fear it would discourage economic growth. As a result, the rate structure has often allowed large users to benefit because of a system that charges the user less the more water is used. Favored customers often receive preferential pricing, and some cities served by the same water district often unknowingly subsidize the water costs of other cities in their area through complex pricing arrangements. Residential users tend to subsidize industrial users throughout most of the United States today.

Another new wrinkle has been the development of "water markets"— transactions ranging from transfers of water rights to the sale and lease of those rights or the land above the water source. Market transfers are dependent upon the concept of reallocating water supplies, rather than coming up with new sources of water. Part of the affection for the market concept was purely economic—new capital projects were becoming increasingly expensive and politically unpopular in much of the West. One group even began purchasing water rights in Colorado as an investment, with the expectation that as supplies diminished, the rights could be sold for a tidy profit. Cities like Phoenix and Scottsdale have also been active in the water market, buying thousands of acres of farmland outside their city limits in order to have a water source as their population increases and water within city boundaries runs short. Reallocation is gradually being looked upon as an alternative to finding new allocations as the primary mode of water development.[18]

One of the more recent battles in the water wars has involved the rights of native Americans to water resources. In 1908, in a far-reaching U.S. Supreme Court case,[19] the Winters Doctrine granted Indians the right to all waters that arise under, border, traverse, or underlie a reservation, and requires that they must continue to be made available to serve the current and future needs of the reservation. Historically, Indian claims to water rights were ignored by the Bureau of Reclamation and the Army Corps of Engineers, but a 1963 Supreme Court case[20] reinforced Indian authority over their land and water. Several tribes explored the possibility of marketing their water rights, but the issue leaves open the question of what the real value of water is.[21]

The American water wars have also touched our southern border with Mexico, where the Colorado River flows on its way to the Gulf of California. In 1922, Congress approved the Colorado River Compact, which divided up the river's resources, giving the three lower basin states (California, Arizona, and Nevada) and the four upper basin states (Wyoming, Colorado, New Mexico, and Utah) 7.5 million acre-feet each (an acre-foot is the volume of water that covers one acre to a depth of one foot, or 325,851 gallons). It should be noted, however, that the actual flow of the river is closer to fourteen rather than fifteen million acre-feet. Congress also authorized the building of Hoover Dam in 1928, giving the United States total control over the Colorado River—a situation that understandably made our Mexican neighbors nervous. Seeking to keep Mexico as a wartime ally, the United States signed a treaty in 1944 that assigned 1.5 million acre-feet to Mexico and created the International Boundary Water Commission to administer the treaty. In the early 1960s, a combination of population growth, the drilling of wells on the U.S. side, saline runoff from drainage projects, and construction of the Glen Canyon Dam in Utah began affecting both the quantity and quality of Mexico's water allocation. It took nearly ten years for the two sides to come to an agreement that in 1973 guaranteed Mexico a fair share of the Colorado in usable form—a turning point in the region's development. Twenty years later, the treaty has still not been fully implemented, in part because the United States has not held up its end of the bargain to operate a desalination plant in Yuma, Arizona.[22]

IMPACTS AND SOLUTIONS

The growing pressure to tap more and more of the Earth's water resources is having a number of negative impacts on a global scale. More urban communities are tapping into underground aquifers, drying them up as residential and agricultural demand increases. In cases like Mexico City and Phoenix, water levels are dropping due to heavy pumping, leading to subsidence—literally, the sinking of the city. In addition to a reduction in the availability of a valuable commodity, it is unlikely the water in the aquifer will ever be fully replaced.

Among the most important consequences of poor water management are soil erosion and desertification, which threaten nearly a third of Earth's surface. Desertification refers to the process by which the land gradually becomes less capable of supporting life and nonproductive. In one 1992 study, the UN's Global Assessment of Soil Degradation found three billion acres of land have sustained moderate to extreme degradation since 1945, accounting for 10.5 percent of the planet's fertile land. Of that land, 740 million acres are severely degraded and considered useless unless a major international financial and technical campaign is launched to reclaim it. The vast majority of the damaged land is in Asia, with 1.1 billion acres, and Africa, with 792 million, where most of the world's subsistence farmers live. Central America has the highest proportion of damaged land—24 percent of its total, followed by Europe (17 percent), Africa (14 percent), Asia (12 percent), and North America (4.4 percent). More than fifteen million acres worldwide (an area the size of West Virginia) are claimed by desertification every year, primarily due to four causes: overgrazing on rangelands, overcultivation of croplands, waterlogging and salting of irrigated lands, and deforestation.[23]

At least one-sixth of China's land is believed to have been ravaged by soil erosion to the extent where it is no longer productive, with another one-sixth ruined by desertification. Deserts there are expanding at the rate of more than six hundred square miles a year, and by the year 2000 are expected to have doubled in size. In Africa, a 1991 UN study found the area of land classified as arid or hyperarid has increased by nearly fifty-four million hectares since 1931. Some scientists believe there is a link between desertification and drought, pointing to a 30 percent reduction in rainfall in the African Sahel, the semi-arid region on the southern edge of the Sahara.[24] This zone is characterized by high temperatures and a short rainy season that begins and ends very abruptly. The ground is flat and the vegetation consists of strips of steppe interspersed with ruined soil. The scanty resources of the Sahel are the home of a nomadic population who graze cattle, moving their livestock to the areas where water is available. As the area's population has grown, the nomads have increased their herds, which have stripped the soil of its meager vegetation.[25] According to meteorologists, a reduction in vegetative cover due to desertification may reduce rainfall because of an increase in the albedo, the share of sunlight reflected back from Earth. According to the hypothesis, developed by Jule Charney of the Massachusetts Institute of Technology, less of the sun's radiation is absorbed at Earth's surface as albedo increases, so surface temperatures drop, causing a sinking motion in the atmosphere. Since the sinking air is dry, rainfall declines, and a degraded, higher-albedo area begins to feed on itself and become more desertlike.[26] Desertification, may, in turn, have an effect on global warming. Overgrazing and deforestation are thought by one researcher to be responsible for increasing temperatures in the Northern Hemisphere over the past century, although other scientists believe it is too premature to make such conclusions.[27]

Adding to the desertification process are increasing levels of salt in the water. An additional one hundred million acres, mostly in India and Pakistan, is estimated by the UN Environment Programme to suffer from salinization, which occurs in dry regions when evaporation near the soil surface leaves behind a thin salt residue.[28] Salinity also affects water quality in Peru and Mexico, where the annual loss of output due to salinization is estimated at one million tons of food grains, or enough to provide basic rations to five million people.[29]

Water diversion has also led to the destruction of valuable wildlife habitats, as is the case in California. In 1940, the state's Division of Water Resources granted the Department of Water and Power (DWP) of Los Angeles a permit to divert virtually all of the flow from four of the five streams that flow into Mono Lake, the second-largest lake in California. The diversion represents about 15 percent of Los Angeles's total city water supply. The lake is located at the base of the Sierra Nevada near Yosemite National Park, and although saline, its brine shrimp population is the food source for millions of migratory birds and 95 percent of the state's nesting gulls. As a result of DWP's diversion through its Owens Valley aqueduct, the level of the lake has dropped and increased salinity levels, which threaten the entire food chain. The lake's surface level has been diminished by one-third, exposing gull rookeries to predators, and future diversions are expected to reduce the lake even further. The receding lake waters have exposed a lake bed composed of an alkali silt, which when dry becomes airborne and becomes a health hazard.

The Irreplaceable Ogallala

When the early Spanish explorers first visited the Llano Estacado—the area of the Great Plains from what is now Texas to South Dakota—they decided it was uninhabitable because of a lack of water. Today, the region is one of the most agriculturally productive in the world, fed by an underground reservoir known as the Ogallala Aquifer. A cache of three-million-year-old fossil water left over from the Ice Age, the Ogallala is seven hundred miles long, three hundred miles wide, and up to a quarter of a mile deep. Forty percent of American beef cattle are fed corn raised with Ogallala water. Without it, food prices would rise dramatically—and food availability would be nowhere near what it is today.[32] In the early part of this century, farmers assumed they were sitting on an endless river of water, a "hidden Mississippi" they believed originated in the snow mass of the Rocky Mountains and flowed downward to the plains. U.S. Geological Survey reports explained that this was untrue; the Ogallala was more like an underground storage tank than a river, but the perceptions of an endless water supply persisted. The region's agricultural users began drilling more and more wells; in 1930 there were 170, and by 1957, there were 42,225 wells. During the early 1980s, studies began to show the area's water table was falling faster than it was being naturally replenished, with about six million acre-feet pumped out annually, and natural recharge replacing only about 185,000 acre-feet per year. Various proposals to recharge the aquifer have been suggested, including channeling flood waters into shallow wells, and conserving water by using secondary sewage effluent for municipal and residential irrigation. Despite these efforts, it is unknown how long it will be before the Ogallala runs dry, and the effects on the area's cattle and agricultural industries begin to be felt.[33]

In 1983, the National Audubon Society filed suit against Los Angeles to try and stop the diversions,[30] arguing the state had an obligation to protect the public trust embodied by the lake. The California Supreme Court agreed and sent the case back to the state's Water Board to determine whether and to what extent DWP ought to reduce its diversions. Despite nearly a decade of environmental studies, reports, investigations, and litigation, a solution to Mono Lake's dwindling water level still is not forthcoming.[31]

There are two basic solutions to the water scarcity and management problem: conservation and technology. The first is relatively straightforward—convince users to use less. The second involves a wide range of options from ancient to modern technological solutions. Water conservation is being implemented in many regions, ranging from urban communities to irrigation improvements in an attempt to reduce residents' dependency upon existing sources. Some of the easiest conservation efforts have been accomplished by metropolitan water districts that have enacted consumption ordinances or made water-saving showerheads and low-flow toilets available.[34] These efforts are not temporary responses to drought—studies indicate by 2010 southern California will have enough water to fulfill only 70 percent of its needs, making demand management practices a more likely strategy for reducing consumption.[35]

Conservation is not limited to urban areas. One of the most obvious strategies used to reduce seepage from agricultural irrigation was the replacement of unlined ditches with piping. Thousands of miles of earth-wall feeder ditches have been replaced in the United States, saving as much as 25 percent of the water in each one thousand feet of ditch. Improvements in furrow irrigation have resulted in irrigation efficiency improvements on the order of 10–40 percent, and low-head sprinkler systems have reduced loss to evaporation to almost zero. Through such methodologies, farmers can achieve water savings from 25 to 40 percent, leading to a stabilization of the underlying groundwater table in many areas.[36]

There are also a number of innovative solutions designed to increase shrinking supplies. One of the oldest methods involves desalination, long considered as one way in which communities could attempt to keep up with the explosive growth common to coastal regions.[37] There are two basic methods of desalination: distillation (heating ocean water and distilling the vapor) and filtering water through a membrane in a process called reverse osmosis. Distillation produces water that is more pure, but reverse osmosis is more energy efficient and the facilities are smaller and more compact. More than two-thirds of the thousands of desalination plants currently in operation worldwide use distillation, with more than half of all desalination facilities located in the Middle East. Israel, one of the pioneers in desalination technology, opened its first plant in 1965 for the new desert town of Eilat. The first U.S. facility opened in Key West, Florida, in 1967, and over one hundred plants have opened to serve other coastal cities. Although there was widespread interest in desalination during the 1960s,[38] public and government interest (and federal funding for research) seemed to go on hiatus during the 1970s and 1980s. The worldwide drought of the late 1980s, however, rekindled interest, especially in California. In 1992, officials dedicated a plant on Catalina Island, twenty-six miles off the coast of Los Angeles, which will provide 130,000 gallons of water a day, enough for a third of the island's needs. Similar plants are being built or considered in Santa Barbara and Morro Bay, California.

Some water experts argue desalination technology has made little progress in the past ten years, although nuclear powered desalination was considered in the early 1960s.[39] One nuclear facility currently operates in Kazakhstan, but the energy source has not been promoted due to fears about contamination of drinking water with radionuclides.[40] In Keahole Point, Hawaii, a pilot plant is operating using ocean thermal energy conversion (OTEC), a process that takes advantage of temperature gradients in deep tropical oceans. The technology, however, is likely only to be feasible along the Gulf Coast and southern California, where there are great enough temperature differences for OTEC to work.

One still unresolved desalination issue is what to do with the leftover salt—a considerable environmental problem.[41]

Cloud seeding is another strategy that has historically been used to increase rainfall. Airplanes release tiny crystals of silver iodide into clouds with the potential to release water by forming a base of ice crystals, which eventually fall as ice or snow. Cloud seeding, when successful, can lead to a 5–15 percent increase in rainfall. Researchers are also considering the use of dry ice, a type of bacterium, and ground-based seeding programs using propane to trigger precipitation.[42]

There are also several "megaprojects" being considered to transfer resources from water-rich areas to those most in need. Turkey, for example, is studying the feasibility of transporting some of its surplus water through two "peace pipelines" to downstream nations for drinking water and other domestic needs. The estimated $21 billion cost, however, has kept the project on the drawing board thus far. China is attempting a major diversion of the Yangtze River in the central part of the nation, although it still will fulfill no more than 10 percent of Beijing's anticipated needs in 2000 when it is completed. Chinese engineers are also preparing to build a canal from Zhenjiang, on the Yangtze to Tianjin, following the path of the Grand Canal, built in the sixth century C.E. The original canal was built to transport grain; this twenty-first-century version will supply Chinese urban centers and provide water for irrigation.[43]

Restoring degraded land is a much more complex problem, however. Efforts are being concentrated on soil stabilization, diversifying crops, and focusing agricultural production on regions that are the most fertile and least erodible. In China and in Ethiopia, for example, researchers are experimenting with ways to trap soil in shallow dams or terrace crops to increase productivity and hasten land reclamation. Other projects include the planting of soil-trapping grasses that form vegetative barriers, and alley cropping, which involves the planting of food crops between hedgerows of trees—a strategy that has been extensively used in tropical regions. Other UN projects are aimed at reducing the harvest length of certain crops or improving species productivity so that the land can be double- or triple-cropped.

Many of the proposals seem farfetched if not downright silly, such as towing icebergs from the Arctic to California to provide fresh drinking water for thirsty Los Angeles residents. Others get serious consideration from policymakers desperate for innovation. For example, Canada's Medusa Corporation wants to solve California's scarcity problem with floating vinyl water balloons, each the size of twenty football fields. The storage bags (up to twenty-four hundred feet long, six hundred feet wide, and eighty feet deep) would cost $6 million each and would hold a million tons of water from Alaska. The idea would be to tow the balloons, which would be partially submerged like an iceberg, down the coast to water-short cities. The concept was eventually termed "not viable" by representatives of the Metropolitan Water District of southern California, which estimated the region would need at least five balloons a day.

Such fanciful solutions are evidence of the desperate straits many regions are in as they seek an answer to the question of where the water is coming from. Although it is obvious to most that water conservation is the most obvious choice among these strategies, it is also one of the most difficult to implement as long as residents (especially those in the United States) are used to simply turning on the tap. Only when drought conditions force cities to adopt restrictive measures does conservation finally hit home. In summer, 1992, for example, the city of Portland, Oregon, banned all use of water for watering lawns and gardens and washing cars when its Bull Run reservoir began to dry up. The city's Water Bureau established a special late-night patrol to catch flagrant violators—those sprinkling their lawns while the rest of the city slept. A "snitch line" allowed residents to inform the patrols of alleged violations, and some neighbors even turned to vigilante tactics—one woman's new lawn was attacked by vandals who accused her of violating the city's conservation ordinance. She awoke one July morning to find rows of sod neatly rolled up on her porch.

SUMMARY

As population growth swells dramatically, water scarcity has become a critical environmental issue due to increases in the amount of personal water consumption; the increased demand for industrial, commercial, and agricultural use; and natural causes like drought. The scarcity problem is not limited to the United States but is shared by countries in north-central and western Africa suffering from extended periods of drought. American water policy is highly politicized, with the power shifting from the farm and agricultural lobbies at the turn of the century to urban legislators and interests now. Those political pressures have affected the water management activities of the Army Corps of Engineers and the Bureau of Reclamation, the two federal agencies with primary responsibility for water, and led to a change in mission from federally supported construction to resource management. As communities tap into more of Earth's water resources to meet urban and agricultural demands, water levels are dropping, leading to subsidence, soil erosion, and desertification. Water diversion has also destroyed valuable wildlife habitats. The two solutions to ensure an adequate water supply are conservation and technologies like desalination and cloud seeding. Between the two, conservation—convincing users to use less—is the most cost-effective choice, but it will take a considerable effort just to keep up with the population's need for fresh water.

NOTES

1. U.S. Congress, House, Committee on Interior and Insular Affairs, Subcommittee on Water, Power and Offshore Energy Resources, *The Drought in California*, hearing, 102nd Cong., 1st sess., February 19, 1991 (Washington, DC: U.S. Government Printing Office, 1991), 3.

2. William Ashworth, *Nor Any Drop to Drink* (New York: Summit Books, 1982), 19–21.

3. World Resources Institute, *World Resources 1992–93* (New York: Oxford University Press, 1992), 163.

4. Sandra Postel, "Emerging Water Scarcities," in *The World Watch Reader on Global Environmental Issues*, ed. Lester R. Brown (New York: Norton, 1991), 127–143.

5. Montague Yudelman, "Sustainable and Equitable Development in Irrigated Environments," in *Environment and the Poor: Development Strategies for a Common Agenda*, ed. H. Jeffrey Leonard et al. (New Brunswick, NJ: Transaction Books, 1989), 61–85.

6. See William S. Ellis and David C. Turnley, "A Soviet Sea Lies Dying: The Aral," *National Geographic* 177 (February 1990): 70–94. See also Peter Rogers, "The Aral Sea," *Environment* 33, no. 1 (January–February 1991): 2.

7. For an overview of agricultural water use issues in the United States, see Ashworth, *Nor Any Drop to Drink*, 55–68.

8. See Ernest A. Englebert, *Water Scarcity: Impacts on Western Agriculture* (Berkeley: University of California Press, 1984).

9. See Gilbert White, "The Environmental Effect of the High Dam at Aswan," *Environment* 30, no. 7 (September 1988): 5–28.

10. Yudelman, "Sustainable and Equitable Development," 71.

11. Ibid., 62.

12. See "Drought Threatens California Bird Populations," *Nature* 350 (March 21, 1991): 180.

13. See George Wharton James, *Reclaiming the Arid West: The Story of the United States Reclamation Service* (New York: Dodd, Mead, 1917).

14. Robert Gottlieb, *A Life of Its Own: The Politics and Power of Water* (New York: Harcourt Brace Jovanovich, 1988), 48.

15. See Wallace Stegner, *This Is Dinosaur* (New York: Knopf, 1955). At that time, the Bureau of Reclamation also had the proposed Glen Canyon Dam near the Arizona-Utah border on the drawing boards; the project was eventually built after the Echo Park controversy.

16. See Constance Elizabeth Hunt, *Down by the River* (Washington, DC: Island Press, 1988), 11–14.

17. See Tom Harris, *Death in the Marsh* (Washington, DC: Island Press, 1991).

18. Gottlieb, *Life of Its Own*, 270–71.

19. *Winters v. United States*, 207 U.S. 564 (1908).

20. *Arizona v. California*, 373 U.S. 546 (1963).

21. See Marc Reisner and Sarah Bates, *Overtapped Oasis: Reform or Revolution for Western Water* (Washington, DC: Island Press, 1990), 92–98. See also Lloyd Burton, *American Indian Water Rights and the Limits of Law* (Lawrence: University of Kansas Press, 1991).

22. See Jose Trava, "Sharing Water with the Colossus of the North," in *High Country News, Western Water Made Simple* (Washington, DC: Island Press, 1987), 171–81. See also Gottlieb, *Life of Its Own*, 223–28.

23. See David D. Kemp, *Global Environmental Issues: A Climatological Approach* (London: Routledge, 1990), 37–67.

24. See Brett Wright, "Colder Winters for Northern Africa as Deserts Expand," *New Scientist*, January 18, 1992, 20. See also William Langewiesche, "The World in Its Extreme," *The Atlantic* 268 (November 1991), 105–28.

25. For an analysis of the problems of the Sahel, see Malin Falkenmar and Gunnar Lindh, *Water for a Starving World* (Boulder, CO: Westview Press, 1976), 70–74.

26. Postel, "Emerging Water Scarcities," 32.

27. Brett Wright, "Does Overgrazing Make the World Warmer?" *New Scientist*, January 11, 1992, 21.

28. Postel, "Emerging Water Scarcities," 25–42.

29. Yudelman, "Sustainable and Equitable Development," 70.

30. *National Audubon Society v. Superior Court (Mono Lake)*, 33 Cal.3d 419 (1983).

31. See Daniel B. Botkin et al. *The Future of Mono Lake* (Riverside: Water Resources Center of the University of California, 1988).

32. See William Ashworth, *The Late, Great Lakes* (New York: Knopf, 1986), 217–18.

33. See David E. Kromm and Stephen W. White, *Groundwater Exploitation in the High Plains* (Lawrence: University of Kansas Press, 1992); John R. Sheaffer and Leonard A. Stevens, *Future Water: An Exciting Solution to America's Most Serious Resource Crisis* (New York: Morrow, 1983), 171–82; and Charles Bowden, *Killing the Hidden Waters* (Austin: University of Texas Press, 1977).

34. William H. MacLeish, "Water, Water, Everywhere, How Many Drops to Drink?" *World Monitor*, December 1990, 54–58.

35. See Benedykt Dziegielewski and Duane D. Baumann, "Tapping Alternatives: The Benefits of Managing Urban Water Demands," *Environment* 34, no. 9 (November 1992): 6–11.

36. Reisner and Bates, *Overtapped Oasis*, 111–22.

37. See William Fletcher, *The Marine Environment* (New York: Academic Press, 1977), and K. S. Spiegler, *Salt-Water Purification* (New York: Plenum Press, 1977).

38. See, for example, the publications of the U.S. Office of Saline Water, such as its *Research and Development Progress Report*, published annually from 1954 to 1972 by the U.S. Government Printing Office, Washington, DC.

39. See U.S. Office of Science and Technology, *An Assessment of Large Nuclear Powered Sea Water Distillation Plants* (Washington, DC: U.S. Government Printing Office, 1964).

40. See Andy Coghlan, "Fresh Water from the Sea," *New Scientist*, August 31, 1991, 37–40.

41. Roberta Friedman, "Seawater to Drink," *Technology Review* 92 (August–September 1989): 14–15.

42. See Elizabeth Schaefer, "Water Shortage Pits Man against Nature," *Nature* 350 (March 21, 1991): 180–81.

43. Robert Delfs, "The Canal's Siblings," *Far Eastern Economic Review*, March 15, 1990, 23–25.

FOR FURTHER READING

Malin Falkenmar and Gunnar Lindh. *Water for a Starving World*. Boulder, CO: Westview Press, 1976.

David Lewis Feldman. *Water Resources Management*. Baltimore: Johns Hopkins University Press, 1991.

Robert Gottlieb. *A Life of Its Own: The Politics and Power of Water*. New York: Harcourt Brace Jovanovich, 1988.

High Country News. *Western Water Made Simple*. Washington, DC: Island Press, 1987.

Marc Reisner and Sarah Bates. *Overtapped Oasis: Reform or Revolution for Western Water*. Washington, DC: Island Press, 1990.

Constance Elizabeth Hunt. *Down by the River*. Washington, DC: Island Press, 1988.

John R. Sheaffer and Leonard A. Stevens. *Future Water*. New York: Morrow, 1983.

Zachary A. Smith. *Groundwater in the West*. New York: Academic Press, 1989.

CHAPTER 8

Water Quality: From Ground to Tap

It is time to realize that one major, overwhelming reason why we are running out of water is that we are killing the water we have.
—William Ashworth, author[1]

In 1965, when he signed the Water Quality Act, President Lyndon Johnson predicted Washington's Potomac River would be reopened for swimming by 1975.[2] Yet the Potomac's Tidal Basin, with its Japanese cherry trees, has been called "the best decorated sewer in the world," making LBJ's prediction premature and unrealistic, as is the case for most of the legislative attempts to improve the quality of America's water supply. A number of factors have contributed to make America's waterways and drinking water as polluted in the 1990s as they were in the 1960s. Concerns about water quality focus on two issues: first, pollution of surface water (rivers, streams, lakes, wetlands, and even drainage ditches), largely from discharges directly into the waterway, and second, groundwater, which flows beneath Earth's surface and is the source of nearly half of the nation's drinking water. Sources of groundwater contamination include landfills, biocide applications[3] on farmland and urban lawns, underground storage tanks, leakage of hazardous waste, and waste disposal wells.

This chapter examines the politics of water quality of both surface and subsurface issue perspectives. It begins with an explanation of the nature and causes of water pollution, with special emphasis on toxic contamination, and continues with a review of the relevant federal legislation regulating surface and groundwater pollution. It concludes with an analysis of the successes and failures of federal water policy, and an international perspective on water quality issues.

THE NATURE AND CAUSES OF WATER POLLUTION

The current level of water pollution is largely a result of massive industrialization and inadequate waste disposal strategies that took place in the United States during the mid- to late nineteenth century. At that time, local officials were generally reluctant to antagonize industry and try to stop the widespread practice of simply dumping industrial wastes into the closest waterway. Most of the early government concerns dealt more with navigational hazards rather than health. In 1886, Congress prohibited the dumping of waste into New York Harbor, followed by the 1899 Refuse Act, which prohibited the dumping of solid waste into commercial waterways. Not until the U.S. Public Health Service was formed in 1912 was there serious consideration given to monitoring pollution levels. Today, much of what is known about trends in surface water quality comes from the U.S. Geological Survey, which monitors waterways through its National Ambient Stream Quality Accounting Network, or NAS-QUAN, which began collecting information in 1974. Groundwater quality, in contrast, must be monitored from wells, or at the tap.[4] In 1984, the federal Office of Technology Assessment compiled a list of over two hundred contaminants known to occur in groundwater, although the actual number is estimated to be more than three times that figure. Basically, the contaminants can be divided into the following categories:

Organisms

Various biological contaminants including bacteria, parasites, and viruses occur in most water sources, although there are usually fewer in groundwater than in surface water. Human and animal wastes carry fecal coliform and fecal streptococcus bacteria, which may enter the water source from improper sewage treatment, cattle feedlots, or through failing leaching septic tanks. Familiar illnesses caused by waterborne organisms include tuberculosis, cholera, and infectious hepatitis. Parasites like giardia and cryptosporidium can cause gastrointestinal illnesses and may be dangerous for persons with weakened immune systems.

Suspended and Total Dissolved Solids

Soil particles, inorganic salts, and other substances may make water brown or turbid (cloudy) and may carry bacteria and other harmful substances that pollute water with them. The problem is particularly acute in areas with significant erosion, including logged watersheds, construction sites, and abused rangelands. Agriculture is thought to be the largest single source of unregulated water pollution, including the 3.1 billion tons of topsoil eroded annually.

Nutrients

There are a number of contaminants that, in excess, can be harmful to human beings, including phosphorous, iron, and boron. Most of the scientific attention has been focused on nitrates, which are not harmful in limited concentrations, and occur naturally in some vegetables like beets and cabbage, and are used as food additives in the meat-curing process. If imbibed in excess quantities, nitrates form the starting point for a chain of reactions in the digestive tract in which common intestinal bacteria form nitrites, which interfere with the release of oxygen to the cells of the body, or nitrite cyanosis. The main nitrate hazard is to infants because their stomachs lack the necessary hydrochloric acid to stop the nitrate-to-nitrite process.

Metals and Toxics

A wide spectrum of heavy metals are commonly found in drinking water, among the most dangerous of which is lead. Over forty million Americans are estimated to drink water with excessive amounts of lead, which can impair children's ability to learn. New regulations issued by the Environmental Protection Agency in 1991 require municipal water suppliers to monitor lead levels beginning in 1992 and 1993, focusing on households at high risk (those with lead service pipes) and at the location where lead content is likely to be the highest—at the customer's faucet. The regulations also place new limits on tapwater lead levels at fifteen parts per billion (ppb), rather than the existing standard for drinking water of fifty ppb. If these new levels are not met, suppliers must lower the water's acidity chemically by adding bicarbonate and lime.[5] Other contaminants include radioactive minerals and gases, such as radon, which travels through water, primarily in regions in the northeast and western mountain states. The EPA did not propose radon limits for drinking water until 1991, giving suppliers until 1996 to comply. Toxic concentrations usually come from man-made sources like pesticides and chemical solvents used in a variety of manufacturing processes. Organic compounds such as acetone, toluene, and benzene are frequently found in drinking water, and long-term exposure has been found to cause cancer, birth defects, and liver damage.

Municipal Wastewater Discharges

Domestic sewage accounts for a large percentage of the materials handled by municipal wastewater treatment plants, but other substances also routinely enter the wastewater stream, including hazardous chemicals dumped down drains and sewers by individuals, industries, and businesses.

Despite these categorizations, it is not always easy to differentiate what substances and chemicals are actually pollutants. Chlorine, for example, has been added to drinking water as a disinfectant since the early 1900s to control infectious disease organisms. By the 1930s, the use of chlorine was responsible for a tenfold decrease in typhoid fever deaths in the United States. But chlorine is also known to react with organic material in water, producing hundreds of chemical byproducts that are known carcinogens. Despite the potential risk, chlorine has markedly expanded the usability of the nation's water resources by disinfecting sources that are not naturally pristine. Another additive, fluoride, was first added to water systems in 1947 in an attempt to reduce tooth decay in young children. Since then, there has been a spirited debate in many communities whether fluoride is a health danger or has any actual dental benefit.[6]

THE POLITICS OF WATER QUALITY

Like many environmental issues, the politics of water quality is not linked to a single act of legislation. One of the factors that makes water policy somewhat difficult to understand is that Congress has given regulatory responsibility for water quality to the EPA under a number of legislative mandates. The Resource Conservation and Recovery Act, for example, gives the EPA the authority to regulate the treatment, transport, and storage of both hazardous and nonhazardous waste—substances that may find their way into the nation's water supply are discussed at some length in Chapter 5. The Comprehensive Environmental Response, Compensation, and Liability Act, more commonly known as Superfund, gives the EPA responsibilities when groundwater is contaminated by inactive waste sites or accidental chemical releases. The Toxic Substances Control Act (TSCA) gives the EPA regulatory authority over the manufacture, use, and disposal of toxic chemicals (which are often dumped into surface water sources), and the Federal Insecticide, Fungicide, and Rodenticide Act (FIFRA) regulates certain pesticides, which can also enter groundwater. Despite the overlap of these regulatory mandates, Congress has also enacted legislation specifically targeting surface and groundwater pollution.

Surface Water

The process of placing surface water quality on the political agenda has been a long one. Prior to World War II, only a few environmental organizations seemed interested in the deteriorating condition of America's lakes, rivers, and streams. The Izaak Walton League was among the first to draw attention to the contamination problem, noting in a report published in the late 1920s that 85 percent of the nation's waterways were polluted and that only 30 percent of all municipalities treated their wastes, many of them inadequately. Industrial interests like the American Petroleum Institute, the American Iron and Steel Institute, and the Manufacturing Chemists Association insisted "streams were nature's sewers" and convinced key legislators industrial dumping posed no environmental threat.[7] The initial attempts to regulate surface water pollution were weak and ineffective. In 1948, Congress passed the first Water Pollution Control Act, which established the federal government's limited role in regulating interstate water pollution. The law also provided for studies and research, limited funding for sewage treatment, and authorized the surgeon general to prepare or adopt programs for eliminating or reducing pollution in cooperation with other agencies and the industries involved. The emphasis on a cooperative approach, coupled with provisions that were both cumbersome and often unworkable, gave the law little impact. In 1952, a report to Congress indicated not a single enforcement action had been taken, and Congress began to hold hearings on a revision to the legislation. The 1956 amendments to the act eliminated many of the difficulties of the 1948 law, but still limited Congress's role to interstate waters and allowed Congress to delegate much of its authority to implement the law to the states. It did, however, condition federal funding of sewage treatment facilities on the submission of adequate water pollution plans by the states. This provided an incentive for states to write water quality standards to meet state goals for surface water pollution. Still, only one enforcement action was filed under this authority over the next fifteen years.

During the 1960s, Congress, led by Senator Edmund Muskie of Maine, became restless over the slow pace of water pollution control, since it was obvious states were doing an inadequate job. In 1965, passage of the Water Quality Act established a June 30, 1967, water quality standard for interstate waters and streamlined federal enforcement efforts. A year later, the Clean Water Restoration Act provided $3.5 billion in federal grants for the construction of sewage treatment plants and for research on advanced waste treatment.[8] These early attempts at water quality legislation were weak and, for the most part, ineffective. They allowed the states to classify waterways within their jurisdiction, so a state could decide a particular stream was best used for industrial use rather than swimming. The use designation of the Cuyahoga River in Ohio, for example, was waste disposal—a fact that did not seem to bother most residents until the river caught fire in 1969. From an enforcement standpoint, the initial pollution laws were meaningless. For the two decades prior to 1972, only one case of alleged violation of federal water pollution control law reached the courts, and in that case over four years elapsed between the initial enforcement conference and the final consent decree.[9]

President Richard Nixon's February 1970 message to Congress on the environment called for a new water pollution bill, which eventually became the 1972 Federal Water Pollution Control Act. The main emphasis of the legislation was on technological capability. In addition to establishing a regulatory framework for water quality, the bill gave the EPA six specific deadlines by which it was to grant permits to water pollution sources, issue effluent (wastewater) guidelines, require sources to install water pollution control technology, and eliminate discharges into the nation's waterways to make them fishable and swimmable.[10] A key component of the legislation was the establishment of the National Pollution Discharge Elimination System (NPDES), which made it illegal to discharge anything at all unless the source had a federal permit to do so. The NPDES had a historical basis in the 1899 Refuse Act, which had previously been thought to apply only to discharges that obstructed navigation. But the U.S. Supreme Court broadened the interpretation of the act in two cases that made it applicable to any industrial waste.[11]

The Not-So-Great Lakes

While the names Love Canal and Cuyahoga River have become synonymous with toxic pollution, few realize they share another common attribute—they flow into one of the Great Lakes. More like inland seas than lakes, the five bodies of water (Lake Superior, Lake Michigan, Lake Huron, Lake Erie, and Lake Ontario) share a ten-thousand-mile coastline and a boundary with Canada. From an environmental standpoint, the Great Lakes are a disaster. Fishing, which was once one of the region's major industries, is nonexistent; native species like the Atlantic salmon and trout have been overfished and zebra mussels have invaded the basin.[12] The sludge at the bottom of Lake Michigan is made up of PCBs, chromium, zinc, lead, oil and grease, iron and other solids. One chemical plant dumps residues into a tributary that flows into Lake Huron; the floor of Lake Superior is covered with asbestos fibers from the processing and shipping of iron ore; effluent from paper mills along the shores of Lake Michigan's Green Bay contribute to eutrophication—high rates of oxygen-depleting algae growth—and in 1991, pollution levels were even linked to infertility.[13]

How did this environmental tragedy happen? The answer to that question lies with an understanding of the political and historical nature of the issue. The United States and Canada are parties to the International Joint Commission on Boundary Waters (IJC), set up under the Boundary Waters Treaty of 1909 to coordinate the water resources shared by the two countries. In 1912, the IJC began studying water pollution in the area, and in 1919 the group concluded that serious water quality problems required a new treaty to control pollution. However, no agreement was reached. Additional studies in the 1940s led to recommendations that water quality objectives be established for the Great Lakes and that technical advisory boards be created to provide continuous monitoring and surveillance. By the 1950s and 1960s, invasions of sea lampreys had decimated fisheries, and a 1964 study of the lower lakes focused new attention on pollution. Despite the mounting evidence, no one was willing to take responsibility for the pollution and sewage that were killing the lakes. Four legislative agreements were enacted between 1971 and 1972 to provide a legal framework for protecting the Great Lakes: the Clean Water Act (one for the United States and a similar Canadian version), the International Great Lakes Water Quality Agreement between the United States and Canada, and lastly, cooperative agreements among governmental/industry/municipal units around the lakes. Another international treaty, the Great Lakes Water Quality Agreement of 1978, was supposed to be a model political approach to water quality problems. It called for improved pollution control and virtual eliminations of discharges of toxic waste, using an ecosystem approach (a broad, systematic view of the interaction among physical, chemical, and biological components in the Great Lakes basin).[14] But the agreement has failed dismally to live up to its expectations. The treaty is routinely violated by both the United States and Canada, and environmental groups recently petitioned the United Nations to require the two nations to abide by the agreement. Two subsequent documents have been signed and respond to concerns about diversions of water from the Great Lakes to other regions of the United States. The Great Lakes Charter (1985) and the Great Lakes Toxic Substances Control Agreement (1986) have no legal enforcement authority in either country and are dependent upon voluntary good faith. Observers believe the root cause is apathy by both government officials and the public, who seem unconcerned they are pouring more and more chemicals into the lakes and are unable to eat the contaminated fish they catch. The inability of agencies, individuals, and environmental groups to clean up the lakes is due to duplicated services and research, overlapping jurisdictions, and political infighting by many of the organizations which insist they know what's best for the lakes. The bottom line is that political solutions have not translated to environmental solutions, and the Great Lakes are still among the most polluted large bodies of water on Earth.[15]

Water quality continued to capture media interest when consumer advocate Ralph Nader publicized contamination along a 150-mile stretch of the Mississippi River between Baton Rouge and New Orleans known as the "petrochemical corridor." A public outcry after a February 1977 spill of carbon tetrachloride (a potential carcinogen) into the Ohio River contaminated Cincinnati's water supply further fueled the legislative fires, although Congress took no action to strengthen the 1972 law. Although the act was amended in 1977, it was not until the mid-1980s that there was general agreement among policymakers and environmentalists that the 1972 legislation had been overly optimistic in setting target dates for the standards to be met. Little progress had been made in improving the overall quality of the nation's waterways, although given the pace of the country's population growth and economic expansion, the argument could be made that at least the situation did not get much worse, or worse as fast. In 1987, Congress enacted a new legislative mandate—the Water Quality Act—over two vetoes by President Ronald Reagan. The new legislation expanded congressional authority to regulate water pollution from point sources—a confined or other man-made conveyance, such as a pipe, tunnel, well, or floating vessel (such as a ship) that discharges pollutants—as well as from nonpoint sources, which is basically anything else. The Water Quality Act also required every state and territory to establish safe levels for toxic pollutants in fresh water by 1990.

Groundwater and Drinking Water

The main groundwater source of drinking water is aquifers—layers of rock and earth that contain water or could contain water.[16] For most of this century, groundwater was thought to be a virtually unlimited natural resource, constantly filtered and replenished and available for human use and consumption. Currently, about half of all drinking water is supplied through groundwater. When massive contamination was discovered at Love Canal in 1977, political officials realized they could not take such a cavalier attitude toward the nation's public drinking water supplies, which provide between one and two billion gallons of drinking water daily.

As a policy issue, water quality has often suffered from differences of opinion over where the regulatory responsibility ought to lie, with regulatory authority divided between drinking water and groundwater. Federal *authority* to establish primary drinking water standards (those applying to materials that are human health standards) originated with the Interstate Quarantine Act of 1893, which allowed the surgeon general to make regulations covering only bacteriological contamination. But the first U.S. primary drinking water standard was *set* in 1914 by the U.S. Public Health Service, whose main concern was the prevention of waterborne diseases. The federal standards were applicable only to systems that provided water to an interstate common carrier. From 1914 to 1974, the standards were revised four times: in 1925, 1942, 1946, and 1962, and were gradually extended to cover all U.S. water supplies.[17]

Groundwater regulatory authority was treated somewhat differently from the way drinking water was treated. There were those who felt the federal government should not hold the responsibility for regulating and cleaning up groundwater. President Dwight Eisenhower, for example, believed water pollution was a "uniquely local blight" and felt the primary obligation for providing a safe drinking water supply ought to rest with state and local officials, not the federal government.[18] But with the creation of the Environmental Protection Agency in 1970, the federal government reaffirmed its policymaking authority for water quality. With passage of the 1974 Safe Drinking Water Act, the EPA was authorized to identify which substances were contaminating the nation's water supply and set maximum contaminant levels, promulgated as the National Primary Drinking Water Regulations. The act was amended in 1986 to accelerate the EPA's regulation of toxic contaminants, and included a ban on lead pipe and lead solder in public water systems. It mandated greater protection of ground water sources, and set a three-year timetable for regulation of eighty-three specific chemical contaminants that may have an adverse health effect known or anticipated to occur in public water systems.[19]

THE TOXICS LEGACY

Until the early 1960s and the publication of Rachel Carson's *Silent Spring*, Americans paid little attention to the millions of gallons of toxic chemicals that were routinely being poured into waterways or dumped onto remote sites or even stored on private property. The dangers posed by the storage and handling of toxic chemicals were either unknown or ignored. Only a series of highly publicized incidents and disclosures moved the toxics legacy onto the political agenda.

Groundwater can be contaminated from a variety of man-made sources. Although contemporary landfills are engineered and designed with sophisticated leak-protection systems, prior to federal regulation, most dumps were simply that—holes in the ground later covered with a layer of dirt or fill. In rural areas or on private property, landowners disposed of waste however they saw fit, and most municipal or sanitary landfills were almost unregulated. There are also a number of agricultural practices that are known to affect groundwater contamination, such as the use of biocides and fertilizers, livestock operations, and some modern irrigation practices. Over seven hundred million pounds of chemicals are used each year to control biological pests on lawns, farms, along highways, and during home building and renovation. Many of these chemical compounds are regulated under FIFRA and TSCA.

The list of cities with polluted water is not limited to any one region, ranging from Portland, Maine, to California's San Gabriel Valley. Some of the toxic contamination has been deliberate, while in other cases the groundwater was accidentally polluted long before researchers and officials even knew contamination was possible, or the extent to which it could be cleaned up.[20] In Los Angeles in 1979, for example, the state's Department of Health Services requested all major water purveyors conduct tests for two hazardous substances, trichloroethylene (TCE) and perchloroethylene (PCE), both routinely used in dry cleaning, metal plating, and machinery degreasing. The survey found hazardous levels of the two substances in several water production wells and traced them to the period between 1940 and 1967 when disposal of large quantities of chemical wastes was unregulated. The most seriously contaminated wells were shut down, and water from wells with lower contamination levels was blended with untainted water to produce acceptable health levels.[21] Some of the contamination is a result of homeowners unknowingly pouring products down their kitchen drains or toilets. New York's Nassau County Health Department has estimated eighty-three thousand gallons of organic chemicals end up in the city's groundwater supply each year from hazardous household products like drain cleaners, paint, oven cleaners, and solvents.

Other forms of toxic contamination are perfectly legal and permitted by state officials. The nation's one hundred pulp and paper mills have been targeted by environmental groups as among the biggest polluters of U.S. waterways, with bleaching plants the source of approximately four hundred to seven hundred million pounds of chlorinated compounds annually. Among the three hundred different compounds identified in bleach plant effluent are dioxins (a generic term applied to a group of suspected carcinogens that are the byproducts of other substances or processes), which have been shown to cause reproductive disorders in animals and immune system suppression and impaired liver function in humans. Dioxins escaped detection for years because researchers were not looking for them as contaminants. Groups like Greenpeace have called upon the pulp and paper industry to supply consumers with paper products that have not been bleached and an overall reduction in the use of chlorine gas in paper processing.

The pace at which toxic contamination has been regulated and enforced, both at the federal and state levels, has been uneven and decidedly sluggish. The Clean Water Act of 1972 required the EPA to impose the best available pollution control technology standards on industries that discharge toxic waste into rivers, lakes and estuaries, or sewage treatment facilities. The agency did not take action to implement the law until 1976, when a lawsuit forced it to agree to regulate twenty-four of more than fifty industrial categories, including organic chemicals, pharmaceuticals, and pulp and paper industries. In 1987, Congress amended the legislation and ordered the EPA to update the old standards and to begin regulating additional categories by February 1991. When the congressional deadline passed, the Natural Resources Defense Council filed suit in U.S. District Court to force the agency to comply with the 1987 law. In its suit, the NRDC noted that the EPA had not yet developed rules for four out of five, or fifty thousand of the seventy-five thousand industrial plants that dump toxic substances directly into surface waters. In 1992, the EPA agreed to settle the lawsuit and extend federal standards to sixteen additional industry categories between 1996 and 2002, including industrial laundries, pesticide manufacturers, and hazardous waste facilities and incinerators.

Similarly, the states have failed to comply with 1987 Water Quality Act provisions, which require them to impose limits on toxic pollution in their waters by 1990. In 1991, the EPA announced it would impose federal rules on the twenty-two states and territories that had not set their own standards to reduce levels of 105 toxic compounds, including pesticides, solvents, and heavy metals. Most states are now in the process of working to complete regulations, but the EPA's announcements hastened their pace.[22]

Why has toxic pollution taken so long to gain policymakers' attention, and why has the EPA been so reluctant to move forward on the legislative mandates? There are several reasons that may explain the current status of toxic pollution control. One, EPA officials cite manpower and budgetary constraints that virtually crippled the agency during the 1980s, especially under President Reagan. A lack of staff and funds, plus cuts in programs under EPA Administrator Anne Burford, put many water quality initiatives on hold. Two, the federal government has delegated much of its responsibilities to the states, which are required to issue permits to industries that discharge pollution into surface water. The permit limits vary from state to state and have generally been much more lenient than federal controls. Three, water quality issues have tended to take a back seat to air quality issues when it comes to the political arena. Congressional committees have focused on the more politically visible issues of smog and auto emissions rather than water quality. Although the 1972 law eliminated the gross pollutants that cause rivers and lakes to look or smell bad, the more invisible but nevertheless hazardous toxic pollutants have been largely ignored until recently. Lastly, both environmentalists and public officials reluctantly admit the compliance deadlines of the 1972 legislation were extremely unrealistic, forcing the EPA to scramble to come up with new rules that even the agency leadership knew were not attainable.

WATER QUALITY SUCCESSES AND FAILURES

There are a number of reasons why neither federal nor state intervention has made an appreciable improvement in the nation's water quality since 1948. The most obvious problem is the overlapping of jurisdictions and responsibilities between the federal and state governments, which has led to a competition among agencies. At the federal level, there is internal competition within the EPA, since staff responsibility for implementation of the Water Quality Act must be shared by those implementing the 1976 RCRA provisions dealing with water and those implementing the 1980 and 1986 Superfund amendments. The divided authority between the federal and state governments has also been a source of overlap and competition. Since Congress has delegated responsibility for designating the use for all bodies of water and for issuing discharge permits to the states, budget cutbacks in tight economies often affect a state's ability to implement environmental regulations. At the same time, most states have adopted their own laws regulating groundwater and drinking water quality, and some are beginning to regulate chemical compounds that are found in water as well. State and local agencies are much more vulnerable to the pressures of local groups (both environmental organizations and polluters) and therefore more likely to be influenced by them.

Both the federal government and the states are also expanding their sphere of environmental influence where water quality is concerned, moving into the regulation of other sources of contamination, such as abandoned industrial and waste sites, underground storage tanks, and injection wells used for the flushing of liquid hazardous waste into deep aquifers.[23] As a result, staff expertise and resources are being spread even more thinly.

One of the historic failures of American water policy has been the EPA's lack of enforcement capability, although the agency has increased its commitment for the 1990s, toughening its stance on polluters in recent years. In 1991, EPA prosecuted 3,109 cases resulting in $28 million in penalties and 346 months of incarceration for the offending polluters. Similar enforcement problems are faced where drinking water standards are concerned. In 1980, nearly fourteen thousand community water systems were in violation of one or more federal standards, and by 1982, more than seventy thousand violations were recorded by twenty thousand systems. Although some of the violations were of monitoring and reporting standards, the EPA estimated more than nine thousand systems needed to improve treatment facilities in order to meet health-related drinking water standards.[24] As a result of the massive number of violations, small water suppliers are seldom caught or punished. Washington State has only six state employees to oversee the entire network of thirteen thousand public water systems, and in Hanford, California, the local utility has not rid its water of naturally occurring arsenic even though it has violated standards for more than ten years.[25] Despite attempts at innovative conservation strategies and protection of existing sources, one of the compelling factors in water policy today is cost. Many of the new federal requirements place a severe burden on small communities that cannot afford expensive water treatment plants on budgets that are already stretched thin. The EPA is thus exploring more affordable and innovative technologies, although the cost of bringing public water systems into full compliance is $1–2 billion per year. Small communities may not be able to take advantage of some treatment technologies, for example, and may not have access to alternative water supplies. Thus, many of the proposed solutions may benefit large urban areas, leaving smaller, rural communities with few alternatives.

INTERNATIONAL PERSPECTIVES ON WATER QUALITY

As one of the world's most industrialized countries, the United States has the advantage of technology and monetary resources to ensure a safe supply of drinking water. To most Americans, water quality is as much a matter of aesthetics as it is health. Around the globe, however, the concerns and attention paid to the issue are quite different. First, in most developing countries water policy has been almost totally health based, with little attention paid to the recreational or scenic value of waterways—values considered luxuries in economies struggling to fund any type of environmental program at all. What minimal environmental resources there are must be spread thinly between air and water pollution, with groundwater contamination receiving the bulk of funds. Second, even in industrialized areas, a lack of a regulatory framework has allowed decades of industrial and household discharges to take place almost unabated. Some of the effluent problems are due to ignorance about pollution, while in other cases substances are simply dumped into rivers and streams because it is the least expensive and easiest method of disposal, and because it has always been done that way. Many countries have only marginal enforcement operations to handle water pollution, and legislation to control and punish polluters is weak where it exists at all. There is a shortage of lawyers with expertise in environmental law, and even fewer judges who are informed or sympathetic. Third, environmental organizations in the United States have been much more successful than their counterparts in other countries in raising the public's awareness about water quality. In many developing nations, polluted waters have always been a way of life, and there is little knowledge of the care and advantages of clean water. As a result, there have been fewer grass-roots efforts to demand stronger enforcement, and less media attention to gross violations and health risks. As a result of these factors, 31 percent of the people in the developing world lack access to safe drinking water, and 44 percent lack sanitation facilities. Waterborne diseases and illnesses are the cause of high mortality and morbidity rates as well as diminished economic prospects.[26] A sampling of international perspectives explains how these factors come together.

Russia and Eastern Europe

In this area, perhaps more than any other in the world, the population suffers from decades of forced industrialization and unmitigated surface water pollution. The "growth at any cost" mentality that was pervasive since the 1920s practically left environmental concerns off the communist political agenda. Most environmental problems were state secrets, and prior to the dissolution of the USSR, there was little public discussion of what most Soviet citizens already knew—the country was killing its lakes and rivers. American researchers have harsh criticisms for what took place throughout much of this century, noting that no other great industrial civilization so systematically and for so long poisoned its air, land, water, and people.[27]

The entire region is marked with water quality tragedies:

The Aral Sea is slowly evaporating as a result of the diversion of rivers that feed into it, changing rainfall patterns, raising local temperatures, and releasing dust and salt into the atmosphere. One recommendation has been to divert water from the Caspian Sea into the Aral through a 270-mile canal, a proposal that would require the building of a costly network of pumping stations.[28]

The Baltic Sea is dying as a result of years of polluters dumping radioactive wastes, toxic chemicals, heavy metals, and industrial effluent directly into the rivers that feed it. The food chain has been badly disrupted, and levels of dioxin in fish make most inedible. Lead and cadmium levels in the sediment of St. Petersburg harbor have been found to be one thousand times normal levels. The Helsinki-based Baltic Marine Environmental Commission has calculated cleanup costs at $20 billion.

Poland has asked Sweden to help it cope with what has been called "an ecological catastrophe"—chemical waste in the bay off Gdansk from the Vistula River that includes phosphorus, nitrogen, oil, lead, mercury, and other heavy metals. Facing foreign debts of $36 billion, the Polish government has been unwilling to release funds for pollution control.[29]

Lithuania's second-largest city, Kaunas, has no sewage treatment facilities at all, and most other Baltic republics have only rudimentary treatment programs. The situation is typical of most of Eastern Europe's largest cities.

More than three thousand factories along the Volga River, the heart of the Soviet military-industrial complex, have been allowed to pollute for decades in the name of national security, dumping an estimated ten billion cubic yards of effluent and waste into the river yearly. A flurry of hydroelectric dams built in the 1950s and 1960s have allowed pollutants to accumulate, breaking down the ecosystem and threatening the river's famous sturgeon with extinction.[30]

At Lake Baikal, the "Pearl of Siberia" and the world's deepest lake, a huge paper products plant employing thirty-six thousand people, dumps its waste directly into the lake, even in winter, when the surface is covered with three feet of ice. The lake's fish population is dying out, including many species exclusive to Baikal.

There are some glimmers of hope that the situation can be turned around, but there are many barriers to overcome. The fledgling Russian environmental movement supports a law passed by the Russian Federation in 1991 that requires an environmental impact statement to be made before a project can be approved for construction, and the Baikal Fund, which now has one hundred thousand members is campaigning to close down the worst polluting factories. Western governments that decry Eastern Europe's environmental policies have been quick to offer criticism and advice, but little financial support for cleanup. Economic realities have convinced many observers Russian political leaders are still more concerned about rising demands for jobs and consumer goods than they are about environmental degradation. The environmentalists who seemed to get a jump start from the downfall of communism have disappeared, and many organizations have now disbanded. As one Soviet environmental writer put it, "Sausage is in the first place in people's minds."[31]

Europe

One of the factors that has made water quality issues in Europe so pervasive is the fact that pollution ignores international boundaries, and many European nations share the same waterways. The problem was first recognized as early as 1868, when nations along the Rhine River agreed to a treaty that required vessels transporting toxic substances on the river bear the word *poison* in French and German. The problem of transboundary European pollution was also addressed in 1963 with the signing of the Berne Convention and in 1977 by the Rhine Chemical Convention, both of which dealt with deliberate discharge of pollutants. Neither document, however, had effective enforcement mechanisms, nor did they provide any incentives for compliance.

The issue once again received worldwide attention in 1986 when water from fighting a fire at the Sandoz Chemical Company near Basel, Switzerland, mixed with one hundred tons of biocides and other agricultural chemicals, flowed into the Rhine River. The Sandoz spill polluted water supplies and killed hundreds of thousands of fish and birds in four other countries, affecting hundreds of towns along the river. As a result, the European Community has worked cooperatively through the European Parliament to strengthen water quality standards and to make them as uniform as possible. Germany has taken a leadership position within Europe, imposing strict controls on its massive chemical industry and banning the use of phosphates in detergents.

Despite those efforts, there are numerous questions involving international law that make transboundary water pollution an extremely complicated matter. Even if a pollution incident can be brought before a judicial forum, which law should apply—that of the downstream or the upstream nation? The role of the European Court of Justice is just now beginning to evolve, but the law regarding such incidents is still in its infancy. Virtually nothing has been done since 1972, when the United Nations Stockholm Declaration established environmental principles but failed to develop an international law of liability and compensation.

Asia

In Asian nations, surface water pollution continues to pose a serious health threat, and the booming population exacerbates the problem of the quality of drinking water. Despite its reputation for sophistication and prosperity, Hong Kong's rapid development has led to widespread water pollution as well. The island is very densely populated, averaging more than five thousand people per square kilometer, with development centered on the country's harbors. Local officials closely monitor the island's shorelines, since fish and animal carcasses routinely wash up on Hong Kong's beaches, posing additional health hazards. Shellfish sales are routinely halted when algal blooms, red tides, and fish kills occur. Hong Kong's major water pollutants are untreated sewage, livestock wastes (especially from pigs raised in urban areas), and heavy metals, and the region's high temperatures increase volatility, evaporation, and decomposition. Most of the industrial effluent sources bypass sewage treatment facilities, and many sources simply dump contaminants down city drains. Hong Kong produces nearly three hundred tons of chemical wastes daily, and the prevalence of leather tanning, bleaching, and dyeing factories along the Ho Chung River has caused local residents to call it "the black river."

Despite a sincere desire among government leaders to clean up the territory, Hong Kong suffers from a variety of obstacles to cleaning up its water supply. As is the case in other Asian nations, Hong Kong has a proliferation of over forty-five thousand small businesses that employ only a handful of workers and are difficult to monitor, making enforcement a daunting task. The leadership is committed to command-and-control pollution management, and has designated water control zones with the authority to issue discharge permits and to monitor compliance. Attempts at installing pollution control technology have not always been successful. For example, efforts to install modern European waste treatment facilities have been ineffective because they were designed for temperate zones and could not deal with the tremendous volume of waste. Water pollution laws allow for grandfathered exemptions to be granted, and many industries can obtain grace periods for compliance with discharge limits. A more recent problem has been the emigration of Hong Kong's citizens (an estimated four hundred thousand are expected to leave between 1990 and 1997), including young scientists and researchers who are leaving the country before it reverts to Chinese control in 1997. The most educated and affluent, who are leaving in the greatest numbers, are also those most likely to demand environmental controls. Other priorities, such as a $16 billion port and airport development sponsored by the United States are suspected of shifting financial resources and personnel away from environmental protection. Despite these challenges, Hong Kong has adopted the leading industrialized nations' relatively sophisticated approach of carefully assessing research data (such as a study of shellfish pollution absorption rates) before considering environmental management issues and options.[32]

Japan, in contrast, has tended to lag behind other industrialized nations in its water pollution efforts. Business opposition to proposed toxic pollution controls has paralyzed the government's weak attempts to regulate those industries, and the lack of a strong environmental movement has provided little impetus for change. Although Japan has made inroads on controlling toxic contamination in rivers and streams, and the concentration of permitted emissions of toxics from factories has been reduced, those successes must be balanced out against a growing population. Sewer construction has lagged behind population growth, straining existing facilities, and the Japanese agricultural system still relies upon chemical pesticides, an important contributor to groundwater pollution along with leaking toxic organic chemicals.[33]

Less developed countries in Asia face similar problems but have attacked water quality from different directions. In Indonesia, for example, the provincial government has begun withholding construction permits for new industries in order to reduce pollution in the Surabaya River. Unfortunately, despite the government's efforts to force companies to install expensive effluent controls, compliance has been spotty. A paper factory outside Jakarta that had decimated the local shrimp fleet, for example, was able to reduce its discharges by 90 percent. Later investigation, however, revealed the waste treatment equipment was operated only when a government inspection was due.[34] And in Malaysia, severe water shortages in 1991 caused taps in several major cities to run dry. Many urban residents had to transport water from rural areas, and villagers often resorted to using unsafe sources. The cause was a rubber-processing facility that discharged latex waste into the Malacca River, but the government did not take action until it was publicized that the incident was the third in less than a year. Analysts believe the problem is one of overdevelopment in a nation that does not have a sufficient infrastructure to deal with its phenomenal industrial growth, a problem common throughout Asia.[35]

Latin America

Here, the biggest water pollution concern is the quality of its surface water, which is the major source of drinking water for its growing population. Some rivers carry a fecal coliform load that is more than a thousand times beyond that set for safe drinking water. The situation is exemplified by the case of Mexico. In 1946, Mexico embarked upon a period of rapid industrialization, which included government ownership and subsidization of mines, foundries, and petrochemical factories, but little concern for the environmental consequences. Most industries discharged wastes directly into the nearest waterway, and as a result, a recent study found more than three-quarters of the nation's river basins are sufficiently polluted to jeopardize public health. Among the worst polluted is the Lerma-Chapala river system, Mexico's most utilized, which drains through seven states and provides water to the federal district. Its flow is now reduced to a trickle, and an extensive plan for wastewater treatment facilities is yet to be built. Two of Mexico's most famous lakes, Chapala and Patzcuaro, are unsafe and unsightly, and beaches along the coast are fouled with raw sewage. A change in policy and direction appears likely. Mexican president Carlos Salinas de Gortari has embarked upon a new wave of environmental protection policies since his election in 1988, including new water quality standards. Mexico City draws 20 percent of its water from outside the area, and the ancient water system is leaking and in dire need of replacement, so the city's mayor has initiated a water conservation program and a moratorium on new water users.[36]

Africa

The major water quality issue facing the African continent is the lack of adequate drinking water supplies and sanitation facilities. Despite the fact the United Nations designated the decade of the 1980s as the International Drinking Water Supply and Sanitation Decade, millions of Africans still do not have access to resources considered a necessity in the industrialized world. Water-related diseases and illnesses are responsible for the deaths of most of the five million children under five years old who die annually in Africa. Two of the most painful and debilitating parasitic diseases, Guinea worm and schistosomiasis, which affect millions of residents of sub-Saharan Africa, are caused by poor sanitation and unsafe water supplies. The economic impact of such diseases goes beyond children, however. In western Nigeria, farmers inflicted with Guinea worm lose one out of every three days of work due to the disease. Families spend hours of their day carrying drinking water from distant and often contaminated sources.

The water problems of the developing world are best seen in Table 8.1, which indicates the overall shortfalls between growing populations and the availability of water and sanitation services. The greatest shortfalls in these figures are in Africa, where population growth of 3 percent (and an 80 percent increase in urban population between 1980 and 1990) far exceeded system capability to provide safe water and adequate sanitation.

Despite those efforts, there are numerous questions involving international law that make transboundary water pollution an extremely complicated matter. contaminants within their water. Health concerns about giardia or toxic pollutants are more likely to be addressed by industrialized nations with the financial resources to build expensive sewage treatment facilities rather than countries whose economic base is still developing. Thus, solutions like water markets, the transfer of water from agricultural use to other needs, privatization, and user fees are most likely to be considered by developing nations thirsty for this scarce commodity.

Table 8.1 Water and Sanitation Services in the Developing World (in millions)

	1980		1990	
	Number of People Served	Number of People Not Served	Number of People Served	Number of People Not Served
Urban Population				
Water	720	213	1,088	244
Sanitation	641	292	955	377
Rural Population				
Water	690	1,613	1,670	989
Sanitation	861	1,442	1,295	1,364
Total Population				
Water	1,411	1,825	2,758	1,232
Sanitation	1,502	1,734	2,250	1,740

Source: Kenneth D. Frederick, "Managing Water for Economic, Environmental and Human Health," *Resources* 106 (Winter 1992): 24.

SUMMARY

Water pollution in the United States is due to massive industrialization and inadequate waste disposal practices that began in the mid-nineteenth century. A variety of contaminants pollute groundwater, which is the source of about half of our supply of drinking water. The regulatory authority for water quality is divided between groundwater and drinking water, and among several federal and state agencies with often overlapping jurisdictions. Of more recent concern has been the pollution of groundwater by toxic chemicals that are improperly disposed of, leak from underground storage tanks, or contaminate soil from various agricultural practices. Critics note that toxic contamination has not been a governmental priority, with existing laws unevenly applied and enforced, due in large part to a lack of funding and manpower at the EPA and a delegation of federal authority to the states. Water quality issues have also been upstaged by air pollution. From an international perspective, the United States has a considerable advantage over other countries in terms of funding and technology. The water quality issues in other nations vary considerably from region to region. Developing countries have been unable to assure a safe supply of drinking water, while the industrialized states of Europe and the countries of the former Soviet Union face an expensive, long-term cleanup of their water supply from industrial discharges.

NOTES

1. William Ashworth, *Nor Any Drop to Drink* (New York: Summit Books, 1982), 134.

2. "Remarks at the Signing of the Water Quality Act of 1965, October 2, 1965," *Public Papers of the President: Lyndon B. Johnson* (Washington, DC: Government Printing Office, 1966), 1035.

3. The term *biocide* is a more inclusive definition and describes pesticides, fungicides, and herbicides; the term *pesticides* generally refers to the use of chemicals on insect pests only.

4. See Eric P. Jorgensen, *The Poisoned Well* (Washington, DC: Island Press, 1989), 51–70.

5. "New Lead Rules for Water," *Science News* 139 (May 18, 1991): 308.

6. See, for example, Steve Coffel, "The Great Fluoride Fight," *Garbage* 4, no. 3 (May–June 1992): 32; G. L. Waldbott, *Fluoridation: The Great Dilemma* (Lawrence, KS: Coronado Press, 1978); and Colin Ingram, *The Drinking Water Book: A Complete Guide to Drinking Water* (Berkeley: Ten Speed Press, 1991), 24–25.

7. Robert Gottlieb, *A Life of Its Own: The Politics and Power of Water* (New York: Harcourt, Brace, Jovanovich, 1988), 163.

8. See J. Clarence Davies III, *The Politics of Pollution* (New York: Pegasus, 1970).

9. Zygmunt J. B. Plater, Robert H. Abrams, and William Goldfarb, *Environmental Law and Policy: Nature, Law and Society* (St. Paul, MN: West, 1992), 827.

10. See Alfred A. Marcus, *Promise and Performance: Choosing and Implementing an Environmental Policy* (Westport, CT: Greenwood Press, 1980), 141–49.

11. The Court's interpretation is outlined in *United States v. Republic Steel Corporation*, 362 U.S. 482 (1960) and *United States v. Standard Oil Company*, 384 U.S. 224 (1966).

12. See Frank Graham, Jr., "Musseling In," *Audubon* 92 (September 1990): 8–9.

13. See M. Robin Eastwood and Brian Gibson, "Canada: Better Ecologues Than Ecocide," *The Lancet* 339, no. 8792 (February 29, 1992): 544–55; Penny Park, "Great Lakes Pollution Linked to Infertility," *New Scientist*, September 28, 1991, 18; "The Great Lakes: Threat to Human Health?" *The Futurist* 24, no. 3 (May–June 1990): 52–53; Nora Underwood, "A Call to Action: The Great Lakes Are in a State of Crisis," *Maclean's*, October 23, 1990, 56–57; Wayne A. Schmidt, "Are Great Lakes Fish Safe to Eat?" *National Wildlife* 27, no. 5 (August–September 1989): 16–19.

14. See U.S. Environmental Protection Agency and Environment Canada, *The Great Lakes: An Environmental Atlas and Resource Book* (Chicago: Great Lakes National Program Office, 1987). See also Barry G. Rabe and Janet B. Zimmerman, "Cross-Media Environmental Integration in the Great Lakes Basin," *Environmental Law* 22, no. 1 (1992): 253–80.

15. See William Ashworth, *The Late, Great Lakes* (New York: Knopf, 1986); Tom Kuchenberg, *Reflections in a Tarnished Mirror: The Use and Abuse of the Great Lakes* (Sturgeon Bay, WI: Golden Glow, 1978); Michael Keating, *To the Last Drop: Canada and the World's Water Crisis* (Toronto: Macmillan of Canada, 1986); Anne McCarthy, *The Great Lakes* (New York: Crescent Books, 1985); and Don C. Piper, *The International Law of the Great Lakes: A Study of Canadian-U.S. Cooperation* (Durham: Duke University Press, 1967).

16. The science of groundwater analysis is a complex one. See, for example, Martin Jaffe and Frank DiNovo, *Local Groundwater Protection* (Washington, DC: American Planning Association, 1987).

17. See Charles D. Larson, "Historical Development of the National Primary Drinking Water Regulations," in *Safe Drinking Water Act: Amendments, Regulations and Standards*, ed. Edward J. Calabrese, Charles E. Gilbert, and Harris Pastides (Chelsea, MI: Lewis Publishers, 1989), 3–16.

18. James Ridgeway, *The Politics of Ecology* (New York: E.P. Dutton, 1970), 51.

19. See Joseph A. Cotruvo and Marlene Regelski, "Overview of the Current National Primary Drinking Water Regulations and Regulation Development Process," in *Safe Drinking Water Act: Amendments, Regulations, and Standards*, ed. Edward J. Calabrese, Charles E. Gilbert, and Harris Pastides (Chelsea, MI: Lewis Publishers, 1989), 17–28.

20. See Ashworth, *Not Any Drop To Drink*, 156–73.

21. Rogene A. Buchholz, "Groundwater Contamination: A City with Problems," in *Managing Environmental Issues* ed. Rogene A. Buchholz, Alfred A. Marcus, and James E. Post (Englewood Cliffs, NJ: Prentice Hall, 1992), 106–20.

22. Keith Schneider, "U.S. Pushing States to Curb Water Pollution," *New York Times*, November 7, 1991, A-23.

23. The aquifers reached by injection wells cannot possibly be used for human water supply because of pumping depth and because of their natural chemical content, which contains salts, heavy metals, etc. Many of them do not contain water, thus their · suitability for injection of wastes.

24. Edward J. Calabrese and Charles E. Gilbert, "Drinking Water Quality and Water Treatment Practices: Charting the Future," in *Safe Drinking Water Act: Amendments, Regulations, and Standards*, ed. Edward J. Calabrese, Charles E. Gilbert, and Harris Pastides (Chelsea, MI: Lewis Publishers, 1989), 113–42.

25. "Is Your Water Safe?" *U.S. News & World Report*, July 29, 1991, 48–55.

26. Kenneth D. Frederick, "Managing Water for Economic, Environmental and Human Health," *Resources* 106 (Winter 1992): 22.

27. See Murray Feshbach and Alfred Friendly, *Ecocide in the USSR* (New York: Basic Books, 1992). See also Douglas Stanglin, "Toxic Wasteland," *U.S. News & World Report*, April 13, 1992, 40–46.

28. There are a number of articles on the fate of the Aral Sea Basin in the January–February 1991 issue of *Environment* (volume 33). See Peter Rogers, "The Aral Sea," A. U. Reteyum, "The Aral Sea," and V. M. Kotlyakov, "The Aral Sea Basin: A Critical Environmental Zone."

29. See "Poland Seeks Help for an Ecological Catastrophe," *New Scientist*, March 17, 1988, 27.

30. Victoria Pope, "Poisoning Russia's River of Plenty," *U.S. News & World Report*, April 13, 1992, 49–51.

31. Stanglin, "Toxic Wasteland," 44.

32. Peter Hills and William Barron, "Hong Kong: Can the Dragon Clean Its Nest?" *Environment* 32, no. 8 (October 1990): 17–20, 39–45. See also Emily Lau, "A License to Pollute," *Far Eastern Economic Review*, May 10, 1990, 23–25.

33. David Vogel, "Environmental Policy in Europe and Japan," in *Environmental Policy in the 1990s: Toward a New Agenda* ed. Norman J. Vig and Michael E. Kraft (Washington, DC: Congressional Quarterly Press, 1990), 266.

34. Robert Cribb, "The Politics of Pollution Control in Indonesia," *Asian Survey* 30, no. 12 (December 1990): 1123–35. See also Ichiro Kato, ed., *Water Management and Environmental Water Pollution in South East Asia* (Tokyo: University of Tokyo Press, 1983).

35. Doug Tsuruoka, "Back on Tap," *Far Eastern Economic Review*, March 26, 1992, 53.

36. Stephen P. Mumme, "Clearing the Air: Environmental Reform in Mexico," *Environment* 33, no. 10 (December 1991): 6–11, 26–30.

FOR FURTHER READING

William Ashworth. *Nor Any Drop to Drink*. New York: Summit Books, 1982.
Edward J. Calabrese, Charles E. Gilbert, and Harris Pastides, eds. *Safe Drinking Water Act: Amendments, Regulations and Standards*. Chelsea, MI: Lewis Publishers, 1989.
Environmental Law Institute, *Clean Water Deskbook*. Washington, DC: Author, 1988.
Colin Ingram, *The Drinking Water Book*. Berkeley: Ten Speed Press, 1991.
Eric P. Jorgensen, ed. *The Poisoned Well: New Strategies for Groundwater Protection*. Washington, DC: Island Press, 1989.

PART 4

The Air

CHAPTER 9

Urban Air Quality: Getting Better or Getting Worse?

Los Angeles Mayor Fletcher E. Bowron announces at a press conference that the city's smog will be entirely eliminated within four months.[1]
—August 14, 1943

Air quality was a problem long before the mayor of Los Angeles made his optimistic prediction. There are references to the fumes produced at the asphalt mining town of Hit, about one hundred miles west of Babylon in the writings of King Tukulti around 900 B.C.E. In 61 C.E. the philosopher Seneca reported on the "heavy air of Rome" and its "pestilential vapors and soot." Marco Polo refused to use coal as a fuel because of its smoky odors. Foreigners traveling to Elizabethan England were astonished and revolted at the filthy smoke produced by domestic fires and workshops.[2] In the United States, concerns about air pollution increased in almost direct proportion to the nation's growing industrialization. In 1881, the Chicago City Council adopted an ordinance that prohibited dense smoke emissions, and in 1905, Los Angeles enacted a similar measure aimed at emissions of dense smoke from flues, chimneys, and smokestacks in the city.[3] The history of cleaning up urban air pollution is marked by small successes on what has proven to be a much longer road than most early municipal officials ever anticipated.

There are three characteristics that can be used to describe global attempts to improve air quality: One, in the United States, local government historically has been given most of the responsibility for pollution control; two, policy efforts have been split between those wishing improvement because of impaired visibility and those who recognize the health effects of pollution; and three, in most other parts of the world, the national government, rather than municipalities, has taken the initiative for improving air quality, with varying degrees of success. This chapter reviews these characteristics and the challenge of developing policies to control urban air pollution both in the United States and in other urban centers, and explores the ways in which the problem has been expanded to other concerns such as visibility and toxic air pollution. While it is not always possible to answer the question posed in the title to this chapter, it is important to identify the political actors and processes that are attempting to improve global air quality.

WHAT IS AIR POLLUTION?

Until well into the twentieth century, the components of pollution were thought to be primarily smoke and soot (suspended particulate matter) and sulfur dioxide—waste products from home heating, industrial facilities, and utility power plants. With industrialization and the advent of the automobile, that list has expanded to include a broad range of emissions.

As Table 9.1 indicates, today the term is usually applied internationally to the six conventional pollutants identified and measured by the Environmental Protection Agency: carbon monoxide, lead, nitrogen oxides, ozone, particulate matter, and sulfur oxides. Of more recent scientific study are air toxics, such as

Table 9.1   Components of Air Pollution

Criteria Pollutant	Sources	Health Effects
Carbon monoxide (CO)	Motor vehicles	Interferes with ability of the blood to absorb oxygen; impairs reflexes
Lead (Pb)	Motor vehicles, lead smelters	Affects kidneys, reproductive and nervous systems; accumulates in bones; hyperactivity in children
Nitrogen oxides (NOx)	Electric utility boilers, motor vehicles	Causes increased susceptibility to viral infections, lung irritation
Ozone	Formed by a chemical reaction of NO_2 and hydrocarbons	Irritates respiratory system; impairment of lung function; aggravates asthma
Particulate matter (PM10)	Combustion from industry, forest fires, windblown dust, vehicles	Organic carcinogenic compounds can migrate into lungs, increasing respiratory distress
Sulfur oxides (SO_2)	Utility plant boilers, oil and chemical refineries	Aggravates symptoms of heart/lung disease; increases respiratory illnesses and colds

lead and benzene, regional and global pollutants, such as acid rain and carbon dioxide, and atmospherically reactive gases, such as chlorofluorocarbons. The conventional, or "criteria," pollutants are found in the atmosphere, and although most are man-made, some, like particulate matter, include the fine particles of dust and vegetation that are natural in origin and small enough to penetrate the most sensitive regions of the respiratory tract. There are three primary categories of sources for conventional pollutants: stationary or point sources, such as factories and power plants, mobile sources, including cars, trucks, and aircraft, and domestic sources, such as home heating or consumer products.

The EPA sets standards of pollution exposure, and federal legislation sets a target date by which regions must meet those standards. The federal government has a variety of sanctions, ranging from fines to shutting down facilities, which can be levied for noncompliance. During the past two decades, U.S. levels of sulfur dioxide, carbon monoxide, particulate matter, and lead have all been reduced, in some cases sharply. Between 1970 and 1988, estimated emissions of SO_2 dropped 27 percent, particulate matter emissions were down 63 percent, and lead emissions dropped a dramatic 90 percent. Emissions of nitrogen oxides increased slightly (7 percent) since 1970, but all areas of the United States except Los Angeles have met the federal standard during the past ten years.[4]

Ozone remains the country's most serious air pollution problem. In its 1992 report, the EPA found that seventy million people in fifty-six urban areas breathe unhealthy air, which violates federal ozone standards. However, the report noted that forty-one areas marginally out of compliance for the years 1988–90 have met federal health standards for ozone during 1989–91, largely due to cooler weather that cleared the air.

THE RESPONSIBILITY DILEMMA

For most of the twentieth century, air pollution has been considered a local problem, and as a result, most of the efforts to do something about it have been accomplished by municipal governments. By 1912, industrial smoke, the hallmark of urban growth after the turn of the century, was regulated in twenty-eight U.S. cities with populations of two hundred thousand or more. Smoke was the prime target of most ordinances because it was visible, but there was little attention paid to controlling the problem.[5]

The federal government, up until the passage of the Clean Air Act in 1963, took only passing interest in the problem. The Bureau of Mines conducted research on smoke control (which at the time was considered to be the only form of pollution) in 1912, and in 1925, the Public Health Service began to study carbon monoxide in automotive exhaust, but for the most part, the federal role was minor. A six-day smog siege in Donora, Pennsylvania, in 1948, which resulted in the deaths of twenty persons, and illness for six thousand residents, focused national attention on a problem that up until then had been considered to be limited to Los Angeles. The Donora incident was followed in December,

1952 by a similar sulfurous smog episode in London, and in 1953 in New York, resulting in two hundred deaths.[6] All three events lent some urgency to the problem. As city officials began to realize the irrelevance of political boundaries to pollution control, they began to coordinate their regulatory efforts.

The discovery in 1949 that automobiles were a prime source of pollution forestalled statewide controls on industrial sources, and local government stepped in to fill the void left by federal inaction. In 1955, Los Angeles officials began to coordinate their efforts with the nation's top automakers, and Congress appropriated $5 million for research into motor vehicle emissions—the beginning of federal intervention in urban air pollution regulation. Research in the early 1960s debunked the idea that pollution was a problem only in the area immediately adjacent to the source, or in urban areas. Studies began to show that pollution was being transported over long distances, causing environmental damage in regions far removed from the actual source. Long-range transport of sulfur and nitrogen compounds across international boundaries—a phenomenon known as acid rain—made air pollution a global problem (a topic discussed in Chapter 12).[7] These findings made air quality much more than a simple local question, and focused problem solving on Congress.

During the 1960s, four members of Congress did attempt to bring the federal government back into the air pollution policy debate: Edmund Muskie, senator from Maine; Abraham Ribicoff, former secretary of the Department of Health, Education, and Welfare (HEW); Kenneth Roberts, member of Congress from Alabama; and Paul Schenck, member of Congress from Ohio. Their efforts were largely responsible for the passage of the pioneering 1963 Clean Air Act, which expanded research and technical assistance programs, gave the federal government investigative and abatement authority, and encouraged the automobile and petroleum industries to develop exhaust control devices. In November 1967, President Lyndon Johnson signed a second air quality bill, which left the primary responsibility for air pollution control with the state and local governments, suggesting that the federal agencies study, but not establish, national automobile emission standards.

California, meanwhile, was moving ahead on its own. With the nation's worst air quality and with frustration over the slow pace of federal action, the state began a series of "firsts" in an aggressive air pollution control program. In 1961, California began requiring automakers to install crankcase devices to reduce pollution, and in 1963, began to require exhaust control devices. In 1966, the state legislature established the first state auto emission standards—two years ahead of federal efforts to do so.

Meanwhile, environmental groups were pressuring Muskie to produce a new federal bill, and the senator, an early contender for the 1972 Democratic presidential nomination, felt the sting of their criticism. A 1970 report by consumer activist Ralph Nader referred to "the collapse of the federal air pollution effort" and laid the blame squarely on Muskie's shoulders.[8] Muskie and the members of his Public Works Committee staff, relying on estimates provided by the National

Air Pollution Control Administration (a part of HEW), proposed tough new federal standards for air quality and a timetable by which the standards had to be met through the filing of state implementation plans (SIPs). The 1970 Clean Air Act required the newly created Environmental Protection Agency to (a) develop national air quality standards; (b) establish emission standards for motor vehicles, effective with fiscal 1975; and (c) develop emission standards and hazardous emission levels for new stationary sources. The legislation went further than ever before by giving the EPA responsibility for regulating fuels and fuel additives, for certifying and subsidizing on the road inspections and assembly-line testing of auto emission control systems.[9] States faced a formidable task when the 1970 act gave them responsibility for preparing emission reduction plans. In addition to facing tight deadlines for plan preparation, neither the states nor the newly created EPA knew very much about translating federal standards into emission limits on sources. Therefore, relatively crude rules—like requiring all sources to diminish emissions by some specified percentage—were often employed.[10]

Critics charge that the 1970 law had several major faults. First, there was a certain amount of ambiguity over the intent of the act with regard to the setting of auto emission levels. The legislation provided automakers with a one-year extension if they made a good-faith effort to comply but found technology was not available to meet the new standards. Second, Congress appropriated only minimal amounts for research for development of control devices that were in some cases required but that did not yet exist. Third, stationary sources like steel mills and utility power plants faced serious problems because control devices were either prohibitively expensive or technologically unfeasible.[11]

Five major automakers (Chrysler, Ford, General Motors, International Harvester, and Volvo) responded in early 1972 by filing for an extension of the requirement they meet emission standards by 1975, arguing that they needed additional time to comply with the law. Their request for an extension was denied by EPA administrator William Ruckelshaus, so the automakers appealed to the federal court, which ordered Ruckelshaus to review his original denial.[12] The automobile manufacturers argued that the necessary catalyst technology would not be available in time to meet the federal deadline, and Chrysler and American Motors testified that even if the vehicles could be mass-produced in time, they would break down.[13] Ruckelshaus redenied the request for extension, then reconsidered and granted the automakers what they were seeking, setting interim standards that the automobile companies did not appeal.

Implementation of the 1970 law was further hampered by what one observer has called "the enduring reluctance of the public to make significant sacrifices for the sake of healthy air."[14] The nation was locked into a pattern of rapid inflation and high unemployment, which was coupled with the imposition of an oil embargo by OPEC in October 1973. With rising concern over energy supplies, in March 1974, President Nixon proposed a package of thirteen amendments to the 1970 Clean Air Act, which froze the interim 1975 auto emission standards for two more years. In 1975, the automakers applied for another one-year extension, which was granted by new EPA administrator Russell Train, largely due to claims that the catalysts produced a sulfuric acid mist.[15]

In 1977, industry pressure to relax the emission standards on automobiles resulted in the passage of new Clean Air Act amendments. The legislation suspended the deadlines for automakers and also extended the deadlines by which states were to have attained federal standards to 1982. If a state's implementation plan made all reasonable attempts to meet the standards but was unable to do so, the state had to submit a second plan, which would bring the area into compliance no later than December 1987, an issue that primarily affected California. A key element of the 1977 law was a provision, shepherded through Congress by the Sierra Club, that states be required to show that any new sources of pollution would not worsen existing pollution conditions. This complex concept, known as prevention of significant deterioration (PSD), required businesses to install the best available control technology (BACT) to ensure that any potential pollution was minimized.

The concept had first been outlined in a 1972 Sierra Club suit against EPA administrator William Ruckelshaus[16] in which the organization argued that the EPA's guidelines under the 1970 Clean Air Act would permit significant deterioration of the nation's clean air, violating congressional intent. The federal district court agreed, ruling that EPA could not approve state implementation plans that degraded existing air quality even if the region still met national air quality standards. The EPA appealed, but the U.S. Supreme Court's 1973 4-4 ruling upheld the district court. The EPA proposed new regulations to implement the Court's ruling in 1974.

The EPA showed more flexibility toward industry with the introduction in 1979 of a "bubble" policy, which allowed businesses to find the least expensive method of reducing pollution from an entire plant or series of plants, rather than from an individual source (as if the entire facility were under a regulatory "bubble"). The policy allowed companies to choose how to reduce emissions and to use more innovative strategies than was previously required.[17]

The Clean Air Act was scheduled for reauthorization in 1981, but a change in policy direction came with the Reagan administration, and as a result, the 1970 legislation remained virtually unchanged until 1990.[18] Chief among the congressional barriers to a new law were Representative John Dingell, a Democrat from Michigan, chairman of the House Energy and Commerce Committee, who stalled efforts to enact legislation that would impose new standards on automakers, and Senate Majority Leader Robert Byrd, a Democrat from West Virginia, who protected the interests and jobs of coal miners in his region affected by proposed acid rain proposals.

Clean air legislation regained its place on the policy agenda in the late 1980s in part due to changes taking place in Congress. Restless Democrats in the House were openly expressing their hostility to Dingell and Henry Waxman of California, members of the House Energy and Commerce Committee, whose personal battles were perceived as holding up the reauthorization. The result was the formation of the Group of Nine—moderate Democrats hoping to break the legislative logjam over urban smog. In the Senate, Byrd was replaced as majority leader by George Mitchell of Maine, who promised an end to the deadlock. Both houses had the opportunity to do so when the Bush administration unveiled its own clean air proposal, forcing the key players to resolve their differences.[19]

The resulting legislation, signed by President Bush in 1990, contained several far-reaching proposals that went far beyond the 1970 and 1977 acts. The bill established five categories of cities termed nonattainment areas (marginal, moderate, serious, severe, or extreme) and set new deadlines by which they must meet federal standards. Only one region, the Los Angeles/South Coast Air Basin, was classified as extreme by the EPA, and was given twenty years to meet federal standards. In contrast, serious nonattainment areas have fifteen years from November 1990 (the date of the enactment of the amendments), moderate areas have six years to comply, and marginal areas three years. Plants emitting any of 189 toxic air pollutants are required to cut emissions, and would be forced to shut down by 2003 if these emissions posed more than a one in ten thousand risk of cancer to nearby residents. Chemicals that harm Earth's protective ozone layer are to be phased out more rapidly than under the Montreal Protocol, to which the United States is a signator. One of the most contentious portions of the bill dealt with acid rain, requiring an annual reduction of sulfur dioxide emissions by 10 million tons by the year 2000, and annual nitrogen dioxide emission reductions of 2.7 million tons by that same date. The cost of the legislation was hotly debated, ranging from $25 to $35 billion dollars. Much of that burden falls on coal-fired utility power plants, many of them in the East and Midwest, which are required to reduce SO_2 emissions. Automakers estimate the costs of compliance will add hundreds of dollars to the price of new cars, and small businesses will also feel the pinch with controls on dry cleaners, gasoline service stations, and other sources.[20]

President Bush called passage of the 1990 Clean Air Act "the cornerstone of our environmental agenda." But the battle was far from over. The implementation of the 1990 act has been just as controversial as its development. Congressman Waxman has charged, "We'll never see clean air in large parts of the country."[21] There are a number of factors that make implementation difficult. Among the most difficult hurdles the EPA faces is the regulatory time frame of the seven-hundred-page legislation. The EPA must complete 150 regulatory activities, including 100 rule makings, in only two years. To put the process in perspective, consider the fact that in the past, the EPA has issued seven or eight major regulations *per year* on all phases of environmental law—from pesticides to solid waste to air and water pollution.

Second, the implementing regulations will be among the most complex the agency has ever issued. While the issue of nitrogen oxide emissions (one of two acid-rain-causing chemicals) took only two pages of the 1990 act, the regulations crafted by the EPA are expected to take up two hundred or more pages. Due to the large volume and complexity of the rules, the EPA will be forced to rely upon outside consultants for many of its rule makings, and on its advisory committees for assistance in prioritizing what rules to tackle first. Many of those advisory groups, such as the Acid Rain Advisory Committee, which has forty-four members, are packed with industry members and few representatives of environmental groups.[22] Among the most complex provisions of the law are those dealing with air toxics, an area in which EPA staff members are notoriously short on expertise.

There is already some evidence to suggest that Congress is stepping back from the thrust of the 1990 amendments. One portion of the legislation, for example, was designed to require state and local planners to adhere to air quality goals when formulating transportation projects. Theoretically, the intent was to force municipalities to look for alternatives to increased use of single-occupancy vehicles. But in 1991 President Bush proposed, and Congress accepted, plans for a 185,000-mile national highway system that would increase auto use by giving the most funds under the program to those states with the highest gasoline use—at odds with the intent of the air quality act.[23]

Meanwhile, industry's political clout has managed to circumvent some efforts by environmental organizations that worked so hard on the bill initially. Under Vice President Dan Quayle, the Council on Competitiveness, created by Executive Order during the Reagan administration as the Task Force on Regulatory Relief, reviewed the EPA's rulings "to reduce the regulatory burden on the free enterprise system." In 1991, the council rejected one EPA regulation that would have prohibited incineration of lead batteries and another that would have required that recyclables be separated from trash before burning. Both rules had been strongly supported by environmental groups, but were quashed by the council. Congressman Waxman has accused the council of "helping polluters block EPA's efforts,"[24] while the Sierra Club calls it "a pipeline into the federal regulatory apparatus for corporate interests."[25]

That view was reinforced by President Bush's 1992 State of the Union message in which the president announced a 90-day freeze on all federal regulations, and then extended it another 120 days after that. The freeze affected several clean air regulations, including the Pollution Prevention Act, which required polluters to report on the amount of toxic chemicals they generate before they were released. Later that year, the president overruled an EPA regulation that required industries to obtain permits that include limits on the pollution emitted by each plant. Industry had originally sought the right to exceed the limits after minor changes in plant operations, without going through the costly and time-consuming process of obtaining a new permit. Citizen groups considered the permit process an important opportunity for public participation, and the EPA, which drafted the regulation, agreed. Bush then overturned the regulation as a part of his emphasis on deregulation.

The Los Angeles Solution

The South Coast Air Basin, made up of four California counties surrounding Los Angeles, has the worst air quality in the United States, exceeding federal standards for four pollutants: ozone, particulate matter, nitrogen dioxide, and carbon monoxide. In 1977, the state legislature gave the South Coast Air Quality Management District (SCAQMD) the authority to develop air quality control regulations from stationary sources in the basin, which encompasses an area of 13,350 square miles and a population of more than twelve million people. In 1979, SCAQMD and the Southern California Association of Governments (SCAG) adopted the first Air Quality Management Plan (AQMP), emphasizing air pollution control measures targeted by the EPA and the state Air Resources Board, which regulates mobile sources of pollution. The AQMP became part of California's attainment plan required under the federal Clean Air Act. The proposal was revised in 1982 with a strategy to meet all federal air quality standards by 2002. In 1987, the twenty-year plan was challenged by a group of citizens and then rejected by a federal court, which ordered the EPA to disapprove the AQMP because it did not demonstrate attainment by the federal law's 1987 deadline.

The court's action forced the SCAQMD and SCAG to come up with one of the most comprehensive air quality attainment plans in the United States. The new AQMP adopted in 1989 proposed attainment by 2010 (arguing there was no way to comply any earlier) by adopting stringent pollution control measures on virtually every conceivable source of pollutants. In addition to requiring that all known control technologies be implemented within five years (affecting coatings and solvents, petroleum refining, industrial and commercial processes, and other sources), the plan also called for significant advancements in new technology, including some that critics said were still in the "Buck Rogers phase" of development. Those control measures included switching 40 percent of passenger vehicles and 70 percent of freight vehicles to clean fuels, such as methanol or electricity, reducing emission from planes, ships, trains and construction equipment, solvents, coatings, and consumer products by half, and maintaining the number of vehicles miles traveled at 1985 levels through car pooling and other measures. Full implementation was expected to bring the region into compliance with federal standards for carbon monoxide and nitrogen dioxide in five years, with particulate matter in ten years, and with ozone in twenty years.

The 1989 AQMP, which was heavily criticized by labor, business, and industry interests prior to its adoption, has had mixed success. The media have ridiculed many of its control provisions, such as a ban on charcoal lighter fluid, which prompted one politician to print up bumper stickers saying, "Use a barbecue, go to jail." Industry groups argued that the cost of implementing the plan was disproportionate to the small improvement in air quality that might accrue. Many companies have argued that they are unprepared to deal with the confusing and detailed control provisions of the plan, which is constantly under revision. The AQMP was modified again in 1991, and will be revised again in 1994.

Some regulations have already proven to be unworkable. A requirement in the 1989 AQMP that the region's eight thousand employers with one hundred workers or more submit annual ride-sharing plans to reduce the number of cars driven (and the pollution they cause) became an implementation nightmare, and many business owners claimed they did not have the personnel or expertise to comply. Labor unions claimed the rideshare regulation infringed upon collective bargaining agreements, and the agency later modified the requirement. In 1992, the AQMD decided to scrap twenty-four of the AQMP's original regulations in fa-vor of a free-market emissions reduction program that would become the first of its kind in the world.

Despite the setbacks and modifications, the AQMP has become a model of regional cooperation and innovation, and there has been improvement in air quality over the past decade, despite substantial increases in population and the number of vehicles. Other states and air quality districts consider the Los Angeles proposals to be on the cutting edge of air pollution regulation, and have adopted many of the rules to meet their own attainment needs. Initially proposed as "a living document" that would be altered as technology and policies change, the AQMP may be the region's only hope for clean air in the next century.

Even EPA officials admit that Americans will wait years to see cleaner air as a result of the 1990 legislation. One Bush administration official said that in a worst-case scenario, a reduction in carbon monoxide will begin to be seen in 1992 with the wintertime blending of oxygen in fuels. Most of the smog, air toxics, and acid rain initiatives are not required by the law to begin until 1995, and full implementation will not take place until 2005.[26]

ASSESSING THE IMPACT OF URBAN POLLUTION

Why has there been such a concern over the impact of urban pollution? There are five types of environmental damage attributable to air pollution: (a) damage to vegetation, including crops and forests;[27] (b) damage to animals, birds, and insects; (c) damage to synthetic materials, including painted surfaces, rubber, nylon, and metals; (d) soiling of materials, such as clothing and buildings; and (e) weather and climatic changes, including visibility deterioration, surface temperature increases, and reduced solar radiation.[28]

But the most serious impact that concerns policymakers is one of health. It is difficult to pinpoint exactly when concerns about health effects of air pollution made its way to the policy agenda. Smoky chimneys and smokestacks were considered part of the price urban dwellers paid for living in an industrialized society, and most were probably unaware of any damage to their health. One of the earliest efforts tying air pollution to health was that of the Los

Angeles County Medical Association, which supported an ordinance in 1907 which regulated smoke discharges from industrial sources and called for the appointment of the nation's first smoke inspector. The gray haze became known as "smog"—erroneously thought of as a combination of smoke and fog—and it became a hallmark of California living.

One factor that made it difficult for policymakers to reach consensus on what to do about air pollution was the lack of a consensus about its source. As industrialization increased, so too did the need to do something about the "pall of haze" that during World War II was once mistaken for Japanese gas attacks. A particularly heavy layer of smoke on September 8, 1943, called the "daylight dimout," resulted in public calls for action. Southern California Gas Company's synthetic rubber plant was accused of being the source of the pollution, and the firm spent $1.5 million on corrective equipment. Yet the pollution continued, and city officials began to realize that the plant was obviously not the sole source of the problem. Two years later, Los Angeles passed an ordinance limiting smoke emissions from any single source, but it was limited to the city's boundaries, and did not apply to the other forty-five incorporated cities or unincorporated areas surrounding the city.

At the state level, California officials were primarily concerned about visibility and odor. The 1947 Air Pollution Control Act prohibited the discharge of emissions more opaque than prescribed standards, and discharges that were considered to be a nuisance. The state held the police power, and county air pollution control districts simply adopted rules and regulations to carry out the broadly drawn legislative standards.[29] In 1949, A. J. Haagen-Smit, a biochemist at the California Institute of Technology, announced that his research showed that the automobile, which was rapidly becoming a fixture in southern California, was a prime cause of smog. This delighted refineries and utility companies, which were being painted as the air pollution villains. The Western Oil and Gas Association, one of the leading industry lobbies, hired Stanford Research Institute to confirm Haagen-Smit's studies, and they reported that automobiles, not incineration or refineries, were 95 percent responsible for smog.

The mid-1950s mark the search for some kind of technological solution to pollution, since it was obvious that Californians were not about to give up their beloved cars. Local newspapers published dozens of ideas on how best to rid the basin of smog, including circulating the air with helicopters, "smoke umbrellas," huge parasols to block the sun, seeding the clouds for rain, and blowing the smog out to the desert through huge man-made tunnels.[30] The emphasis on the health effects of pollution was due in large part to the role of the U.S. Public Health Service, which was given responsibility for air pollution legislation from 1959 until the passage of the Clean Air Act in 1963. Although there was little policy initiation prior to 1963, the surgeon general did convene the First National Conference on Air Pollution in 1958. Similarly, in 1959 California gave the state's Department of Public Health authority to determine air quality and motor vehicle emission standards that were necessary to protect health and avoid interference with visibility and damage to crops and vegetation.

Now, policymakers have focused on the overall protection of public health and the special problems created by toxic air contaminants. Since 1970, research has shown that many Americans are affected by air pollution. A 1981 study found that asthmatics are especially sensitive to sulfur dioxide, and EPA researchers have discovered that otherwise healthy, exercising individuals show significant effects after six to eight hours of breathing ozone at levels even below the threshold of the current health standard. Still remaining to be answered are the long-term effects of repeated exposures to smog. The American Lung Association, one of the leading organizations to call for more regulation to reduce the health impacts of air pollution, estimates the annual health cost of air pollution at $50 billion.[31] Cost estimates include days lost from work as a result of pollution-related illnesses, as well as the actual cost of care.

The government's concern over public health has most recently been focused on the control of toxic air contaminants. Five metals found in air—beryllium, cadmium, lead, mercury, and nickel—are known to pose various hazards to human health. With the exception of lead, most of these substances pose a risk primarily to those living adjacent to the source, such as a waste dump or factory. Lead, however, is much more widely dispersed as a component of vehicle fuels and paints. Lead poisoning is characterized by anemia and may lead to brain dysfunction and neurological damage, especially in children. The elimination of lead from automobile fuels in the United States, Japan, and Canada have reduced emissions significantly, but few developing countries have made an attempt to phase out lead in gasoline. The problem is compounded by a lack of emission controls on lead smelters, battery manufacturing plants, and paint production facilities.[32]

Little is known about the health risk posed by the tens of thousands of synthetic chemicals available today. Although research is ongoing, many of the effects of toxic contamination, such as cancer, are not apparent for decades after exposure. Although many of these substances are produced by factories and industrial processes, such as pulp and paper processors, smaller sites, such as municipal waste dumps, dry cleaners, and print shops are also responsible for toxic emission releases. Pesticides and herbicides used in agricultural application also are released into the atmosphere.

As is often the case in policy development, government regulation of toxics has typically come on the heels of crisis, and in this case, events outside the United States. In July 1976, an explosion at a herbicide manufacturing facility in Sevesco, Italy, released a toxic cloud of dioxin and other chemicals that spread downwind. Dioxin is a generic term applied to a group of suspected cancer-causing substances that are known to cause severe reproductive disorders as well as immune system problems and impaired liver function. Although no deaths were directly attributed to the incident, within two weeks plants and animals were dying and residents were admitted to local hospitals with skin lesions. More than seven hundred persons living near the plant were evacuated, and five thousand others in the surrounding area were told not to garden or let their children play outside. It took two weeks for local authorities to discover a toxic chemical had been involved and to implement effective safeguards.[33] The incident resulted in the Sevesco Directive in 1984—an agreement by members of the European Community that plants using hazardous chemicals must inform residents of the nature and quantity of the toxics they use and the risks they pose. Later that year, the accidental release of a forty tons of isocyanate at a Union Carbide facility in Bhopal, India, refocused attention on the need to require safeguards in developing nations as well. The incident resulted in death or injury to hundreds of thousands of residents near the plant.

Two landmark pieces of U.S. legislation, the Federal Insecticide, Fungicide and Rodenticide Act (FIFRA) of 1972 and the 1976 Toxic Substances Control Act (TSCA), which regulates how toxic chemicals are to be used, were a result of such incidents. The laws allow the EPA to regulate chemicals that pose an unacceptable health risk, such as PCBs, which were first regulated in 1978. In addition, the Emergency Planning and Community Right-to-Know Act of 1986 now provides communities with access to information about toxic chemicals in their region. The law calls for extensive data collection and for the creation of state emergency response commissions to plan for chemical release emergencies. The federal government also conducts an annual inventory of toxic releases and transfers of about three hundred toxic chemicals from over twenty thousand manufacturing facilities nationwide, called the Toxics Release Inventory. As information about the health effects of each substance is gathered, chemicals of little or no toxic concern are removed from the list, while others are added. Before a new pesticide may be marketed or used in the United States, it must first be registered with the EPA after a series of health, economic, and cost-benefit studies. If the studies indicate that the risks outweigh the benefits, the EPA can refuse to register the product or regulate the frequency or level of application. This process was used to ban the pesticide DDT in 1972, and to cancel registrations for thirty-four other potentially hazardous pesticides.[34]

Yet some observers believe the United States's progress toward controlling toxic air pollutants has been glacially slow. Before the passage of the 1990 Clean Air Act, the EPA had completed regulations for only seven toxic chemicals,[35] and no information is available on the toxic effects of nearly 80 percent of the chemicals used in commerce.[36] Information generated from the Superfund Right-to-Know rule indicates that more than 2.7 billion pounds of toxic air pollutants are emitted annually in the United States. EPA studies indicate exposure to such quantities of air toxics may result in one thousand to three thousand cancer deaths each year.[37] The 1990 legislation, however, does offer a comprehensive plan for reducing hazardous air pollutants from major sources and includes a list of 189 toxic air pollutants for which emissions must be reduced. In addition to publishing a list of source categories that emit certain levels of these pollutants, the EPA must develop standards for pollution control equipment to reduce the risk from the contaminants.

Reductions in the EPA's budget and costly and time-consuming studies of the health effects of toxics are the chief culprits behind the federal government's inaction to date. Some toxics, such as mercury and lead, last a long time in the atmosphere before they are deposited in bodies of water where they are ingested by fish or plants, later harvested for human consumption. The new law will fund studies by the National Academy of Sciences and the EPA that will review and recommend improvements to current techniques for estimating risks to public health from exposure to air toxics. The Council of Economic Advisers has estimated that the cost to industry of the air toxics program would be as much as $1 billion in 1995 and $6–7 billion in 2005. It is impossible to quantify, however, the potential health benefit costs, since the results of reducing the damage may not be seen for many years.[38]

VISIBILITY

Although policymakers have placed public health risks at the top of their list of concerns relating to air quality, environmental groups also point to the problem of visibility as a reason why pollution must be controlled, and the issue is not limited to urban areas. In 1975, Gordon Anderson, representing the group Friends of the Earth, took photographs of the haze that was obscuring the views of Bryce Canyon. The photographs, published by the National Parks and Conservation Association,[39] focused public attention on the growing problem of visibility impairment.

There are three major sources of pollutants that impair visibility: sulfur dioxide from fossil-fueled power plants, copper smelters, industrial boilers, and chemical production; nitrogen dioxide from coal-fired power plants and vehicle fuel emissions; and fine particulates from both man-made and natural sources, many of which can travel a long distance when airborne. The 1977 Clean Air Act amendments included regulations to control visibility that were promulgated by the EPA in December 1980. But it has been the National Park Service that has taken the leadership role in visibility research, largely in part due to complaints that visitors to the national parks could not see the great canyons and monuments they believed were being protected.

The National Commission on Air Quality was asked to provide Congress with information on the Four Corners area, where power plant emissions were suspected of polluting the Grand Canyon, Canyonlands, Bryce, and Mesa Verde National parks. But a 1985 National Park Service study found that contrary to what many groups believed, visible plumes from stationary sources were not the most important source of visibility impairment. The NPS attributed the problem to regional haze,[40] including soil-related materials and blowing dust. The issue arose again in 1987 with the WHITEX (Winter Haze Intensive Tracer Experiment), which attempted to determine if emissions from the Navajo Generating Station near Page, Arizona, contributed to the Grand Canyon's haze.[40] The study found visibility was impaired by manufactured as opposed to natural sources only 15–30 percent of the year. Concerned about the impact of costly pollution control equipment, Interior Secretary Manuel Lujan called for further studies, in part due to the fact that the department's Bureau of Reclamation owns 24 percent of the Navajo facility. Finally, in 1991, the EPA adopted a final regulation to cut sulfur dioxide emissions generated by the Navajo facility by 90 percent. The regulations are expected to impose additional costs of $89 million a year, and will take effect in 1997 under a compromise agreement between the federal government, environmentalists, and the owners of the plant. It marked the first time the agency had issued a major regulation solely to improve visibility, although the cutbacks will improve visibility by only 7 percent on the average winter day.[41]

But the National Park Service considers the visibility problem to be worst at Shenandoah National Park, which extends eighty miles along the crest of the Blue Ridge mountains in Virginia. The superintendent of the park, J. William Wade, believes that the park is under siege, saying, "We're right on the edge of disaster."[42] The problem is so severe that twice in recent years park officials have been forced to issue health warnings to hikers, climbers, and joggers. The park service says Shenandoah ranks first among major federal parks in the amount of sulfates in its air, and second in the levels of ozone.

As a result, in 1991 the NPS took the unprecedented step of opposing two new power plants in southern Virginia that it believed would contribute to the visibility problem, even though the plants would be equipped with pollution control devices. Both the EPA and the Virginia Department of Air Pollution Control dispute the park service's concerns that the new facilities would cause further damage. Fifteen environmental groups led by the Southern Environmental Law Center appealed and have urged the EPA to reassess the situation.[43] NPS officials also plan to review applications for new industrial sites and power plants planned near other national parks, including Great Smoky Mountains National Park on the Tennessee–North Carolina border and Maine's Acadia National Park. For the most part, however, the EPA has not placed visibility on a par with its health protection programs, although the problem did get some funding during the Carter administration. The National Park Service, however, has filled the void in visibility research and has done more than any other agency to bring the problem to the attention of Congress.[44]

INTERNATIONAL AIR POLLUTION EFFORTS

Much of what is known about urban air pollution in nations other than the United States comes from the Global Environmental Monitoring System (GEMS) established under the auspices of the World Health Organization (WHO) and the United Nations Environment Programme (UNEP). GEMS/Air is active in over fifty countries representing different climatic conditions, levels of development, and pollution situations. GEMS/Air data are available for five pollutants: sulfur dioxide, suspended particulate matter, nitrogen dioxide, carbon monoxide, and lead.

In its most recent report, the GEMS assessment report found that world-wide, an estimated six hundred million people live in urban areas where average SO_2 levels exceed recommended levels of exposure. Most urban populations reside in cities where particulate levels are unacceptably high, and residents in rapidly industrializing countries are being exposed to higher levels of NO_2. Although the data are not complete, there is evidence that people living in as many as half the cities in the world may be exposed to excessive carbon monoxide levels, with one-third of the world's city dwellers exposed to marginal or unacceptable lead concentrations.[45] Smog can travel for hundreds of miles and last for many days, growing as it passes over new sources of pollutants. As a result, "modern" smogs frequently cross international boundaries, such as a 1976 smog that began in central Europe and was tracked several days later crossing the shores of Ireland from the Atlantic Ocean.[46]

The air quality issue has been approached differently between developed and less developed nations throughout the world. In the developed regions, environmental deterioration emerged as a political issue more or less simultaneously in the late 1960s, and many countries introduced protective legislation.[47] But the nature of the air quality problems in developed countries is quite different from that of Third and Fourth World nations. Japan, which has traditionally been a pioneer in requiring industrial pollution controls, has made progress, but it is being countered by emissions of pollutants from household energy consumption and the transportation sector. A 1991 study by the nation's Environment Agency found that although industrial emissions have dropped considerably over the past twenty-five years, increased electricity use (from air conditioning and household appliances) and diesel truck emissions (which are not controlled by Japan's strict automotive exhaust regulations) have increased dramatically.[48]

Great Britain has been at the forefront of European regulatory programs, enacting the Alkali Acts in 1863, which required that 95 percent of the emissions from industrial alkali facilities be controlled. In 1956, the Clean Air Act granted local authorities power to regulate "smoke control areas" and a 1968 law expanded those powers. Pollution episodes in London in 1972 and 1974, caused largely by fuel oil emissions, resulted in legislation in 1974 that reduced the sulfur content of fuel.[49] British scientists have been active in air pollution studies and have brought together researchers from all over the world.

European Community members began to recognize the health effects of urban air pollution in the early 1970s and set maximum smoke and sulfur dioxide levels for urban areas in 1980 with a 1983 compliance date. The method of compliance was left up to individual member countries. The emissions of sulfur dioxide in Norway are among the lowest in Europe, achieved largely through the use of low-sulfur oils. The country's leaders have also made planning decisions to site industrial plants to mitigate the local effects of SO_2 emissions. The government also provides financial incentives for firms that use new pollution control technology.[50] In 1992, Italy, which faces one of the most critical pollution problem because of its twenty-five million vehicles on the road, began implementing alternate-day driving, using an odd/even license plate system. Residents have attempted to circumvent the new laws by altering their plates, borrowing a friend's car with the correct plate, or bribing officials. The real problem, however, is that Italy has been slow to impose any long-term pollution control measures on automobiles. Only 1 percent of the cars are equipped with catalytic converters to reduce pollution, and EC regulations requiring new cars to have converters are unlikely to make much of a difference, since old cars will continue to spew noxious fumes and the average Italian car is on the road for fourteen years.[51]

In the Commonwealth of Independent States and other regions of Eastern Europe, industrialization has been of paramount importance, with both air and water pollution control near the bottom of the political agenda.[52] The Soviets began to establish strict emission standards in 1951, but they have frequently been ignored. They differ from the standards in most other countries in that they have been based on toxicological evidence, rather than on epidemiology studies.[53] Transportation accounts for many of the air quality problems in that region, since vehicles there are not equipped with pollution control devices and rely upon leaded fuels. Stationary sources, such as the Astrakhan gas processing plant, which uses high-sulfur content fuels, also are known polluters. But the actual amount of pollution caused by such facilities is largely unknown because scientists there do not have access to accurate emission inventories like those available in the West. Similarly, in most of Eastern Europe, figures on emissions were kept secret during the communist regime, and local leaders often had no idea how much air pollution was being emitted by factories in their area. Near Nowa Huta in southern Poland, for example, more than 170 tons of lead were leased from the air annually, and the electrostatic precipitators installed on factory chimneys to control dust were switched off at night to save electricity.[54]

Katowice, a city of 370,000 in the Silesia region of Poland, is reputedly Eastern Europe's most polluted city. But it is also becoming one of the region's rare air quality success stories. The reason is due to the phasing out of government subsidies and government-controlled energy prices, which have driven costs up and forced Polish citizens to conserve. Coal, which fills 80 percent of the nation's energy needs, is now being used more efficiently as prices have gone up. It is an example where letting the market do the job of providing an incentive for control is more effective than government intervention.[55] Other Eastern European nations, recognizing the degree of environmental degradation, are also making efforts to bring pollution technology to the region. During a 1989 trip to the area, President Bush offered U.S. assistance, and the EPA has provided support to establish the East European Environmental Center in Budapest, Hungary. The facility opened in September 1990 to develop programs to improve both air and water quality. The opening of trade channels with the West is also expected to impact pollution. Most of Eastern Europe's vehicles, like the Trabant, emit masses of dirty smoke, and several firms are hoping to capitalize on increased demand for new cars. Volkswagen and Renault hope to engage in joint ventures in Czechoslovakia, and Japan's Suzuki is negotiating to build cars in Hungary.

But these efforts to bring pollution technology to the East have a high price tag. One environmentalist estimates the cost of stopping Russian air pollution at more than $350 billion, and the World Bank expects the cost of bringing Polish industry up to Western environmental standards at more than $20 billion. The cost is complicated by the fact that many of these nations already suffer from indebtedness and a lack of hard currency.[56]

Even though air pollution is almost as serious in the urban areas of less developed countries—Mexico City, Sao Paulo, Lagos, Cairo, Beijing, and Bangkok—the problem has taken a backseat to efforts to increase economic development. Attempts by international organizations such as the United Nations to protect the environment are often met by skepticism in Third and Fourth World countries where political leaders have a less global view. They argue that attention to environmental matters should follow the attainment of a higher standard of living for their people.[57]

Private cars and geography are the primary pollution culprits in both Mexico City and Sao Paulo. Mexico City's twenty million residents are crammed into a valley ringed by mountains—the same conditions responsible for Los Angeles's notorious smog. Vehicles at the high altitude burn fuel inefficiently, releasing unburnt hydrocarbons, which are then trapped at street level, especially during the winter. In winter 1990, the city suffered from the most polluted conditions ever, and the nation's ecology ministry twice declared an emergency, requiring industries temporarily to cut their operations by half. In response, Mexico's president announced a five-year, $4.6 billion program to clean up dirty industries or move them out of the city entirely. In addition, the city has enacted a mandatory program restricting automobile usage and forced Pemex, the government-owned petroleum company, to reduce the lead content in gasoline and shut down its city refinery, the largest single source of industrial pollution. Hundreds of thousands of trees are also being planted in a companion effort to create a green belt.[58] Sao Paulo, the world's second-largest city, is the headquarters for thirty of Brazil's fifty largest companies, responsible for emitting 350,000 tons of smoke into the air each year. Most workers drive old, exhaust-producing cars, and the city's buses are equally antiquated. By 1997, however, Brazilian cars will be required to use pollution control equipment as strict as those of the United States and Japan.[59]

One reason why urban air pollution is approached differently outside the United States is that the sources of pollution in developing countries are somewhat different from those in more developed ones. The fuels used for cooking in China and India, for example, are usually coal based, which results in high emissions of SO_2 and particulate matter. However, some progress has been made in recent years in replacing domestic coal-burning stoves with gas. The number of urban households in China using gas for cooking increased from 15 percent in 1980 to 22 percent in 1985.[60] In Africa and other Fourth World countries, wood is the primary cooking fuel, also resulting in high concentrates of PM10. Diesel engines, which generate ten times the particulates of gasoline-powered vehicles, are much more common in countries such as Mexico, as is leaded gasoline (where Mexico is the exception), which has been eliminated in the United States.[61]

In China, pollution was long considered a problem of capitalist societies that exploited workers and resources, when China, in contrast, managed its environment. But the expansion of the Chinese population has outgrown its meager attempts at environmental management, and most of its air pollution control policies have had only limited success. The major difficulty is China's reliance upon coal as a fuel source and the high level of suspended particulates result in tremendous visibility impairment. China has very few privately owned vehicles, so there is less of a need to control mobile sources than in more developed nations. But Chinese vehicles are also considerably more polluting (estimates indicate that they produce from fifteen to fifty-five times the amount of hydrocarbon emissions as comparable Japanese models), so any increase in vehicles within the cities will sharply affect pollution levels.[62]

Indonesia suffers from a variety of pollution sources that are common to developing nations. The country faces formidable environmental challenges because of its large geographic coverage and fragmentation of its land masses. In addition to the traditional sources of urban pollution like poorly tuned vehicles and uncontrolled rubbish burning, the country's air is also poisoned by clouds of dust and fumes from erupting volcanoes. Cement factories on the outskirts of Jakarta blanket residents with a layer of fine dust, with recent surveys indicating that a quarter of the population suffers from acute respiratory distress.[63] Although other nations in Southeast Asia are making a concerted effort to reduce air pollution, they face not a lack of regulations, but enforcement capabilities. Many of them enacted environmental legislation on the heels of more industrialized countries in the early 1970s. Thailand, for example, enacted an Environmental Conservation and Promotion Act in 1975 and has repeatedly passed laws to reduce industrial pollution. But regulations for pesticide and fertilizer use, and controls on emissions from domestic and agricultural sources have yet to be adopted.[64] Malaysia adopted its Environmental Quality Act in 1974 to coordinate regulatory activities in response to extensive economic development. In the twenty-five years since independence, the nation has made considerable efforts to integrate environmental considerations in planning and investment decisions and is ranked among the most environmentally progressive countries in the region.[65]

Yet Southeast Asia has two examples of countries where pollution concerns are somewhat different from their less developed neighbors: Singapore and Hong Kong. Both have faced rapid industrialization in a more urban setting, combined with a lack of the natural resources common to other countries in that region. But what makes these countries unique is that the ethical values of their societies, along with the law-abiding attitudes of the residents, have made persistent pollution offenders almost rare. They have become cultural exceptions to the air pollution rules.[66]

The most recent international air pollution problem involves the Middle East and the 1991 Gulf War. When Iraq's Saddam Hussein ordered more than seven hundred of Kuwait's oil fields set ablaze in February 1991, smoke from the burning of over four million barrels of oil per day emitted massive amounts of hydrocarbons, sulfur dioxide, and nitrogen oxide into the atmosphere. More than twelve thousand metric tons of particulate matter were released daily, equal to about 10 percent of biomass burning worldwide. When the oil fires were extinguished in November 1991, researchers from the World Health Organization, Greenpeace, the EPA, and other agencies were just beginning to study the health effects of the conflagration. The studies are being hampered by a lack of information on the toxicity of the smoke from the Kuwaiti crude oil, and it may be several decades before scientists know the long-term impacts. Since many residents evacuated the region, risk assessments will be haphazard at best. There is also concern about the international impact of increased carbon dioxide emissions, which might contribute to global warming, and the "black rain," which fell in Saudi Arabia and Iran.[67]

SUMMARY

Of the six known air pollutants, ozone is the most serious health hazard and the major component of urban smog. Even though efforts to combat air pollution have existed for decades, researchers have continued their research on the causes of air pollution. Most recently, regulatory efforts have focused on mobile sources like trucks and automobiles, and stationary sources, like factories and other industrial emission sources. There have also been shifts in why policymakers are concerned about pollution. At some decision points the concern has been health, and at others, visibility. As the cost of controlling pollution has gone up, attention is now being paid to more innovative control measures, such as paints and solvents and consumer products. In the United States, air quality legislation has been fine-tuned over the past forty years, with the 1990 Clean Air Act amendments the most comprehensive regulatory framework to date. Despite its sweeping controls, however, critics argue the act was being undermined through the implementation process and decisions made by the Bush administration to deregulate. On the international front, the United States is far ahead of other industrialized nations in controlling pollution, although technology is rapidly advancing throughout developed countries. But in the Third World, the cost of installing pollution control equipment and changing to less polluting fuels thwarts advances made elsewhere.

NOTES

1. Ed Ainsworth, "Fight to Banish Smog, Bring Sun Back to City Pressed," *Los Angeles Times*, October 13, 1946, 7.

2. For examples of the earliest awareness of air pollution, see Donald E. Carr, *The Breath of Life* (New York: Norton, 1965), 28–34; and Arthur C. Stern et al., *Fundamentals of Air Pollution* (New York: Academic Press, 1973), 53–59.

3. For a chronology of the early air pollution control efforts, see James E. Krier and Edmund Ursin, *Pollution and Policy*. (Berkeley: University of California Press, 1977), 46–47.

4. "Air," *EPA Journal* 16, no. 5 (September–October 1990): 16.

5. Krier and Ursin, *Pollution and Policy*, 47.

6. For a description of the London episode, see Peter Brimblecombe, *The Big Smoke* (London: Methuen, 1987), and Fred Pearce, "Back to the Days of Deadly Smogs," *New Scientist*, December 5, 1992, 25–28.

7. Derek Elsom, *Atmospheric Pollution* (New York: Basil Blackwell, 1987), 4–5.

8. John C. Esposito, *Vanishing Air: The Ralph Nader Study Group Report on Air Pollution* (New York: Grossman, 1970), vii.

9. John C. Whitaker, *Striking a Balance: Environment and Natural Resources Policy in the Nixon–Ford Years* (Washington, DC: American Enterprise Institute, 1976), 94.

10. Marc K. Landy et al., *The EPA: Asking the Wrong Questions* (New York: Oxford University Press, 1990), 205.

11. See Alfred Marcus, "EPA," in *The Politics of Regulation*, ed. James Q. Wilson (New York: Basic Books, 1980), 267–303.

12. *International Harvester v. Ruckelshaus*, District of Columbia Court of Appeals, February 10, 1973.

13. Whitaker, *Striking a Balance*, 100.

14. Alfred A. Marcus, *Promise and Performance: Choosing and Implementing an Environmental Policy* (Westport, CT: Greenwood Press, 1980), 123.

15. Whitaker, *Striking a Balance*, 104.

16. *Sierra Club v. Ruckelshaus*, 344 F.Supp. 253 (1972). For an analysis of the case, see Thomas M. Disselhorst, "Sierra Club v. Ruckelshaus: On a Clear Day . . .", *Ecology Law Quarterly* 4 (1975): 739–80.

17. For examples of how the "bubble" policy has affected industry, see Elsom, *Atmospheric Pollution*, 176–77.

18. See Arnold W. Reitze, Jr., "A Century of Air Pollution Control Law: What's Worked; What's Failed; What Might Work," *Environmental Law* 21, no. 4:II (1991): 1549–1646.

19. For a detailed chronology of these events, see Richard E. Cohen, *Washington at Work: Back Rooms and Clean Air* (New York: Macmillan, 1992).

20. See Norman W. Fichthorn, "Command-and-Control vs. the Market: The Potential Effects of Other Clean Air Act Requirements on Acid Rain Compliance," *Environmental Law* 21, no. 4:II (1991): 2069–84; and Alyson Pytte, "A Decade's Acrimony Lifted in the Glow of Clean Air," *Congressional Quarterly Weekly Report*, October 27, 1990, 3587–92.

21. Michael Weisskopf, "Writing Laws Is One Thing—Writing Rules Is Something Else," *Washington Post National Weekly Edition*, September 30–October 6, 1991, 31; see also Henry Waxman, "An Overview of the Clean Air Act Amendments of 1990," *Environmental Law* 21, no. 4:II (1991): 1721–1816.

22. Henry V. Nickel, "Now, the Rush to Regulate," *The Environmental Forum* 8, no. 1 (January–February 1991): 19.

23. Mark Mardon, "Last Gasp Next 185,000 Miles?" *Sierra* 76, no. 5 (September–October 1991): 38–42.

24. "Quailing over Clean Air," *Environment* 33, no. 6 (July–August 1991): 24.

25. "Industry's Friend in High Places," *Sierra* 76, no. 5 (September–October, 1991): 42.

26. "Questions and Answers: An Interview with William G. Rosenberg," *EPA Journal* 17, no. 1 (January–February 1991): 5.

27. See James J. Mackenzie and Mohamed T. El-Ashry, *Air Pollution's Toll on Forests and Crops* (New Haven: Yale University Press, 1989).

28. Elsom, *Atmospheric Pollution*, 13.

29. Krier and Ursin, *Pollution and Policy*, 62–63.

30. Ibid., 93–94. Although such ideas may seem farfetched today, similar proposals were received by the South Coast Air Quality Management in 1989 when the agency sought public input for its Air Quality Management Plan.

31. John R. Garrison, "Will the New Law Protect Public Health?" *EPA Journal* 17, no. 1 (January–February 1991): 58.

32. Alan J. Krupnick, "Urban Air Pollution in Developing Countries: Problems and Policies," *Discussion Paper QE91-14* (Washington, DC: Resources for the Future, 1991), 8.

33. Elsom, *Atmospheric Pollution*, p. 58. See also Angela Liberatore and Rudolf Lewanski, "Environmental Disasters and Shifts in Italian Public Opinion," *Environment* 32, no. 5 (June 1990): 36.

34. "Chemicals," *EPA Journal* 16, no. 5 (September–October 1990): 27.

35. The EPA has set standards for arsenic, asbestos, benzene, beryllium, mercury, radionuclides, and vinyl chloride.

36. Walter A. Rosenbaum, *Environmental Politics and Policy*, 2nd ed. (Washington, DC: Congressional Quarterly Press, 1991), 149.

37. U.S. Environmental Protection Agency, *The Clean Air Act Amendments of 1990: Summary Materials* (Washington, DC, November 15, 1990), 4.

38. Lydia Wegman, "Air Toxics: The Strategy," *EPA Journal* 17, no. 1 (January–February 1991): 32–33.

39. See for example, "Smog Alert for Our Southwestern National Parks," *National Parks and Conservation Magazine* 49 (July 1975), 9–15.

40. See Barbara Rosewick, "Air Pollution at Grand Canyon," *Wall Street Journal*, August 30, 1989, A-20.

41. "Grand Canyon Visibility to Improve under EPA Rule," *EPA Journal* 17, no. 4 (September–October 1991): 2.

42. B. Drummond Ayres, "Battle Flares over Air Pollution in Shenandoah National Park," *The Oregonian*, May 5, 1991, E-3.

43. Ibid., E-5.

44. See John Freemuth, "Visibility Protection and the National Parks of the United States," in *Regulatory Federalism, Natural Resources and Environmental Management*, ed. Michael S. Hamilton, (Washington, DC: American Society for Public Administration, 1990), 97–116.

45. "Monitoring the Global Environment: An Assessment of Urban Air Quality," *Environment* 31, no. 8 (October 1989): 6–37.

46. Pearce, "Back to the Days of Deadly Smogs," 28.

47. Elsom, *Atmospheric Pollution*, 6–7.

48. See David Swinbanks, "Pollution on the Upswing," *Nature* 351 (May 2, 1991): 5.

49. Elsom, *Atmospheric Pollution*, 194–208.

50. See "SO2 Levels in Norway," *Environment* 31, no. 8 (October 1989): 13.

51. See Angela Liberatore and Rudolf Lewanski, "The Evolution of Italian Environmental Policy," *Environment* 32, no. 5 (June 1990): 12.

52. See Joan De Bardeleben, *To Breathe Free: Eastern Europe's Environmental Crisis* (Washington, DC: Woodrow Wilson Center Press, 1991).

53. Elsom, *Atmospheric Pollution*, 220–24.

54. See Jon Thompson, "East Europe's Dark Dawn," *National Geographic*, June 1991, 42–68.

55. Peter Fuhrman, "Breathing the Polish Air," *Forbes*, January 24, 1991, 40–42.

56. Debora MacKenzie, "The Green Wave Heads East," *New Scientist*, June 16, 1990, 2–3, 10.

57. Elsom, *Atmospheric Pollution*, 9.

58. See "Smog City," *The Economist*, May 18, 1991, 50. See also Stephen Baker, "Mexico's Motorists Meet the Smog Patrol," *Business Week*, June 25, 1990, 100–101; Christine Gorman, "Mexico City's Menacing Air," *Time*, April 1, 1991, 61; and Mark A. Uhlig, "Mexico City: The World's Foulest Air Grows Worse," *New York Times*, May 12, 1991, 1.

59. See "Cough City," *The Economist*, March 16, 1991, 40.

60. "SPM Levels in China," *Environment* 31, no. 8 (October 1989): 30.

61. See Krupnick, "Urban Air Pollution in Developing Countries," 5–8.

62. Elsom, *Atmospheric Pollution*, 235.

63. Robert Cribb, "The Politics of Pollution Control in Indonesia," *Asian Survey* 30, no. 12 (December 1990): 1123–35.

64. See Surin Setamanit, "Thailand," in *Environmental Management in Southeast Asia*, ed. Lin Sien Chia (Singapore: Singapore University Press, 1987), 169–211.

65. See Augustine Ong et al., "Malaysia," in *Environmental Management in Southeast Asia*, ed. Lin Sien Chia (Singapore: Singapore University Press, 1987), 14–76.

66. For an analysis of the differences in pollution control in the urbanized nations of Southeast Asia, see Lin Sien Chia and Chionh Yan Huay, "Singapore," in Chia, 109–68; and Peter Hills and William Barron, "Hong Kong: Can the Dragon Clean Its Nest?" *Environment* 32, no. 8 (October 1990): 17–20, 39–45.

67. There is an extensive literature on the Kuwaiti disaster. See, for example, Thomas Y. Canby, "After the Storm," *National Geographic*, August 1991, 2–32; Stephanie Pain, "Is Kuwait's Foul Air Fit to Breathe," *New Scientist*, October 26, 1991, 13; Michelle Hoffman, "Taking Stock of Saddam's Fiery Legacy in Kuwait," *Science* 253 (August 30, 1991): 971.

FOR FURTHER READING

Richard E. Cohen. *Washington at Work: Back Rooms and Clean Air.* New York: Macmillan, 1992.

Derek Elsom. *Atmospheric Pollution.* New York: Basil Blackwell, 1987.

Hilary French. *Clearing the Air: A Global Agenda.* Washington, DC: Worldwatch Institute, 1990.

Philip E. Graves and Ronald J. Krumm. *Health and Air Quality.* Washington, DC: American Enterprise Institute, 1981.

Charles O. Jones. *Clean Air: The Policies and Politics of Pollution Control.* Pittsburgh: University of Pittsburgh Press, 1975.

Jack Fishman and Robert Kalish. *Global Alert: The Ozone Pollution Crisis.* New York: Plenum Press, 1990.

A. J. Krupnick. *Urban Air Pollution in Developing Countries.* Washington, DC: Resources for the Future, 1991.

CHAPTER 10

Indoor Air: Pollution and Health

The right of Americans to breathe clean air does not end the moment they walk indoors.
  —Representative Joseph P. Kennedy II, author of H.R. 1066, the Indoor Air Quality Act of 1991[1]

While most of the world's attention to air quality has been focused on ambient, or outdoor, air pollution, health experts have sought to interest policymakers in what many consider to be the more serious problem of indoor air pollution. One report[2] by the Environmental Protection Agency has even suggested indoor air risks are, in fact, higher than most other environmental risks. Coupled with the fact, one study found, on average an employed person spends 28 percent of the day indoors at work and 63 percent indoors at home,[3] indoor pollution would conceivably be a high policy priority. The key question is if the problem is serious enough to warrant government intervention, and if so, in what way.

The subject of indoor air pollution gained attention during the late 1960s when concerns about workplace safety grew, eventually leading to the 1970 passage of the Occupational Safety and Health Act and a federal mandate to study occupational hazards like indoor air pollution. Legislation to provide funds for the EPA to conduct further research was introduced in 1983, but although there are ventilation guidelines, there are no universally accepted standards for indoor air quality. Congressional hearings on H.R. 1066, the Indoor Air Quality Act of 1991, found there is even disagreement whether such standards are needed for comfort or health reasons.

In July 1968, an epidemic of illness characterized by fever, headaches, and muscular pains affected nearly 150 people in a single building in Pontiac, Michigan, but no source could be found and the incident was simply called "Pontiac fever." In 1976, twenty-nine people attending an American Legion convention in Philadelphia died from a previously unknown pneumonia-like illness that affected nearly two hundred people. The cause was later traced to a bacterium, now identified as Legionella pneumophila (Legionnaire's disease), found in a defective air-conditioning system. These two events began to call attention to the problem of indoor air pollution—a term applied to a wide spectrum of substances found in residential and commercial buildings.

214

The contaminants found in a home may be different from those found in a grocery store, bank, or government office. Generally, however, pollutants may be divided into fourteen primary pollutant types emanating from fifteen major sources, as seen in Figure 10.1. Classifications like those found in the figure are not totally satisfactory, since some pollutants, such as environmental tobacco smoke, are both particulates and gases, and passive smokers may also be exposed to various types of volatile organic compounds.

In 1989 and 1990, *New Yorker* columnist Paul Brodeur wrote a series of articles,[4] warning the American public about a previously unpublicized threat to human health. Suddenly, attention was focused on yet another environmental hazard, with both the utility industry and public officials accused of hiding information and suppressing scientific studies about the dangers of electromagnetic fields, or EMFs. This chapter identifies the major sources of indoor air pollution and the related issue of electromagnetic fields, and explains why these two environmental problems have received so little attention from public officials.

THE "SICK BUILDING SYNDROME"

The indoor air pollution problem seems to have been exacerbated with the development of new energy-efficient buildings. Prior to the energy crisis of the 1970s, most conventional buildings relied upon natural ventilation (e.g., open windows and doors) so the quality of the air indoors was basically the same as what was being breathed outdoors. But energy efficiency (and high fuel costs) demand less fresh air enter the building, so architects and engineers are taking a new look at ventilation, although some researchers believe even increasing ventilation will not significantly benefit indoor air quality.[5]

The World Health Organization has estimated as many as 30 percent of all new and renovated office buildings emit some type of toxic contaminant, exposing workers in those buildings to what has now come to be known as the "sick building syndrome" (SBS). The term is usually applied to situations where 20 percent or more of a building's occupants exhibit symptoms such as headaches, nausea, dizziness, sore throats, dry or itchy skin, sinus congestion, nose irritation or excessive fatigue, and the complaints persist for more than two weeks. An associated problem has been termed building related illness (BRI), which is a clinically verifiable disease when signs of actual illness are present and can be attributed to a condition in the facility. The difference between the two is that in SBS there may be no known causal agent. In BRI, affected persons may experience allergic reactions or infections, such as "humidifier fever," which produces flulike symptoms.

While several types of pollutants are usually responsible for both SBS and BRI, the indoor air quality problem is best viewed as a result of a multiplicity of factors, rather than any single pollutant. Respirable particles, formaldehyde, and bioaerosols, or airborne biological agents like yeasts and molds are typically

Figure 10.1 Sources of Indoor Air Pollution

SOURCES \ POLLUTANTS	Respirable Particles	Env. Tobacco Smoke	Radon	Asbestos	Volatile Organics	Pesticides	Formaldehyde	Polycyclic Hydrocarbons	Carbon Monoxide	Nitrogen Dioxide	Sulfur Dioxide	Ozone	Lead	Biological Agents
AC Systems	■	■												■
Outdoor Air	■								■			■	■	■
Building Materials	■		■	■	■	■	■							■
Copying Machines					■							■		
Earth/Ground			■		■			■					■	
Furnishings	■				■		■							■
Kerosene Heaters								■	■		■			
Gas Stoves	■				■				■	■				
Gas Heaters								■	■	■				
Consumer Products	■				■		■							
Insulation				■			■							
Moist Materials						■								■
Tobacco Smoke	■	■			■									
Vehicle Exhaust	■				■		■	■	■	■			■	
Woodstoves	■							■	■					

Source: Dennis F. Naugle and Terrance K. Pierson, "A Framework for Risk Characterization of Environmental Pollutants," *Journal of the Air Waste Management Association* 41, No. 10 (October 1991): 1299.

suspected. But the problems may also be due to stagnant water in air conditioners, wall and floor coverings, insect infestations, and the incomplete combustion of cooking or heating fuels, resulting in a variety of illnesses. Trapped indoors in modern office complexes with windows that do not open, pollutants can reach concentrations twenty times higher than are found outdoors. One of the few studies that has actually measured exposure within buildings was conducted in 1990 by the Ontario Ministry of the Environment. Using samples collected from offices during normal working hours, researchers concluded indoor levels of pollutants were highly variable, but appeared to be as much as two to five times worse than the outdoor air quality.[6] This does not mean, however, that SBS is limited to air-conditioned buildings; in fact, similar problems have been observed in those that are naturally ventilated.

Why has the issue been of somewhat recent concern? When energy prices jumped by as much as 600 percent during the 1970s, building managers and developers sought to find ways of reducing heating and cooling costs. Schools, in particular, tried to balance utility budgets by sealing windows, adding insulation, and blocking ventilation grills and ducts. Buildings saved energy, but also trapped all sources of contamination tightly inside. A study conducted from 1978 to 1983 by the National Institute for Occupational Safety and Health (NIOSH) found nearly half of the buildings classified as "sick" were found to be inadequately ventilated.[7] As budget woes mounted, many public agencies and school districts responded by cutting back on maintenance and operations, further exacerbating the problem.

In addition, technological advances have brought more contaminants into buildings, ranging from special carpet adhesives and backing to office equipment like copiers, facsimile machine, and computers, along with the chemical agents needed to service them and keep them clean. Formaldehyde, for example, is a volatile organic compound and colorless gas with a pungent odor. It is used in a wide variety of building materials like plywood, fiberglass, and in furniture, ceiling tiles, and upholstery. Canada has stopped using urea formaldehyde foam insulation (UFFI), which may be carcinogenic, and the U.S. Consumer Products Safety Commission (CPSC) has considered a similar ban.[8]

Since most of the indoor air contaminants are odorless and invisible, it may be virtually impossible to try to track down their source. It is believed, however, that up to 10 percent of office workers suffer from symptoms like those mimicking the flu to major respiratory attacks. When an incident takes place, researchers usually begin by interviewing the affected workers to try to find a common denominator, such as employees affected on a particular floor of a building. They will also investigate the building's ventilation and cooling systems to make sure they are working properly to filter the air.[9] Once the source is found, ventilation systems are cleaned to remove offending particles, and the source (such as carpeting) is replaced. Research is also being conducted to determine if even simple strategies, like adding green plants to a room, can help to remove pollutants and improve indoor air quality.[10]

Equally important to assessing the magnitude of the indoor air quality problem has been the development of sophisticated monitoring equipment—a process that began in the mid-1970s. In addition to stationary equipment, which must operate from a fixed location, researchers use portable units that can be hand-carried from one location to another. The newest sampling devices are personal units that have been miniaturized and are usually attached to clothing. This allows for samples to be taken in a variety of microenvironments—at work, home, outdoors, or while commuting—to give a more accurate assessment of total human exposure to contaminants.[11]

Policymakers seeking to deal with the indoor air pollution problem are divided in their approach. Some believe the emphasis should be on the sources of pollution: removing the offending pollutants from the building materials, furnishings, office, and consumer products and chemicals. Others feel the emphasis should be on a "building systems approach"—the design, maintenance, and operation of the building's heating, ventilation, and air conditioning (HVAC).[12] This latter group, led by the Business Council on Indoor Air, points to the fact during construction, dirt may be literally built in to a new building's vents, or filters may be poorly installed or left out entirely.

There has been little regulation of indoor air quality for a number of reasons. Historically, the United States has focused on "end-of-pipe" controls on air pollution—the cleanup of pollutants after they have been generated. But the Research Strategies Committee of the EPA's Science Advisory Board has concluded there should now be an emphasis on reducing pollutants before generation, known as risk reduction. This includes strategies such as materials substitution instead of air cleaning, localized mitigation options over rigid federal regulations, and participation by professional organizations such as the American Society of Heating, Refrigerating and Air Conditioning Engineers (ASHRAE). The group's predecessor organization, the American Society of Heating and Ventilating Engineers, first adopted ventilation standards in 1895. In 1973, ASHRAE promulgated standards for minimum and recommended ventilation rates for occupied areas and has continually updated those standards to take into account pollutants such as environmental tobacco smoke.[13] Other groups, like the Sheet Metal and Air Conditioning Contractors' National Association and the National Energy Management Institute, have been involved in research and development.[14] Congress, in contrast, has focused on minimal funding for research rather than regulation.

Unlike other forms of pollution control, regulations to control indoor air pollution in residential and nonoccupational buildings exist almost exclusively in densely populated and industrialized nations such as Japan, Sweden, and Canada. European nations have made efforts to restrict smoking in public places, but have never moved into residential air quality. Some researchers believe the problem of indoor air pollution is one that needs to be addressed in developing countries as well. In those cultures dependent upon coal or animal dung as a source of fuel for cooking and heating, exposure to emissions from biomass

Bobbie's Building

Bobbie Lively-Diebold is a victim of sick building syndrome. Like many office workers who have suffered from this illness, she experienced a number of puzzling symptoms when she came to work each day. Her nose twitched at the carpet, and suddenly her body began to shut down. Her throat tightened, her eyes burned, her lungs heaved, her mind fogged up, and she was forced to tell her employer she was going home sick. What makes the situation somewhat ironic, however, is that Bobbie Lively-Diebold worked at the Washington, DC, offices of the U.S. Environmental Protection Agency.

An investigation into the source of her complaints traced the likely source of the problem to a specific chemical in the backing of the office's carpet called 4-phenylcyclohexane. The agency agreed to remove the carpet from the building, but Bobbie was unable to return to work in her office until the building was completely decontaminated. The incident has caused considerable embarrassment for the EPA and exemplifies how indoor air pollution can strike even the guardians of the nation's environmental quality.[17]

burning is an important contributing factor to the incidence of respiratory infections, and possibly even the beginnings of chronic lung disease in children. In some regions of the world, the indoor concentrations of particulate matter may be ten to one hundred times that found in homes with modern cooking appliances,[15] and children living in homes with gas stoves have been found to have significantly lower lung capacity than children living in all-electric homes.[16]

ENVIRONMENTAL TOBACCO SMOKE

Environmental tobacco smoke (ETS) is perhaps the most heavily polarized issue involving indoor air pollution. On the one side is the tobacco industry, which argues smoking is like a lot of other risky activities that individuals freely and knowingly undertake but that so far do not seem to raise similar concerns of public policy.[18] On the other side is a great body of literature arguing that ETS may be responsible for a wide range of health effects, including reduced pulmonary function, age at menopause, cardiovascular disease, and prenatal development and birth weight.[19]

ETS is used to describe side-stream smoke emitted from the burning end of cigars, cigarettes, and pipes, as well as the smoke exhaled from smokers themselves, and is usually considered "passive" or involuntary smoking.[20] The contaminants that make up ETS include irritating gases and carcinogenic tar particles. Since tobacco does not burn completely, other contaminants are also given off, such as sulfur dioxide, ammonia, nitrogen oxides, vinyl chloride, hydrogen cyanide, formaldehyde, radionuclides, benzene, and arsenic. A lighted cigarette, for example, can give off nearly five thousand chemical compounds.[21]

One of the factors that has made it difficult for researchers to come up with a definitive ruling on the impact of ETS is the level of exposure. Most of the studies have not controlled for other factors that may also have a negative health impact, such as diet, life-style, and exercise. Although the dangers of ETS have been thoroughly reported by the media, some scientists believe the studies are inconclusive. One study found ETS was a major contributing factor to indoor air quality problems in only 3 percent of the cases.[22] Still, despite industry claims, in 1986 the U.S. surgeon general felt the evidence was strong enough to issue a warning that passive smoke could be dangerous to health.[23]

In 1993, the EPA released a report that may provide in its assessment of the respiratory health risks of passive smoking the most compelling reasons of all for limiting tobacco use. The study concluded that ETS is a human lung carcinogen, responsible for 3,000 lung cancer deaths annually in nonsmokers, and impairs the respiratory health of hundreds of thousands of children in the United States. The report admitted that although the EPA does not have any regulatory authority for controlling ETS, there was sufficient evidence that ETS presents a serious and substantial public health risk.

Despite such evidence, the federal government has done little to regulate environmental tobacco smoke, largely because the issue has strong political ramifications and is closely tied to the regulation of smoking itself. The tobacco lobby is one of the most powerful in the country, and supporters point to the fact that the industry is responsible for more than one million jobs, $11 billion in government revenue and tens of millions of dollars in donations to minority causes and public schools. Antismoking advocates, like the American Lung Association, admit the tobacco industry's political action committees contribute significantly to members of Congress, making them unlikely to support smoking bans. As a result, U.S. policy is inconsistent: Some federal agencies are responsible for publicizing the health hazards of smoking, while others promote the tobacco industry at home and abroad.[24] The only two agencies with authority to regulate tobacco are the Federal Trade Commission, which oversees health warning labels on cigarettes, and the Justice Department, which enforces the ban on broadcast advertising. Neither is likely to venture into the ETS arena. The one area in which Congress has acted is the 1989 ban on smoking in the cabins on domestic airline flights of six hours or more. The legislation, which had the support of the Association of Flight Attendants and public health officials, had started out as a trial two-hour ban in 1988. Predictions of widespread public resistance to the trial ban proved inaccurate, and Congress extended the ban to virtually all U.S. flights.[25]

The most recent targets of antismoking advocates have been public places and the workplace. Local ordinances are being enacted to ban smoking in restaurants and public buildings, and even jails are moving toward smoking bans. Studies have shown that smoke-free jails have reduced maintenance and cleaning costs, and have had significant gains in inmate and staff health care.[26] The reason why these measures are being considered at the state and local levels, rather than by Congress, may be that these policymakers are less influenced by the tobacco lobby, although states where tobacco is a major industry have been reluctant to impose smoking bans. In addition, protecting public health is the traditional domain of state and local governments under their police powers, rather than a concern of federal officials.

Internationally, ETS is an issue that has not reached the policy agenda in most countries, despite warnings that "the twentieth century's brown plague" will kill twelve million people annually by the year 2050. Health costs from smoking-related disease are estimated at over $50 billion a year in the United States alone, but most cases of disease occur in Third World countries. Although U.S. tobacco consumption has declined, worldwide tobacco use, especially in Asia, rose by 75 percent during the 1970s and 1980s, and the figures continue to rise. The industry has targeted developing countries as its most promising new market, and unlike their practices in the United States, tobacco companies do not have to carry a consumer warning and their products have a higher tar content, making them even more harmful.[27] China is one of the few Asian countries that has begun to recognize the health threat posed by smoking and ETS, but the large number of smokers makes change glacial at best.[28]

European attempts to curb smoking, and therefore the impact of ETS, are slow as well. Alitalia and Scandinavian Airline Systems have banned smoking on domestic flights, and Air France is testing similar restrictions. Restaurants in Belgium are instituting no-smoking sections, and in Britain, some companies are experimenting with workplace bans. Sweden has adopted the world's strongest warning labels, but the tobacco industry is extremely strong in Europe and is fighting back at restrictions on advertising and trade.[29]

Canada has been successful at regulating ETS using a totally different strategy. The government imposes a tax of approximately $3 on each pack of cigarettes sold and restricts advertising. Employers under federal jurisdiction (which account for 9 percent of all workplaces) have banned smoking, and smoking is also banned in all public spaces. The result has been a 10 percent decline in the number of smokers in only two years. Still, ETS remains one type of indoor air pollution where political forces are shaping legislation and regulation, making an outright ban nearly impossible to implement.

RADON

After eleven accident-free years of working at the Limerick Nuclear Power Plant in Pottstown, Pennsylvania, Stanley Watras assumed the plant's radiation monitoring equipment had made a mistake when its alarms sounded in December 1984, indicating radiation exposure. But several days later, the alarms continued to go off, even though the plant was on inactive status at the time, and he was apparently the only employee affected. Acting on a hunch on December 14, he entered the radiation monitoring room *before* he reported for his shift, and the alarm immediately went off. It was obvious he was picking up radiation from some source besides the plant, and his house was a suspected location. When his employer sent a team over to measure radiation in the Watrases' residence, they found radiation levels seven hundred times higher than the maximum considered safe for human exposure.[30]

The Watras incident focused public attention on an issue that has been hiding just beneath the surface of the planet since Earth was created. Although radon was first discovered in 1900 by Friedrich Dorn, a German physicist who described the "emanations" of radon from the decay of uranium-238, its effects were described as early as the sixteenth century. Radon is found in more than 150 types of rocks, although it is most concentrated in granite, phosphate, shale, and uranium ore—deposits of which are found throughout North America and in various regions in Europe.

Indoor radon, most commonly used to describe radon-222, is an inert colorless, tasteless, odorless gas that decays and emits radioactive particles called "radon progeny," which are hazardous when inhaled directly or when attached to dust particles that are lodged in the lungs. As early as the Middle Ages, miners in regions of Germany and Czechoslovakia were known to suffer from "Bergkrankheit," or "mountain sickness," a lung disease attributed to working with pitchblende, the ore in which uranium is found. Despite numerous studies of the causes of death among miners, especially after World War II, when widespread uranium use began, the role of radon as a causative agent was not generally accepted until the 1960s. It was not until 1971 that the EPA issued federal guidelines limiting exposure for uranium miners after numerous studies showed a causal link between radon exposure and an increased incidence of lung cancer. Similar epidemiological analyzes in Czechoslovakia, Sweden, and the Canadian provinces of Newfoundland, Saskatchewan, and Ontario confirmed the U.S. studies.[31]

Other research has indicated the radon risk must be considered separately for smokers versus nonsmokers, since lung cancer from smoking is now the leading cause of cancer death in the United States. There is evidence smoking and radon exposure are interactive—that is, the risk of death from lung cancer for smokers, already much greater than for nonsmokers, is multiplied further by radon exposure.[32] The National Council on Radiation Protection and Measurements estimates up to ten thousand lung cancer deaths per year may be attributed to indoor radon,[33] and EPA estimates the figure may be as high as thirteen thousand.[34]

Radon travels in a number of ways, but it is impossible to predict exactly where it will show up next. For example, the home next to the Watrases' was tested and found to have only low levels of radon. It may diffuse through permeable soils and porous rock, or may "hitchhike" in groundwater that passes through uranium-containing granite or other rocks. Radon has been detected in natural gas, although some regions produce natural gas that is relatively free of radon. Radon can enter residential dwellings through cracks, loose caulking or sealants, pipe fittings, or in building materials, such as hollow rock blocks, concrete, or brick. Higher concentrations may be found in homes that are energy efficient, especially in the first two stories due to decreased ventilation rates, although uncovered crawl spaces are also culprits. It is important to note, however, that indoor radon is but one source of radiation, since a variety of natural and man-made sources can affect the amount of exposure humans receive in an average lifetime. Cosmic rays constantly bombard Earth, and other naturally occurring radioactive gases and materials are present in the air we breathe. The higher the altitude, the higher the level of dosage. Radon accounts for 55 percent of all radiation exposure, although smoke detectors, color televisions, watches, and medical diagnostic and therapeutic X-rays also contribute to a lesser extent.

Indoor radon is measured in picocuries per liter (pCi/l), a term used to describe the amount of radon atoms disintegrating per minute in every liter of air in a room. To put the figure in perspective, breathing air in a house that contains 10 pCi/l carries the same lung cancer risk as smoking one pack of cigarettes a day. The critical aspect of radon risk, however, is exposure, which is measured as working level (WL). In a typical house, a level of 200 pCi/l converts to 1 WL, or conversely, 1 pCi/l converts to 0.005 WL.[35] Outdoor radon levels throughout the United States range from about 0.10 to 1.5 pCi/l.

One factor making indoor radon exposure unique among environmental hazards is that it is naturally occurring, so there is no technological "bad guy" to point to or regulate. Radon is simply *there*, emanating from the ground for millions of years. A group of University of Washington analysts believe that although radon is the most important radiation problem, it is by no means the greatest public health problem. A 10 percent reduction in smoking would probably reduce lung cancer incidence by as large an amount as the elimination of all radon. Still, they recommend indoor radon levels should be mapped nationwide to provide an accurate characterization of the problem, and more studies are needed to reduce radon levels in new homes and in existing dwellings. They also believe further epidemiological studies are needed to establish the relationship between radon and the incidence of cancer.[36]

Excessive indoor radon levels can be mitigated in a variety of ways, some of them simple and others requiring more extensive remedial action. Some homes may reduce levels simply by diluting indoor air with outdoor air, either by opening windows or turning on a fan to mix the indoor air. EPA recommends, for example, that earthen floors be covered with a cement slab or layers of gas-proof plastic lining, and most home mitigations involve a subslab depressurization system rather than the costly excavation or removal of soil. It has become a specialized field within the home-building industry and has produced scores of home radon detection kits, some of them of questionable utility. The EPA has a listing process for both mitigators and test-kit manufacturers, and many states now have certification programs as well.

From a regulatory standpoint, radon, unlike other carcinogenic substances, has not been a target of congressional action.[37] Although considered a Class A, or known human carcinogen, there are no federal exposure standards for radon, though the EPA has established a guidance level of 4 pCi/l. Other organizations, such as ASHRAE, have proposed a guideline of 0.01 WL (2 pCi/l), while the Bonneville Power Administration recommends action be taken at a level of 0.025 WL (5 pCi/l).

Under the 1986 Superfund Amendment and Reauthorization Act (SARA) amendments, EPA conducted a national radon survey and technology demonstration programs, and 1988's Indoor Radon Abatement Act (IRAA) primarily expanded the agency's outreach efforts. The IRAA also established a program by which states could apply for funds to survey buildings, operate public information programs, and purchase testing equipment. The IRRA, which was scheduled for reauthorization in 1992, is unlikely to be expanded into a more proactive regulatory mode. While the IRAA made it a national goal to virtually eliminate all traces of indoor radon,[38] existing mitigation systems make that goal virtually unreachable. It is more likely that technology will allow levels to be reduced to 4 pCi/l.

The most politically interesting aspect of this policy issue, however, is that although indoor radon is unparalleled as an indoor health hazard, it has failed to capture the interest of the public, environmental organizations, or regulators. Analysts have outlined a number of reasons why this has occurred. First, although researchers are in agreement as to the link between radon and lung cancer, they have not reached a consensus on the real extent of risk from exposure. Second, unlike other environmental issues, which are characterized by confrontation, the radon danger was never really captured by advocacy groups, because both opponents and proponents of nuclear energy agreed on the problem. Third, the public has remained unconvinced that radon is a serious health hazard, because it is not "sensed" and therefore virtually invisible even after decades of exposure. Lastly, no federal agency has attempted to expand its bureaucratic turf by claiming radon as its own. The EPA has concentrated on ambient air; although the Department of Energy's radon budget is bigger than the EPA's, the agency has shifted attention to nuclear power; the Department of Housing and Urban Development and other agencies have chosen not to become involved for fear of the issue draining their already limited resources. Historically, the major battle among the agencies has been one of exposure levels. Radon has become an environmental orphan, with few champions either within the bureaucracy or among organizations and groups.[39]

ASBESTOS: "DISEASE OF SLAVES"

One of the most publicized of the indoor air pollution health issues is asbestosis, but it is not wholly a contemporary concern. The ancient Roman historian Pliny referred to the use of transparent bladder skin as a respirator to protect slaves weaving asbestos. Roman slaves were becoming disabled to the point they eventually died from breathing asbestos dust, a malady referred to as the "disease of slaves."[40]

Asbestos is a mineral produced in various regions of the world, although the chief exporters have been the former Soviet Union, Quebec, China, and Zimbabwe. It is found in serpentine, the official state rock of California, and was once referred to as the "wonder fiber" because of its multiplicity of uses. Historically, it has been used most often in two ways: one, in construction, with fibers used in acoustic ceilings, roofing and flooring felt, floor tiles, asbestos-cement pipe, shingles, and thermal insulation; and two, in automotive parts like drum brake linings and disc brake pads. It is resistant to heat and chemicals and relatively low cost. Asbestos has also been used in a variety of other applications, many of which are not obvious to most consumers. Long, thin, microscopic asbestos fibers are found in table salt, intravenous drugs, drywall patching compounds, electric hair dryers, fake fireplace logs, and clothing. U.S. consumption of asbestos fiber peaked in 1974 and has decreased dramatically since then for two reasons: Government regulations have limited asbestos use, and substitute materials are now available.

The modern asbestos industry began to flourish in the 1870s, but attempts to control the pulmonary diseases that were a consequence of working with the substance did not really begin until the 1920s, when the first death from pulmonary asbestosis was recorded. It was not until ten years later that asbestosis became classified as an occupational disease.[41] Today, medical researchers attribute a wide spectrum of illnesses to asbestos. Asbestosis is a lung disease that is caused when the mineral fibers scar delicate tissue, gradually choking off the air supply. What makes the disease especially disturbing is that even under conditions of extreme exposure, symptoms may not be evident for at least ten years. Some medical researchers believe deaths due to exposure to asbestos are substantially lower than published risk estimates from common causes,[42] but there is substantial agreement that no level of exposure can be considered safe. The mineral is also suspected of causing lung cancer and mesothelioma, a rare disease of the lining of the lungs and intestinal tract. Studies have found smoking increases the risk of asbestosis death by a factor of two to three. Risks of lung cancer among smoking asbestos workers also were found to be eight times greater than among the smokers in the general population, and ninety-two times greater than for nonsmokers in the general population.[43]

Occupational exposure ranges from school custodians working in buildings insulated with asbestos to more than one million U.S. workers doing brake repair work. While there is obvious concern about workers who handle asbestos (referred to as "direct" occupational exposure), studies have also shown risk for those who work nearby but do not handle asbestos themselves ("indirect" occupational exposure), for asbestos workers' family members (household contact exposure), and for neighbors of sources of asbestos air pollution.[44]

During the 1980s, policymakers responded to what some have called a virtual "asbestos panic" in their attempts to solve what was at the time perceived as a crisis. Fueled by media hype and horror stories, asbestos removal programs were undertaken throughout the United States. One of the most visible efforts to deal with the issue has involved schools. A 1983 U.S. Department of Education report found fourteen thousand schools were affected, with an abatement cost estimate of $1.4 billion. That figure was later revised in 1986 to thirty-five thousand schools, with the cost of cleanup in school buildings alone reaching $3.1 billion.[45]

Despite the fact only about one out of every three U.S. schools is estimated to contain "friable" (crumbling) materials that may release asbestos fibers into the environment of schoolchildren and school employees,[46] many schools rushed to remove the substance without seeking expert advice or consultation, often hiring firms with no experience. One source estimates fewer than a quarter of the firms dealing in asbestos abatement are competent, many of them "rip-and-skip" companies that later disappear. Careless removal can result in airborne asbestos levels three to four times higher than before the work was done.[47] But the rush to remove seems to have faded; annual spending on asbestos removal leaped from $1.8 billion in 1987 to $4.2 billion in 1989, but dipped to $2.7 billion in 1991 after stories began circulating that removal was not always necessary.[48]

At the federal level, regulatory action has been initiated by the Occupational Safety and Health Administration (OSHA) and by the EPA. OSHA has set inhalation and exposure limits, but Congress, in contrast, has been slow to respond. In 1980, it enacted the Asbestos School Hazard Detection and Control Act, which assisted states and localities in the evaluation of asbestos pollution and possible remedies, such as renovation. The funding of these projects, however, was stalled until the passage of the Asbestos Hazard Emergency Response Act in 1986, which allocated $600 million for removal. In 1986, the EPA announced a total ban that was to take effect by 1996, but major parts of the law were struck down be a federal court in late 1991. The U.S. Court of Appeals ruled the EPA could legally prohibit new uses of asbestos and imports, but the agency failed to adequately consider alternative regulations short of a ban on other uses.[49]

There is no complete record on how many other buildings, many of them public, are also in need of asbestos removal. One 1988 EPA study estimated there are 501,000 commercial and public buildings with damaged friable asbestos materials.[50] Yet now virtually everyone involved, on both sides of the issue, agrees asbestos need not be removed from buildings unless it has been damaged or disturbed. Because the exact extent of the amount of asbestos in buildings (and its condition) is so uncertain, final figures on the total cost of removal range from $30 billion[51] to as high as $150 billion.[52]

Thousands of workers exposed to asbestos have also sought legal remedies and compensation. As a result of a landmark 1973 federal court decision more than twenty-five thousand lawsuits were filed over the next ten years as word spread that asbestos manufacturers could be held strictly liable for damages incurred by those who had worked with the substance. Many sympathetic juries began handing out hefty awards to victims and their families, including a Marshall, Texas, case in which three asbestos installers and the widow of another were awarded $7.9 million, including $1 million each in punitive damages.[53] The cost to the manufacturers has been high, although attempts have been made to reduce their overall liability and to speed up claims to the neediest victims. In 1985, thirty-four asbestos manufacturers and sixteen insurance companies agreed to set up a claims facility to handle all future litigation. A number of victims' groups have been established to provide counseling and to promote asbestos compensation legislation. Groups like the White Lung Association and the Asbestos Victims of America have sought to educate the public and have served an important function in keeping pressure on Congress and suppliers. The EPA has also set up an Asbestos Ombudsman Clearinghouse and Hotline to provide consumers on remediation and risk.

Outside the United States, international efforts to control asbestos use have had only moderate success, with world asbestos consumption remaining steady at about 4.5 million metric tons per year. But although industrialized nations have reduced their consumption, developing countries are using more of it. Sweden, for example, virtually eliminated its use as a result of a trade union campaign which began in 1975. Thailand, which imports more Canadian asbestos per capita than any other nation except Malaysia, originally sought a warning label on bags of imported cement, but was convinced by the Canadian government not to do so because the idea was "excessive."

U.S. manufacturers with plants abroad have also been accused of blatant environmental and health abuses. New and expanded asbestos plants are under construction or operation in Tunisia, Kuwait, the Sudan, the Philippines, Nigeria, Malaysia, South Africa, Thailand, India, and Sri Lanka.[54] The Canadian government is facing considerable pressure from the world's environmental and health organizations, which argue that the country has become a "merchant of death" for selling asbestos to Third World nations that are not aware of the health risks of the mineral.[55] By the late 1980s, half of Canadian asbestos exports were being sent to the Third World.[56] The Asbestos Institute, the promotional arm of the industry, argues a 1990 study, known as the Mossman Paper,[57] exonerates Canada's "good" serpentine asbestos, as compared with the spiky fibers of amphibole asbestos mined primarily in Africa. The institute says its products are actually a boon to developing nations, since they are used to provide fresh drinking water and sewer service at a quarter of the cost of plastic pipe. Although litigants have been successful in the United States, that has not been the case in other nations. There has been no asbestos product liability litigation in Great Britain, and most Australian claims have been settled out of court. In 1986, a Tokyo District Court ordered an asbestos manufacturing firm and its parent company to pay $1.2 million to ten former asbestos plant workers, but such examples are rare.[58]

EMFs: WAVES OF THE FUTURE

Utility transmission lines represent to many a sign of creeping civilization— their metallic skeletons bringing electric power across the miles for residential and commercial use. But as the boundaries of urban growth come closer to not only transmission lines but to utility substations, and as electric appliances and computers proliferate, the fears often associated with electricity are magnified. Part of the problem is that the term is often referred to as electromagnetic radiation, which conjures up images of nuclear power and radiation from fallout. Electricity is a cornerstone of modern living, powering appliances and providing illumination and energy for virtually every aspect of human existence. It is also an aspect of science that can be intimidating, frightening, and complex.

Scientists have been studying man-made and naturally occurring electric and magnetic fields since the nineteenth century. In the United States and Canada, utility power plants produce electricity, which is sent out at a frequency of 60 hertz (Hz), which means the current in the circuit reverses direction (called alternating current, or AC) sixty times each second. Nations in other parts of the world generally use 50 Hz power. The term *electromagnetic fields* (a combination of electric and magnetic fields) usually refers to extremely low frequencies (ELFs)—the portion of the electromagnetic spectrum from 0 to 100 Hz, as opposed to X-rays at the other end of the spectrum, with radio, television, and microwave frequencies in between. The strength of the field is measured in gauss, with the field strength usually measured in milligauss, which is one-thousandth of a gauss. There is an ambient or natural magnetic field that surrounds us, normally measuring about three milligauss in an urban area and less than one in a rural area, depending upon the proximity to power transmission lines.

Most of us are exposed to additional electromagnetic radiation depending upon the kind of life-style we lead and the number of household appliances we use. An electric toothbrush, for example, produces 7–10 milligauss, a toaster up to 60 milligauss, and an electric stove 5–7. The strength of EMFs drops rapidly with distance so someone working twelve inches away from a computer video display terminal (VDT) would be exposed to 2.5–3.5 milligauss, but the exposure would be half that if the screen was twenty-four inches away. A child sitting four inches from a television screen could be exposed to up to 100 milligauss, but at three feet, the exposure is less than 2. Prolonged exposure, like someone sleeping under an electric blanket overnight, could amount to up to 10 milligauss. A person outdoors standing underneath a utility power pole might be exposed to 7–10 milligauss, and in the front seat of a car, 3.5–5.

The controversy is over what effect EMFs (magnetic fields, primarily, although little research has been done on the effect of electric fields) have on human beings, if any, and if so, what dose presents a risk to human health. The term commonly used to determine the effects of EMFs is *dose-response*—a small level of exposure produces no response, and too much exposure yields an adverse response. The key is to determine what the effect is in between. Even that issue is complicated, since there are questions about whether there are differences between long-term and short-term exposure, or brief intense bursts compared with low-level ones. Some exposure, for example, has proved to have beneficial effects. Man-made pulsed electromagnetic fields (PEMFs) have been used to treat patients with bone fractures that have not healed normally, and research indicates PEMFs may be useful in treating osteoporosis, severed nerves, chronically unhealed diabetic ulcers, and coronary artery disease.[59]

The U.S. Department of Energy has supported EMF research since the mid-1970s, as have a number of electric utilities,[60] the National Cancer Institute and the National Institutes of Health, and the U.S. Navy. Most studies are generally of two types: those that measure the potential health risks of EMF exposure within the home, and those that are primarily occupational, based on the exposure of those working directly with power sources, such as linemen or electricians. Several foreign studies have also been completed, notably in Sweden, the United Kingdom, Germany, Canada, France, Italy, Japan, and Norway.

Past studies have been inconclusive and often contradictory about the relationship between EMFs and cancer.[61] Although Soviet researchers first suggested a human health effect in 1972, their reports were met with skepticism by American scientists. Similarly, a 1979 study linking childhood cancer and proximity to high-current electrical wires was dismissed because it did not rely upon experimental evidence.[62] One of the first studies to gain some scientific acceptance was published in 1982, suggesting men whose occupations required them to work in electric or magnetic fields died from leukemia proportionately more often than men in ten out of eleven occupations studied.[63] Other studies have shown a link between EMF exposure and brain tumors.[64] One researcher, Dr. Robert O. Becker, turned to the popular press in the 1970s and 1980s to warn the public of what he called "the perils of electropollution." He now advocates a maximum field strength of 1 milligauss for continuous exposure, and believes residential exposure to ambient fields greater than 3 milligauss are significantly related to increases in the incidence of childhood cancer.[65] Several early studies of childhood exposure to EMFs showed no adverse relationship,[66] but a five-year, $1.7 million study completed in 1991 by the University of Southern California and sponsored by the electric utility industry found children who live close to high-voltage powerlines may have twice the normal one in twenty thousand chance of getting leukemia. The study of children in Los Angeles, considered one of the most comprehensive to date, found only a weak link, however, between leukemia and the strength of magnetic fields measured in the children's homes, and no link between the cancer and the intensity of electric fields.[67] A followup study of utility employees, published in 1993, found no linkage between exposure and the number of cancers observed in the group.

In 1990, a landmark EPA study concluded there is a significant link between exposure to extremely low frequency electromagnetic radiation and the occurrence of cancer in humans.[68] A subsequent 1992 report concluded that there was some epidemiological evidence of an association between cancer and EMFs, but that there was insufficient information to conclude that EMFs are carcinogenic.[69] The largest research project, expected to be completed by the National Institutes of Health in 1995, will study possible links between childhood leukemia and magnetic fields. In 1993, the EPA also called for both human and animal studies, emphasizing links to higher rates of cancer and reproductive harm to women.

Groups like the Electromagnetic Energy Policy Alliance, however, have characterized many of the studies as "alarmist,"[70] and critics argue that given the nature of possible risk, not enough federal money is going into research. The United States is currently spending about $10 million a year on the problem, with half of that sum supplied primarily by utilities. Some community organizations, like New Jersey–based RAGE (Residents against Giant Electric) are putting pressure on federal officials to fund more research because they fear the government is not telling them the truth about EMFs risks. No one is seriously considering a ban on the use of electricity. Still, despite some degree of uncertainty over the nature and magnitude of risk, many individuals are taking action to limit exposure, and some manufacturers are redesigning their products to reduce EMFs. Sunbeam, for example, made changes in the company's electric blankets to reduce fields, and some computer manufacturers now offer products which claim to reduce EMF exposure from VDTs. Consumers can purchase gaussmeters to measure electromagnetic fields in their homes, offices, or child's schools, although some devices are more reliable than others.[71] The best advice is usually "prudent avoidance"—limiting a child's play with video games, phasing out use of nonessential electric appliances, and moving further away from the screen when watching television, for example. Many of these strategies simply require a change in behavior, such as using a battery-operated clock radio rather than an electric one, or replacing an electric razor with a safety razor.

From a political and regulatory standpoint, there are growing pressures for government agencies to take action. The federal government has, for the most part, abdicated its leadership role to state and local governments, which are taking it upon themselves to develop and implement EMF regulations. Public officials facing the unknown (and worried constituents) have often reacted by enacting ordinances to bar the construction of utility substations, or by banning the placement of transmission lines through residential areas. Several states have adopted field strength limits for new transmission lines, even though many of the regulations lack any scientific basis.

There is no doubt the issue is impacting utility operations. One 1991 study found that EMF concerns have contributed to delays or failures in attempts to site new transmission and distribution facilities in one out of three cases.[72] The EMF issue has also reached the judicial arena. In 1985, Houston Lighting and Power was ordered to pay $25 million in punitive damages because the company had built a transmission line near a school (and in full compliance with Texas law) but with "callous disregard for the safety, health, and well-being of . . . the children." The Texas Court of Appeals later denied the award but affirmed the lower court's finding there are potential health effects associated with exposure to powerline fields. Declining property values are also a potential problem. Approximately ten million acres of land and one million homes lie close enough to a transmission line in the United States to have higher than normal EMF levels. A decline of just 1 percent in property values could amount to a nationwide market loss of $1 billion. As a result, many utilities are changing the design of their distribution circuits and placing more lines underground, measures that may increase costs by as much as $1 billion per year.

The concerns are not limited to the United States. British environmentalists have been extremely active in the anti-EMF debate. In Beckton, East London, for example, a group of citizens campaigned to have a 400-kv transmission line removed because residents feared it was responsible for symptoms ranging from headaches to cancer. Another group in Great Yarmouth was successful in rejecting a proposed transmission line through their area. In Sweden, a new group has formed, the Union of Those Injured by Electricity and Video Display Terminals. Similar disputes are being waged in Western Australia.[73]

What are the policy and political implications of the EMF issue? It has been argued that the public perception of EMF risk is far ahead of scientific knowledge.[74] There is unanimous agreement from all sides that more research is needed to determine the nature and existence of any risk posed by human exposure to EMFs. Even if a risk is determined to exist, the follow-up questions are whether the risk is significant, whether the risk can be reduced, and if so, at what costs. Within the past few years, utility companies, which had previously been on the defensive in the EMF debate, have taken a more proactive approach, communicating directly with consumers and sharing information extensively with other researchers. Some power companies have agreed to measure EMF levels for residential customers, and others have developed extensive public outreach efforts. A 1991 study of sixty-five public and investor-owned utilities found the industry considers the EMF issue "very serious," with one out of five of the companies assigning at least one professional to deal with the issue on a full-time basis.[75] There is also a sociopolitical dimension to the problem, since EMF represents the traditional battle between consumers and large corporations and public agencies—a battle typical of other environmental issues as well.

POLICY AVOIDANCE AND NONDECISIONMAKING

One characteristic common to both EMF and indoor air pollution is they are exemplary of "policy avoidance"—a subject most public officials have managed to finesse for decades without being forced to make policy.[76] This tendency has also been called "nondecisionmaking" —the ways in which problems are kept off the policy agenda, often before they even have a chance to be heard, a problem common to many public policy issues.[77] Why is this so?

First, despite the fact the negative effects of indoor air pollution were identified more than sixty years ago, the pollutants themselves have never been systematically *monitored*. Most research has involved isolated case studies of single pollutants, rather than comprehensive testing of a wide spectrum of irritants. Coupled with the fact most airborne contaminants have a long latency period (the period between first exposure and the manifestation of any health effects), it may take as many as forty years for there to be evidence of any risks from exposure, and evidence may be hidden in interacting causes of disease, such as smoking.[78] The difficulties of *identifying* the nature and extent of the problem allow it to remain unresolved. Even if the monitoring problem were to be dealt with, however, it is unlikely there will be consensus on the risk factor. In the case of radon, for example, there has never been scientific agreement on the dose-response relationship. With EMFs, many studies are inconclusive.

Second, these issues have often been lumped along with a host of other problems routinely labeled as "occupational health" rather than as environmental problems. As such, they may have captured the interest of health professionals, but not the mainstream environmental groups that have been responsible for bringing similar issues to the top of the policy agenda and to the attention of the media. On an already crowded environmental policy agenda, indoor air quality and EMFs have been edged aside by more potent issues. There may also be a concern tackling indoor air quality would increase pressure to weaken ambient air quality standards.

Third, indoor air pollution and EMFs lack the graphic visibility that initially focused attention on urban air quality. There are no tall smokestacks spewing smoke, nor dirty emissions from automobiles and city buses. It has virtually been taken for granted because it cannot be seen, nor, for the most part, smelled, touched, or tasted. Victims do not die overnight, and it is often hard to link their deaths to a specific source or cause. Many homeowners may be reluctant to admit pollution or EMFs have invaded their residences, preferring to believe they are safe there. As a result, policymakers have not been forced to confront angry constituents pointing to a municipal blight and demanding it be shut down. This allows the issue to languish at the bottom of the policy pile, overwhelmed by more "dirty" pollution sources.

Fourth, ambient or "outdoor" air is generally thought of as common property, meaning there is a justification for regulation because all of society benefits from cleaner air. Cleaning up the emissions from one factory improves the air all of us breathe. Not so with indoor air, however, except in "public" spaces. An argument can be made it is the responsibility (financial and moral) of the homeowner or landlord or building owner to maintain whatever interior atmosphere he or she chooses. For that reason, there is less public acceptance of either government intervention and enforcement or promulgation of standards of what constitutes acceptable indoor air quality.

Lastly, although the 1990 Clean Air Act amendments provide the regulatory structure needed to clean up ambient air, there is no similar mechanism in place for indoor air. As is the case with several environmental concerns, indoor air quality comes under the jurisdiction of a multitude of federal agencies, fragmenting responsibility and making coordination difficult. While the EPA has taken the lead, other agencies involved include NIOSH, which investigates problem buildings, OSHA, which is responsible for safeguarding worker health, and the Department of Housing and Urban Development, which has issued regulations on emission limitation in some building materials. Other related concerns are handled by the CPSC, which often issues warnings on products like home radon test kits and humidifiers, and the Federal Home Loan Mortgage Corporation, which sets standards for environmental hazard evaluation when reviewing mortgages backed by the Federal Housing Administration. Interagency research has involved the Department of Education, General Services Administration, and the National Institute for Standards Technology.

More than a half dozen others have also been involved in the controversy, ranging from the General Services Administration and the Department of Energy to the Tennessee Valley Authority, Bonneville Power Administration, the National Bureau of Standards, and the National Aeronautics and Space Administration. At the state level, the New York State Energy Office has been involved in radon research, and California, Maine, Minnesota, New Jersey, Vermont, and Wisconsin have actively pursued antismoking legislation or other efforts to deal with indoor air quality. In addition, there is a professional chasm that exists among those working with ambient air and those specializing in indoor air quality issues. At some agencies, the two technical staffs are isolated from each other, both physically and politically. As a result, there is little sharing of data or research as might be expected in an agency dealing with the general issue of air quality.

With such a wide spectrum of administrators involved, it has been difficult for regulators to come to an agreement on what kinds of indoor air quality standards are needed. Along with jurisdictional disputes and turf battles common to most policy issues are the political ones as well. Attempts to reach consensus on this issue are likely to continue well into the next century as the research community develops further scientific data on the nature and extent of the problem.

The challenge with EMF is for political leaders to avoid succumbing to the hysteria that has often permeated the media, allowing them to jump into the fray before sufficient evidence has been gathered. Setting standards for high-voltage transmission lines, for example, may prove to be both expensive and ineffective. Policymakers have several options before them:

- Do nothing at this point, waiting for the scientific evidence to be more clearly defined.
- Continue scientific investigation and allow the public to make exposure decisions based on the "prudent avoidance" concept.
- Allow the utility industry to take voluntary steps to reduce exposure from EMFs.[79]
- Adopt regulations anyway based on a lack of scientific evidence.

Unfortunately, many legislators and regulators have chosen the last option, feeling administrative convenience (based on numbers that have no scientific basis) is preferable to the political pressures they face from constituents. Rather than routing transmission lines away from residential areas, or redesigning appliances, which are less costly and have at least a minimal scientific rationale, there are some political leaders who prefer to take immediate and dramatically visible action, even if it's wrong.

SUMMARY

Until recently, policymakers have not recognized indoor air pollution as a significant environmental health problem, and attempts to regulate indoor contamination have not been nearly so successful as ambient air controls. Part of the difference is that indoor air pollutants are regulated by a number of federal agencies, each with its own political agenda and clientele. One notable exception has been the involvement of various industry groups that have drawn up their own standards, primarily based on ventilation. Other indoor pollution hazards, such as radon, environmental tobacco smoke, asbestos, and electromagnetic radiation, are still being researched to determined the nature of the risk they pose for human exposure. What makes indoor pollution unique among environmental protection issues is that the topic has never captured the interest of organizations as have other problems like water quality and endangered species. Aside from a handful of specialized organizations representing victims, indoor air pollution is still struggling to gain the attention of mainstream groups.

NOTES

1. U.S. Congress, House, Committee on Education and Labor, Subcommittee on Health and Safety, *Legislative Hearings on H.R. 1066, The Indoor Air Quality Act of 1991*, hearing, 102nd Cong., 1st sess., June 26, July 10, 17, 24, 31, 1991 (Washington, DC: U.S. Government Printing Office, 1991), 4.

2. U.S. Environmental Protection Agency, *Comparing the Risks and Setting Environmental Priorities* (Washington, DC: Office of Policy, Planning, and Evaluation, 1989).

3. The findings are reported in W. R. Ott, "Human Exposure to Environmental Pollutants" (Paper presented at the Eighty-first Annual Meeting of the Air Pollution Control Association, June 1988).

4. Paul Brodeur, "Annals of Radiation," *The New Yorker*, July 9, 1990, 38.

5. Alan Hedge, "Statement and Comments on H.R. 1066, The Indoor Air Quality Act of 1991," in *Hearings*, 187–97.

6. R. W. Bell et al., *The 1990 Toronto Personal Exposure Pilot Study* (Toronto: Ontario Ministry of the Environment, 1991), 18.

7. See Gray Robertson, "Building Related Illnesses," in *Clearing the Air: Perspectives on Environmental Tobacco Smoke*, ed. Robert D. Tollison (Lexington, MA: D.C. Heath, 1988), 30–32.

8. John D. Spengler and Ken Sexton, "Indoor Air Pollution: A Public Health Perspective," *Science* 221 (July 1, 1983): 9–16.

9. For a summary of the methodology of investigating and monitoring indoor air quality, see John F. McCarthy, David W. Berg, and John D. Spengler, "Assessment of Indoor Air Quality," in *Indoor Air Pollution: A Health Perspective*, ed. Jonathan M. Samet and John D. Spengler. (Baltimore: Johns Hopkins University Press, 1991), 82–108.

10. See, for example, B. C. Wolverton, Rebecca C. McDonald, and E. A. Watkins, "Foliage Plants for Removing Indoor Air Pollutants from Energy-Efficient Homes," *Economic Botany* 38 (April–June 1984): 224–28.

11. For a complete description of commercially available monitoring equipment and the use of monitoring plans, see Niren L. Nagda, Harry E. Rector, and Michael D. Koontz, *Guidelines for Monitoring Indoor Air Quality* (Washington, DC: Hemisphere, 1987).

12. See "Ventilation and Problem Buildings: A Self-Serving Approach?" *Indoor Air Bulletin* 1, no. 1 (May 1991): 1.

13. For a sampling of ASHRAE standards, see *Thermal Environmental Conditions for Human Occupancy*. ASHRAE 55-1981, and *Ventilation for Acceptable Indoor Air Quality*, ASHRAE 62-1989. The organization also publishes guidelines for contractors and developers, *Energy Efficient Design of New Buildings Except New Low-Rise Residential Buildings*, ASHRAE 90.1-1989.

14. Dennis F. Naugle and Terrence K. Pierson, "A Framework for Risk Characterization of Environmental Pollutants," *Journal of the Air Waste Management Association* 41, no. 10 (October 1991): 1298.

15. See Kirk Smith, *Biofuels, Air Pollution and Health* (New York: Plenum Press, 1987). Smith advocates use of a "total exposure assessment" (TEA) as a way of reducing pollution levels in developing countries. See also "Air Pollution: Assessing Total Exposure in Developing Countries," *Environment* 30, no. 10 (December 1988): 16–20, 28–35.

16. See Laurence S. Kirsch, "Behind Closed Doors: Indoor Air Pollution and Government Policy," *Harvard Environmental Law Review* 6 (1982): 339–94.

17. Michael Weisskopf, "Pollution Strikes the EPA," *Discover*, January 1989, 32–33.

18. For an example of this literature, see Robert D. Tollison ed., *Clearing the Air: Perspectives on Environmental Tobacco Smoke* (Lexington, MA: D.C. Heath 1988). The book was supported by Philip Morris, Inc.

19. Many of these studies are outlined in the proceedings of the International Symposium on Tobacco Smoke at McGill University in 1989. See Donald J. Ecobichon and Joseph M. Wu, eds., *Environmental Tobacco Smoke* (Lexington, MA: D.C. Heath, 1990). See also Jonathan M. Samet, William S. Cain, and Brian P. Leaderer, "Environmental Tobacco Smoke," in *Indoor Air Pollution: A Health Perspective*, ed.

Jonathan M. Samet and John D. Spengler (Baltimore: Johns Hopkins University Press, 1991), 131–69; M. L. Slattery et al., "Cigarette Smoking and Exposure to Passive Smoke Are Risk Factors for Cervical Cancer," *Journal of the American Medical Association* 261 (1989): 1593–98.

20. See Hans Ole Hein, Poul Suadicani, and Peder Skov, "Indoor Dust Exposure: An Unnoticed Aspect of Involuntary Smoking," *Archives of Environmental Health* 46 (March–April 1991): 98–101.

21. Shirley J. Hansen, *Managing Indoor Air Quality* (Lilburn, GA: Fairmont Press, 1991), 61.

22. Gray Robertson, "Indoor Pollution: Sources, Effects, and Mitigation Strategies," in *Environmental Tobacco Smoke*, ed. Donald J. Ecobichon and Joseph M. Wu (Lexington, MA: D.C. Heath, 1990).

23. U.S. Public Health Service, "The Health Consequences of Involuntary Smoking," *Surgeon General's Report* (1986).

24. See Alyson Pytte, "Tobacco's Clout Stays Strong through Dollars, Jobs, Ads," *Congressional Quarterly Weekly Report*, May 19, 1990, 1542–48.

25. See "Ten Year Lobbying Effort Results in Smoking Ban on Most U.S. Flights," *Aviation Week and Space Technology*, October 23, 1989, 71; and "Leave the Butts Behind," *Time*, October 30, 1989, 59.

26. See Andrew Skolnick, "Jails Lead Prisons in Smoking Bans," *Journal of the American Medical Association* 264 (September 26, 1990): 1514. The American Jailers Association passed a resolution calling for all U.S. jails to be smoke free.

27. Seth Shulman, "Global Smoke Out," *Technology Review* 94 (May–June 1991): 20–21. See also Marsha F. Goldsmith, "Fight against Tobacco Addiction Moving into International Arena," *Journal of the American Medical Association* 263 (June 11, 1990): 2989–90.

28. See Phyllida Brown, "Cancer Threat Prompts China to Curb Smoking," *New Scientist*, August 25, 1990, 15.

29. "Europe Tries to Clear the Air," *Business Week*, February 12, 1990, 14.

30. For an account of what happened at "the most radioactive house in America" see Michael Lafovore, *Radon: The Invisible Threat* (Emmaus, PA: Rodale Press, 1987).

31. Kenneth L. Jackson, Joseph P. Geraci, and David Bodansky, "Observations of Lung Cancer: Evidence Relating Lung Cancer to Radon Exposure," in *Indoor Radon and Its Hazards*, ed. David Bodansky, Maurice A. Robkin, and David R. Stadler (Seattle: University of Washington Press, 1987), 91–111.

32. See Jonathan M. Samet, "Radon," in Samet and Spengler, 342.

33. *Evaluation of Occupational and Environmental Exposures to Radon and Radon Daughters in the United States*. National Council on Radiation Protection and Measurements, NCRP Report No. 78, May 1984.

34. U.S. Environmental Protection Agency, *A Citizen's Guide to Radon: What It Is and What to Do about It*, Pamphlet no. OPA 86-004 (Washington, DC: Government Printing Office, August 1986).

35. Some researchers now use a different method of expressing exposure, systeme international (SI) units. In SI units, the concentration of radon in air is expressed as Becquerels per cubic meter (Bq/m^3); 1 WL corresponds to 3.7 X 10^3 Bq/m^3. See Samet, "Radon," 342.

36. David Bodansky, Maurice A. Robkin, and David A. Stadler, eds., *Indoor Radon and Its Hazards* (Seattle: University of Washington Press, 1987), 14–15. For a slightly different perspective, see Philip H. Abelson, "Radon Today: The Role of Flimflam in Public Policy," *Regulation* 14, no. 4 (Fall 1991): 95–100.

37. This is not to say, however, that Congress has not investigated the issue. See U.S. Congress, Senate, Committee on Environment and Public Works, Subcommittee on

Superfund, Ocean and Water Protection, *Pending Radon and Indoor Air Legislation*, hearing, 102nd Cong., 1st Sess., May 8, 1991 (Washington, DC: U.S. Government Printing Office, 1991).

38. See Judith E. Cook and Daniel J. Egan, Jr., "Mitigation," in *Environmental Radon*, ed. C. Richard Cothern (New York: Plenum Press, 1987), 249–72.

39. For an explanation of why radon has failed to attract more interest among policymakers, see Denise Scheberle, "Stalking the Deadly Intruder: Agenda-Setting for Radon" (Paper presented to the 1992 Annual Meeting of the Western Political Science Association, San Francisco, March 20, 1992).

40. For a complete history of the development of knowledge about asbestosis, see Barry I. Castleman, *Asbestos: Medical and Legal Aspects* (Englewood Cliffs, NJ: Prentice Hall Law and Business, 1990).

41. The story is retold in Irving J. Selikoff and Morris Greenberg, "A Landmark Case in Asbestosis," *Journal of the American Medical Association* 265 (February 20, 1991): 898.

42. This view is taken by Brooke T. Mossman and J. Bernard L. Gee in "Asbestos-Related Diseases," *New England Journal of Medicine* 320 (June 29, 1989): 1721.

43. Kirsch, "Behind Closed Doors," 369.

44. Castleman, *Asbestos*, 424.

45. Ibid., 663.

46. See Diana Goodish, "Asbestos Exposure in Schools," *Journal of School Health* 59, no. 8 (October 1989): 362–63.

47. Louis S. Richman, "Why Throw Money on Asbestos?" *Fortune*, June 6, 1988, 155.

48. Jay Mathews, "To Yank or Not to Yank? *Newsweek*, April 13, 1992, 59. Death from exposure to asbestos in buildings is estimated to be highly unlikely. You are more likely to be struck and killed by lightning (3 in 100,000 cases) or die in motor vehicle accidents (400 per 100,000) than die from asbestos exposure in a school building (1 per 100,000).

49. Warren E. Leary, "Appeals Court Strikes Down Major Parts of Federal Asbestos Ban," *New York Times*, October 22, 1991, A-20.

50. "Damaged Material in 501,000 Buildings, Potential Worker Hazard, Seen in EPA Report," *Occupational Safety and Health Reporter*, March 9, 1988.

51. Castleman, *Asbestos*, 664–67.

52. Brooke T. Mossman et al., "Asbestos: Scientific Developments and Implications for Public Policy," *Science* 247 (January 19, 1990): 294.

53. For an account of the litigation involving the asbestos industry, see Paul Brodeur, *Outrageous Misconduct: The Asbestos Industry on Trial* (New York: Pantheon Books, 1985).

54. Castleman, *Asbestos*, 696–97.

55. "Canadian Asbestos: Export and Die?" *The Economist*, September 26, 1987, 82–83.

56. Paul Rauber, "New Life for White Death," *Sierra* 76, no. 5 (September–October 1991): 63–111.

57. Mossman et al., "Asbestos," 294.

58. Castleman, *Asbestos*, 675.

59. C. Andrew Bassett, "Premature Alarm over Electromagnetic Fields," *Issues in Science and Technology* 6 (Spring 1990): 37–39.

60. The first utility studies were those funded by the American Electric Power Company at Johns Hopkins University in 1962, one of lineworkers and one of mice exposed to strong electric fields. The Bonneville Power Administration has done significant livestock studies, and Southern California Edison has been involved in several

research projects. The Electric Power Research Institute (EPRI) has been involved with EMF research at its Massachusetts facility since 1975. Despite the fact that it is funded by utilities, which have an obvious stake in the outcome of any findings, the group is considered to be one of the most reputable in the country. See "Exploring the Options for Magnetic Field Management," *EPRI Journal*, October–November 1990.

61. For a comprehensive and objective view of the most significant studies, see Gordon L. Hester, "Electric and Magnetic Fields: Managing an Uncertain Risk," *Environment* 34, no. 1 (January–February 1992): 6–11, 25–32. See also U.S. Congress, Office of Technology Assessment, *Biological Effects of Power Frequency Electric and Magnetic Fields—Background Paper*, OTA-BP-E-53 (Washington, DC: U.S. Government Printing Office, May, 1989).

62. Nancy Wertheimer and Ed Leeper, "Electrical Wiring Configurations and Childhood Cancer," *American Journal of Epidemiology*.109 (March 1979): 273.

63. Samuel Milham, Jr., "Mortality from Leukemia in Workers Exposed to Electrical and Magnetic Fields," *New England Journal of Medicine* 307, no. 4 (July 22, 1982): 249. The study examined all deaths of Washington State men twenty years and older from 1950 to 1979, coded by occupation and cause of death. Most of the deaths to leukemia occurred in men working in aluminum reduction processing and as arc welders, motion picture projectionists, and hydroelectric generating plant employees.

64. See for example, R. S. Lin et al., "Occupational Exposure to Electromagnetic Fields and the Occurrence of Brain Tumors: An Analysis of Possible Associations," *Journal of Occupational Medicine* 27 (1985): 413–15, and T. L. Thomas et al., "Brain Tumor Mortality Risk among Men with Electrical and Electronics Jobs: A Case-Control Study," *Journal of the National Cancer Institute* 799 (1987): 233–36.

65. Becker has published several books on the subject, including *The Body Electric: Electromagnetism and the Foundation of Life* (New York: Morrow, 1985), and *Cross Currents: The Promise of Electromedicine, the Perils of Electropollution* (Los Angeles: Jeremy P. Tarcher, 1990).

66. See for example J. Fulton et al., "Electrical Wiring Configurations and Childhood Leukemia in Rhode Island," *American Journal of Epidemiology* 11 (1980): 292–96.

67. Stephanie London et al., "Exposure to Residential Electric and Magnetic Fields and Risk of Childhood Leukemia," *American Journal of Epidemiology* 134 (1991): 923–37.

68. U.S. Environmental Protection Agency, *An Evaluation of the Potential Carcinogenicity of Electromagnetic Fields: Review Draft*, EPA/600/6-90/005B. (Washington, DC, October 1990).

69. U.S. Environmental Protection Agency, *An SAB Report: Potential Carcinogenicity of Electric and Magnetic Fields* (Washington, DC, January 1992).

70. A general summary of the views of environmental groups, health experts, and industry analysts can be found in U.S. Congress, House, Committee on Interior and Insular Affairs, Subcommittee on General Oversight and Investigations, *Electric Powerlines: Health and Public Policy Implications*, hearing, 101st Cong., 2nd sess., March 8, 1990 (Washington, DC: U.S. Government Printing Office, 1990).

71. Cynthia Hacinli, "A Gauss in the House," *Garbage* 4, no. 1 (January–February 1992): 38–43.

72. "Utilities Agree: The EMF Issue Is 'Very Serious,' " *Electrical World* 256 (September 1991): 14.

73. See "International EMF," *Microwave News*, May–June, 1991, 3.

74. Hester, "Electric and Magnetic Fields," 30.

75. "Utilities Agree: The EMF Issue Is 'Very Serious,' " 14.

76. See, for example, Charlotte Twight, "From Claiming Credit to Avoiding Blame: The Evolution of Congressional Strategy for Asbestos Management," *Journal of Public Policy* 2, no. 8 (September 1991).

77. See Peter Bachrach and Morton S. Baratz, *Power and Poverty* (New York: Oxford University Press, 1970).

78. The problems of identifying workplace illnesses are identified in Laura Punnett, "Airborne Contaminants in the Workplace," in *To Breathe Freely: Risk, Consent and Air*, ed. Mary Gibson (Totowa, NJ: Rowman & Allanheld, 1985): 31–51.

79. This policy is outlined in M. Granger Morgan et al., "Controlling Exposure to Transmission Line Electromagnetic Fields: A Regulatory Approach That Is Compatible with the Available Science," *Public Utilities Fortnightly*, March 17, 1988, 49–58.

FOR FURTHER READING

David Bodansky et al., eds. *Indoor Radon and Its Hazards*. Seattle: University of Washington Press, 1987.

Paul Brodeur. *Currents of Death*. New York: Simon & Schuster, 1989.

Paul Brodeur. *Outrageous Misconduct: The Asbestos Industry on Trial*. New York: Pantheon Books, 1985.

Barry I. Castleman. *Asbestos: Medical and Legal Aspects*. Prentice-Hall, Englewood Cliffs, NJ: 1990.

Frank B. Cross. *Legal Responses to Indoor Air Pollution*. Westport, CT: Quorum Books, 1990.

Shirley J. Hansen. *Managing Indoor Air Quality*. Lilburn, GA: Fairmont Press, 1991.

Michael Lafovore. *Radon: The Invisible Threat*. Emmaus, PA: Rodale Press, 1987.

Jonathan M. Samet and John D. Spangler. *Indoor Air Pollution: A Health Perspective*. Baltimore: Johns Hopkins University Press, 1991.

PART 5

Globalized Environmental Issues

CHAPTER 11

Oceans: The Largest Environment

> The use of the sea and air is common to all; neither can any title to
> the ocean belong to any people or private man, for as such as neither
> nature nor regard of the public use permitted any possession thereof.
> —Queen Elizabeth I, 1580[1]

The news about the oceans is not good. The headlines of the 1990s have been filled with stories of medical waste washing up on beaches along the Atlantic coast, of deadly red tides and algal blooms along the Adriatic, and of Filipinos starving due to the loss of fish from threatened coral reefs. Once thought of as an abundant and virtually limitless resource, the reality is that the oceans of the world have been damaged and ravaged to a point where emergency action must now be taken to restore them.

Three-quarters of the planet's surface is covered with seawater, causing one observer to suggest that "Planet Water" is a more accurate title than "Planet Earth." For centuries, the oceans have played a central role in human development, serving as a transportation network, as a food source, and as a spiritual element in many cultures. But the oceans have also served as humanity's dumping ground, and except for the past twenty to thirty years, we have ignored the results of our actions. Waste thrown into the ocean simply floated away, sank, got eaten by marine creatures, was dissolved, or otherwise disappeared from view. Because the world's oceans are so vast, the common belief was that they could assimilate waste without significant harm. "The solution to pollution is dilution"—just dispose of wastes far enough from shore and dilution would make them disappear. The oceans are what is commonly known as a common pool resource, a term used by biologist Garrett Hardin in his 1968 essay, "The Tragedy of the Commons."[2] Using as an analogy the medieval practice of grazing cattle on an open pasture, Hardin theorized that each individual livestock herder would graze as many cattle on the pasture (the commons) as possible, acting purely from economic self-interest. The result, of course, would be overgrazing of the commons to the point where all the herds would starve. The metaphor is applicable to the marine environment as well. For years, waste and chemicals have been dumped into the oceans with little thought as to the eventual result for all who use it as a resource. The marine environment that makes up the oceans of Earth is not a static one, but rather an ever-changing, dynamic system. It is affected by both physical and chemical changes as substances are added to it, intentionally and otherwise. The ocean environment is also affected by another common pool—the atmosphere—so that changes in one affects the other. In this cycle, water evaporates from the surface of the ocean, is carried by the winds over the continents, where it falls to Earth as rain, which then enters the oceans again from streams and rivers. Pollution of the atmosphere thus becomes a common pool problem as well.[3]

This chapter takes a look at this largest environment of all, the oceans, and the problems that threaten its existence. Three issues are at the forefront of the oceanic agenda: marine pollution, overfishing, and the destruction of coral reefs. The chapter also reviews the international agreements and regimes that have been developed to try to protect marine resources.

MARINE POLLUTION: SOURCES AND EFFECTS

The small coastal town of Minamata, Japan, brought worldwide attention to marine pollution in the early 1950s. Starting about 1953, the town's cats began to die of some mysterious ailment, and residents contracted severe neurological diseases. Between 1953 and 1968, thousands of residents suffered severe permanent nerve damage or died, with the cause later traced to the consumption of seafood contaminated with dimethyl mercury. A manufacturing plant on the shores of the bay was suspected as being the source of the mercury poisoning, but tests revealed it discharged only modest quantities of inorganic mercury, which was relatively safe. It took fourteen years for Swedish scientists to conclude that fish and shellfish in the bay had somehow stored mercury from the facility in their flesh, which had then been eaten by the residents and their cats. The Japanese government, in what became its most notorious environmental disaster, agreed to award compensation to the Minamata victims, but has been slow in doing so.[4]

The incident led to a global call for a more complete understanding of the oceanic food web and the man-made pollution that threatens the marine environment. Since then, oceanographers, biologists, meteorologists and politicians have developed a different perspective on the ocean, viewing it as one large ecosystem. Some environmental issues affect the "blue water" deep oceans, while others impact coastal zones, which include estuaries, deltas, reefs, and the continental shelf. One of the most important problems that affects both is marine pollution, which can be categorized as follows:

Floating Debris

The incidence of pieces of plastic, fishing nets, bottles, and other nonbiodegradable materials is alarming many marine biologists. Studies have shown that many marine species have become entangled, and then drowned and choked on human debris that is discarded into the ocean, such as plastic rings from six packs of soda or beer. Indiscriminate discharges by fishing vessels as well as beachgoers pose a significant threat to marine mammals and birds.

Petroleum

An estimated four million tons of petroleum products are discharged annually into the ocean, partially from shipping operations or bilge washings, although a significant amount also comes from land-based industrial charges that find their way to the sea and some natural seepage. Nearly 70 percent of the world's petroleum output is transported by sea, making tanker spills an additional source of oil pollution worldwide.

Nutrients

One of the most difficult coastal pollution problems to deal with comes from an overload of nutrients, primarily nitrogen and phosphorous from sewage, agricultural runoff, and erosion, which overfertilize an area. The problem grows along with the world's population. The resulting algal blooms deplete oxygen as they decay, leading to mass kills of fish and other marine invertebrates, and making beaches unsafe for swimming.

Heavy Metals and Trace Elements

These pollutants are usually found in coastal zones, and include lead, mercury, aluminum, copper, and zinc. The source is usually local industrial facilities. Excessive concentrations can lead to a variety of health ailments.

Radiation

From 1946 to 1970, the United States was among the nations that routinely dumped steel drums of low-level radioactive waste off the Atlantic and Pacific coasts. A legacy of weapons testing, radioactive isotopes have been found in fish harvested from open oceans, although levels of radiation have declined as the testing programs ended. A more contemporary concern is the danger of radiation leakage into coastal zones adjacent to nuclear power plants, although this has not been shown to be a problem at U.S. power plants.

Dredged Materials

In order to keep maritime shipping lanes open, ports and harbors are regularly dredged of their natural sand and sediments, which are dumped in deeper waters. The dredged spoil, as it is known, may be contaminated by toxic metals and chemicals, which then contaminate the marine life where they are dumped.

Toxic Chemicals

Synthetic organic compounds pose a threat when they are taken up through the food chain and become a human health hazard when accumulated in food fish. Those most affected are fishermen and coastal residents who depend upon fish as a primary food source.

Marine pollution poses a number of serious environmental policy issues that are complicated by the nature of the oceans themselves. First, there is a great deal of uncertainty about the short- and long-term effects of ocean pollution. Scientists are still not sure of the potential impacts on human health, or of the ability of the oceans to adapt to change. There is a great deal of evidence that suggests that the marine food chain is very easily disrupted, and that any major changes could affect the chemical balance that exists between marine organisms and seawater.

Second, many policymakers are grappling with the issue of what to do about waste generally. Is it better to dispose of man-made waste on land, which is expensive but where it can be confined, or dump it in the ocean, which is free but where the effects are unknown? Or is it better yet to minimize the generation of waste by changing industrial processes or recycling? As the volume of waste grows, and as land-based disposal becomes less acceptable and costly for urban residents (a subject that was discussed in Chapter 5), ocean dumping begins to look somewhat more attractive, although in the long run it may be the most costly alternative.[5]

Third, the marine pollution issue is not just what is dumped into the oceans, but also the effect it has on coastal zones and beaches. Millions of dollars of tourist business are estimated to be lost every time beaches are closed because of pollution of when debris washes ashore. The problem became a key issue in the 1988 presidential campaign, and continues to plague Boston Harbor.[6]

Although there is no international body that regularly monitors the ocean's health, several organizations and agreements have been established to gather information and make recommendations. There is, however, no true global assessment of whether or not the ocean environment is truly endangered. In

1972, the United Nations Conference on the Human Environment recommended that there be an overall assessment of global oceanic health, which later was adopted as the Global Investigation of Pollution in the Marine Environment (GIPME) program. GIPME's objective is to assess, regulate, and monitor marine pollution, as well as to develop research activities. One of the most common local monitoring efforts is through the observation of various organisms and their response to pollutants. Petroleum pollution has been monitored in the Wider Caribbean, which includes the Gulf of Mexico, the Straits of Florida, and the eastern approaches to the Caribbean Sea, by the World Meteorological Organization's Marine Pollution Monitoring Pilot Project. The group analyzes tar on beaches, floating tar, and dissolved/dispersed petroleum hydrocarbons. Other research is being conducted by the UN's Global Environment Monitoring System, the International Council for the Exploration of the Sea, which studies contamination of fish and shellfish, and the Baltic Monitoring Programme, which began in 1979 among the seven Baltic Sea states.

MARINE REGIMES

A number of international agreements have been developed to protect the ocean environment from pollution, with varying degrees of effectiveness. Initially, these agreements were focused on oil spills, a very visual marine pollution problem. In the 1950s and 1960s, eight of the nine multilateral agreements signed involved oil pollution; from 1970 to 1985, only thirteen of thirty-six dealt with oil.[7] Oil tanker spills have attracted environmental interest even though they account for only 12 percent of global marine oil pollution. But it is the image of oil-soaked birds and tar on beaches that captures the public's (and thus policymakers') attention much more than dry statistics. The environmental damage caused by highly publicized spills like the Torrey Canyon in 1967, the Amoco Cadiz in 1978, or the Exxon Valdez in 1989 often pale in comparison to less publicized ones like the 1972 Sea Star spill in the Gulf of Oman and an incident off South Africa's coast involving the supertanker Castello de Belver in 1983.

One of the first agreements was the 1954 International Convention for the Prevention of the Pollution of the Sea by Oil, which was limited to a zone fifty miles from any coast, and had no enforcement capabilities. It was replaced in 1973 by the International Convention for the Prevention of Pollution by Ships, also known as the MARPOL Convention, which set limits on discharges from land and at sea for various pollutants. An addition to the MARPOL Convention, Annex V, prohibited the discharge of plastics by ships effective in January 1989. In 1972, the Convention on the Prevention of Marine Pollution by Dumping of Wastes and Other Matter, more commonly called the London Dumping Convention (LDC), set limitations on the disposal of many pollutants at sea, including high-level radioactive waste at sea. In 1988, the accord was modified to prohibit ocean incineration of toxic substances by 1994. The agreement is administered by the International Maritime Organization (formerly called the Intergovernmental Maritime Consultative Organization, or IMCO). The LDC prohibits the dumping of certain hazardous substances and establishes a five-tier permit system for other types of ocean dumping, and keeps records of all dump sites throughout the world. In the United States, the permit process is administered by the Environmental Protection Agency under the Marine Protection, Research, and Sanctuaries Act of 1972.

In 1972, the United Nations Environment Programme chose the oceans as one if the priority areas in which it would focus efforts to fulfill its coordinating role, and in 1974, it established the Regional Seas Programme. The program covers ten regions and involves more than 120 coastal states, as seen in Table 11.1. What sets this issue apart in terms of environmental protection is that it is one of the few global environmental problems where a regional approach has been taken, rather than a global one. Typically, a group will begin with a framework convention (as is the case with East Asia and South Asia), followed by progressive agreements to establish scientific cooperation and monitoring efforts.

The first major project of the group was the Mediterranean Action Plan (MedPlan), adopted in 1975 in Barcelona, to prevent, abate, and combat pollution of the Mediterranean Sea, and to enhance the marine environment of the area. The MedPlan includes participation by all eighteen Mediterranean nations (including Israel and Lebanon), which coordinate their pollution control practices and sponsor joint research programs. The accord covers oil and marine dumping and well as land-based sources of marine pollution, such as agricultural spraying, and municipal and industrial wastes. It is considered to be a model for other international conventions, and for the other nine regions of the Regional Seas Programme.[8] Despite the lengthy nature of regional negotiations, these

Table 11.1   UNEP Regional Seas Program Agreements

Area	Dates Adopted
Mediterranean	1976, 1980, 1981, 1982
Persian Gulf/Gulf of Oman	1978, 1989, 1990
West and Central Africa	1981
Southeast Pacific	1981, 1983, 1989
Red Sea and Gulf of Aden	1982
Wider Caribbean	1983, 1990
East Africa	1985
South Pacific	1986
East Asia	Draft Convention
South Asia	Draft Convention

Source: World Resources Institute, *World Resources 1992–93.* New York: Oxford University Press, 1992, p. 183.

regimes have managed to overcome intense animosities among individual countries to form alliances, as seen in agreements formed by the United States and Cuba, Iran and Iraq, and Israel and Syria.[9]

In 1982, after nearly ten tumultuous years of negotiation, the UN Convention on the Law of the Sea was formulated as a major treaty defining the economic uses of the sea. The convention granted coastal nations the right to control resource development within two hundred miles of their shores, but obligated them, in exchange for that right, to protect the marine environment within those boundaries. The document also encourages the development and transfer of marine technology from industrialized to less developed countries. The most controversial portion of the document was a provision creating an International Seabed Authority that would cooperatively mine the seabed for minerals if it became economically attractive to do so. Under the international agreement, private mining ventures would be licensed and a share of the profits given to developing countries. The United States, Germany, and the United Kingdom chose not to ratify the treaty, in large part due to provisions dealing with what they felt was exploitation of the sea floor, even though such mining is unlikely to occur for decades. To date, the convention has not received the approval of the minimum of sixty nations required to ratify it, but there is some hope that the seabed provisions can be eliminated in order to gain full ratification.[10]

OVERFISHING

One of the earliest occupations, fishing contributes significantly to the economic development of Third World countries as well as being a major source of income for industrialized nations. Fishing is a major base for employment and is a principal food source for many developing nations as well. In Southeast Asia, fish makes up 55 percent of the residents' annual intake of animal protein, and 19 percent in Africa. In some developing countries, fish is the only real source of "meat."

There are approximately thirty thousand species of fish in the world's oceans, and their numbers are estimated to be in the billions. At one time, the great sea fisheries were considered to be inexhaustible, and statistics on the number of fish caught each year have been rising, in some decades very dramatically. In 1900, for example, the world catch was four million metric tons; between 1950 and 1970, the figures rose from twenty-one million metric tons to seventy million annually. But by the late 1960s and 1970s, scientists began to realize that the catch levels were just barely increasing, even with technological advances like fish-finding instruments and improved fishing gear.

In 1990, the total global fish catch declined for the first time in thirteen years. The UN's Food and Agriculture Organization (FAO), which monitors world fishing harvests, reported a total catch of 99.6 million metric tons of fish, crustaceans, and mollusks in 1989, but only 95.2 million in 1990. The FAO reported that most traditional marine fish stocks have reached full exploitation, meaning that an intensified fishing effort is unlikely to produce an increase in catch. The FAO divides the ocean into seventeen major fishing areas, and its study shows that between 1988 and 1990, the fish catch declined in nine areas, remained stable in three, and increased in five. Four of the areas are now classified as overfished. The largest decreases occurred in the Southeast Pacific, which is heavily influenced by the anchovy catch off Peru, and in the Northeast Atlantic off Europe, where the most commercially valuable species are found.

Fishermen in the United States have been affected for the last fifteen years. Since 1977, when the United States extended its jurisdiction to two hundred nautical miles, 30 percent of the species, stocks, or species groups caught by U.S. fishermen have declined. Nearly two-thirds of U.S. fish species are fully or overexploited. In 1990, the Massachusetts Offshore Groundfish Task Force found that landings of commercially valuable fish, such as cod, haddock, and flounder, had reached their lowest reported levels, resulting in a loss of $350 million in income and fourteen thousand jobs.[11]

Peru was one of the first nations to experience a massive, economic loss due to overfishing by its anchovy fleet. In the early 1950s, the catch was minimal, but by 1960 it became the world's largest fishery. Ten years later, over twelve million metric tons of anchovy were captured in Peruvian waters, representing nearly a fifth of the world's total fish catch. Peru capitalized on the anchovy catch (which was used as high-protein feed for poultry and pigs) and made it the nation's number one export. Environmental groups pressed for a 9.5-million ton limit on the yearly catch, but by 1972 the catch plummeted to less than half that amount, and by 1980 dropped to only three-quarters of a ton. Part of the blame was placed on El Nino—changes in the weather and currents off the Pacific coast in 1972–73 that caused a mild winter, warm spring, and water shortages in the Pacific Northwest—but overfishing was a key element of the decline.[12] No significant recovery of fish (or the Peruvian economy) has taken place since then. Similar fates are behind the loss of the Pacific sardine fishery in the 1940s and the halibut catch in the mid-nineteenth century.[13]

Complicating the problem is the use of drift nets, nets that hang vertically like curtains in the open ocean and stretch for twenty to forty miles, sweeping an area the size of Ohio. The nets are suspended by floats at the ocean's surface, and catch fish by their gills as they attempt to swim through. In addition to being extremely efficient at catching fish, the drift nets also capture marine mammals, birds, and nontarget fish. Between three hundred thousand and one million cetaceans, mainly dolphins, were killed by drift nets worldwide between 1988 and 1989. Drift nets were blamed for a 1988 crash in the Alaska pink salmon fishery, when only twelve million fish, rather than an expected forty million, were taken by Alaskan trawlers.[14]

A number of factors led to an increase in the use of drift nets in the mid- and late 1980s within the Asian fishing industry. Initially, many of the trawlers used a seine in search of squid, but as supplies dwindled, the boats ventured further into the Pacific to catch salmon and tuna, and began using drift nets. The fishing industry worldwide was caught in a cost crunch as seafood demand rose but prices plummeted, and crews demanded higher wages at a time of labor shortages. By the end of the decade, there was a glut on the seafood market, and many large companies found they had overextended themselves by investing in massive cannery operations.[15] In recognition of the impact of driftnet fishing, the UN General Assembly and several regional conventions have called for limitations or a total ban. South Pacific region nations agreed to restricted driftnet use in November 1989, and in December, 1989, the UN urged major fishing nations to accept a moratorium on high seas drift netting as of June 1992. The European Economic Community and the United States imposed bans on the use of drift nets within their waters, but Japan and Korea, two of the major users of drift nets, did not bow to international pressure until late 1991 to stop drift netting in the South Pacific.[16] Taiwan continued the practice despite pressure from environmental organizations and the threat of UN sanctions.[17]

The United States has entered into more international agreements pertaining to fish than it has for any other type of wildlife, beginning with a 1923 agreement with Canada to protect the Pacific halibut fishery. Current agreements focus on the management of a particular fishery so as to achieve its maximum sustainable yield. The overriding legislative basis for regulating overfishing, however, is the Fishery Conservation and Management Act, passed in 1976, which gives the United States exclusive management authority over not only fish, but all other forms of marine animal and plant life other than marine mammals, birds, and highly migratory species. One of the key provisions of the legislation is a requirement that each of the eight Regional Fishery Management Councils, composed of both state and federal officials, develop comprehensive species management plans for the fish in its region. Foreign fishing is prohibited in all areas where the United States claims jurisdiction unless there is an international agreement in effect. This obligates foreign nations, and their vessels, to abide by U.S. regulations, including permit fees, catch limits, and inspections. But it also requires the secretary of state, upon a request from the secretary of commerce, to initiate agreements with other nations to secure American fishing fleets "equitable access" to the fishery conservation zones established by other countries.[18]

Although political agreements are one way to deal with the problem of overfishing and drift net use, there is some evidence that treaties alone are not enough. The United States is using satellites to monitor compliance with the drift-net restrictions as part of the bilateral agreements with Japan and South Korea. Fishing boats using drift nets are required to carry radio transmitters so their movements can be tracked to detect fishing in waters that are off-limits. Coast Guard officials are given authority under the agreements to board and detain suspicious ships if necessary, a system that has proved successful in preventing fishing by pirate vessels.[19]

Scientists are also exploring a variety of ways in which the ocean environment can be better understood and managed. One of these methods is the large marine ecosystem (LME) concept. An LME is a broad geographic region distinguished by a self-contained food web and by oceanographic properties such as currents and surface temperatures. LME management involves the collection of a vast amount of data on the number of species in the region, the effects of pollution, the nature of the food chain, and what oceanographic factors influence marine animals and plants. So far, LME management is practiced in only one region—the Southern Ocean—by the nations that are signatories to the convention for the Conservation of Antarctic Marine Living Resources (CAMLR), signed in 1982. The parties who have signed the CAMLR have agreed to regulate fishing to maintain all ecological relationships and have set up a structure to obtain data on all Antarctic species. The ecosystem approach is considered the wave of the future by many experts in international law, despite obstacles such as a lack of funds for gathering information.[20]

DESTRUCTION OF CORAL REEFS

One of the newest marine environmental issues is the potential destruction of coral reefs, which form natural breakwaters around islands in many parts of the world. Coral reefs are living organisms made up of calcium carbonate, which grow just a few feet under the ocean's surface. They need to be near the surface in order to provide adequate sunlight for the algae that live in their tissues. The coral and algae live in a symbiotic relationship—the coral providing shelter and the algae providing essential nutrients for their host. Their destruction is tied to a number of factors, many of them man-made. Over the past few years, researchers in the Caribbean and the eastern Pacific have observed a phenomenon called "bleaching" in which the coral loses it color, evidence that its algae population has abandoned it or been expelled, leaving it to die. The bleaching may be due to pollution, but there is new evidence that the cause may be an increase in the water temperature, perhaps due to global warming.[21] Other studies show that whole chains of islands, such as the Maldives, may be lost as the sea rises over the coral reefs and inundates them.[22]

In 1992, a five-year study of the Florida Keys concluded that the two-hundred-mile-long reef, which is the nation's largest marine sanctuary, is dying at a faster pace that it was five years ago, and could be doomed by the year 2000. The Florida Institute of Oceanography found that pollution, primarily from human sewage and agricultural runoff, sedimentation from accelerated erosion and shoreline destruction, disease, and weather have all led to losses in the range of 10 percent per year. Some scientists believe the gloomy forecast is unwarranted, and that the current situation is simply part of a natural cycle of reef growth and death over thousands of years. Still, there is agreement that conservation measures are necessary to protect water quality, even if the exact condition of the reef is still under debate. A similar picture exists in the Philippines, where the government estimates that 71 percent of the reefs are in "poor to fair" condition, and only 6 percent are considered "excellent." Much of the damage there is attributed to sedimentation caused by upland logging, which can completely bury a reef or block needed sunlight.[23]

The damage being done to coral reefs can be attributed to both wealth and poverty. In affluent tourist areas like the Caribbean, coral reefs are being destroyed by divers, snorkelers, and boat owners who drop anchor on the delicate coral. Shell and coral collectors are often more interested in their "prizes" than in the reefs from which they came.[24] Sometimes, the damage is inadvertently caused by fishermen who lose their lobster traps, which bounce along the reef, or the nylon fishing line, which catches on crags and is whipped by the wind. The construction of resort hotels in areas like Fiji and the Maldives produces additional waste, which is often drained directly into lagoons, polluting the coral. Sometimes the destruction is due to people's insatiable desire for gourmet food. Taiwanese poachers have attacked reefs in the western Indo-Pacific in search of giant clams, a delicacy that has virtually disappeared from China. And in Japan, one of the last undisturbed coral reefs is threatened by the construction of an airport. Despite protests from dozens of organizations, including the Friends of the Earth Japan, labor unions, the Japan Nature Conservation Society, and consumer groups, the plans are proceeding. As mitigation, the developers plan to build a "coral museum" on the paved-over reef.

The most serious problems are those of poverty-stricken Third World nations. In the Philippines, where the situation is particularly acute, local residents squirt liquid cyanide into the coral to flush out fish for the lucrative aquarium trade. The practice not only kills nonaquarium fish, but the coral as well. Divers often suffer skin lesions and hair loss from the cyanide, and there have been some fatalities. In regions where there is no other rock, miners use crowbars to strip the reefs for use as building material. In Tanzania, five of the seven reefs recommended for World Heritage status are now dead, blasted by fishermen using dynamite.[25]

There are some success stories, such as the Great Barrier Reef Marine Park, established by Australia in 1975. The park protects not only the marine life within the reef, but the coral itself. It is considered a model of what could be accomplished if the damage has not already been done. Other attempts to protect coral reefs have met with significant opposition and controversy. The Philippines' largest coral reef atoll, the 33,200-hectare Tubbataha Reef in the middle of the Sulu Sea, is the first and only protected marine park in that nation. The atoll is home to 46 genera and 300 species of coral, along with 379 species of fish, and is considered the richest, most environmentally diverse reef in the Philippines. It gained protected status after the nation's largest seaweed company announced plans to develop the atoll and settle twenty-four thousand people there. The plans pitted owners of luxury boats, tour operators, and divers against powerful business owners who planned to create jobs for unemployed fishermen.[26]

A great deal of attention has been focused on the creation of artificial reefs using old tires—a solution that helps by finding a use for waste that is difficult to dispose of. But scientists also point out the fact that while the native fish population will thrive on the tires, and abundantly breed there, the tires do not regenerate corals—they simply replace them. It is but a partial solution to a much deeper environmental problem.

THE FUTURE OF THE OCEANS

The Romans and the Greeks worshipped the oceans and their gods of the seas, Neptune and Poseidon, holding them in high esteem because of their tremendous power over their lives. Today, we have shown little respect for the world of these gods, plundering the ocean's resources as if there was little we could do to harm them. Is there any question why the future of the oceans is so in doubt, given our attitudes and past record?

There are several reasons why the oceans pose a somewhat distinct political challenge. One, the oceans represent a truly global resource. Their waters touch on every continent, affecting the lives of all human beings in one form or another. Unlike the atmosphere, however, which is also considered a common pool issue, the oceans can be mined, farmed, fished, and exploited for their resources. Whether the prize is offshore oil, minerals found on the seabed, fish for food, or room for waste products and chemicals, the ocean is becoming increasingly valuable. Two, the oceans have no political constituency. No one lives on them, or votes there, or except for waters over continental shelves, presides over the waters. So far, the international community has had only moderate success at establishing protocols to protect the marine environment, and national self-interest is still the rule in many parts of the world. Environmental organizations with an interest in the ocean do exist, but they are vastly outnumbered by groups whose focus is air or land based. Three, for centuries, mankind has relied upon the old Latin dictum of *mare liberum*—the sea is free. Attempts to regulate its waters have been, for the most part, unsuccessful. The creation of an Exclusive Economic Zone of two hundred miles from each nation's coast through the Law of the Sea Treaty underscores international intent to give each country a piece of the oceanic "pie." Without full international cooperation, protection of the seas will continue to be accomplished on an incremental, document-by-document basis—a strategy that offers little security at all.

SUMMARY

There are three major environmental protection issues that pertain to the ocean: marine dumping, overfishing, and the destruction of coral reefs. Historically, the ocean has been a gigantic dumping ground for various kinds of human debris, both solids and liquids. The resulting marine pollution is of global concern because researchers are not yet certain what effect the pollutants have on the food chain and on fragile marine ecosystems, beaches, and coastal zones. International efforts to control ocean pollution have been focused on assessments of how various pollutants affect marine organisms, and fish and shellfish contamination. The first international regimes in the 1950s and 1960s were designed to protect the oceans from oil spills, and after highly publicized incidents in the 1970s and 1980s, there was general agreement on the need for more stringent restrictions. Other regimes designed to control the ocean dumping of pollutants, including radioactive waste, have been only moderately successful, and there has not yet been full ratification of the UN's Convention on the Law of the Sea. Treaties alone have not been able to convince nations which rely upon fishing as a major source of food and export income to reduce their catch, although international pressure finally convinced Japan and Korea to end the use of drift nets in 1991. More recently, attention has turned to coral reefs, which are being destroyed by tourists, development, poachers, and fishermen. The creation of marine parks is one possible alternative to protect the reefs, but the situation is already considered acute in many regions.

NOTES

1. M.C.W. Pinto, "Emerging Concepts of the Law of the Sea: Some Social and Cultural Impacts," in *Managing the Ocean: Resources, Research, Law*, ed. Jacques G. Richardson (Mt. Airy, MD: Lomond, 1985), 298.

2. Garrett Hardin, "The Tragedy of the Commons," *Science* 162 (December 13, 1968): 1243–48.

3. For a discussion of the common pool resource theory, see Zachary A. Smith, *The Environmental Policy Paradox* (Englewood Cliffs, NJ: Prentice Hall, 1992), 5.

4. See "Japan's Green Tinge," *The Economist*, February 2, 1991, 32.

5. See Michael A. Champ and Iver W. Duedall, "Ocean Waste Management," in *Marine Pollution*, ed. J. Albaiges (New York: Hemisphere, 1989), 305–45; and Steven J. Moore, "Troubles in the High Seas: A New Era in the Regulation of U.S. Ocean Dumping," *Environmental Law* 22, no. 3 (1992): 913–52.

6. See Eric Jay Dolin, "Boston Harbor's Murky Political Waters," *Environment* 34, no. 6 (July–August 1992): 6–11.

7. Peter M. Haas, *Saving the Mediterranean: The Politics of International Environmental Cooperation* (New York: Columbia University Press, 1990), 11.

8. Ibid., 214–23.

9. World Resources Institute, *World Resources 1992–93* (New York: Oxford University Press, 1992), 181.

10. Hilary E. French, *After the Earth Summit: The Future of Environmental Governance*, Worldwatch Paper 107 (Washington, DC: Worldwatch Institute, March 1992), 16.

11. *World Resources 1992–93*, 180.

12. See D. H. Cushing, *The Provident Sea* (Cambridge: Cambridge University Press, 1988), 253–56.

13. See Anne W. Simon, *Neptune's Revenge: The Ocean of Tomorrow* (New York: Franklin Watts, 1984), 32–33.

14. Nicholas Lenssen, "The Ocean Blues," in *The Worldwatch Reader on Global Environmental Issues*, ed. Lester R. Brown (New York: Norton, 1991), 53.

15. Lincoln Kaye, "A Quest for Net Profits," *Far Eastern Economic Review*, September 28, 1989, 138–39.

16. Steven R. Weisman, "Japan Agrees to End Use of Huge Fishing Nets," *New York Times*, November 27, 1991, A-3.

17. See Albia Dugger, "Gillnet Fisheries: A Worldwide Concern," *Sea Frontiers* 36, no. 1 (January–February 1990): 20–21; and Colin James and Lincoln Kaye, "A Catch-All Dilemma," *Far Eastern Economic Review;* September 28, 1989, 139–40.

18. See U.S. Executive Office of the President, Council on Environmental Quality, *The Evolution of National Wildlife Law* (Washington, DC: U.S. Government Printing Office, 1977), 423–43.

19. French, *After the Earth Summit*, 30.

20. T. M. Hawley, "Managing the Oceans," *Technology Review* 92, no. 2 (February–March 1989): 18.

21. See Leslie Roberts, "Greenhouse Role in Reef Stress Unproven," *Science* 253, July 19, 1991, 258–59.

22. Sue Wells and Alasdair Edwards, "Gone with the Waves," *New Scientist*, November 11, 1989, 47–51.

23. Jon Miller, "Troubled Waters," *Far Eastern Economic Review*, March 15, 1990, 34.

24. See Mark Derr, "Raiders of the Reef," *Audubon* 94 (March–April 1992): 48–55.

25. See Kenneth Brower, "State of the Reef," *Audubon* 91 (March 1989): 56–81.

26. Yasmin D. Arquiza, "Toll on the Atoll," *Far Eastern Economic Review*, March 15, 1990, 32–34.

FOR FURTHER READING

J. Albaiges, ed. *Marine Pollution*. New York: Hemisphere, 1989.

David K. Bulloch. *The Wasted Ocean*. New York: Lyons and Burford, 1989.

D.H. Cushing. *The Provident Sea*. Cambridge: Cambridge University Press, 1988.

Art Davidson. *In the Wake of the Exxon Valdez*. San Francisco: Sierra Club Books, 1990.

Peter M. Haas. *Saving the Mediterranean: The Politics of International Environmental Cooperation*. New York: Columbia University Press, 1990.

Jacques G. Richardson, ed. *Managing the Ocean: Resources, Research, Law*. Mt. Airy, MD: Lomond, 1985.

Boyce Thorne-Miller and John G. Catena. *The Living Ocean: Understanding and Protecting Marine Biodiversity*. Washington, DC: Island Press, 1990.

CHAPTER 12

Acid Rain:
What's Ours Is Yours

These buildings are melting away like sugar candy.
—comment of a Danish architect on the effect of acid rain on the
Acropolis, the Tower of London, and Cologne Cathedral.[1]

In Germany's Fichtelgebirge forest, the normally green needles of Norway spruce began yellowing around 1979, turning the forest floor into a pile of yellow and brown litter. The blight spread year by year until the canopy of trees was thin and living trees the exception rather than the rule. Surveys in 1982 showed about 8 percent of all trees were affected; by 1987, more than half were damaged. It was on the slopes of this Bavarian ridge that scientists first spotted the effects of transboundary air pollution we now call acid rain.[2]

"Acid rain" and "acid deposition" are terms that are often used interchangeably to describe the emissions of sulfur dioxide and nitrogen dioxides, primarily from man-made sources, which react in the atmosphere and return to Earth. The oxidized "wet" form (created when the emissions dissolve in clouds and rain droplets) is usually referred to as acid rain, and the dry form is called acid deposition. Since the early 1980s, scientists have suspected the resulting pollution damages lakes, streams, forests, and soils, with potential harm to human health. This chapter outlines the nature of the acid rain problem, both in the United States and in Europe, and what is being done to reduce its potential for destruction.

THE NATURE OF ACID RAIN

Acid rain is invisible, and cannot be smelled or tasted. For many years, it has been undetected because in its early stages, there is little evidence of its impact. It did not become a potent policy issue in the United States until the late 1970s, and now researchers are finding that many other regions of the world also face an acid rain problem.

There are three primary components of acid rain: sulfur dioxide, nitrogen oxides, and volatile organic compounds (VOCs). The most common of the pollutants, sulfur dioxide, comes primarily from the combustion of coal which reacts with oxygen in the air. The sulfur content of coal varies considerably with the geographic region in which it is mined, so not all areas experience acid deposition to the same degree. Coal from the western portion of the United States, for example, typically has a sulfur content of about 0.5 percent, which is considered to be very low. In contrast, that mined in the northern region of Appalachia and some midwestern states has a sulfur concentration of 2 to 3 percent.

Coal has become an increasingly significant source of energy in the United States ever since the oil embargo of the early 1970s and Americans' fear about dependence on foreign sources of fuel. Fuel burned in utility power plants is responsible for about two-thirds of the nation's sulfur dioxide emissions, followed by industrial processes (16 percent), nonutility fuel combustion from stationary sources (14 percent), and transportation sources (4 percent). Acid rain also becomes an issue for those regions or countries that import coal, since they may, in effect, be importing the resultant sulfur emissions as well. More recent attention has been focused on emissions of nitrogen oxides, produced primarily from the exhaust of motor vehicles. In the atmosphere, nitrogen oxides are converted into nitric acid and nitrates.

Acidity is measured on a pH scale from 0 to 14, with lemon juice measured at 1, vinegar at 3, and "pure" (nonacid) rain at 5.6. Readings below 7.0 are acidic; readings above 7.0 are alkaline. The more pH decreases below 7.0, the more acidity increases. Because the pH scale is logarithmic, there is a tenfold difference between one number and the next one to it. Therefore, a drop in pH from 6.0 to 5.0 represents a tenfold increase in acidity, while a drop from 6.0 to 4.0 represents a hundredfold increase. Rain with a pH below 5.6 is considered "acid rain."

THE EFFECTS OF ACID RAIN

Acid rain causes several types of environmental damage. First, it contributes to growing acidity levels in bodies of water that are fed by rainfall, damaging the fish population in lakes and streams. Some species of fish have disappeared from lakes in Sweden and Norway, as well as Scotland and England.[3] Recently the Environmental Defense Fund has reported that airborne nitrogen oxides, mainly from automobiles and electric utilities, have affected sea life in eastern coastal waters near the Long Island Sound, the New York Bight, and North Carolina's Albermarle-Pimlico Sound. The damage is caused not from acidity but from eutrophication, in which excessive growth of algae, stimulated by nitrate salts and other nutrients, chokes off the oxygen supply, blocking sunlight required by other animals and plants.[4]

Second, acid rain damages flora and fauna, such as spruce forests in the eastern United States,[5] and more than half of the forests in Germany have been affected by *Waldsterben*, or "forest death." Growing levels of nitrogen oxides are also reported to cause an aluminum-induced calcium-deficiency syndrome, which causes stunted growth in trees. The impact of acid rain also shows up in various links in the food chain. One Dutch study found, for example, that there was a direct relationship between acid rain and bird eggs. In areas where acid deposition was a known problem, eggs were being laid without shells or with shells so thin that the embryo evaporates.[6] Researchers in the United States have also found reduced yields of crops such as winter and spring wheat, barley, potatoes, beets, radishes, and certain species of grass.[7]

Third, acid rain is believed to contribute to health problems. It facilitates the accumulation of mercury, a toxic metal, in fish that are found in inland lakes, particularly in the states of Minnesota, Wisconsin, and Michigan, and that are then ingested by humans. Downwind derivatives of acid rain—acid aerosols—may lead to bronchitis in children and decreased lung function in adults. Other researchers have discovered that a potential threat to human health may occur as a result of exposure to a higher heavy metal intake from drinking water provided in lead or copper plumbing—a concern raised in Sweden and the United Kingdom.[8]

Yet there is general agreement it is virtually impossible to establish a direct link between health and acid rain because of the limits of human health research. Scientists obviously cannot carry out potentially lethal studies on human beings, and research involving lab animals is often criticized because of a belief that their respiratory systems may respond differently. Still, many health officials believe the evidence is now too compelling to ignore.[9]

Scientists are also concerned about the long-term impact of acid precipitation on the world's cultural heritage. In Greece, for example, home to some of the most beautiful historical artifacts in the Western world, wet and dry acid precipitation has damaged the delicate stonework on the Acropolis and the Parthenon. Similar pollution has damaged Rome's monuments, and in Venice, palaces and frescoes have been discolored and destroyed. In addition, visibility is reduced when the byproducts of sulfur dioxide, called sulfates, contribute to regional haze.

Various studies have been undertaken to quantify the extent of these types of damage. The ten-year long National Acid Precipitation Assessment Program (NAPAP), which was sponsored by the Environmental Protection Agency, the National Oceanic and Atmospheric Administration, the Departments of Agriculture, Energy, and the Interior, and the Council on Environmental Quality, is the most comprehensive source of information about acid rain in the world. The study was initiated in 1980 when acid rain became the subject of bitter debate in New England and Canada, where the impact was thought to be the most acute. Over two thousand researchers spent $570 billion to create elaborate models to determine how best to solve the acid rain problem. The 1985 NAPAP emissions inventory, which is considered to be the most accurate assessment of how much acid deposition occurs, found that the United States emits 23.1 million tons per year of sulfur dioxide (75 percent of which comes from large factories emitting ten thousand tons per year or more), 20.5 tons per year of oxides of nitrogen, and 22.1 tons per year of VOCs. These figures are lower than those for the early 1970s when emissions peaked, but twice as high as levels found in 1900. Sulfur emissions have decreased by 27–29 percent since the passage of the 1970 Clean Air Act, but NOx and VOC emissions have gone up due to increased fuel consumption.[10]

The study's findings have been the subject of some controversy, especially after one 1987 interim report seemed to downplay the problem.[11] James Mahoney, who served as director of the program during its last two years, reported in February 1990 that although acid rain is a problem, "the good news is that it is not as bad as we thought."[12] Although the study was considered excellent from a purely scientific standpoint, it never provided policymakers with what they needed most—recommendations on how best to control acid rain and at what cost.

A PROBLEM WITHOUT POLITICAL BOUNDARIES

One of the reasons why acid deposition has become such a critical international issue is that it knows no political boundaries.[13] Power plants along the Ohio River Valley are suspected of causing acid rain in Canada, and Eastern European emissions have been traced throughout Europe. Even Asian nations are now measuring significant levels of acidification, although the European situation appears most severe. Coal emissions from the "dirty triangle" of northern Czechoslovakia, eastern Germany, and the Silesian district of northern Poland result in highly acidic rain, and prevailing winds carry the smoke to the east, where forests are dying. So many trees were being killed in the southwestern Polish resort town of Jelenia Gora, near the Czechoslovak border, that the army was brought in to fell them in 1990.[14] The problem is due to the fact that great quantities of poor-quality coal are burned locally, and the more expensive low-sulfur coals are exported for foreign currency.

The republics of the Commonwealth of Independent States are usually thought of as importers of pollutants from other parts of Europe which are carried on the prevailing westerly winds. Samples of snow on the ridges of the Carpathian mountains, which are just next to the Russian/Romanian border, have a pH level of 3.8 to 4.0, even though there are no utility plants within the region.[15] However, near Lake Baikal, the "Pearl of Siberia," pollution from aluminum smelters and chemical plants has caused acid rain to fall just ten miles away. The lake's fish population, including many species found only in Baikal, is dying out. Local residents, led by the Baikal Fund, composed of over one hundred thousand members, are campaigning to close down factories that

The Canadian Controversy

Among the most extensive bilateral efforts to deal with acid deposition have been the negotiations between the United States and Canada. Environmentalists have argued that acid rain emanating in the United States has damaged as many as sixteen thousand Canadian lakes. Attempts to deal with the transport of American emissions across Canadian borders began in 1978 with the signing of the Great Lakes Water Quality Agreement. The treaty required both nations to take appropriate measures to control airborne contaminants. But such cooperative agreements bogged down considerably in February 1980 when President Jimmy Carter announced plans to convert one hundred U.S. oil-fired plants to coal. Congress blocked Carter's proposals, but Canadians were offended by what they considered to be an insensitivity on the part of the president to their environmental problems.[18]

During the Reagan administration, there was less of a sense of urgency about the issue, in large part due to the fact that Reagan's environmental appointees differed in their assessment of the nature of the acid rain problem. Interior Secretary James Watt and EPA Administrator Anne Burford argued that the United States should undertake more intensive research efforts before embarking on expensive control measures, a position which later became the U.S. negotiating team's primary issue. After two years of preliminary negotiations, no agreement appeared to be forthcoming, although the Canadian's hopes were raised in May 1983, when former EPA administration William Ruckelshaus was named to replace Burford. Despite his efforts to craft a plan that would require modest reductions in coal-fired utility emissions, other Reagan appointees (namely, Budget Director David Stockman and Secretary of Energy Donald Hodel) argued the proposed changes would be too costly for electric utilities and their customers.

A more conservative administration was elected in Canada in 1984, and Prime Minister Brian Mulroney and President Reagan met several times to discuss bilateral issues, culminating in a March 1985 meeting on acid rain. It resulted in a statement acknowledging the problem of acid rain, but did not make any recommendations for solutions. The situation deteriorated to the point where Ontario, Canada's wealthiest province, decided in 1988 to take the EPA to court for the agency's failure to admit that American companies were polluting their northern neighbor.[19] No progress on the acid rain issue was really made until the passage of the Clean Air Act amendments in 1990. For the first time, the United States made a serious attempt to do more than just appropriate more funds for research into the problem. President Bush subsequently visited Mulroney in March 1991 to sign an acid rain accord, which commits both nations to halve 1980 emission levels of sulfur dioxide by 1994. Critics believe that the treaty lacks enforcement and monitoring measures, but administration officials believe it is an important step forward.[20]

are heavy polluters near the lake, and were successful in stopping a proposed expansion of the Baikal Paper Complex in 1988.

Transboundary environmental pollution has also developed into a political confrontation in Finland along the seven-hundred-mile-long border with Russia. Military factories along the Kola Peninsula emit seven hundred tons of corrosive sulfur dioxide emissions into Finland each year—far more than is produced in all of Finland. Forests within a three-hundred-mile radius of the factories have been ravaged, and the Finnish Green party reports that there is clear damage in an additional fifty thousand square miles, with an estimated 30 percent of the firs in Finnish Lapland in danger of dying. What makes the Finnish situation unique in Europe is the almost spiritual relationship of the people to their forests. Although the nation is highly dependent upon trees as the largest exporter of paper products in Europe, there is an almost mystical environmental consciousness among its residents. The governments of Norway, Sweden, and Finland (all of whom are affected by the acid rain problem) were finally able to convince the Russians to accept a $1 billion loan in September 1990 to install sophisticated Finnish antipollution equipment.[16]

One of the problems facing Eastern European nations is the question as to whether old power plants should be refurbished or replaced. Electricity production in what was formerly East Germany is among the most polluting in the region, but Western investors have found that the costs of modernization are prohibitive. Hungary, which is desperate for outside investment, is less concerned about pollution control laws than its staggering debt of $20 billion and a 23 percent inflation rate.[17]

STRIVING TOWARD SOLUTIONS

Title IV of the 1990 Clean Air Act amendments marks the first real effort by Congress to address the acid rain issue. Its passage came after bitter debate, pitting groups like the National Clean Air Coalition (made up of environmentalists who believe that acid rain causes serious health problems or threatens recreational areas) against the Electric Power Research Institute, the Edison Electric Institute, the National Coal Association, and the American Electric Power Service Company. The new law requires significant reductions in sulfur dioxide emissions. Industry must reduce emissions by ten million tons from 1980 levels by the turn of the century in a two-phase process. One, 110 coal-burning electric utility plants in twenty-one eastern and midwestern states that emit high levels of sulfur dioxide must reduce emissions beginning in 1995. Two, those plants face tighter controls and another one thousand utility facilities must reduce emissions in 2000. The law requires utilities to install monitoring equipment to ensure compliance. The amendments also address nitrogen dioxide emissions, which must be reduced by two million tons by the year 2000. Utility boilers, which are the primary source of these pollutants, will face new emission limitations and must also be monitored for compliance.

What is unique about the law is that it implements a market-based allowance-trading system to reduce emissions in the most cost-effective manner. The EPA will annually allocate allowances to those utility companies affected by the law that permit a plant to emit one ton of sulfur dioxide. The number of allowances the EPA will issue is capped at 8.95 million beginning in 2000. To be in compliance with the law, utilities may not emit more sulfur dioxide than they hold allowances for, which requires them to either reduce emissions or obtain additional allowance permits from other firms. This process allows companies to trade allowances if they meet emission levels, bank them for future use and expansion, or sell them at market rates. The buying and selling of allowances will be done on a nationwide basis, so that a firm may buy or sell its allowances with a utility in another state, or may purchase one from a broker, private citizen, or environmental group. The EPA will hold some allowances back that will be sold at a fixed rate of $1,500 per allowance.[21]

Rather than installing expensive pollution control equipment, a utility might choose to purchase allowances from another company or a broker. The Chicago Board of Trade has announced that it will also buy and sell allowances. Starting in 1993, the EPA will begin to hold auctions and sales of allowances to establish a market price early on in the process. The EPA will also record all emission allowance transfers so that at the end of each year, a firm's emissions do not exceed the number of allowances it holds. If a company does not comply, it faces a $2,000 per ton excess emission fee and must then offset the emissions in the following year—a figure substantially higher than the expected cost of compliance.

In order to implement the complex provisions of Title IV, the EPA will require utility companies to obtain emission permits and to keep comprehensive records of emissions. To assist the agency in drawing up these regulations, the EPA created an Acid Rain Advisory Committee months before the amendments were signed into law by President Bush. The forty members, representing utilities, environmental organizations, consumer groups, and air pollution control officials, are now developing what is considered a prototype for incentive-based pollution control programs.

This is not, however, the first time that the EPA has implemented an economic incentive approach, although it will be the first done on a large scale.[22] In 1974, the EPA experimented with emissions trading by allowing firms that reduced emissions below required levels to receive emissions "credits" that could be traded among sources within the firm. The level of emissions, however, must comply with the aggregate total allowed for the firm. Credits may also be "banked" or stored for future use or sale. Under the 1976 "offset" program, firms in regions that do not meet air quality standards were allowed to expand or establish new pollution sources only if they reduced their existing emissions by an equal or greater amount. They could do that by cleaning up their own pollution sources, or by agreeing to clean up the pollution of another source in the same region.

The acid rain issue has focused attention on the economic side of environmental pollution control. In his 1989 testimony before Congress, NAPAP Director Jim Mahoney noted that the proposed ten-million-ton reduction in sulfur dioxide emissions "would benefit aquatic resources and would mitigate other environmental effects caused by acid deposition and its precursors." The only question Mahoney raised is, "How much reduction is appropriate and how much benefit are we going to get from the cost?"[23] There is no disagreement that acid rain control is possible. Industry sources admit that existing pollution control equipment, once installed, can reduce 95 to 98 percent of the sulfur dioxide being emitted. Studies by Resources for the Future indicate the benefits of acid rain control will be worth approximately $5 billion per year, about 50 percent greater than the costs of control, a conclusion reached by a 1988 EPA study as well. The significance of the acid rain legislation, then, is that it allows for innovation and market-based forces to control pollution, rather than the traditional command-and-control approach of past regulatory efforts. The legislation marks a turning point in air quality regulations, which may result in a real "clearing of the air."

One of the most ambitious international efforts to control acid rain has been quietly taking place in Europe. Two organizations have been at the forefront of these negotiations: the UN Economic Commission for Europe (ECE), which comprises both Eastern and Western European nations, and the twelve member nations of the European Community (EC). In 1979, the members of the UN body enacted the Convention on Long-Range Transboundary Air Pollution, which served as a declaration of intent for development of an acid rain control strategy. However, it left up to each member nation the decision as to what the "best" strategy for control might be. Yet it did establish a framework for further scientific cooperation and consultation.[24]

Efforts moved a step further in Helsinki in 1985 with the adoption of a protocol reducing sulfur emissions by 30 percent no later than 1993—a document signed by thirty nations. Nations signing the treaty are referred to as members of the "30 percent club." It is a political, rather than science-based target, and the United Kingdom, Ireland, Spain, Portugal, and Greece never signed the protocol. European leaders have also failed to take the initiative in reducing nitrogen oxide emissions, the other major cause of acid precipitation, although some countries have set more ambitious sulfur emission reduction targets. The EC, meanwhile, has used the Treaty of Rome as a mechanism for bringing uniformity to the development of environmental laws in the region. Most of the body's efforts to date have focused on conventional air pollutants, and it has been difficult for the members to agree on uniform, across-the-board reduction targets.

Both Sweden and Norway have set the pace for acid rain control and are considered by some to be ten years ahead of the United States in their education and research programs.[25] Not only are they working to control their own emissions, but they are also attempting to convince other European nations to do the same. The United Kingdom, which is Western Europe's largest producer of SO_2, seems to be the least willing to change, despite a history of disastrous consequences. In 1952, London was struck by a "killer fog" that resulted in the deaths of thousands of residents, but most British officials still do not consider acid rain to be a serious problem. One study found that acid "clouds" in upland areas of Britain are likely agents responsible for the accelerating decline of forests, but another research project concluded that clear evidence to link acid deposition with tree health does not yet exist. Despite a 1990 Austrian study which reported "huge economic losses" if acid rain was not dramatically controlled,[26] government officials still believe that many factors affect the growth of a tree and that no one understands fully how these factors interact. The British government has only recently set up a network of monitoring stations to determine the nature and extent of acid deposition throughout the country. Still, Britain has made some attempts in recent years to accelerate its control of sulfur dioxide emissions, most of which come from coal-fired utility power plants. The Central Electricity Generating Board started a desulfurization program in 1988, but despite costly technological improvements, the nation is still far from joining the 30 percent club.[27] The UN Convention is expected to be revised in 1993–94 with the addition of a "sulfur protocol," which will set targets for reducing emissions of sulfur dioxide for Europe and North America by 2000. The protocol's targets will be based on assessments of the critical loads of acid deposition that habitats can absorb without sustaining substantial damage.[28]

NEW THREATS/NEW SOLUTIONS

Although acid rain has traditionally been associated with the industrialized nations of Europe and the United States, there is new evidence that damage is also being done in other regions of the world as well. A survey conducted by the International Union for Conservation of Nature and Natural Resources has found acid-rain-related threats in Brazil, Australia, Thailand, and South Africa. In the heavy coal-mining region of Santa Catarina, Brazil, the environmental secretary estimates that 80 percent of the local hospital patients have respiratory ailments caused by acidic pollutants.[29]

One of the least publicized threats of acid rain is in Asia, where prevailing winds carry sulfur particles from coal-burning power plants in China to Japan and South Korea. Japan has been quietly working behind the scenes to install desulfurization technology on Chinese facilities, which are responsible for about 70 percent of the sulfur oxides emitted in Asia. The Chinese-Japan Friendship Environmental Protection Center, expected to open in Beijing in 1995, will also bring Japanese commercial technology to China, which plans to increase its coal-burning capacity by 40 percent by 2000. Japanese officials, however, believe these projects are not sufficient to solve a problem that is growing so rapidly.[30]

Scientists are also looking at various ways to restore lakes that have been determined to be excessively acidic, and are finding that some bodies of waters cannot be recovered at all. An international and interdisciplinary study, the Surface Waters Acidification Programme (SWAP) has found that some highly acidified bodies of water may result not only from acid rain, but from large accumulated stores of sulphur compounds in deep soils. In some cases, the surrounding soils may be so acidified that it may take decades for the compounds to be leached out, and even a 60 percent reduction in acid deposition would not be enough to create conditions suitable for fish.[31] One proposed solution is to add lime to the lake waters to neutralize the acid, with some success. Sweden has limed five thousand of its sixteen thousand acidified lakes usually by dropping in powdered limestone. Repeat doses are needed every few years, and it is extremely costly to attempt to lime free-flowing bodies of water like rivers and streams. But Swedish researchers report that invertebrates and fish have returned to lakes that have been limed.[32] Similar projects have been attempted in Canada and in the Adirondack lakes of New York. The downside of the strategy is lime itself can damage wetlands around lakes and rivers, and researchers are not sure what effect the increased calcium from the lime will have on the overall ecology of the watershed. Treatment, which depends on the volume of water, its chemistry, and its turnover time, is often crude at best. In the end, liming only treats the symptoms while the cure is to reduce emissions of acid at their source.[33]

This is, perhaps, where the bottom-line environmental protection question really remains unresolved. Since the acid rain problem is not shared equally by all regions of the United States (or of the world, for that matter), should the financial burden of solving it be borne only by those sources that contribute to it? This is the approach taken by the 1990 Clean Air Act, and somewhat grudgingly agreed to by utilities and coal producers. What of transboundary pollution that flows across state and national borders? Is there a responsibility for those sources to make sure that their pollution does not negatively impact their neighbors? Who should pay the cost of acid rain pollution in such cases? As the U.S.-Canadian negotiations point out, hammering out such agreements may take years of diplomatic effort in addition to millions of dollars of control costs.

SUMMARY

The issue of acid rain did not become a part of the environmental protection agenda until the late 1970s, partly because unlike some other forms of pollution, it cannot be smelled or tasted. But the damage it causes the ecosystem by raising acidity levels in lakes and waterways, as well as suspected harm to human health, is only now beginning to be realized. Researchers are also studying the long-term effects of acid rain, such as damage to historical artifacts. What the studies have failed to provide however are political solutions—how best to control acid rain and what cost. Acid rain has also become a global issue, with disputes between the United States and Canada typical of the type of transboundary air pollution issues that are developing in industrialized regions. However, new evidence suggests acid rain may also be threatening other parts of the world as well.

NOTES

1. Anne La Bastille, "The International Acid Test," *Sierra*, May–June 1986, 51.
2. Janet Raloff, "Where Acids Reign," *Science News* 136 (July 22, 1989): 56–58.
3. See Environmental Resources Limited, *Acid Rain: A Review of the Phenomenon in the EEC and Europe* (New York: Unipub, 1983), for a discussion of the impacts of acid rain on the region.
4. "Acid Rain Affects Coastal Waters Too," *Environment* 30 (June 1988): 22. See also Philip Shabecoff, "Acid Rain Is Called Peril for Sea Life on Atlantic Coast," *New York Times*, April 25, 1988, A-1.
5. See Robert A. Mello, *Last Stand of the Red Spruce* (Washington, DC: Island Press, 1987).
6. P. J. Drent and J. W. Woldendorp, "Acid Rain and Eggshells," *Nature* 339 (June 8, 1989): 431.
7. *Acid Rain: A Review of the Phenomenon in the EEC and Europe*, 24.
8. Ibid., 119.
9. See Jon R. Luoma, "The Human Cost of Acid Rain," *Audubon* 90 (July 1988): 16–27; see also Luoma, *Troubled Skies, Troubled Waters: The Story of Acid Rain* (New York: Viking Press, 1984).
10. Patricia Irving, ed., *Acid Deposition: State of Science and Technology, Summary Report of the United States National Acid Precipitation Assessment Program* (Washington, DC: U.S. Government Printing Office, September 1991), 26–27.
11. See Leslie Roberts, "Learning from an Acid Rain Problem," *Science* 251 (March 15, 1991): 1302–05.
12. Leslie Roberts, "How Bad Is Acid Rain?" *Science* 251 (March 15, 1991): 1303.
13. For an assessment of the global nature of the problem, see John McCormick, *Acid Earth: The Global Threat of Acid Pollution* (Washington, DC: International Institute for Environment and Development, 1985).
14. See Jon Thompson, "East Europe's Dark Dawn," *National Geographic*, June 1991, 36–68.
15. See "Environmentalism in the Soviet Union," *Environment* 32, no. 2 (March 1990): 8.
16. Gordon Sander, "No Friends to the Fir," *Sierra*, May–June 1991, 36–39.
17. Debora MacKenzie, "The Green Wave Heads East," *New Scientist*, June 16, 1990, 3.
18. For an extensive analysis of the U.S.-Canadian negotiations, see Jurgen Schmandt, Judith Clarkson, and Hilliard Roderick, eds., *Acid Rain and Friendly Neighbors: The Policy Dispute between Canada and the United States* (Durham, NC: Duke University Press, 1988).
19. See "Government Agency in Court Over Acid Rain Damage," *New Scientist*, October 29, 1988, 26.
20. See Norman W. Fichthorn, "Command-and-Control vs. the Market: The Potential Effects of Other Clean Air Act Requirements on Acid Rain Compliance,"

Environmental Law 21, no. 4:II (1991): 2069–84; and Glen Allen, "Savoring Victories," *Maclean's*, March 25, 1991, 14–15.

21. See Robert Pool, "Polluters Pay at Auction," *Nature* 351 (May 30, 1991): 337.

22. For an explanation of the economic incentive concept, see Robert N. Stavins, "Harnessing Market Forces to Protect the Environment," *Environment* 31, no. 1 (January–February 1989): 5–7, 28–29.

23. Ned Helme and Chris Neme, "Acid Rain: The Problem," *EPA Journal* 17, no. 1 (January–February 1991): 20.

24. See Marc Pallemaerts, "The Politics of Acid Rain Control in Europe," *Environment* 30, no. 2 (March 1988): 42–44.

25. La Bastille, "International Acid Test," 52.

26. William Bown, "Europe's Forests Fall to Acid Rain," *New Scientist*, August 11, 1990, 17. The report estimates that acid rain will cost Europe 118 million cubic meters of wood every year for the next century.

27. "Clean Up," *The Economist*, June 16, 1988, 62.

28. Fred Pearce, "Will Britain Fail the Acid Test?" *New Scientist*, December 5, 1992, 11.

29. La Bastille, "International Acid Test," 54.

30. Clayton Jones, "Acid Rain Looms as Newest Threat to Japan's Island of Kyushu," *The Oregonian*, November 8, 1992, A-14.

31. For an explanation of the SWAP study and its findings, see B. J. Mason, ed., *The Surface Waters Acidification Programme* (Cambridge: Cambridge University Press, 1990). The study focused on highly acidified sites in Norway, Scotland, and Sweden.

32. "A Twist of Lime in a Cocktail of Troubles," *The Economist*, May 27, 1989, 85–86.

33. For a summary of liming attempts, see Sarah Woodin and Ute Skiba, "Liming Fails the Acid Test," *New Scientist*, March 10, 1990, 50–54.

FOR FURTHER READING

Jutta Brunnee. *Acid Rain and Ozone Layer Depletion*. Ardsley-on-Hudson, NY: Transnational, 1988.

John Firor. *The Changing Atmosphere*. New Haven: Yale University Press, 1990.

Roy Gould. *Going Sour: Science and Politics of Acid Rain*. Boston: Birkhauser, 1985.

Gwyneth Parry Howells. *Acid Rain and Acid Waters*. New York: E. Horwood, 1990.

Jon R. Luoma. *Troubled Skies, Troubled Waters: The Story of Acid Rain*. New York: Viking Press, 1984.

John McCormick. *Acid Earth: The Global Threat of Acid Pollution*. Washington, DC: International Institute for Environment and Development, 1985.

Chris Park. *Acid Rain: Rhetoric and Reality*. New York: Methuen, 1987.

James L. Regens and Robert W. Rycroft. *The Acid Rain Controversy*. Pittsburgh: University of Pittsburgh Press, 1988.

Jurgen Schmandt, Judith Clarkson, and Hilliard Roderick. *Acid Rain and Friendly Neighbors: The Policy Dispute between Canada and the United States*. Durham, NC: Duke University Press, 1988.

CHAPTER 13

Climatic Change:
Challenges and Options

We really are changing our earth in measurable ways, so we better
damn well know what we are doing to it.
 —Dr. Ralph Kahn, climate scientist, California Institute of Technology[1]

Ever since the 1860s, when British scientist John Tyndall first described a
phenomena we now call the greenhouse effect, the public has been alerted to
imminent doom caused by climatic change. Unfortunately, researchers have been
unable to agree whether our future is tied to an impending ice age that will
result in continental glaciation or a warming trend that will melt the glaciers and
send coastal cities into the sea. The debate flourished around the turn of the
century when Nobel Prize–winning Swedish scientist Svante Arrhenius calculated that a doubling of the carbon dioxide in the atmosphere would raise the
average surface temperature of Earth. His calculations were confirmed by American geologists Thomas Chamberlin and C. F. Tolman, who studied the role that
the oceans play as a major reservoir of carbon dioxide. In the 1930s, after three
decades of warming temperatures and the development of a massive dustbowl in
the central United States, other scientists warned of the dangers of rising temperatures, which had already been tied to increasing levels of carbon dioxide in
the atmosphere. But between the 1940s and 1970s, global temperatures fell, and
many reputable scientists prophesied a new ice age rather than a warming
trend.[2] The global warming forecast was resurrected again in June 1988 when
Dr. James Hansen, director of the National Aeronautic and Space Administration's (NASA) Institute for Space Studies told a Senate Committee, "The greenhouse effect is here."

Humans' ability to cause changes in the atmosphere is a relatively recent
phenomenon—primitive peoples did not have the technology to alter the environment as we do today. With the Industrial Revolution came technological
devices like the steam engine, electric generator, and internal combustion engine,
which have forever altered the planet, the water we drink, and the air we
breathe. That ability to alter the environment is threatening to some, but considered a natural part of the evolutionary process by others. Some believe that

Earth exists as a living organism in which internal control mechanisms maintain the stability of life—a theory called the Gaia hypothesis.[3] According to this theory, environmental problems like ozone depletion will be brought under control naturally by the environment itself, which will make the necessary adjustments to sustain life. Critics of the theory, however, refer to policies built on such optimism as "environmental brinksmanship" and warn that we cannot rely upon untried regulatory mechanisms to protect the planet from large-scale human interference. This chapter looks at two issues with obvious global dimensions: global warming and stratospheric ozone depletion. It provides an overview of the scientific controversy and identifies the ways in which the two issues differ politically.

GLOBAL WARMING

Although global warming is ostensibly a subject for scientific debate, it has become one of the most politicized environmental issues of this decade.[4] It is also part of the evolution of environmental concerns from pollution in the 1960s to energy (beginning with the oil crisis of 1973) to the more global concerns of the 1980s. It became the focus of attention at the Earth Summit in Rio de Janeiro in June 1992 and is likely to remain near the top of the political agenda well into the twenty-first century.

Global warming refers to the process by which solar radiation passes through Earth's atmosphere and is absorbed by the surface or reradiated back into the atmosphere. The phenomenon is also called the "greenhouse effect" because certain gases in the atmosphere act like the panels of a greenhouse, letting some heat in but keeping some of it from going back out.

There are about twenty so-called greenhouse gases that make up Earth's atmosphere, with the five major sources identified in Table 13.1. Changes in the volume of these gases affect the rate at which energy is absorbed, which then affects Earth's temperature. Greenhouse gases are emitted or absorbed by virtually every form of human activity, as well as by oceans, terrestrial plants, and

Table 13.1   Major Greenhouse Gases

Gas	*Where It Comes From*
Carbon dioxide	Fossil fuel sources including utility power plants, refineries, automobiles
Chlorofluorocarbons (CFCs)	Solvents, foam insulation, fire extinguishers, air conditioners
Halons	Compounds used in fire extinguishers
Methane	Natural sources like decaying vegetation, cattle, rice paddies, landfills, oil field operations
Nitrogen oxides	Fertilizers, bacteria

animals, which contribute to the carbon dioxide cycle. Scientists are primarily concerned about increases in levels of carbon dioxide, since it is difficult to quantify the exact cause and effect of other greenhouse gases. The more carbon dioxide builds up, the more heat is trapped near Earth. The buildups have been monitored since 1958 at facilities on Mauna Loa on the big island of Hawaii.

Although researchers began studying the effect of carbon dioxide on climate in the early part of this century, the implications of such changes were not seriously considered until the early 1970s. A World Climate Conference in Geneva in 1979 was one of the first efforts at organizing international research, followed by a series of studies and conferences over the next ten years. One of the most respected reports was published in 1987 by the World Commission on Environment and Development, which recommended a global approach to a broad spectrum of environmental problems, including greenhouse warming.[5] In December 1988, the UN General Assembly unanimously passed a special resolution calling for a framework convention on climate change, which was implemented through the Intergovernmental Panel on Climate Change (IPCC). The IPCC was initially formed to develop a scientific consensus on the danger of greenhouse warming stemming from the use of fossil fuels.

Researchers have relied upon a variety of tools to help them understand the impact of climate change, with general circulation models (GCMs) the most commonly used ways of forecasting the results. The models allow scientists to predict what would happen when carbon dioxide levels are increased to specific levels, but the models are not foolproof.[6] They are limited by a number of factors, including our incomplete knowledge of atmospheric and ocean processes, heat transfer in the atmosphere, details of the effects of clouds, and the nature of ocean currents. Any one of these factors could alter the results reached by the modeling process.[7]

One of the most vocal critics of the models is scientist Sherwood Idso, who believes that the predicted rates of warming are inaccurate and that, in fact, some cooling trends may occur. He is joined by several other credible researchers, including meteorologist Richard Lindzen of Harvard, who wrote President Bush saying current forecasts of global warming "are so inaccurate and fraught with uncertainty as to be useless to policy makers."[8] Other models show that certain types of human activities, such as sulfur emissions from the burning of fossil fuels, may increase the rate of cloud condensation and clouds' reflecting power may actually cool Earth, offsetting any predicted temperature increases. Other researchers believe temperature increases, which began around 1880, are not the onset of greenhouse warming but rather a retreat from the "Little Ice Age," which is a part of an interglacial interval, with the onset of the next glacial cycle near.[9] Scientists acknowledge it is difficult to use GCMs to predict regional changes that may occur, rather than global ones, and when they are used to "hindcast" (look backward to analyze trends in temperature that have already occurred) the models are notoriously inaccurate.[10]

There is little controversy over the scientific evidence that the levels of carbon dioxide have increased by about 50 percent since the late 1700s, 25 percent over the past century, and are now increasing at the rate of 0.5 percent each year. Most of the studies agree that continued emissions of greenhouse gases will lead to a warming of Earth's temperature between 1.5 and 4.5 degrees Celsius (or 2.7–8.1 degrees Fahrenheit). So far this century, global average temperatures have risen between .5 and 1 degree Fahrenheit, consistent with the GCM predictions.

In his congressional testimony, Hansen claimed that he was 99 percent certain that Earth was getting warmer, that the warming could be associated with the greenhouse effect, and that there was a noticeable increase in the frequency of drought based on climate models. The disputes that have politicized this debate involve the amount of warming, when it will occur, and the impact of that temperature increase.

Why should we be concerned about what seem like relatively small changes in temperature? There are a number of possible scenarios attributed to global climate change. One of the most respected scientists who has studied the issue, Dr. Stephen H. Schneider of the National Center for Atmospheric Research, believes the temperature increases would lead to a rise in sea levels through the heating of the oceans, and possibly higher levels from the melting of polar ice as well. Drought and prolonged heat would be expected to lead to a greater likelihood of fire damage, more severe air pollution and air stagnation, and increased energy use leading to a need for more power production. Some of the changes forecast to occur might not be as negative. Global warming might lengthen the growing season for grain in Siberia, allowing some nations to increase their food production. The flip side of the equation, however, would be a loss to U.S. farmers, who are currently the world's leading grain exporters, with an accompanying impact on our economy.[11]

Other scientists using case studies of climate-related events like rising levels of the Great Lakes and the Great Salt Lake, are attempting to predict how society might react to global warming using "forecasting by analogy."[12] Some analysts, however, believe that people can adapt to climate change, and that such apocalyptic predictions are unwarranted. They believe there are ways in which we can reduce dependence upon fossil fuels without taking the kinds of draconian measures that would damage our standard of living.[13] Some studies show that even if temperatures rise as predicted, the effect will be more subtle, with gradual adaptation by humans and other species. For example, the more industrialized nations like the United States, Great Britain, and Japan will be better able to adapt to rising sea levels than will, for example, Bangladesh.[14]

Are the models of doom correct? Despite human advances and technological breakthroughs, weather and climate remain elements of the environment that remain imperfectly understood and uncontrolled by humankind. The uncertainty over global warming comes from three sources: predicting future climate, predicting future impacts, and assessing costs and benefits of policy responses.[15] Some scientists, for example, have predicted the eruption of Mt. Pinatubo in the Philippines in June 1991 will lead to a cooling of Earth's temperatures. NASA researchers believe that the volcano's eruption has led to an increase in the amount of dust and aerosols in the stratosphere, resulting in a cooling over the next three years.[16] The polarization among the members of the scientific community has spilled over to the political arena, where policymakers are trying to decide which view is the most reliable. The debate is joined by industry representatives (primarily electric utilities) who argue that it is foolhardy to make costly changes in technology or life-style changes until all the evidence is in. They seek support and funding for further study and analysis until there is a general scientific consensus.

Nonetheless, there is a growing body of scientific evidence that given the various scenarios, it is imperative that steps be taken immediately to avoid the devastating effects of climatic change being forecast with general agreement of a need for a major reduction in carbon dioxide emissions. Such a strategy would require substantive (and costly) changes in the way we live, and not only in the United States. Although the burden of cost is likely to fall disproportionately on the industrialized nations of the North, developing countries in the South will be asked to make drastic changes in their current patterns of energy use. This raises a whole host of policy questions. Will industrialized nations share their technology and expertise with the less developed countries? If so, will they also give their financial support to those nations to help them reduce their dependence upon fossil fuels? Could developing countries, already facing massive foreign debt, afford to switch to alternative fuels without aid from the North? Is the United States willing to set an example with its policies and rely more on energy conservation and non-fossil fuel sources?

The answers to those questions are at the heart of the international debate over global warming. Though industrialized countries have been dealing with the issues for over a decade through bodies like the IPCC, and are aware of the ramifications of the problem, developing nations are less likely to perceive global warming as a potential risk. They are less represented on various international study boards and have devoted fewer resources to research on the potential impact of global climate change. As a result, they are understandably less concerned and less anxious about finding a solution.[17]

Despite these uncertainties, opinion appears to be focusing on the need for an "insurance policy" approach to greenhouse warming. Such a strategy calls for reductions in energy consumption and enhanced conservation—policies that would benefit the United States by reducing the nation's dependence upon foreign oil. The energy savings would have spillover effects as well, such as reducing the need to drill for oil in environmentally sensitive areas and reducing the emissions that contribute to acid rain. Such policies would not solve global warming, advocates say, but would buy more time for additional research and the opportunity to come up with better solutions.[18] Even though most scientists admit additional research is needed to predict the timing and magnitude of global warming, there is a growing consensus that some initial steps like these to reduce carbon dioxide emissions can be taken now without a major economic disruption. This view appears to be gaining more acceptance. A 1991 study by the National Academy of Sciences marked a decided shift in policy. The group, which had previously concluded that additional research into greenhouse warming was needed, recommended that "despite the great uncertainties, greenhouse warming is a potential threat sufficient to justify action now."[19]

STRATOSPHERIC OZONE DEPLETION

Ozone is an element of Earth's atmosphere caused by a photochemical reaction of hydrocarbons (produced mainly from the burning of fossil fuels) and sunlight. In one sense, there is "bad" ozone and "good" ozone. At the surface of Earth, ozone is one of the major components of smog, but higher up in the stratosphere (between six and thirty miles above Earth's surface), the ozone layer provides a filtering layer of protection against the harmful effects of ultraviolet radiation. Without such protection against ultraviolet radiation, medical experts believe there would be a substantial increase in skin cancers and genetic changes in some types of plants and animals.

In the early 1970s, scientists warned that the exhaust gases from high-flying supersonic transport planes could damage the ozone layer. Studying components of the high-altitude atmosphere, they discovered that CFCs, which are synthetic, reacted with ultraviolet light when released into the atmosphere, forming chlorine. Chlorine is known to attack ozone molecules, and the researchers warned that unless steps were taken to reduce CFC production, between 7 and 13 percent of Earth's protective ozone layer would be destroyed.[20] CFCs are found in thousands of synthetic products, and are used primarily in air conditioning and refrigeration, foam packaging, and insulation. They are also used in cleaning the sides of the space shuttles, in sterilizing whole blood, and as a solvent in cleaning computers. Congress responded in 1977 by including provisions in the Clean Air Act amendments, which authorized the EPA administrator to regulate substances affecting the stratosphere, and in 1978, the EPA banned the use of CFCs in most aerosols. At the time, scientists were unable to measure the damage to the ozone layer, but on the strength of the theoretical evidence alone, Congress responded.[21]

With the election of Ronald Reagan in 1980, research into CFCs came to a virtual standstill and the search for substitute compounds subsided. Even though the United States had banned CFCs in aerosols, the nonaerosol use grew to record levels with the United States producing about one-third of the world total.[22] The issue gained new prominence in 1985 when a group of British scientists in Antarctica, who had been monitoring ozone levels for thirty years, found a "hole" in the ozone layer approximately the size of North America above the continent that lasted nearly three months each year.[23] The National Science Foundation sent its own team of researchers to Antarctica later that year,

The Rush to Refrigerate

While Americans take their refrigerators for granted as one of the necessities of modern living, that is not the case in most developing countries, where cooling appliances are luxury items in increasing demand by consumers. More and more countries are seeking to upgrade their standard of living, and that means owning a refrigerator. The refrigerator debate is based on the fact refrigerant technology now accounts for one of the largest and fastest-growing uses of CFCs in the developing world. As scientists learn more and more about the impact of CFCs on stratospheric ozone depletion, they are more concerned about the growing use of refrigerators.

How many refrigerators are we talking about? China and India represent about 40 percent of the world's population but currently consume only about 5 percent of all CFCs. If the two countries are successful in supplying refrigerators to a majority of their citizens, CFC use would rise rapidly. India's 6 million refrigerators are projected to increase to eighty million by 2010, and in China, the thirty million refrigerators now in operation are expected to double by 1996, with production capacity reaching eleven million units per year.

As a result, the rush is on to find safe substitutes for existing technology, fueled in part by funds generated through the 1990 amendments to the Montreal Protocol. The treaty created a $160 million fund to compensate developing countries for the additional costs they incur in using non-CFC products. Chemical companies in the industrialized nations are, understandably, somewhat reluctant to share their CFC-substitute technology (developed after years of costly investment) for free, so some of the Protocol funds can be used to purchase patent rights and licensing agreements. This allows less developed countries to purchase cutting-edge technology and shift to less damaging substitutes. Ammonia, for example, is being considered as a replacement refrigerant, since it is abundant and more energy efficient. The disadvantage is that ammonia is also toxic and flammable, making it inappropriate for some domestic uses. China has redirected its research and is already testing new types of refrigerators, which it hopes to export to the United States and Europe, and other developing countries are also experimenting with CFC substitutes. They are expecting a lucrative market for alternative refrigerators as the Protocol deadline approaches.[24]

and although they could not agree on an exact cause, they concluded that chlorine chemistry was somehow involved and that the hole was getting larger. In 1992, one study by the European Ozone Secretariat and another by NASA concluded that the ozone shield had also thinned markedly over the Northern Hemisphere. Although researchers were unable to discover a similar ozone hole over North America like that over the Antarctic, they warned that the increased levels of ozone-destroying chemicals were cause for alarm. As the scientific evidence of stratospheric ozone depletion mounted, the environmental protection wheels began to turn in the political arena.

BALANCING OUT THE OPTIONS

Even though the evidence that CFCs are responsible for ozone depletion is not irrefutable, there were a number of differences in the response of the government and industry from that of global warming. First, the issue of stratospheric ozone depletion was perceived as a more "manageable" problem than global warming, which is a much more complex and multifaceted problem than developing substitutes for CFCs. While industry officials called for more research into global warming before they were willing to accede to costly changes in production and technology, CFC manufacturers almost immediately agreed that CFC production should be reduced, even in the absence of proof that CFCs were damaging the ozone layer.

In 1988, the DuPont Company, the inventor and world's largest user of CFCs, announced it was phasing out production of two types of CFCs altogether. Other manufacturers and users of CFCs followed suit, and competition began to find replacement products and processes. The significance of the CFC strategy, from a political standpoint at least, is the United States and its industry leaders were willing to take action even before all of the scientific evidence was in. This "preventive action on a global scale" was a unique approach to environmental protection. Rather than bucking the trend and refusing to cooperate, companies like DuPont immediately began researching alternatives and substitutes for CFCs. And rather than stalling for time, the U.S. government took a leadership role and sought the strongest action possible—a complete ban on CFCs. The cost of finding replacements for the estimated thirty-five hundred applications where CFCs are used could reach $36 billion between now and 2075, according to the EPA.[25] As a result, what might initially be seen as an unreasonable cost of compliance is now being viewed as a new marketplace by many in the chemical industry. Forced to find substitutes for products and processes, some companies anticipate higher profits, while others fear that substitute substances will have their own complications. For example, one substitute—hydrochlorofluorocarbons, or HCFCs—are being criticized by environmentalists because they still contain ozone-damaging chlorine. But they are less damaging than CFCs and may prove to be a valuable transitional substitute while industry research continues.

Second, the U.S. government accepted the premise that a unilateral phase-out of CFCs was not acceptable for solving such a global problem. The United States initiated an international agreement to phase out CFC production within ten years, a move that led to the signing in September 1987 of the Montreal Protocol on Substances That Deplete the Ozone Layer. The document set a strict timetable of step-by-step reductions in CFCs and other ozone-depleting substances leading to a complete production ban by 2000. Developing nations were given a ten-year grace period before full compliance is required, but many have refused to sign the treaty because of the expense involved in switching to new technology.

After scientists warned that the 50 percent reduction was not adequate to reduce the destruction of the ozone layer, the United States enacted even more stringent domestic legislation with passage of Title VI of the Clean Air Act amendments of 1990.[26] The legislation required an accelerated phase-out of the compounds that pose the greatest threat to the ozone layer: CFCs, halons, carbon tetrachloride, and methyl chloroform, with elimination as soon as possible and no later than 2002. Under the terms of the amendments, the EPA now requires the mandatory nationwide recycling of CFCs in motor vehicle air conditioners, the biggest user of CFCs in the United States. The American efforts were not designed to replace a stronger version of the Montreal Protocol, but instead were expected to serve as a model for future international agreements. Subsequent negotiations among the parties to the protocol in London in 1990 and Copenhagen in 1992 led to a speeding up of the CFC phase-out. Delegates in Copenhagen also agreed to reduce HCFCs by 35 percent by 2004, by 99.5 percent by 2020, and to a total ban by 2030. The parties also added methyl bromide, which may be responsible for 10 percent of the ozone lost so far, as a "controlled substance," which means emissions will be frozen at 1991 levels by 1995. Methyl bromide is used to fumigate soils and crops in some less industrialized countries. The Copenhagen amendments are expected to reduce deaths due to the thinning of the ozone layer by forty thousand.[27]

The United States has not pursued a similar strategy with regard to greenhouse warming.[28] While the United States took a leadership position with ozone depletion, the United Nations has been the vanguard for development of an international regime to address global climate change. Members of the European Community and Japan have also agreed to adopt greenhouse gas stabilization or reduction targets, and have attempted to capture U.S. support. Led by Germany, delegates to the UN's Earth Summit in June 1992 sought approval of a convention that would reduce emissions of carbon dioxide to 1990 levels by the year 2000. The United States refused to ratify the document, arguing that the emission reduction proposal would hurt economic growth—a position underscored by President George Bush in his appearance before the delegates. As a result, a watered-down version of the agreement emerged without specific targets, with Bush agreeing to urge the Senate to ratify the treaty as soon as possible. The United States's position was sharply criticized by other nations, but EPA administrator William Reilly promised delegates that the United States would complete a detailed action plan for reducing emissions of greenhouse gases by January 1, 1993, and would spend $1.4 billion for climate change research—the largest such effort in the world.

Third, media coverage of the ozone-depletion issue kept attention focused on the U.S. efforts to develop an international agreement and prevented the administration negotiators from weakening the proposed CFC controls. For example, on May 29, 1987, the media published reports that Interior Secretary Donald Hodel was attempting to revoke the authority of the U.S. delegation to negotiate significant reductions in ozone-destroying compounds. After newspaper headlines reading "Advice on Ozone May Be: 'Wear Hats and Stand in Shade' " and "Administration Ozone Policy May Favor Sunglasses, Hats; Support for Chemical Cutbacks Reconsidered," the public outcry over the apparent change in the U.S. position created a backlash that virtually guaranteed the imposition of stringent controls.[29] Media coverage of global warming, in contrast, has been colored by the lack of scientific consensus on the rate of onset and the potential magnitude of the problem. The attention given to global warming has not been as focused, if only because the potential impacts are more uncertain, less tangible, and less immediate than those of ozone depletion. Global warming lacks an equivalent to the ozone hole upon which the media and public can focus their attention.[30]

It is this lack of scientific consensus that is perhaps the most important difference in how the policy debate has developed. At least initially, concerns about global warming were dominated by scientists who debated the consequences of human interference in the environment. There were many more attempts to measure the nature of global climate change before taking action than had been the case with CFCs. Increased production of carbon dioxide and rising atmospheric turbidity were recognized as two important factors capable of causing climate change, but there was uncertainty whether the result would be a warming or a cooling of the atmosphere. There have been dozens of scientific congresses and meetings, but the task of building consensus among scientists has been formidable.

Equally difficult has been the task of agreeing on what should be done about greenhouse warming. For example, the National Academy of Science report made several recommendations to Congress, including a phase-out of CFCs and other halocarbon emissions and the development of substitutes that minimize or eliminate greenhouse gas emissions; enhanced energy conservation and efficient development of a new generation of nuclear reactor technology that is designed to deal with safety, waste management, and public acceptability; and reduction of global deforestation, initiation of a domestic reforestation program, and support for international reforestation efforts to restore the cleansing capacity of forests.

Critics argue that while several of these proposals may have some merit, others do not. For example, a UN Environment Programme study has noted that while reforestation is probably a good idea on its own merits, it probably cannot do much to slow the accumulation of carbon dioxide in the atmosphere. A much larger area than France would have to be reforested annually to "mop up" the carbon dioxide released from the burning of fossil fuels.[31] The most likely option is to reduce source production of greenhouse gases through energy conservation and a switch to cleaner-burning fuels such as natural gas and nuclear energy, an alternative discussed in Chapter 6. If the experts cannot agree on the nature and extent of the problem, it is unlikely that they will agree on solutions as well.

Lastly, the global warming issue lacks the support of major actors in the political arena, including the United States. In order for an international agreement to be effective, it must also have the support of the developing countries, which are becoming dependent upon fossil fuels. This was not the case with CFCs and the Montreal Protocol. In that instance, sufficient concessions could be made outside the fishbowl of media publicity to allow room for negotiation and compromise. Global warming does not have a similarly low profile.[32] What that means is that the process of reconciling differences among developing and industrialized nations to produce a global warming agreement will be much more politicized and therefore much more difficult.[33] Until there is sufficient scientific consensus on the problem itself, there is little foundation for future policymaking.

SUMMARY

The twin problems of global warming and stratospheric ozone depletion are examples of the globalization of an environmental issue, as well as a contrast in perception and response. Global warming, which some researchers believe will result in dramatic climate change, has become one of the most controversial environmental protection issues, with scientists polarized over the nature and extent of the forecast impacts. As a result, policymakers have been unable to gain acceptance of an international agreement to reduce emissions of carbon dioxide, the most abundant synthetic greenhouse gas. The United States has continually refused to accept proposals to reduce its emissions of greenhouse gases, citing the adverse economic impacts that would occur. At the UN Conference on Environment and Development in Rio de Janeiro in June 1992, the United States was alone among the industrialized nations in rejecting specific targets for greenhouse gas emission reductions. The U.S. position continues to be that the problem needs additional research. In contrast, the issue of stratospheric ozone depletion, although only recently verified by scientific evidence and research, immediately gained acceptance among policymakers, who rushed through international agreements to phase out and eventually ban the use of ozone-depleting compounds. In addition, there was agreement that only a global approach would be successful, rather than unilateral action by the United States, the world's largest contributor to ozone depletion. There are various explanations for the difference in the way the two issues were handled, ranging from the more extensive media coverage of the ozone depletion problem, the difference in the manageability of the two issues, and the lack of scientific consensus on the nature and extent of greenhouse warming. Lack of scientific consensus looms as a major obstacle to the acceptance of an international agreement on greenhouse warming like that of the Montreal Protocol limits on CFC production.

NOTES

1. Quoted in Christopher Flavin, *Slowing Global Warming: A Worldwide Strategy.* (Washington, DC: Worldwatch Institute, October 1989), 15.

2. See, for example J. D. Hays, John Imbrie, and N. J. Shackleton, "Variations in the Earth's Orbit: Pacemaker of the Ice Ages," *Science* 194 (December 10, 1976): 1121–31. The authors conclude, "A model of future climate based on the observed orbital-climate relationships, but ignoring anthropogenic effects, predicts that the long-term trend over the next several thousand years is towards extensive Northern Hemisphere glaciation."

3. See James E. Lovelock, *Gaia* (Oxford: Oxford University Press, 1979).

4. See U.S. Congress, Senate, Committee on Commerce, Science and Transportation, *Policy Implications of Greenhouse Warming*, hearing, 102nd Cong., 1st sess., 25 April 1991 (Washington, DC: U.S. Government Printing Office, 1991).

5. World Commission on Environment and Development, *Our Common Future* (Oxford: Oxford University Press, 1987).

6. See Jon R. Luoma, "Gazing into Our Greenhouse Future," *Audubon*, March 1991, 52–59, 124–29.

7. See S. Fred Singer, "Global Climate Change: Fact and Fiction," *You and I*, July 1991, 284–91.

8. See Sherman Idso, *Carbon Dioxide: Friend or Foe?* (Tempe, AZ: IBR Press, 1982). See also D. S. Halacy, Jr., *Ice or Fire: Can We Survive Climatic Change?* (New York: Barnes and Noble Books, 1978). Lindzen is quoted in William K. Stevens, "Skeptics Are Challenging Dire Greenhouse Views," *New York Times*, December 13, 1989, A-1.

9. S. Fred Singer, Roger Revelle, and Chauncey Starr, "What to Do about Global Warming: Look Before You Leap," *Cosmos* 1, no. 1 (1991): 28–31.

10. Ibid., 286.

11. See Stephen H. Schneider, *Global Warming: Are We Entering the Greenhouse Century?* (San Francisco: Sierra Club Books, 1989).

12. For an explanation of this concept as it is used in ten case studies, see Michael H. Glantz, ed., *Societal Responses to Regional Climatic Change* (Boulder, CO: Westview Press, 1988).

13. See, for example, Dixy Lee Ray, "The Greenhouse Blues: Keep Cool about Global Warming," *Policy Review* 49 (Summer 1989): 70–72.

14. For this view, see Thomas Levenson, *Ice Time: Climate, Science, and Life on Earth* (New York: Harper & Row, 1989).

15. See E. William Colglazier, "Scientific Uncertainties, Public Policy, and Global Warming: How Sure Is Sure Enough?" *Policy Studies Journal* 19, no. 2 (Spring 1991): 61–72.

16. Jeff Hecht, "Pinatubo Cooling Will Test Greenhouse Models," *New Scientist*, January 11, 1992, 20.

17. See David Feldman, "Tracking Global Climate Change Policy," *Policy Currents* 1, no. 4 (November 1991): 1–5.

18. See Schneider, *Global Warming*, 238–85.

19. National Academy of Sciences, *Policy Implications of Greenhouse Warming* (Washington, DC: National Academy Press, 1991), 72.

20. For a narrative description of the rise of the ozone depletion issue to the top of environmental protection agenda, see John J. Nance, *What Goes Up: The Global Assault on Our Atmosphere* (New York: Morrow, 1991).

21. For an account of the early scientific evidence and the political debates that followed, see Paul Brodeur, "Annals of Chemistry: In the Face of Doubt," *The New Yorker*, June 9, 1986, 70.

22. Steven J. Shimberg, "Stratospheric Ozone and Climate Protection: Domestic Legislation and the International Process," *Environmental Law* 21, no. 2175 (1991): 2184.

23. See Susan Solomon et al., "On Depletion of Antarctic Ozone," *Nature* 321 (June 19, 1986): 755–58.

24. See Debora MacKenzie, "Cheaper Alternatives for CFCs," *New Scientist*, June 30, 1990, 39; and Armin Rosencranz and Reina Milligan, "CFC Abatement: The Needs of Developing Countries," *Ambio* 19, nos. 6–7 (1990): 312–15.

25. Martha M. Hamilton, "The Challenge to Make Industry Ozone-Friendly," *Washington Post National Weekly Edition*, October 7–13, 1991, 21.

26. For an analysis of the Title VI amendments, see Shimberg, "Stratospheric Ozone and Climate Protection," 2193–2214.

27. Debora MacKenzie, "Agreement Reduces Damage to Ozone Layer," *New Scientist*, December 5, 1992, 10.

28. For a summary of the U.S. position, as well as that of other countries, see Peter M. Morrisette and Andrew J. Plantinga, "Global Warming: A Policy Review," *Policy Studies Journal* 19, no. 2 (Spring 1991): 163–72.

29. Shimberg, "Stratospheric Ozone and Climate Protection," 2188.

30. Peter M. Morrisette, "The Montreal Protocol: Lessons for Formulating Policies for Global Warming," *Policy Studies Journal* 19, no. 2 (Spring 1991): 152–61.

31. Levenson, *Ice Time*, 204.

32. Morrisette, "Montreal Protocol," 158.

33. For an explanation of the difficulties of reaching an agreement on greenhouse warming, see James K. Sebenius, "Designing Negotiations towards a New Regime: The Case of Global Warming," *International Security* 15, no. 4 (Spring 1991): 110–48.

FOR FURTHER READING

Dean Edward Abrahamson, ed. *The Challenge of Global Warming*. Washington, DC: Island Press, 1989.

Richard Benedick. *Ozone Diplomacy: New Directions in Safeguarding the Planet*. Cambridge: Harvard University Press, 1991.

Gary C. Bryner, ed. *Global Warming and the Challenge of International Cooperation*. Provo, UT: Kennedy Center for International Studies, 1992.

Christopher Flavin. *Slowing Global Warming: A Worldwide Strategy*. Washington, DC: Worldwatch Institute, October 1989.

John J. Nance. *What Goes Up: The Global Assault on Our Atmosphere*. New York: Morrow, 1991.

National Academy of Sciences. *Policy Implications of Greenhouse Warming*. Washington, DC: National Academy Press, 1991.

Sharon L. Roan. *Ozone Crisis: The Fifteen Year Evolution of a Sudden Global Emergency*. New York: Wiley, 1989.

Stephen H. Schneider. *Global Warming: Are We Entering the Greenhouse Century?* San Francisco: Sierra Club Books, 1989.

CHAPTER 14

Tropical Forests:
On the Cutting Edge

Poverty forces the poor to destroy the environment. It would be absurd to think that someone who is dying of hunger will think about protecting the environment before satisfying his basic needs.
  —Venezuela foreign minister Armando Duran, commenting on efforts by industrialized nations to impose ecological controls on developing nations[1]

The fate of tropical forests is a classic example of the conflict that has erupted between the "haves" of the industrialized countries of the North and the "have-nots" of the developing South. The issue has often pitted environmental activists from industrialized nations against policymakers from Third and Fourth World nations who have accused the United States of "environmental imperialism" in its attempts to control the fate of other countries' resources.

The term *tropical forests* usually refers to a wide belt of land circling the equator between the Tropic of Cancer and the Tropic of Capricorn—areas with consistently high temperatures averaging 80 degrees Fahrenheit. Scientists further delineate between tropical dry forests, tropical moist forests, and true tropical rainforests, a term applied to areas that receive 120 to 235 inches of rain per year. Four-fifths of the world's rainforests are concentrated in nine countries: Bolivia, Brazil (with one-third of the worldwide total), Colombia, Gabon, Indonesia (with one-third), Malaysia, Peru, Venezuela, and Zaire. China's Yunnan Province along the border with Laos and Myanmar is considered a north tropics rainforest, once home to half of China's fifteen thousand species of plants and more than half the nation's five hundred species of mammals and two-thirds of its one thousand kinds of birds. The United States also controls four tropical forest regions of its own: American Samoa, Hawaii, Puerto Rico, and the U.S. Virgin Islands.[2]

There are two major problems currently being addressed by global policymakers. One, although there is a lack of precise information about the rate of loss, there is consensus among scientists that tropical forests are disappearing at an alarming and ever-increasing rate. Two, there is also agreement that failure to effectively manage tropical forests can result in a number of negative impacts, including the loss of wood products for fuel and other uses, soil erosion, global warming, shrinking populations of plants in the wild, destruction of fish-breeding areas, and loss of biological diversity and wildlife habitat.

Estimates as to how much tropical forest remains are notoriously unreliable and depend in large part on what definition of *forest* is used. One researcher believes that only 57 percent of Earth's original 8.65 million square miles of moist tropical forest remains, meaning that an area the size of the former Soviet Union has disappeared, much of it since 1945. The rate of worldwide tropical deforestation was about 120,000 square miles per year in 1979, between 175,000 and 220,000 square miles per year just ten years later, and may range from 1 to 1.8 percent per year now.[3] An unpublished study by the World Bank, in contrast, says that the levels of deforestation have been grossly exaggerated, and that there is evidence of the beginning of a long-term slowdown in forest clearing.[4] While most of the loss is due to burning for agricultural purposes, with another 20–25 percent of the deforestation attributable to commercial logging, some losses are not the result of human actions. In 1983, for example, a forest fire in northeastern Borneo during a period of severe drought resulted in the loss of an area of tropical forest the size of Belgium.

Deforestation in tropical areas occurs primarily on lands not held by private citizens, especially in developing areas, where over four-fifths of closed forest area is public land. In some countries, nearly 100 percent of all natural forest is government owned, giving officials total authority over the use and preservation of the lands. Thus, the rates of deforestation vary considerably from one region of the world to another. The Ivory Coast, for example, is considered to have the fastest rate of deforestation, with estimates ranging from 7 to 15 percent per year. In Southeast Asia, rates range from less than 1 percent in Kampuchea to 8 percent in Thailand. China is estimated to have lost nearly 40 percent of its rainforest to rubber plantations, logging, and the pressures of feeding a rapidly increasing population. In the Philippines, natural forest cover has shrunk from two-thirds of total land areas to only 22 percent since 1945, while in Central America, forest areas declined by 38 percent between 1950 and 1983. Western Ecuador is estimated to have less than 10 percent of its original forests, and Madagascar about 7 percent.[5]

This chapter outlines key issues including the unique characteristics of the tropical forest ecosystem, the development of political awareness and control over tropical forests, the groups (both international and indigenous) involved in the controversy, and proposed solutions to reducing the rate of tropical deforestation, the term applied to a change in land use from forestry to other uses, such as agriculture, grazing, or the creation of human settlements.

THE TROPICAL FOREST ECOSYSTEM

Antarctica and tropical forests are both examples of ecosystems that are so valuable and biologically diverse that scientists are in unanimous agreement that extraordinary measures must be taken to preserve them. But unlike Antarctica, which is geographically remote, uninhabited, marginally valuable for its natural resources, and a single physical entity, tropical forests cross political borders, are home to millions of native populations, and are accessible to developers seeking to exploit their resources.

People

An estimated 140 million people live within the world's tropical forest zones, making up more than a thousand indigenous tribal groupings. Many of these native populations have been practicing sustainable management for centuries, using the forest for all their daily needs while maintaining its variety and size, and many possess sophisticated knowledge of forest use. To some, the forest has unique spiritual and cultural value as well.

Yet the destruction of tropical forests has disturbed and in some cases decimated indigenous peoples. Some die as a result of being exposed to infectious diseases carried by colonists because they have no resistance. Others are forced to change their way of life as they are relocated or resettled, often losing their memory of ancient ways—a loss that is felt by contemporary society as well. Indonesia, for example, has resettled 3.5 million peasants from the inner islands of Bali, Java, and Madera to the outer islands of Irian Jaya, Timor, Sulawesi, and Sumatra—a change in life-style that has destroyed the cultural heritage of many of the nation's people.

Protection of the rainforest people is critical because they have so much to offer. Perhaps most valuable is their knowledge of sustainable forest management and agriculture—a skill that allows them to live off their natural environment without destroying it. These people are an irreplaceable resource, such as Thailand's Lua tribe, which grows seventy-five food crops and twenty-one different medicinal plants, or the Hanunoo of the Philippines, who grow 430 rainforest crops. Protection of their life-style and culture is an essential element of any program to protect the rainforest's resources.

Flora and Fauna

Researchers can only estimate the number of species of plants and animals that exist on Earth, with the total ranging anywhere from five to thirty million. Of that number, only about 1.4 million species have been identified and named thus far, which means that millions more have yet to be discovered. At least half to two-thirds of the world's species are found in tropical forests, and many of them are found nowhere else. Many of them are already extinct, and thousands more are being lost every year.

Many of contemporary society's needs are filled by products originally found and cultivated in tropical forests, ranging from coffee and citrus fruits to chocolate and rice. Only 2 percent of the crop production in the United States is based on native species, and new varieties of edible fruits are being introduced into American markets every year. Latex from rubber plants finds its way into vehicle tires and paints, and as a renewable resource now accounts for over $3 billion in yearly exports from Third World countries.

Of critical importance is the role of tropical forests in providing biodiversity—the gene pool that allows nature to adapt and respond to changing environmental conditions. Although scientists do not fully understand the role of genes, genotypes, species, and communities, they recognize that there is some urgency in learning how changes in biodiversity affect Earth's ecosystem.[6] The destruction of animal and plant habitat through deforestation is resulting in the extinction of an estimated seventeen thousand species per year, and a large number of species currently considered endangered live only in the rainforest. Many species found in tropical forests are endemic to a single region. The 3,435-square-mile island of Puerto Rico, for example, is home to 3,000 species of plants, 232 native bird species, 13 types of bats, and 78 species of reptiles and amphibians, many of them unique to the island.[7]

Medicinal Value

The tropical rainforest has been described as nature's medicine cabinet, and its value is only beginning to be appreciated by pharmacologists. One of the earliest rainforest plants discovered to have medicinal value was quinine, a product of the cinchona plant found in certain areas of South America. For some time, it was the only known treatment for malaria. The National Cancer Institute has identified three thousand plants that have cancer-fighting properties, 70 percent of which are found in rainforests. Vast plantations of the Madagascar (or rosy) periwinkle, which had disappeared completely in the wild, are now commercially harvested for use in a compound that is used in treating leukemia. Rainforest plants found in Belize, Guatemala, and Mexico are the source for diosgenin, the active ingredient in cortisone and birth control pills. Plants with medicinal qualities that could treat humans' most deadly diseases could be awaiting discovery in a rainforest even now.[8]

Climate Control and Erosion

Tropical forests play an important role in the hydrological cycle that controls Earth's climate, and deforestation has several negative impacts. Loss of rainforest cover, which both reflects and absorbs sunlight, may disrupt wind circulation and change rainfall patterns, which contributes to surface drying. Deforestation is also estimated to contribute to up to 30 percent of the world's carbon dioxide emissions, which are believed to contribute to global warming, a subject discussed in Chapter 13. One scientist believes that deforestation contributes twice as much carbon dioxide into the air as had originally been estimated.[9]

Trees have a secondary benefit because they absorb the brunt of the force of tropical storms, reducing the damage to human settlements and populations.

The forests also receive more than half of the world's rainfall, which is absorbed by trees and slowly released into the watershed. When the trees are logged, flooding results and the soil is rapidly eroded. Thailand was forced to ban logging throughout most of the country after a 1988 storm degraded the soil and severe flooding left hundreds dead and thousands homeless. Soil erosion also contributes to changes in sedimentation rates, blocking streams and dams and destroying fish habitats.

THE DEVELOPMENT OF POLITICAL AWARENESS AND CONTROL

Logging of tropical forests and their products has been occurring for nearly five hundred years, beginning with the collection of rare and valuable spices like pepper and cinnamon by Southeast Asian traders. However, early merchants tended to collect only what they wanted and did not destroy the forests in their search for spices. During most of the nineteenth century, Europeans sought African hardwood for furniture but left the rest of the forest intact. Latin American forests, in contrast, were often burned to the ground as Spanish settlers established colonial outposts and set up plantation agriculture. The export of agricultural commodities quickly proved a lucrative enterprise for several nations. The Portuguese, for example, leveled Brazilian rainforests and turned the land into sugar plantations to satisfy the needs of European consumers, bringing in African slaves when the native people were unwilling to work the land. The Dutch brought sugar farming to the Caribbean, clearing the islands' fragile ecosystems for firewood as well, as did the Spanish in Cuba. British pirates plundered the Central American forests for wood for European furniture, and European demand for coffee resulted in more clearing of the land.

The United States entered the picture in the 1880s when U.S. investors edged out their Spanish competitors and built huge sugar processing facilities dependent upon crops in Cuba and in the Pacific islands of Hawaii and the Philippines. The sugar barons' quest for increased profits meant that more and more forest acreage was cleared and sugar cane became the primary vegetation in many areas, pushing out tropical woods. The logging of native forests for sugar cane was followed by massive acreage devoted to tropical fruits, such as banana plantations in Costa Rica and Nicaragua.[10]

In the 1920s and 1930s, international journals of forestry documented the rapid destruction of tropical forests, but there was little political attention to the problem at that time. Four reasons have been suggested to explain the huge losses of tropical forests throughout the globe that have occurred primarily since World War I:

- Population growth, especially in regions of the world where vast tracts of forest land have been cleared for new roads, farming, cattle grazing, and as new settlements are established
- Demand for wood as a fuel source, especially in Africa, Asia, and the Caribbean, and for furniture, especially by Japan.[11]
- Lack of expertise in forest management, and a scarcity of professionals in developing countries
- A lack of citizen participation in land planning and resource extraction decision making

Much of the tropical deforestation that took place between World War I and the advent of the international environmental movement in the early 1970s occurred with little or no political debate. The more highly publicized issues of pollution crowded the top of the environmental protection agenda, especially in industrialized nations. Attention to the environmental concerns of Third and Fourth World countries is a recent phenomenon. It was not until the early 1980s that international organizations, such as the UN's Food and Agriculture Organization (FAO) began to systematically review scientific literature on deforestation. In 1985, the FAO announced that the problem was due to the poverty of native peoples, who cleared the forest for food. The FAO proposed that the forest should be used commercially for timber production, which would be sold and would produce higher incomes and therefore improve the living standard of the regions' peoples. Also in 1985, a report prepared by the World Bank, World Resources Institute, and the UN Development Programme called for the implementation of new forestry practices and creation of timber plantations.

The two proposals were combined into the Tropical Forestry Action Plan (TFAP), which sought the support of member nations to slow deforestation—a process that now involves nearly a hundred nations holding over 85 percent of the world's tropical forests. The TFAP has come under growing criticism, however, from the World Wildlife Fund, the World Rainforest Movement, and the Conservation Foundation, among others, which no longer support the plan. They have urged the International Union for the Conservation of Nature and Natural Resources to reform TFAP by involving local peoples in the decision-making process and to compare logging's economic gains to community-based forest management, including income from nontimber forest products such as rubber and nuts.[12] Some groups believe that the responsibility for administering the TFAP should be moved from the FAO to a more "green" body, such as the UN Development Programme.[13]

There have been some attempts, however, to change long-standing practices that have contributed to deforestation. Some recent efforts have been made to transfer property rights from the government to local residents, returning at least some sense of local control. In 1990, for example, the government of Colombia awarded land rights to half that nation's Amazonian forest to Indian groups, and Peru has also announced plans to transfer land to small-scale local farmers.

Other governments have attempted to make their logging industries self-supporting by banning the export of raw logs and placing heavy levies on the export of sawn timber. In Indonesia, loggers must pay a reforestation fee, and the government fined Barito Pacific, one of the world's biggest logging companies, $10 million for its failure to log selectively. The government has also privatized control of its customs operations (reducing widespread corruption, which shortchanged government revenues on timber) and monitored its logging operations, which is ending underreporting of logging and increasing revenues as well.[14]

Some of the deforestation issues are of relatively recent origin. In southern Chile, for example, widespread logging did not begin until the late 1980s, when native trees were cut and ground into small chips that are shipped to Japan to be processed into paper. Although thirty million acres of Chilean forest are protected in reserves, the nineteen million acres estimated to be in private hands are often destructively cut by landowners seeking quick profits. The forestry industry has grown into one of Chile's main export earners, generating $913 million in 1991, more than twenty times its annual foreign revenues in the early 1970s. Attempts by groups such as California-based Ancient Forests International and Chile's National Committee for Defense of the Flora and Fauna have been largely unsuccessful in convincing the Chilean government to enforce existing regulations that limit cutting and provide for reforestation. Few violators are prosecuted and even fewer are convicted by Chilean courts. Fundacion Lahuen, a Chilean nongovernmental organization (NGO) that advocates a moratorium on all industrial logging of native forest land, is attempting to acquire some forest areas privately—a tactic successfully used in the United States by groups like the Nature Conservancy.

Now, as some countries' forest resources are being depleted, international attention is being focused on countries where commercial logging was previously limited or inaccessible. Since the demand for tropical woods has not slowed, logging cartels are looking at regions in New Guinea, China, and New Caledonia, considered "hot-spot" regions of destruction.[15] This means that more nations, by necessity, will become stakeholders and involved in the debate over the future of tropical forests.

INDIGENOUS REVOLT

The exploitation of natural resources has slowly led to revolts by the indigenous people of the tropical forest countries. The best known of the struggles—the *chipko* movement—began in India as part of a century-long peasant movement offering resistance to state encroachment in a region embracing the eight hill districts in the state of Uttar Pradesh. This area of the Himalayas is one of the most densely forested on the Asian continent, with vast parcels of cedar, oak, and fir. The trees were initially logged by the state during the 1860s in order to supply timber for the Indian railway system, built with the assistance of German engineers and forestry experts who surveyed timber resources throughout the country. The turn of the century marked the expansion of the lumber industry into supplying resin and turpentine to Europe and the Far East, the takeover of timber management by the government, and a gradual loss of local peasant control over the forests.

The chipko movement began with a series of peasant uprisings, termed *andolan*, in 1904, including incidents in which local villagers refused to help the government fight fires in government-owned preserves, as they were required to do by law. After World War II, loans from the World Bank for road building further opened up the Himalayan forests and increased tourism. This brought about a greater demand for firewood, but little of the economic development benefited the local area or its residents. Meanwhile, although the native population was increasing exponentially, agricultural productivity was decreasing with the deterioration of the hill ecosystem due to excessive logging. In 1958, the Indian government convened a committee to investigate the complaints of local residents about forestry practices, but the result was only a generalized commitment to meeting the needs of the villagers.

The disastrous floods of 1970 marked a turning point, as residents began to see the causal linkage between logging and erosion, and led to demonstrations demanding local control of forests. The leadership of the movement was the cooperative organization Dashauli Gram Swarajya Sangh (DGSS), which discussed options ranging from lying down in front of timber trucks to burning resin depots. They finally adopted a strategy to "hug the trees even if axes split open their stomachs," and thus chipko ("to hug") was born. Demonstrations against continued logging began in 1973, and in 1974, native women became actively involved in the andolan when the government tried to log at a time when the men were absent from the village. More floods during the late 1970s and 1980s led to an expansion of the chipko andolan throughout India.[16]

Chipko was followed by a rapid succession of similar movements around the world directed at the environmental consequences of mining and the siting of dams, as well as other indigenous efforts to halt deforestation. In 1985, along the Pacific coastal rainforest of Ecuador, the Awa people began battling the *colonos* (colonists) who cleared trees, overhunted game, fished with dynamite, and settled wherever they chose. The land, which receives three hundred to four hundred inches of rain per year, is one of the most biologically diverse areas in Ecuador if not in all Latin America. It is home to thousands of plant species, many rare fish and amphibians, and more than six hundred species of birds, many of which are found nowhere else in the world. Led by former Peace Corps volunteer Jim Levy, the twenty-two hundred Awa who make their home in Ecuador established the *manga*, a 150-mile-long swath encircling their territory, now designated an Ethnic Forest Reserve by the Ecuadorean government. The manga is in one sense a moat that surrounds Awa lands and serves as a line of demarcation and a claim to ownership, allowing the natives to manage their own

Saga of a Seringuerio

One of the most highly publicized of the indigenous people's revolts took place in 1988 along Brazil's westernmost border with Bolivia and Peru, in the state of Acre. When the government began its National Integration Program in 1969 to colonize the region, the local rubber tappers, called *seringuerios*, were forced from their homes by cattle ranchers and settlers who came to clear the land.[19] When told by the government that they would have to relocate, many complied, but one group, led by Chico Alves Mendes Filho, refused. Mendes, known to his friends as Chico, was head of the local rubber tappers union, and began a fight to save the forest, which was the economic lifeline for his family and thousands of fellow workers.

During a thirteen-year period, Mendes and his followers organized forty-five human, nonviolent *empates*, (blockades) against bulldozers brought in to clear the rainforest, and he gained international acclaim for his efforts to save the region. He became the darling of American environmentalists, who invited him to Washington and Miami and to international conferences to speak of his struggle. He proposed the creation of "extractive reserves" where local people could practice sustainable-use management, including a sixty-one thousand-acre tract in his own region, Seringal Cachoeira. Darly Alves da Silva, who headed a group of wealthy ranchers, the Rural Democratic Union, had often threatened Mendes, who continued to organize the seringueiros blockades. Alves, who lived nearby on a ten-thousand-acre ranch, had a reputation for murdering those who got in his way. On December 22, 1988, Mendes was shot at close range as he left his home, and Darly's son, Darci Alves, later confessed to the killing. After the Western media pressured reluctant local officials to uncover the facts about the case, the Brazilian government stepped in, captured, questioned, and finally arrested Darly as well. A trial date has still not yet been set, and it is unlikely that there will ever be a complete accounting of who was involved.[20]

The murder of Chico Mendes had a profound effect thousands of miles away from the Amazon rainforest. His notoriety with American and global environmental organizations made his death an international event and brought media and public attention to the death of the rainforest as well, making the name Chico Mendes synonymous with tropical forest protection— a legacy he no doubt never imagined.

natural resources.[17] Another revolt took place in 1992 when several thousand Amazonian Indians from three tribes marched three hundred miles demanding that Ecuador's president grant them territorial rights to the Pastaza rainforest as well as permission to govern themselves within its boundaries. The march was organized by the Organization of Indian Peoples of Pastaza, but was largely unsuccessful.

In Asia, the Penan people represent one of the last of the few remaining hunting and gathering tribes, with the forest the source of all their basic needs. The Penan live in the forests of Kalimantan (Indonesia) and Sarawak (Malaysia), areas that produce 80 percent of the tropical hardwoods traded globally. In March 1987, the Penan banded together to form human barricades in an attempt to block further logging in their homeland. There are estimates that Sarawak will be logged out by 2002, and Kalimantan, by 2010. The Malaysian government has proposed moving the Penan into new areas, some of which have already been logged, so the natives continue to battle the government, even though hundreds have been imprisoned under a federal law that makes it a crime to interfere with logging operations.[18]

INTERNATIONAL ACTIVISM

The protection of tropical forests is an issue that has generated global levels of support. Environmental organizations throughout the world have rallied against tropical deforestation, agreeing, for the most part, on the urgency of the problem. But there is also a gulf that separates the groups in their approaches to what needs to be done.

In the United States, the Natural Resources Defense Council has used its extensive legal expertise to seek a tripling of the federal government's financial commitment to saving the American tropical forests. The group has also monitored the U.S. Forest Service's plans for the Caribbean National Forest (El Yunque) in Puerto Rico, and is working to find alternative energy sources in Hawaii that would reduce the need for additional geothermal exploration within the rainforests.[21]

Globally, efforts to save the rainforests are split between more radical groups seeking to ban trade in timber from virgin rainforests and an end to large aid programs (such as the World Rainforest Movement) and more traditional groups, primarily in the United States, that believe that the solution is to "green" the development process. Mainstream groups like the World Resources Institute and Friends of the Earth have supported the World Bank's efforts to improve economic conditions in developing countries. Other groups like Greenpeace have established tropical forest units within their organizations, and a host of smaller organizations are involved in other projects. The Washington, DC–based Better World Society, chaired by television executive Ted Turner, has produced and distributed a film on the murder of Chico Mendes, and the Rainforest Action Network has put pressure on companies like Burger King, which was urged to stop buying $35 million in rainforest beef. The Rainforest Alliance, which links groups and researchers, has established fellowships for conservation researchers, and has raised funds to add lands to Costa Rica's Monteverde Cloud Forest Reserve. Most of these organizations are new (post-1985) and are struggling to keep media attention focused on the issue.

In order to slow the world demand for exotic woods, the more radical environmental groups have proposed a ban on the sale of tropical timber. They want the International Tropical Timber Organization (ITTO), made up of forty-seven producing and consuming nations, to severely restrict timber harvests and trade. The organization, which administers the 1984 International Tropical Timber Agreement, is dominated by Japanese interests and by the United States, which is the world's largest importer of tropical hardwood products. The ITTO has the somewhat contradictory role of both protecting forests and regulating the timber trade upon which many of its member nations depend. It has as its goal bringing all tropical forests under sustainable management by 2000. Neither Japan nor the United States seems to be willing to agree to a reduction in trade or imports, with the current agreement scheduled to expire in 1994. After its December 1991 meeting in Yokahama, Japan, one observer commented that although the ITTO is not dead, the organization is certainly in trouble, and making little progress toward sustainable forestry.[22]

Many developing nations are highly critical of foreign attempts to restrict further logging—another illustration of the growing divide between the North and South. Malaysia, which now accounts for nearly 60 percent of the world's exports, has attacked proposed trade restrictions as arbitrary and discriminatory.[23] Malaysia's leadership role is likely due to the fact that it has been singled out as the worst offender in tropical deforestation, while countries like Brazil are gradually beginning to slow logging rates.[24] Other countries have criticized North American environmental organizations for failing to recognize the desire of developing countries to overcome widespread poverty. The economy of many of these nations is dependent upon forest products and their allied jobs, including shipping and processing industries, although local residents often do not benefit from employment opportunities. The lumber potential of the Amazon, for example, is estimated at $600 billion, a figure that could mean economic prosperity for millions of Brazilians. Meeting in Manaus, Brazil, in February 1992, Latin America's eight Amazonian nations endorsed sustainable development and blamed the environmental problems of their countries on industrialized countries.[25]

Several proposals have been launched to provide aid to tropical nations to fund forest protection, but for the most part, they have received only token support. In 1990, German Chancellor Helmut Kohl suggested the creation of a fund to find alternative sources of revenues for ranchers, loggers, and others whose livelihood is dependent upon the rainforest, with a pilot program to begin in Brazil.[26] In 1991, a draft program drawn up by the World Bank to funnel $1.5 billion for rainforest protection was criticized by groups like Friends of the Earth as doing nothing to change the base economic conditions that led to the initial destruction of the forest. Despite a pledge by Germany to provide $150 million to save the Brazilian rainforest, and a $15 million commitment from the European Community, the president of Brazil accused the world's seven richest nations (the Group of seven, or G-7) of showing a "lack of urgency" in finding funds for the project.[27]

Other than an outright ban on timber, other solutions to deforestation vary in their practicality and level of international support. The World Wildlife Fund and Friends of the Earth, for example, believe that the equipment and the types of forestry management being used in these regions need to be modernized. Current harvesting practices, they argue, are inefficient and waste much of the forest's resources. They have called for an end to existing logging practices and feel that technological advances could bring about extraction that is more compatible with sustainable management.[28] Other observers believe that a complete restructuring of timber taxing and sales practices is needed, since governments in these areas receive only a fraction of the rents from logging. Virtually all tropical countries also provide generous tax incentives for timber processing and logging, with the benefits accruing to the wealthiest strata of the population. In Indonesia and Ghana for example, the government captures, through royalties and taxes, only 38 percent of the total estimated rents, with the rest accruing to investors in logging firms. In the Philippines, only 11 percent goes to the government, with similar rates applicable in Liberia, Ivory Coast, Cameroon, and Gabon.[29]

Some of the proposed solutions are highly innovative. In an attempt to diversify the economy of tropical regions, researchers are experimenting with different land uses. In Costa Rica, where cattle ranching is prevalent, the Tropical Agricultural Research and Training Center is promoting the conversion of beef to dairy cattle, which provides a more steady income, stable markets, and predictable prices. Many rural people are unable to meet their minimum protein requirements, due in large part to their dependence on slash-and-burn agriculture, leading to soil erosion, poor crop yields, and general poverty. Wildlife habitats are often decimated through deforestation, reducing another traditional source of protein. But in Panama, commercial ranching of the green iguana, a traditional tropical protein source, is a promising way of introducing the reptile to the area and shows some economic viability.[30]

The most commonly voiced solution is the creation of forest reserves, which many researchers argue is the only way to save tropical forests at this point. They believe that destruction is proceeding too fast for reforestation to be effective because a damaged tropical forest does not regenerate quickly. One model that is currently being used is the UN Man and Biosphere concept, in which the center of the reserve is strictly set aside for preservation, with areas of increasing use working out toward the boundary in concentric circles. Examples where the concept is already being tried are the La Amistad Biosphere Reserve in Costa Rica, Korup National Park in Cameroon, and Khao Yai Park in Thailand.[31] One of the barriers to the creation of forest preserves is cost. Ira Rubinoff, director of the Smithsonian Tropical Research Institute, has proposed that temperate-zone nations create an international conservation bank similar to the World Bank to fund reserves. A tax would be levied on industrialized countries, based on their gross national product, which Rubinoff estimates could raise as much as $3 billion a year. Such proposals may be unrealistic, however, at a time when many nations are cutting back their foreign aid obligations or redirecting them toward the support of developing democracies, such as the Commonwealth of Independent States.

DEBT-FOR-NATURE SWAPS

Many of the world's industrialized nations and lending institutions have given developing countries loans that have resulted in more than $1.3 trillion in foreign debt, much of it incurred in the early 1970s in an attempt to offset the rising price of oil. Many of these Third World countries do not have now, and are unlikely to have in the future, the ability to repay the loans while their economic systems are in disarray. In an attempt to pay off foreign debt while at the same time establishing tropical forest preserves, several environmental organizations and some governments have engaged in debt-for-nature swaps. Among the first to propose the concept in 1987 were British environmentalists Teddy Goldsmith and Nick Hilyard.

Here's a hypothetical example of how they work: A developing country borrows $1 million from an industrialized country to purchase medical equipment and supplies. Because of changing economic conditions, it later is unable to pay back the loan. The industrialized country decides that it is better to sell the loan on the world secondary market at a discount rather than not having the loan repaid at all. An environmental group purchases the debt at a greatly discounted rate, for example, paying only $200,000, or 20 percent. The environmental group agrees to forgive the loan in exchange for a promise from the developing country that a region of tropical forest will be set aside in a reserve.

Although the practice sounds simple, there are a number of economic and political drawbacks to debt-for-nature contracts. For example, questions have been raised about the enforceability of such agreements. What happens if five years later, the developing country decides that the land is needed for livestock grazing, and begins logging operations? Does the industrialized country or the environmental organization that purchased the debt have any legal recourse? What effect do such economic machinations have on the inflationary spirals of these countries? And lastly, what right do outsiders have to impose their will and values on the sovereignty of other nations? Do such trades constitute environmental/economic blackmail? What happens if the leadership of either nation changes its policies?

One of the groups supporting the debt-for-nature concept is the World Wildlife Fund. It helped to arrange a deal in which Costa Rica agreed to spend $17 million on its Guanacaste National Park in return for being relieved of $24 million in debt, and negotiated the purchase of $10 million worth of Ecuadorean debt with Fundacion Natura, an Ecuadorean environmental group, which will use the funds to support conservation activities in conjunction with the national government. On a smaller scale, Conservation International helped negotiate the purchase of $650,000 worth of Bolivian debt for $100,000, exacting a promise by the government that it would expand the Rio Beni reserve in the northwestern part of the country. Goldsmith and Hilyard favor "big and systematic" swaps, criticizing what has been accomplished thus far as being so small they fail to challenge the development process.[32]

Two developments underscore the continued salience of deforestation as a global issue. In 1992, George Bush announced a "Forests for the Future" initiative—a unilateral pledge to increase forest conservation efforts from $120 million to $270 million. The most important aspect of the initiative, however, was not the monetary commitment but the pledge that aid would be further increased in the future if other countries contributed. A more general and nonbinding "Statement of Forest Principles" was adopted at the Earth Summit, stressing sustainable management that does not cause environmental damage. Key to the Earth Summit, however, was an acknowledgment of the sovereign right of countries to exploit their own forest resources. That concept, pressed by Malaysia and other exporters of tropical woods, precluded any binding agreement in Rio.

As a result, a more likely outcome would be a form of voluntary forest partnership in which developed countries would finance forest protection and conservation projects proposed by developing countries. Such a proposal was endorsed by the G-7 member nations Munich in July 1992.[33]

SUMMARY

Exemplary of the political disputes between the industrialized "haves" of the North and the "have-nots" of the developing nations of the South is the fate of tropical forests. The world's rainforests, which are concentrated in nine countries, are known to be disappearing at an alarming rate, although there is disagreement as to exactly how fast deforestation is occurring. In the past ten years, there has also been a growing awareness, fueled by environmental organizations and indigenous groups, of the impact of deforestation on the ecosystem as a whole. Researchers have only vague estimates about the number of species of plants and animals on Earth, but they do know that perhaps as many as two-thirds of them are found in rainforests, and that destruction of those habitats means a potential loss of species diversity, products, and medicines, as well as effects on global warming and climate. Efforts by the United Nations and environmental groups (many of them based in the United States) to limit logging have been joined by various indigenous people's groups, generating global support. They are pressing for a ban on the sale of exotic woods and timber but face resistance from tropical nations that resent external interference. Proposals like debt-for-nature swaps and the creation of forest preserves are meeting with some acceptance, and some progress is being made, largely through voluntary forest partnerships, to develop a long-term solution for tropical deforestation.

NOTES

1. Quoted in Associated Press wire story, February 10, 1992.
2. For an overview of U.S. tropical forests, see Scott Lewis, "Red, White and Blue Rainforests," in *The Rainforest Book: How You Can Save The World's Rainforests* (Los Angeles: Living Planet Press, 1990), 72–86.
3. Malcolm Gillis, "Tropical Deforestation: Economic, Ecological, and Ethical Dimensions," *The South Atlantic Quarterly* 90, no. 1 (Winter 1991): 7–38.
4. "Empires of the Chainsaws," *The Economist*, August 10, 1991, 36.
5. Gillis, "Tropical Deforestation," 13–14. See also "Half of World's Deforestation Occurs outside the Amazon," *National Wildlife* 27 (August–September 1989): 25.
6. See Otto T. Solbrig, "The Origin and Function of Biodiversity," *Environment* 33, no. 5 (June 1991): 16–20, 34–38.
7. Lewis, "Red, White and Blue Rainforests," 79–83.
8. See "Seeking Medical Secrets in the Rain Forest," *National Wildlife* 30, no. 3 (April–May 1992): 44.
9. See Fred Pearce, "Felled Trees Deal Double Blow to Global Warming," *New Scientist*, September 16, 1989, 25.
10. See Richard P. Tucker, "Five Hundred Years of Tropical Forest Exploitation," in *Lessons of the Rainforest*, ed. Suzanne Head and Robert Heinzman (San Francisco: Sierra Club Books, 1990), 39–52.
11. See Jan G. Laarman, "Export of Tropical Hardwoods in the Twentieth Century," in *World Deforestation in the Twentieth Century*, ed. John F. Richards and Richard P. Tucker (Durham, NC: Duke University Press, 1988), 146–63.
12. "UN Forestry Plan Under Fire," *Environment* 32 (November 1990): 21. See also Jay Hair, "Global Unity for Local Action," *International Wildlife* 20 (November–December 1990): 26.
13. "Empires of the Chainsaws," 36.
14. "Lost in the Forest," *The Economist*, August 31, 1991, 30.
15. "Half of the World's Deforestation Occurs outside the Amazon," *National Wildlife* 27 (August–September 1989), 25.
16. An extensive survey of the Chipko movement and its predecessor rebellions is chronicled by Ramachandra Guha, *The Unquiet Woods: Ecological Change and Peasant Resistance in the Himalaya* (Berkeley: University of California Press, 1990). See also Vandan Shiva, *Ecology and the Politics of Survival: Conflicts over Natural Resources in India* (New Delhi: Sage Publications of India, 1991); and Renu Khator, *Environment, Development and Politics in India* (Lanham: University Press of America, 1991).
17. David Schwartz, "Drawing the Line in a Vanishing Jungle," *International Wildlife* 21 (July–August 1991): 4–11.
18. See Michael Cross, "Logging Agreement Fails to Protect Sarawak," *New Scientist*, December 1, 1990, 23.
19. See Kat McKenna, "Seringueiros—The Rubber Tappers," *Whole Earth Review*, Fall, 1989, 79.
20. See Andrew Revkin, *The Burning Season: The Murder of Chico Mendes and the Fight for the Amazon Rain Forest* (Boston: Houghton Mifflin, 1990). See also Brian Homewood, "Ranchers Jailed for Mendes Murder," *New Scientist*, December 22, 1990, 5; and John Maier, Jr., "Justice Comes to the Amazon," *Time*, December 17, 1990, 76.
21. Lewis, "Red, White and Blue Rainforests," 84. See also Michael D. Lemonick, "Hot Tempers in Hawaii: Exploiting Clean Geothermal Energy Could Threaten a Rain Forest," *Time*, August 13, 1990, 68; and Bill McKibben, "Power Play Endangers Hawaii's Rain Forest," *Rolling Stone*, May 31, 1990, 41–42.
22. Peter Hadfield, "Forest Watchdog Fails to Show Its Teeth," *New Scientist*, December 14, 1991, 12.

23. Gareth Porter and Janet Welsh Brown, *Global Environmental Politics* (Boulder, CO: Westview Press, 1991), 101.

24. Ibid., 102.

25. See Rachel McCleary, "The International Community's Claim to Rights in Brazilian Amazonia," *Political Studies* 39, no. 4 (December 1991).

26. Stephen Kinzer, "Aiding Amazon Forest Gains Support in the West," *New York Times*, November 7, 1991, A-5.

27. Sylvia Hughes and Debora MacKenzie, "Greens Damn Kohl's Rainforest Pledge," *New Scientist*, November 9, 1991, 18. The G-7 nations are Canada, France, Germany, Italy, Japan, the United Kingdom, and the United States.

28. See Francois Nectoux and Nigel Dudley, *A Hard Wood Story: Europe's Involvement in the Tropical Timber Trade* (London: Friends of the Earth, 1987).

29. Gillis, "Tropical Deforestation," 19–20.

30. Judith Gradwohl and Russell Greenberg, *Saving the Tropical Forests* (Washington, DC: Island Press, 1988), 116–22. See also Noel Vietmeyer, "Iguana Mama: Dagmar Werner Has 18,000 Delectable Lizards and Bright Idea for Saving Latin America's Forests," *International Wildlife* 19 (September–October 1989): 24–27.

31. See Gradwohl and Greenberg, *Saving the Tropical Forests*, 57–101.

32. Pearce, "Felled Trees Deal Double Blow," 41.

33. Roger A. Sedjo, "A Global Forestry Initiative," *Resources*, Fall 1992, 16–19.

FOR FURTHER READING

Mark Collins, ed. *The Last Rain Forests: A World Conservation Atlas.* New York: Oxford University Press, 1990.

Al Gedicks The New Resource Wars: Native and Environment Struggles Against Multinational Corporations. Boston: South End Press, 1993.

Robert Goodland, ed. *Race to Save the Tropics.* Washington, DC: Island Press, 1990.

Judith Gradwohl and Russell Greenberg. *Saving the Tropical Forests.* Washington, DC: Island Press, 1988.

Susanna Hecht and Alexander Cockburn. *The Fate of the Forest.* New York: Verso, 1989.

Arnold Newman. *Tropical Rainforest: A World Survey of Our Most Valuable Endangered Habitat.* New York: Facts on File, 1990.

Mark Plotkin and Lisa Famolare. *Sustainable Harvest and Marketing of Rain Forest Products.* Washington, DC: Island Press, 1992.

Andrew Revkin. *The Burning Season: The Murder of Chico Mendes and the Fight for the Amazon Rain Forest.* Boston: Houghton Mifflin, 1990.

CHAPTER 15

Endangered Species and Habitats

Nobody's told me the difference between a red squirrel, a black one or a brown one. Do we have to save every subspecies?
—Manuel Lujan, secretary of the interior under President Bush[1]

In the long, hot summer of 1988 the Socorro isopod (Thermosphaeroma thermophilium), a tiny, water-dependent crustacean, had its closest brush with extinction in a million years. Roots clogged the water pipe leading to the cement horse-watering trough where the only known population of the species survived, thus drying out its entire habitat. City officials in Socorro, New Mexico, removed the roots and restored the water flow, but no isopods could be found. Extinction was averted, however, because the University of New Mexico had established a laboratory colony of isopods, 555 of which were restocked into the trough, where the species is once again clinging to survival.[2] It may sound as if the U.S. Fish and Wildlife Service paid an exorbitant amount of attention to this lilliputian water creature, but the isopod's survival is but one example of the efforts now being undertaken on a global scale to protect wildlife and their habitats.

We have only the beginning of an understanding of the diversity and numbers of forms of life that currently exist on this planet. There may be as many as thirty million species currently in existence, primarily insects and marine invertebrates, with only about 5 percent of them named and identified. That number is thought to be only a tiny percentage of the species that have inhabited Earth during its millions of years of history—perhaps less than 1 percent of as many as four billion. Some species have disappeared due to cataclysmic change, such as changes in the level of the seas, or massive ice movements, while others can be attributed to the appearance (and often, the intervention) of humans.[3]

Estimates as to the current rate of species extinction vary considerably from one source to another, and are largely dependent upon the period of time covered. From 1600 to 1980, for example, nearly two hundred vertebrate extinctions were documented, over half of them birds. But since 1980, habitat destruction, hunting, pesticide use, pollution, and other man-made causes have led to the extinction of as many as one thousand species per year, primarily in tropical regions. The *Global 2000 Report to the President* projected between a half million and two million species extinctions would occur by the turn of the century. Most of those losses were attributed to the clearing or degradation of tropical forests, although marine species are threatened by damming, siltation, and pollution.[4]

It is almost impossible to discuss the status of endangered animals and plants without discussing the status of their habitats as well. Similarly, it is difficult to discuss habitats without examining the factors that threaten them. For example, the need for additional sources of energy has led utility companies to build more transmission lines, which often attract eagles, hawks, and other raptor species. The companies now routinely conduct surveys of these birds' habitats and may reroute a line to avoid breeding areas, or may install nesting platforms or equipment to protect the birds from electrocution. Thus, this chapter's review of the efforts being made to preserve wildlife includes a review of the loss of their habitats as well.

This chapter focuses on the history of legislation, both in the United States and internationally, to protect wildlife, plants, and their habitats, and looks at the wildlife bureaucracy and the role of nongovernmental organizations, and gives a report card on the status of endangered species today.

PROTECTIVE LEGISLATION

The development of laws protecting wildlife can be traced back to earliest legal history, but those laws have often differed in terms of what has been protected and why. Under Roman law, wild animals, or *ferae naturae*, were given the same status as the oceans and air—they belonged to no one. As Anglo-Saxon law developed, however, an exception was made: Private land-owners had the right to wildlife on their property. As land was parceled out to the nobility as "royal forests" around 450 C.E., hunting restrictions began to be imposed, and only the king was given sole right to pursue fish or game anywhere he claimed as his realm. As the English political system developed, there were very few changes in this theory except to perpetuate a system by which only the wealthy or nobles were qualified to take game. Those same restrictions found their way to American shores and flourished until the mid-nineteenth century, when a major policy shift occurred as the U.S. Supreme Court established the basis for a doctrine of state ownership of wildlife. The federal government's role in defining the legal status of wildlife was limited to a 1868 statute prohibiting the hunting of furbearing animals in Alaska and in 1894, a prohibition on hunting in Yellowstone National Park. The states began to regulate fishing within their waters just after the Civil War, a policy that was upheld by the Court using the commerce clause of Article 1, section 8 of the

Constitution. What is important about the decisions of this period, however, is the states' regulatory authority was based on a fundamental nineteenth-century conception of the purpose of wildlife law—the preservation of a food supply.[5]

That policy changed slightly as the concern for wildlife for other than purely commercial reasons broadened. In 1900, Congress passed the Lacey Act, which prohibited the interstate transportation of any wild animals or birds killed in violation of state law, and the importation of birds or animals deemed by the secretary of agriculture to be injurious to agriculture or horticulture. The law was aimed at starlings and English sparrows, which threatened farms throughout the eastern and midwestern states. It was also a response to the decimation (and eventual extinction) of the passenger pigeon, whose numbers had at one time been so pervasive the sky had darkened when they took flight. The Lacey Act authorized the secretary to adopt measures necessary to preserve and restore game and wild birds—the first movement toward affirmative wildlife management.

Contemporary U.S. legislation protecting plants and animals can be divided into four categories: migratory and game birds, wild horses and burros, marine mammals, and endangered species. What is unique about these legislative provisions is the fact that in addition to offering protection for reasons of aesthetics or biological diversity, Congress has also sought to regulate the commerce and trade in these species. Generally, it is illegal to possess, offer for sale, sell, offer for barter, offer to purchase, purchase, deliver for shipment, ship, export, import, cause to be shipped, exported, or imported, deliver for transportation, transport or cause to be transported, carry or cause to be carried, or receive for shipment, transport, carriage, or export any of the protected plants and animals.

The first category, migratory and game birds, gained protection with the 1918 Migratory Bird Act, which limited hunting and prohibited the taking of nests or eggs. Similar conventions were signed with Mexico in 1936 and with Japan in 1972. In 1940, Congress enacted the Bald Eagle Protection Act after scientists voiced concerns the national symbol was in danger of becoming extinct. The act was amended in 1962 to protect young eagles, and in 1972 after the widely publicized death of several dozen eagles in Wyoming that ate poisoned bait designed to attract coyotes.

In 1971, Congress passed another largely symbolic measure, the Wild Free-Roaming Horses and Burros Act. This legislation was preceded by a 1959 bill that made it a crime to use aircraft or a motor vehicle to hunt wild horses or burros on public lands but otherwise gave the animals little federal protection. The issue struck a responsive chord in the public after the media focused attention on the plight of the animals, which symbolized the spirit of the western pioneer. Under the 1971 law, burros and horses gained protection even when they wandered onto private lands or mixed with nonwild animals.

Marine mammal protection laws were enacted as the result of three somewhat different interests. One group, composed largely of commercial fishing interests, believed marine resources, including mammals, should be viewed as an important food resource with commercial value. The other group, made up of biologists and environmentalists, felt the entire marine ecosystem needed protection for ecological reasons. And a third, made up of a wide spectrum of the public, wanted whales and dolphins protected because they felt an emotional kinship to them for their intelligence and almost-human personalities. But these three groups put aside their individual interests to support a comprehensive marine mammal protection policy. The United States had taken some steps to regulate harvesting of marine animals under the Endangered Species Act, and a variety of state laws were in effect as well. Protection had been afforded the manatee, the Mediterranean monk seal, Pacific fur seals and some species of whales. But the laws produced a patchwork of protection, with some species falling through the legislative cracks. In 1972, after compromises were agreed to among the various interest groups, Congress enacted the Marine Mammal Protection Act, totally preempting the states' role. It established a moratorium on the taking of marine mammals, with exceptions made for scientific research, and for natives of the Arctic and Pacific coasts. One notable feature of the act is that it provided protection for species that, though not yet in danger of extinction, might become so in the future.

That element was critical to the fourth major category of U.S. wildlife protection, endangered species. Three separate legislative efforts have been enacted—all within the past thirty years—which indicates how recently American concern for endangered species has reached the political agenda. The first, the Endangered Species Preservation Act of 1966, mandated the secretary of the interior to develop a program to conserve, protect, restore, and propagate selected species of native fish and wildlife. Its provisions were primarily designed, however, to protect habitats through land acquisition, and little else. The species protected under the law were those "threatened with extinction" based on a finding by the secretary in consultation with interested persons, but the procedures for doing that went no further. It did not limit the taking of these species, or commerce in them, but it was an important first step in the development of the law.

The Endangered Species Conservation Act of 1969 attempted to remedy those limitations by further defining the types of protected wildlife, and more importantly, by including wildlife threatened with worldwide extinction and prohibiting their importation into the United States—an international aspect not included in the earlier legislation. Instead of using the broad term *fish and wildlife* (which was interpreted as only vertebrates) the 1969 law included any wild mammal, fish, wild bird, amphibian, reptile, mollusk, or crustacean. The list of species was to be developed using the best scientific and commercial data available, with procedures for designation pursuant to the rule making in the Administrative Procedure Act. This formalized a process that had been haphazard and highly discretionary under the 1966 act.

President Richard Nixon warned that the two laws did not provide sufficient management tools needed to act early enough to save a vanishing species and urged Congress to enact a more comprehensive law, which became the Endangered Species Act (ESA) of 1973. There are several notable features in the law that distinguish it from previous efforts. One, it required all federal agencies, not just the two departments identified in the 1966 and 1969 acts, to seek to conserve endangered species, broadening the base of protective efforts. Two, it expanded conservation measures that could be undertaken under the act to include all methods and procedures necessary to protect the species, rather than emphasizing habitat protection only. Three, it broadened the definition of wildlife to include any member of the animal kingdom. Four, it created two classes of species: those "endangered" (in danger of extinction throughout all or a significant portion of its range) and those "threatened" (any species likely to become an endangered species within the foreseeable future).

From an administrative standpoint, the 1973 law was considerably more complex than previous legislative efforts. It included a circuitous route by which a species was to be listed by the secretary of the interior, de-listed when the species' population stabilized, and changed from threatened to endangered and vice versa. The secretaries of commerce and the interior have virtually unlimited discretion in deciding when to consider the status of a species, since the law did not establish any priorities or time limitations.

Generally, a species is considered for listing upon petition of an interested group that has developed scientific evidence regarding the species' population. In 1992, for example, a single biologist working in Oregon's Willamette Valley discovered specimens of Fenders' blue butterfly, a one-inch-long species thought to be extinct. Researchers found ten spots where the butterfly was found, estimating there are only two to two and a half thousand of the insects in existence. The biologist prepared a report for the Fish and Wildlife Service on the butterfly's status as the first step toward possible designation as threatened. The report will be considered by the secretary of the interior, although the time frame for consideration is totally discretionary. Some species have become extinct while waiting to be listed.

Listing, however, is but the first phase in a very lengthy process. Once a species is added to the list (which is made official by publishing a notice in the *Federal Register*), the federal government must decide how much of its habitat needs to be protected. The 1973 law is somewhat vague in indicating how "critical" habitat is to be determined, and when that determination must be made. The law then requires the government to develop a recovery plan for the species. Recovery is defined by the law as the process by which the decline of an endangered or threatened species is arrested or reversed, and threats to its survival are neutralized to ensure its long-term survival in the wild. The plan delineates, justifies, and schedules the research and management actions necessary to support the recovery of a species, including those that, if successful, will permit reclassification or de-listing. Typical recovery plans involve extensive public participation and include the cost of each strategy. One of the most controversial aspects of the planning process is the assignment of individual species recovery priorities, which signifies the imminence of extinction, and the designation of those species where a known threat or conflict exists (usually from development projects). About one-quarter of the listed species are in conflict with other activities and receive the designation. The law was amended in 1988 to make more specific the requirement that the secretaries of the interior and commerce develop and implement recovery plans, and requires a status report every two years on the efforts to develop recovery plans for all listed species and on the status of all species for which recovery plans have been developed. An analysis of those efforts is discussed later in this chapter.

Plants are also protected under the ESA, with the first four plants (all found on San Clemente Island off the California coast) listed in 1977. Before the 1988 amendments, it was illegal only to "remove and reduce to possession" listed plants, and then, only those on lands under federal jurisdiction. Under the amended provisions, there is a prohibition against maliciously damaging or destroying plants on federal lands, and makes it illegal to remove, destroy, or damage any listed plant on state or private land in knowing violation of state law.

INTERNATIONAL PROTECTION AGREEMENTS

The development of an international regime to protect endangered species has come largely from the leadership of the United States. The 1969 Endangered Species Conservation Act included a provision directing the secretaries of the interior and commerce to convene an international meeting prior to June 30, 1971, to develop an international agreement on the conservation of endangered species. Although it was a year and a half late, that meeting produced the Convention on Trade in Endangered Species of Wild Fauna and Flora, or CITES as it is better known. The United States was the first nation to ratify the convention in January 1974, and it became effective July 1, 1975; 117 nations are currently parties to CITES.

It is important to note, however, that CITES is not strictly a conservation agreement; it focuses on matters of international trade rather than preservation per se. One of the key aspects of the CITES treaty is that it creates three levels of species vulnerability: Appendix I (all species threatened with extinction that are or may be affected by trade), Appendix II (all species that are not now threatened with extinction but that may become so unless trade in specimens is strictly regulated), and Appendix III (species subject to regulation for the purpose of preventing exploitation). Within ninety days of the date when a species is added to an appendix, and upon a showing of an overriding economic interest, party nations may make a "reservation" to the convention. The reservation means that they do not accept the listing of a species in a particular appendix, and therefore are not subject to the trade prohibitions.

CITES establishes an elaborate series of trade permits within each category, and between importing and exporting authorities. Exempt from the trade restrictions are specimens acquired before the convention applied to that species, specimens that are personal or household effects, and specimens used in scientific research. The CITES agreement is supported by a secretariat, provided through the UN Environment Fund, and a Conference of the Parties, which meets every two years for the purpose of regulating trade in each species.

When the CITES agreement was first ratified, it received the support of the majority of nations which are active in wildlife trading because it helps them to protect their resources from illegal traders and poachers. Several countries, however, such as Mexico and South Korea, both of which are deeply involved in wildlife trading as importers and exporters of products, have not signed on to CITES. The result is an active animal-smuggling industry, much of it centered in Southeast Asia.[6] Japan, the world's biggest importer of illegally traded goods, initially made twelve reservations to the convention, including two species of endangered sea turtles, although it agreed to phase out its trade in those species by the end of 1992.[7] The sea turtle shells, primarily those of the hawksbill and olive ridley species, are made into eyeglass frames, cigarette lighters, combs, handbags, belts, and shoes.

Perhaps the most publicized and controversial listing under CITES is the African elephant. The elephant had already been listed by the United States as a threatened species in 1978, but in 1988 the World Wildlife Fund and Conservation International sponsored a scientific study of the African elephant population and recommended it be listed under CITES Appendix I—threatened with extinction. The listing was supported by the United States and several other nations (including Kenya and Tanzania) at the October 1989 Conference of the Parties, along with a proposed ban on trade in ivory products, a position opposed by Botswana, Malawi, Mozambique, South Africa, Zambia, and Zimbabwe. Their opposition was due to the fact that several of the nations had managed to increase their elephant herds through nationally supported economic incentives. They felt there was no need for their countries to suffer the loss of the lucrative ivory trade because herds in other African states were being diminished through poor wildlife management practices.

In the end, the U.S.-led position won, and the elephant achieved Appendix I status. The opposing African nations made reservations and announced they would continue to sell ivory, but the impact of that decision was made moot when Japan, the largest ivory importer, decided against filing a reservation of its own. Efforts by the United States and several European diplomats appear to have convinced the Japanese that their image in the global environmental community would be further tarnished had they tried to go against the ivory ban. Prices in African raw ivory dropped by as much as 90 percent, reducing any real incentives for poaching and smuggling, and it appeared the issue was resolved.[8]

In 1992, when the Convention of the Parties reconvened in Kyoto, Japan, ninety-seven species were on the agenda for discussion, including seventeen kinds of frogs, eleven species of hornbill birds, a carnivorous plant, an orchid, a viper, and a type of herring. But the "megafauna"—like the elephant—once again dominated the debate. Once again, the same six African nations sought relief from CITES to sell ivory from culled elephants, arguing they had managed their herds effectively to stabilize the population. They felt as if they were being penalized for their efforts, and denounced efforts by countries without elephants to lay down conservation rules for them. But other member nations, fueled by the protests of environmental organizations, pointed out the elephant population still had declined from an estimated 2.5 million animals in 1950 to only about 350,000 today, voting to keep the ivory trade ban in effect.[9]

The issue of endangered species was also raised at the Earth Summit in Rio de Janeiro in June 1992. Unlike the dissension that marked the initial reservations to CITES, the biodiversity convention gained the support of 153 nations. Under the terms of the agreement, the parties agree that a state has sovereignty over the genetic resources within its borders, including any valuable drugs and medicines produced from endangered animals and plants that may be developed. The United States, however, declined to sign the document, arguing that it made unfair demands on the industrial nations who would be required to fund habitat protection programs.

Before the Earth Summit, habitat protection found international support largely through organizations like the International Union for Conservation of Nature and Natural Resources (IUCN) and by regimes such as the International Convention concerning the Protection of World Cultural and Natural Heritage, which entered into force in 1972. To date, nearly twelve hundred national parks have been established worldwide, covering nearly 2.7 million square kilometers—an area larger than Alaska, Texas, and California combined. One of the challenges facing global efforts to preserve wildlife habitats is basically one of economics: in times of declining budgets, many governments are finding it difficult to support parks and reserves over human needs. Countries like New Zealand, for example, are reorganizing their parks to earn more revenue from them, and several African nations are using tourism as a way of financing wildlife refuges. But there are less obvious problems as well. Most national parks are outlined by some type of physical barrier, such as a fence or moat, but animals within do not always respect those limitations. Large mammals and birds of prey, for example, demand a large ecosystem for their habitat, which may cross national borders. This makes it unlikely that even when strictly protected, national parks by themselves will be able to conserve all, or even most, species.[10]

Other European organizations are working to create *ecological bricks*, a term first developed by Hanns Langer of the World Wide Fund for Nature. The concept involves the development of nature preserves on the borders of countries to substitute ecological for military security along river floodplains, mountain ranges, and forests. Many of the parks and preserves are in areas that were once military staging areas. One such "brick," established along the borders of what was once Czechoslovakia, stretches from Bohemia to the Carpathian mountains along the border with Hungary and Ukraine. The preserve, which is a natural habitat for animals, is funded by a $7 million World Bank contribution. Other preserves are being planned for the Danube delta, on the shores of the Black Sea in Romania, and the forests in Bulgaria and Poland. As transportation systems between East and West are developed, the preserves may be the only way of protecting endangered species in a region that has been at war for decades. The new peace of the 1990s provides an opportunity, albeit a costly one, to protect the habitats of plants and animals that have also been victims of the cold war.[11]

THE MAKING OF WILDLIFE POLICY

Federal authority for the regulation and protection of wildlife is a case study in the growth of bureaucracy, characterized by name changes and power struggles within the agencies. Power is shared by a number of agencies, most of which have their counterparts at the state level. Until 1939, the Bureau of Biological Survey in the Department of Agriculture held regulatory authority for all wildlife, with the exception of marine fisheries, which were under the jurisdiction of the Bureau of Fisheries in the Department of Commerce. Both agencies were absorbed by the Department of the Interior, and then consolidated into the U.S. Fish and Wildlife Service in 1940, but in 1956, the Fish and Wildlife Act divided authority into a Bureau of Sports Fisheries and Wildlife and a Bureau of Commercial Fisheries, much as had been the case prior to 1939. President Richard Nixon's federal reorganization of 1970 transferred the Bureau of Commercial Fisheries to the National Oceanic and Atmospheric Administration and the agency became the National Marine Fisheries Service, once again under the Commerce Department. The Bureau of Sports Fisheries and Wildlife went back to its previous designation as the Fish and Wildlife Service in 1974, remaining in the Department of the Interior.

This truncated division of responsibility is best seen in the implementation of the Marine Mammals Protection Act. Under the 1972 legislation, the secretary of commerce, through the National Marine Fisheries Service, has responsibility for protection of whales, porpoises, and seals. The secretary of the interior, through the Fish and Wildlife Service, is responsible for all other marine mammals, such as manatees, dugongs, polar bears, sea otters, sea turtles (on land), and walruses. The two departments must, however, consult with the Marine Mammal Commission, an independent body created by the act, which is in turn supported by the scientific community through the Committee of Scientific Advisors on Marine Mammals.

The implementation of the CITES agreement is equally disjointed. The Office of Management Authority of the U.S. Fish and Wildlife Service monitors the international trade in species protected by CITES, and the Department of the Interior routinely receives petitions from groups seeking certification from foreign countries for trade. Additional responsibility for CITES implementation is held by the Department of Commerce, which is required under the Pelly amendment to the Fishermen's Protective Act of 1967 to inform the president when foreign nations are engaging in trade or taking that diminishes the effectiveness of any international program for endangered or threatened species. Upon that finding, the secretary of the treasury then becomes involved, with authority to prohibit the importation into the United States of wildlife products originating in the offending country.

While government agencies are responsible for implementing the legislative aspects of wildlife protection, environmental organizations and industry interests have been at the vanguard of ensuring that the legislation is carried out effectively. Wildlife protection groups began to flourish in the late nineteenth century, and many of them survived to become the mainstays of the contemporary environmental movement, such as the National Audubon Society, founded in 1905. Others, such as the Wilderness Society (1935) and the National Wildlife Federation (1936) were products of the surge of interest instigated by Teddy Roosevelt. The vast majority of wildlife organizations, however, have a more recent origin, due in part to a spate of legislative activity just after Earth Day 1970. The National Wildlife Federation, which monitors environmental organizations, reports that of the 108 national wildlife and humane organizations identified in its study, 14 percent had been founded before 1940, and 68 percent since 1966. The decade surrounding Earth Day (1965–75) accounted for the founding of 38 percent of all groups with a species orientation.[12]

Those with a single species focus, such as the Mountain Lion Preservation Foundation, the Society of Tympanuchus Cupido Pinnatus (prairie chicken), or Whitetails Unlimited (whitetail deer) are much more recent in origin, dating from the 1980s. Some groups have expanded their initial concerns to encompass a broader interest, as is typical of interest group behavior. The Peregrine Fund, for example, which was founded in 1970 to prevent the extinction of the peregrine falcon, has now expanded its operations with the opening of the World Center for Birds of Prey. Similarly, Greenpeace has expanded its range of interests from whales to virtually the entire spectrum of environmental issues. Groups that might have folded for lack of interest, membership, or resources thus keep their organization intact by expanding their scope to cover a broader overall base.

Wildlife protection groups have been successful at focusing attention on their issues in large part because of the emotional appeal of the subject. Graphic photographs of baby harp seals being clubbed on the head, or of seabirds trapped in oil washing up on beaches, are certain to raise the public's ire. The fate of three whales trapped under the Arctic ice, or of the last California condor trapped in the wild, captured national news attention for weeks while other environmental problems went largely unnoticed. Sometimes the appeal is symbolic—the bison represents our western heritage—other times, it is the perceived human qualities of a smiling dolphin or plaintive sound of a whale. That concern is not unilateral, however. There tends to be much more public interest in protecting mammals than insects, or birds over plants. Whatever the reason, Americans have a devoted (some might say obsessive) interest in the preservation of species.

The tactics used by these groups range from the traditional to the radical. Some organizations see their role within the context of legislation, lobbying to get protective legislation for a particular species enacted, or pressuring Congress to increase appropriations for habitat protection. One target of these groups has been the Land and Water Conservation Fund, which is the primary source of funding for the National Wildlife Refuge System. Other organizations such as the Natural Resources Defense Council rely upon the legal arena to ensure that wildlife laws are fully implemented and enforced.

One of the strategies used by these interest groups is the citizen suit, made possible by a provision in the 1973 Endangered Species Act, which allows individuals to enjoin the government for violating the provisions of the law. For example, the Sierra Club sued the government in 1976 when the group claimed a proposed Army Corps of Engineers dam near St. Louis would flood caves inhabited by the endangered Indiana bat.[13] A similar suit was brought that same year by the National Wildlife Federation, which opposed construction of an interstate highway in Mississippi because it would impact the endangered Mississippi sandhill crane.[14]

The Nature Conservancy, founded in 1951, now has over a half million members whose goal is using their funds to buy up endangered habitats to save the species on them from extinction. They have managed to purchase or negotiate donations of more than five million acres worldwide, making the group the custodian of the largest private nature sanctuary in the world. Another notable accomplishment of the group is their Biological and Conservation Data System, a biogeographic data base or more than four hundred thousand entries that can be used to assess species diversity on a region-by-region basis. It allows the group to establish protection priorities and is also used by public agencies and resource planners in preparing environmental impact studies.[15]

Somewhat ironically, hunting organizations, such as Ducks Unlimited and the Boone and Crockett Club, organized by Teddy Roosevelt in 1887, have also been active in species preservation. Many of the national hunting organizations have dedicated their efforts to preserving wildlife habitat and the enforcement of game laws. They have been instrumental in advocating management policies for species such as the North American deer, the wild turkey, the pronghorn antelope, and migratory waterfowl.[16]

Other nonprofit organizations seek to pressure those countries that have not joined as parties to CITES or that have reservations to a species listing. The San Francisco–based Earth Island Institute's Sea Turtle Restoration Project, for example, has urged its supporters to donate funds to the preparation of a lawsuit to stop Japan from buying turtle products. It also asks members of its group to send letters to the Japanese minister of international trade and economy condemning Japan for its trade in endangered wildlife. Similar efforts have been directed toward Mexico, which allowed the turtles to be killed at their nesting sites until international pressure led to a ban on the practice by the president of Mexico in May 1990.

Environmental organizations have been joined in their efforts by a number of corporate interests seeking to capitalize on Americans' love of wildlife. Firms like the DuPont Chemical Company and General Wine and Spirits (bald eagle), Manhattan Life Insurance Company (peregrine falcon), Sony Corporation (California condor), and Martin-Marietta (bighorn sheep) have made significant financial contributions to species restoration. As one publicist suggested, "People simply love animals. If your company is associated with kindness to animals, some of that love will rub off on you."[17]

AN ESA STATUS REPORT

How successful have government agencies and interest groups been in their efforts to protect endangered species and their habitats? The record thus far is one of mixed success and many failures, depending upon which species is involved, and where. By 1989, the Fish and Wildlife Service estimated it had identified twenty-five hundred plants and fifteen hundred animals worldwide for possible listing under the Endangered Species Act, with enough data accumulated on 950 of the total to warrant listing. However, the agency's resources allowed it to complete only fifty listings per year, resulting in a huge backlog of species. A 1992 General Accounting Office report sharply criticized the Bush administration for dragging its feet on implementing the act, noting that six hundred species have been accepted by federal agencies as candidates for listing, but their official designation is expected to be held up in paperwork until the year 2006 or beyond.

Under the 1988 amendments to the Endangered Species Act, the secretary of the interior is required to report to Congress every two years on the status of the Recovery Program; the first report was published in 1990. The agency also publishes a monthly "box score" of endangered and threatened species and recovery plans, a sample of which is seen in Table 15.1. As the table indicates, as of January 1993, the United States has designated a total of 758 species as threatened or endangered, evenly split between plants and animals. Another 532 foreign species have been designated, almost all of them animals, for a total of 1,290 endangered and threatened species listed.

Congress, in the 1988 amendments to the act, directed the agency to more closely monitor those species facing substantial declines of their populations and to carry out emergency listings when necessary. Generally speaking, the longer a species has been listed, the better its chances for its population stabilizing or improving. For the most part, those species listed less than three years do not yet have final approved recovery plans, although they may have plans in some stage of development. Recovery outlines are developed within sixty days of

Table 15.1 Endangered and Threatened Species and Recovery Plans as of January 31, 1993

Group	Endangered U.S. Only	Endangered Foreign Only	Threatened U.S. Only	Threatened Foreign Only	Listed Species Total	Species with Plans
Mammals	56	249	9	23	337	33
Birds	73	153	13	0	239	67
Reptiles	16	64	18	14	112	26
Amphibians	6	8	5	0	19	8
Fishes	55	11	36	0	102	54
Snails	12	1	7	0	20	8
Clams	42	2	2	0	46	38
Crustaceans	9	0	2	0	11	5
Insects	15	4	9	0	28	13
Arachnids	3	0	0	0	3	0
Subtotal	287	492	101	37	917	252
Plants	298	1	72	2	373	149
Total	585	493	173	39	1290	401

Note: Separate populations of a species, listed both as endangered and threatened, are tallied twice. Those ten species are as follows: chimpanzee, grizzly bear, leopard, gray wolf, bald eagle, piping plover, roseate tern, Nile crocodile, green sea turtle, and olive ridley sea turtle.
Source: U.S. Fish and Wildlife Service.

publication of the final rule listing a species and are submitted to the director of the Fish and Wildlife Service to be used as a guide for activities until recovery plans are developed and approved. Of the 581 species in the 1990 report, 352 (61 percent) had approved recovery plans, with an additional 22 percent having draft plans, 14 percent with plans pending, and 3 percent with no plans developed, often because the species is believed to have become extinct. As of January 1993, 334 recovery plans had been approved covering 401 species. Some recovery plans cover more than one species, and a few species have separate plans covering different parts of their ranges.[18]

A different perspective on status shows an inconsistency in the number of species added to the list since it was first created in 1967. As Table 15.2 indicates, a historical review of the number of species listed shows that after the first group of wildlife species were listed in 1967, there was a two-year gap and then an explosion of listings in 1970, and another surge of activity in 1976. Since 1983, listing activity has leveled off with between fifteen and thirty-five wildlife or plant species added each year, with an exception to this pattern being a big increase in plant listings in 1991.

One other important difference in the preservation effort is where the wildlife and plant species habitats are being protected. While the list of threatened

Table 15.2   Threatened and Endangered Species Listings by Year, 1967–1991

Year	Wildlife Listings	Plant Listings
1967	69	
1968	0	
1969	0	
1970	304	
1971	0	
1972	6	
1973	17	
1974	3	
1975	9	
1976	190	
1977	15	4
1978	18	17
1979	30	35
1980	19	2
1981	1	3
1982	6	6
1983	22	2
1984	32	15
1985	25	35
1986	22	23
1987	28	34
1988	20	27
1989	17	17
1990	25	24
1991	22	63

Source: Code of Federal Regulations, Title 50, Part 17 (July 15, 1991) and supplement to July 1, 1991 Reprint (March 15, 1992).

and endangered wildlife represents habitats throughout the globe, all but three of the listed plant species have critical habitats within the United States and its territories, Mexico, or Canada.[19] Despite the attention being paid to the loss of plant biodiversity within the tropical forests, resources have limited the government to researching and protecting only those species habitats within U.S. borders and our geographic neighbors.

The United States can, with some justification, point to some successes in its efforts. The Aleutian Canada goose, for example, was once widespread through Alaska but began to decline when commercial fox farmers introduced nonnative foxes from about 1836 to 1930. The geese made easy prey for the foxes who decimated their numbers. When the species was listed as endangered in 1967, only about two hundred to three hundred birds were estimated to remain, restricted to a single island in the Bering Sea. But by relocating wild family groups on additional islands and protecting the wintering flock from hunting in Oregon and California, the current population is about fifty-eight hundred birds. Other success stories include the peregrine falcon, the Gila trout, the piping plover, the red wolf, and the American alligator, which was reclassified from endangered to threatened.

Some efforts to preserve a species have been highly publicized and equally controversial, such as attempts in 1987 by the San Diego Wild Animal Park to capture the last of the known wild California condors. The 1985 decision by the U.S. Fish and Wildlife Service to remove the last six condors from the wild prompted an injunction by the National Audubon Society and years of legal wrangling.[20] Another controversial project involved the translocation of the California sea otter. The Fish and Wildlife Service began capturing the animals in 1987 to move them to a protected habitat area on San Nicholas Island, off the coast of southern California, but the effort was largely ineffective because the otters returned to their old hunting grounds and others died.

In contrast, protection of some species may have come too late. The carcasses of the last two female Florida panthers known to exist in the wild were found in 1991 in the Florida Everglades, and preliminary analyses of the cause of death appeared to be mercury poisoning. Only two panthers, both of them male, are thought to remain in the southeast Everglades. Other species, such as Bachman's warbler and the Scioto madtom (a rare fish found in Ohio waters), are believed to be extinct, and unless representatives of these species are found in the wild, recovery plan preparation is curtailed. Outside the United States, extinction has already claimed hundreds of species, best exemplified perhaps by the dodo. The most famous of all animals on the island of Mauritius, the dodo was a dovelike flightless bird about the size of a turkey. Since it had no natural predators, it was naturally curious of the Dutch colonists who came to settle the island. The colonists did not kill the dodo for its meat (which is tough and bitter) but for sport, clubbing the last one to death around 1680.[21]

The bottom line on effectiveness, however, is a criticism shared by everyone who comes into contact with the Endangered Species Act. After twenty-five years, the United States has de-listed only four species as recovered—three birds (the Palau dove, the Palau owl, and the Old World flycatcher), and a plant, the Rydberg milk-vetch. Seven other species have become extinct while awaiting protection. These "successes" have come at a cost of millions of dollars in recovery programs, staff time, and private and public studies. The ESA was scheduled for reauthorization in 1992, but a campaign-conscious Congress chose to defer action on new amendments, fearing both voter revolt and a Bush veto. Environmentalists were elated when President Bill Clinton promised to make the legislation a priority of his new administration. Meanwhile, the Department of the Interior agreed to a December 1992 out-of-court settlement with environmental groups to speed up designation of four hundred varieties of plants and animals that had already been proposed for consideration as endangered species, setting a September 1996 target. In addition, nine hundred more will be given priority for evaluation, an action termed a major victory by environmentalists who feel Clinton is more sympathetic to this issue than his predecessor.

The Clinton administration's approach to balancing species protection and local economic needs has been unprecedented. Several actions by the president have underscored his determination to find a way out of the morass of regional disputes that have jeopardized implementation of the ESA. At a one-day Forest Conference in Portland, Oregon, in April 1993, Clinton, Vice President Al Gore, and five members of the president's cabinet listened to both environmentalists and timber workers express their frustration regarding their long-simmering dispute over the protection of habitat for the northern spotted owl. Giving his staff only two months to come up with a solution, Clinton accelerated the policy process through direct personal intervention.

Equally notable was a March 1993 announcement by Interior Secretary Bruce Babbitt that the California gnatcatcher, a four-inch long, blue-gray songbird that lives on prime development land in southern California, would be designated a threatened species. The significance of the announcement was not in the designation itself, but in the fact that Babbitt agreed to allow state and local governments to set aside some land as a protected habitat, while at the same time allowing development to proceed in less critical areas.

A similar U.S. Fish and Wildlife Service habitat conservation plan was developed to protect the threatened desert tortoise. Using a process approved by Congress as part of the 1982 revision of the ESA, the government agreed to a plan that allows for development on about twenty-two thousand acres of tortoise habitat near Las Vegas in exchange for strict preservation on four hundred thousand acres of federal Bureau of Land Management land south of the city. The ten million dollar habitat conservation plan, funded by development fees of $250 to $550 an acre, requires the elimination of livestock grazing and limits on off-road vehicle use—both prime hazards for the tortoise.

Babbitt's desire to avoid the "environmental and economic train wrecks" that were exemplified by the owl debate is praiseworthy but not easy. Although some developers have been willing to set aside voluntarily land for habitat protection in exchange for the right to develop elsewhere, thus far only a few dozen such agreements have been approved, most of them in California. But as multiple-species ecosystems begin to clash and the Clinton administration accelerates the listing process, habitat conservation plans may require developers to give up considerably more of their valuable landholdings.

THE CONTINUING SAGA OF SPECIES PROTECTION

Much of the opposition to the ESA is not whether it has been effective in restoring or preserving species, but its impact on development and jobs. The celebrated case of the snail darter is an example of how protection of a single species can affect a major federal project. In the late 1960s, the Tennessee Valley Authority (TVA) initiated its Tellico Development Project in the eastern part of the state, with plans to flood a valley behind the $120 million dam to make it a booming recreational area. The dam would also be part of a massive hydroelectric project that would bring power to the region.[22] In 1971, opponents to the project, led by the Environmental Defense Fund (EDF), successfully sued to stop the project on the grounds that the TVA had failed to file an environmental impact statement. The TVA complied and filed a report that mentioned a rare species of fish, the snail darter, was found in the river just above the dam site. In the interim, the Endangered Species Act was enacted in 1973, and biologists argued the completion of the project would destroy the snail darter's habitat. The TVA attempted to transfer the fish to other streams nearby, but was unsuccessful, yet at the same time refused to consider any alternative to completing the dam. The EDF and various citizens' groups sued again, and after working its way through the legal system, the U.S. Supreme Court ruled in favor of the environmentalists in June 1978.[23]

At the same time, Congress amended the 1973 legislation to create a special committee to review disputed projects like Tellico, nicknamed the "God Squad" because its members could grant an exemption from the protection provisions of the ESA. The committee ruled in favor of the snail darter, but a separate piece of legislation, signed by President Jimmy Carter in September 1979, exempted the Tellico project from not only the act, but from all other laws that blocked its completion as well. The project continued, with some transplanted snail darters surviving in nearby waters.

Critics of the ESA often point to projects discontinued or stalled because of habitat protection requirements. When the golden-cheeked warbler was listed under the act, it brought a halt to residential and commercial development on some of the choicest real estate in Texas, and led to an announcement by the 3M Company that it was delaying a multi-million-dollar expansion of its research and development center until the habitat issue was settled. Similarly, a spate of petitions to list species found only in the Pacific Northwest has caused a virtual crisis among the federal and state agencies that use the region's waters for hydroelectric power and agriculture.[24] California is believed to have more endangered species within its borders than any other state, with species affecting housing developments (the gnatcatcher and the Stephens kangaroo rat) and agriculture (the Delta smelt).[25] In one of the more dramatic examples of dissatisfaction with the law, a disgruntled Florida land developer shot at several endangered red-cockaded woodpeckers and destroyed nesting sites because he believed concern for the birds was unduly delaying his application for a building permit on his property.

Fishermen, too, have denounced the act for its impact on their livelihood, with the controversy focused on the protection of sea turtles. All six species of sea turtles found in U.S. waters have been listed since 1978, but their populations have been in decline as the beaches where they lay their eggs have been developed, or as they were caught by shrimp trawlers. The shrimping industry has grown as Americans' diets have changed to include more seafood, and now accounts for an estimated thirty thousand jobs.

In order to save both the turtles and the shrimp industry, the National Marine Fisheries Service spent $3.4 million over a three-year period to develop a technological solution—the turtle excluder device, or TED. The device is a panel of large mesh webbing or a metal grid inserted into the shrimp nets which deflects out large species like sea turtles and sharks. The devices were made available at no charge, although their use was purely voluntary. Fishermen, who preferred the term *trawler elimination device*, argued as much as 20 percent of the catch is deflected out the shrimp nets as well. When it appeared the voluntary approach had failed and dead turtles continued to wash ashore, groups like the Center for Marine Conservation and Greenpeace threatened to sue the government and shut down the shrimp industry completely. Despite numerous lawsuits of their own, the industry was unsuccessful and turned to Congress for help. A series of amendments to the ESA in 1988 made the devices mandatory in offshore waters by May 1989 and inshore a year later. In the meantime, dead turtles washed up on Florida beaches in record numbers, and the state was pressured by environmental groups to require emergency use of TEDs in its waters in advance of the federal deadline. A coalition of industry representatives then convinced the Louisiana congressional delegation to persuade the secretary of commerce to delay implementation of the law. The secretary later reversed himself, which led to a blockade of ports along the Gulf coast and some violence, which led to another reversal and a suspension of TED use until the National Academy of Sciences completed a study of TEDs' effectiveness. After several unsuccessful attempts were made by the secretary of commerce to restrict shrimp trawl times and force the use of TEDs, the industry sued the federal government in February 1990, saying the TED laws placed an unconstitutional burden on their businesses. The action is still pending in federal court.[26]

Despite examples like these, however, the actual number of projects blocked because of provisions in the ESA is very small. A 1992 study by the World Wildlife Fund found only nineteen federal activities and projects out of a potential pool of almost seventy-five thousand were blocked or terminated in the past five years because of irreconcilable conflicts over species protection. The study tracked the results of more than two thousand formal consultations between other federal agencies and the Fish and Wildlife Service or the National Marine Fisheries Service required under Section 7 of the law, which calls for a determination as to whether a proposed activity would jeopardize a species. Only 353 "jeopardy opinions" were issued, and of those, the overwhelming majority did not result in a cancellation of the project or activity. In most of the cases, the government was able to find alternatives that allowed the actions to go forward without threatening protected species.[27]

There is a growing wave of opinion, however, that the debate over the future of endangered species (and biodiversity in general) is becoming more

Seven Men and an Owl

On May 14, 1992, a panel of seven men met in Washington and made a decision on the fate of a two-pound bird that, if only symbolically, may change American environmental policy for decades to come. The Endangered Species Committee met for only the second time in history to exempt Endangered Species Act protection for the northern spotted owl on thirteen timber tracts in southwest Oregon. Unlike the snail darter incident, however, the controversy over the spotted owl marks a dramatic departure from political decisions of the previous twenty years. Although the immediate impact of the committee's vote is negligible, affecting only 1,742 acres of timber land and a thousand jobs, it was the first such exemption ever granted in the history of the legislation. More importantly, the decision represents the choice that must be made between forest products jobs and preservation of the owl's habitat, a choice exemplary of many environmental issues today.

The northern spotted owl's habitat ranges along the Pacific Coast from Canada to the San Francisco Bay area. Fewer than three thousand breeding pairs are estimated to exist, preferring to nest in tree holes or snags, preying on flying squirrels and rodents. One of the keys to the owls' survival are its young; 70 to 90 percent die, mostly from starvation and predation. Research shows the surviving young owls must be dispersed in a range of about three thousand acres each to replace dead owls and mix the genetic pool. Concerns about the future of the bird convinced the U.S. Fish and Wildlife Service to declare the owl "threatened"

in 1990 and to begin development of a recovery plan and designation of critical habitat for its protection.

At issue in the 1992 hearing was a request by the Bureau of Land Management for forty-four timber sales in western Oregon to be exempted from the act. In an internal battle between competing federal agencies, the Fish and Wildlife Service had issued an opinion that the proposed sales would jeopardize the long-term survival of the owl by fragmenting forests that provide important dispersal routes for young owls. In the interim, a federal court granted environmental groups' requests for an injunction to block timber sales on all forty-four parcels. After a month-long series of hearings that produced fifty thousand pages of exhibits and a four-thousand-page transcript at a cost of $1.5 million, the committee met to weigh the alternatives.

In order to grant an exemption, the Endangered Species Commitee must make three findings:

- That there is no "reasonable and prudent" alternative to the proposed action
- That the benefits of the action "clearly outweigh" any other alternatives
- That the action is in the public interest, and of regional or national significance

The committee deciding the fate of the owl was made up of seven members: the secretaries of agriculture, army, and interior, the administrators of the Environmental Protection Agency and the National Oceanic and Atmospheric Administration, the chairman of the Council of Economic Advisers, and a representative of the state of Oregon, designated by the governor. Meeting far from the site of the controversy, the committee deliberated at the same time the Department of Interior was releasing two other owl plans—a long-awaited Fish and Wildlife Service recovery plan and a proposed alternative plan prepared by Interior Secretary Manuel Lujan. The Fish and Wildlife Service plan is expected to cost the region an additional thirty-two thousand jobs, while the Lujan preservation plan is expected to cut job losses by half that number. Since the Lujan proposal violates the Endangered Species Act and the National Forest Management Act, it would require congressional approval.

In a 5 to 2 vote, with EPA Administrator William Reilly and Oregon's representative Tom Walsh dissenting, the committee denied thirty-one of the forty-four timber sales for which the Bureau of Land Management had sought exemption. Reilly admitted in later interviews the amount of timber involved would not seriously hurt Oregon jobs or the spotted owl, but the exemptions would set an unwise precedent. In May 1992, the issue was complicated further when a federal judge ruled in response to lawsuits by several environmental organizations that the Fish and Wildlife Service protection plan for the owl was insufficient because it failed to take into consideration new scientific evidence about the owls' declining population. Although the judge issued a ban on further logging, the case is likely to be tied up in litigation for years to come as both sides debate the jobs versus owls issue.

political and less scientific in nature. Critics of the process believe many of the most important decisions about species survival are being made by political appointees who make policy only in response to the groups that provide financial support for their benefactors. This produces, they argue, a system in which there is a natural tension between politicians and scientists, and as the issue of conserving biodiversity becomes more important, it inevitably becomes more political.[28]

Conservationists also note there are three factors that make it difficult to keep biodiversity on the public agenda: a lack of an easy identifiable opponent, a lack of any immediate impact on human life-styles, and a lack of cohesiveness by large groups around the widespread preservation of species. It is difficult, they say, to generate support or to motivate groups to mobilize to action when dozens of species are becoming extinct every day and their daily lives don't appear to be affected. The most difficult task seems to be convincing people, despite their concerns for endangered species, that there is a relationship between their own activities and the causes of endangerment. As a result, public attention begins to dissipate as policymakers realize the full costs of implementing protection measures.

A good example of this disparity between opinions and actions is the grizzly bear. Although environmentalists and the general public appear to be in agreement about the abstract benefits of protecting the bear, the people who are expected to make economic sacrifices by restricting their activities in bear habitat are likely to be ranchers, developers, and timber owners, who can lobby their concerns to political leaders extremely effectively.

One of the paradoxes of both the ESA and the CITES agreements is that a species is not protected until its population becomes so low that it is likely to become extinct. When that happens, recovery becomes both inefficient and costly. Recovery then begins to compromise the activities of other agencies (international, federal, state, and local), which must change their policies to accommodate the situation, increasing the probability of conflict. What this tells us about the future of endangered species and their habitats is that their protection requires the building of a much broader political constituency than currently exists. The actions of isolated organizations dedicated to the preservation of an individual species are unlikely to convince policymakers there is a need for change. Instead, public policy is more likely to be politicized by groups whose economic prospects are influenced by what happens to their future.

SUMMARY

Efforts to protect endangered species, both domestically and internationally, also involve protection of species habitats. Historically, animals gained protection because they were considered property of the king, and later, the landowner. Later, that responsibility fell to the government, which protected public lands (and the animals upon them) in trust for the public. U.S. policy has focused on protecting four categories of species: migratory and game birds, wild horses and burros, marine mammals, and endangered plants and animals. Legislatively, protection efforts are relatively new, with the most significant bills passed within the past thirty years. The United States has been at the forefront of international efforts to preserve species, but its own record is considered dismal by environmentalists. They cite the fact that few protection plans have been developed, and even fewer species have recovered from the brink of extinction as evidence that current legislation does not adequately protect species and their habitats. Critics of the law believe that trade-offs must be made between protecting species and balancing economic growth. Thus far, neither side of the controversy is satisfied with the law or how it is being implemented.

NOTES

1. The comments were made in an interview with the *Denver Post*, and quoted in Joe Hallinan, "Manuel Lujan: Genial Tender of the Interior," *The Oregonian*, December 5, 1991, A-3.

2. "Region 2 Report," *Endangered Species Technical Bulletin* 13, nos. 11–12 (1988), 3.

3. See Paul Ehrlich and Anne Ehrlich, *Extinction: The Causes and Consequences of the Disappearance of Species* (New York: Random House, 1981).

4. U.S. Executive Office of the President, Council on Environmental Quality, *The*

Global 2000 Report to the President, vol. 1 (Washington, DC: U.S. Government Printing Office, 1980), 37.

5. U.S. Executive Office of the President, U.S. Council on Environmental Quality. *The Evolution of National Wildlife Law* (Washington, DC: U.S. Government Printing Office, 1977), 17. One of the critical decisions of this period, *Geer v. Connecticut*, 161 U.S. 519 (1896), upheld a state law regulating the transportation of game birds outside Connecticut. Despite the narrow legal issue raised in the case, it is considered to be the bulwark of the state ownership doctrine even today.

6. See John Nichol, *The Animal Smugglers* (New York: Facts on File, 1987).

7. Susan Lieberman, "Japan Agrees to Phase Out Trade in Endangered Sea Turtles," *Endangered Species Technical Bulletin* 16, nos. 7–8 (1991): 4–6.

8. See Gareth Porter and Janet Welsh Brown, *Global Environmental Politics* (Boulder, CO: Westview Press, 1991), 82–85; Nick Cater, "Preserving the Pachyderm," *Africa Report* 34, no. 6 (November–December 1989): 45–48; Sue Armstrong and Fred Bridgland, "Elephants and the Ivory Tower," *New Scientist*, August 26, 1989, 37–41.

9. See "Elephant Skin and Bones," *The Economist*, February 29, 1992, 48; Peter Aldhous, "Critics Urge Reform of CITES Endangered List," *Nature* 355 (February 27, 1992): 758–59; Peter Aldhous, "African Rift in Kyoto," *Nature* 354 (November 21, 1991): 175; and Steven R. Weisman, "Bluefin Tuna and African Elephants Win Some Help at a Global Meeting," *New York Times*, March 11, 1992, A-8.

10. Jeffrey A. McNeely, "The Future of Natural Parks," *Environment* 32, no. 1 (January–February 1990): 17–20, 36–42.

11. See Fred Pearce, "Europe Discovers the Debt-for-Nature Swap," *New Scientist*, January 11, 1992, 50–51.

12. James A. Tober, *Wildlife and the Public Interest: Nonprofit Organizations and Federal Wildlife Policy* (New York: Praeger, 1989), 24.

13. *Sierra Club v. Froehlke*, 534 F.2d 1289 (8th Cir. 1976).

14. *National Wildlife Federation v. Coleman*, 529 F.2d 359 (5th Cir. 1976).

15. See John Cordell, "The Nature Conservancy: Databanking on Diversity," *Computerland Magazine*, November–December 1990, 19–20.

16. For a perspective on the role of hunters in wildlife conservation, see Roger L. Disilvestro, *The Endangered Kingdom: The Struggle to Save America's Wildlife* (New York: Wiley, 1989). For specific specie protection issues, see for example, Oliver H. Hewitt, ed., *The Wild Turkey and Its Management* (Washington, DC: Wildlife Society, 1967); Douglas L. Gilbert, *White-Tailed Deer: Ecology and Management* (Harrisburg, PA: Stackpole Books, 1984); William J. Chandler, *Audubon Wildlife Report* (San Diego: Academic Press, 1988); and Jim Robbins, "When Species Collide," *National Wildlife* 26 (February–March 1988): 20–27.

17. Tober, *Wildlife and the Public Interest*, 48.

18. U.S. Department of the Interior, U.S. Fish and Wildlife Service, *Report to Congress: Endangered and Threatened Species Recovery Program* (Washington, DC: U.S. Government Printing Office, December 1990), 12.

19. The exceptions are the Chilean false larch (found in Chile and Argentina), the Costa Rican jatropha (Costa Rica), and the Guatemalan fir (Mexico, Guatemala, Honduras, El Salvador). For a complete listings of the species, refer to the *Code of Federal Regulations*, Title 50, Part 17, and its supplements.

20. See Tober, *Wildlife and the Public Interest*, 59–83; Mark Crawford, "The Last Days of the Wild Condor?" *Science* 229 (August 30, 1985): 845; David Phillips and Hugh Nash, *The Condor Question: Captive or Forever Free?* (San Francisco: Friends of the Earth, 1981); and William W. Johnson, "California Condor: Embroiled in a Flap Not of Its Own Making," *Smithsonian*, December 1985, 73–80.

21. For a journalist's account of the plight of endangered species like the dodo, see

Douglas Adams and Mark Carwardine, *Last Chance to See* (New York: Harmony Books, 1990).

22. See William B. Wheeler, *TVA and the Tellico Dam* (Knoxville: University of Tennessee Press, 1986); and William Chandler, *Myth of the Tennessee Valley Authority* (Cambridge, MA: Ballinger, 1984).

23. Ehrlich and Erhlich, *Extinction*, 182–86.

24. See John M. Volkman, "Making Room in the Ark: The Endangered Species Act and the Columbia River Basin," *Environment* 34, no. 4 (May 1992): 18.

25. See Tom Horton, "The Endangered Species Act: Too Tough, Too Weak, or Too Late?" *Audubon* 94 (March–April 1992): 68–74.

26. See Rogene A. Buchholz, Alfred A. Marcus, and James E. Post, "Save the Turtles," in *Managing Environmental Issues* (Englewood Cliffs, NJ: Prentice-Hall, 1992), 61–70.

27. Donald J. Barry, *For Conserving Listed Species, Talk Is Cheaper Than We Think* (Washington, DC: World Wildlife Fund, 1992).

28. Jeffrey A. McNeely, "Report on Reports," *Environment* 34, no. 2 (March 1992): 25. See also Richard Tobin, *The Expendable Future: U.S. Politics and the Protection of Biological Diversity* (Durham, NC: Duke University Press, 1991).

FOR FURTHER READING

Douglas Adams and Mark Carwardine. *Last Chance to See.* New York: Harmony Books, 1990.

Paul Ehrlich and Anne Ehrlich. *Extinction: The Causes and Consequences of the Disappearance of Species.* New York: Random House, 1981.

Wendy E. Hudson, ed. *Landscape Linkages and Biodiversity.* Washington, DC: Island Press, 1991.

Kathryn A. Kohn, ed. *Balancing on the Brink of Extinction: The Endangered Species Act and Lessons for the Future.* Washington, DC: Island Press, 1990.

Jeffrey A. McNelly et al. *Conserving the World's Biological Diversity.* New York: International Union for Conservation of Nature, 1990.

Richard Tobin. *The Expendable Future: US Politics and the Protection of Biological Diversity.* Durham, NC: Duke University Press, 1991.

CHAPTER 16

The Frozen Environment: Arctic and Antarctic Protection

Hell, this country's so goddamn big that even if industry ran wild we could never wreck it.
—Comment voiced by the executive assistant to the governor of Alaska[1]

For many, the frozen polar regions represent an environment that is virtually unknown. We may have an image of a white wasteland inhabited by flora and fauna unlike any other place on Earth, or visions of brave explorers and sub-freezing temperatures. But the arctic and antarctic regions are unique in many ways, and thus present an uncommon opportunity for both exploitation and preservation. It is these two conflicting agendas that will be discussed in this chapter. What makes the topic particularly relevant is that the frozen environment gives us a chance to demonstrate what we have learned from other environmental experiments on the rest of the planet. Before tackling the issue of protection, however, it is necessary to know the background of these two regions, since they are in many ways as different as they are alike.

ARCTIC REGIONS

Unlike Antarctica, which is definable as a separate continent, the Arctic is delineated by somewhat arbitrary and often conflicting criteria. One commonly used definition is that the Arctic comprises those regions above the tree line, while another measure is temperature, which defines the Arctic as those regions in which the mean temperature for the warmest month is not greater than ten degrees Celsius. This line of temperature, or isotherm, incorporates various regions with similar climates and thus, similar plant and animal life. Others believe a more accurate description is the boundary in North America between the Eskimo and Indian cultures.

The most understandable definition, however, is the Arctic is made up of all lands and seas lying to the north of sixty degrees north latitude. Generally speaking, the Arctic is made up of a central sea surrounded by land masses, including parts of Eurasia and North America, Greenland, and Iceland. The greatest length of Arctic coastline belongs to Russia (about four thousand miles), Canada (fifteen hundred miles) and Alaska (nine hundred miles). The main body of the Arctic Ocean is covered by pack ice, from a few feet to many miles across, continually in motion, separating and refreezing. Even though the topography of the region varies considerably, there is a uniformity of vegetation— tundra and forest. The tundra consists of small shrubs, grasses, lichens, and mosses, while the forest, or taiga, is made up of coniferous trees, with tamarack, spruce, and pine the predominant species. Total precipitation is low, ranging from about five to fifteen inches per year, with about half of it falling as rain. The Arctic regions are inhabited, with the population estimated at sixty-four thousand Inuit from Alaska, fifty-two thousand in the Canadian Arctic, fifty-three thousand in Greenland, fifty thousand Sami of the Scandinavian Arctic, and the remaining one million peoples in the Eurasia-Siberian Arctic (Komi and Yakuty), and whites from the south.[2] The region has been extensively explored by more than a dozen nations in hopes of finding a trade route from East to West and in search of natural resources.[3]

Among the first to recognize the geopolitical importance of the Arctic was Vilhjalmur Stefansson, whose writings during the 1920s increased awareness of the region for policymakers.[4] Three issues have dominated the political landscape of the arctic regions over the past fifty years: strategic security, the fate of its indigenous peoples, and environmental protection. What all three issues have in common is they are basically conflicts over the allocation of resources among competing groups.

Eight Arctic Rim nations have played a role in the region's development: the former Soviet Union, Finland, Sweden, Norway, Iceland, Denmark (Greenland), Canada, and the United States, which has had a stake in the Arctic since 1867 when it purchased Alaska from Russia. The Eurasian Arctic region— which makes up three-quarters of the land area and by far the majority of its population—has been of critical importance from a strategic standpoint, especially since World War II. The coast of western Alaska is only fifty-seven miles from eastern Siberia, and the polar route marks the shortest distance between the United States and Western Europe and their former cold war enemy. With the development of intercontinental ballistic missiles and the possibility of nuclear confrontation, the Arctic's potential was primarily a military one.[5] The United States for example, set up bases on Greenland to defend against the Germans during World War II, ending 250 years of isolation, and Canada has allowed U.S. submarines to patrol through its territorial waters. In the 1970s and 1980s, the United States enacted the statutory framework to provide for the implementation of a comprehensive arctic policy. This led to a 1990 summit agreement with then-Soviet president Mikhail Gorbachev, which included a bilateral maritime boundary agreement and provision for the establishment of an international park in the Bering Strait region. Despite various agreements, however, environmental pollution is rampant and commercial exploitation is totally unregulated, especially within the Russian/Siberian arctic. Scientists have found that the Arctic air is loaded with pollutants carried there from industrial regions in the northern hemisphere, creating a massive haze.[6]

Of more contemporary importance has been the dispute between the United States and Canada over the Northwest Passage. It was not until 1903–06 that the first full transit of the passage was made by Norwegian Roald Amundsen, and the commercial and strategic value of the passage has been at issue ever since. The waterway is commercially significant for the transportation of oil and gas from the North American Arctic to markets in the eastern United States and Western Europe. It is strategically important for use by nuclear submarines, although that has become less of an issue as the cold war has wound down. The issues involved are primarily jurisdictional, with the focus on Canada affirming its control over the region.[7]

The second major Arctic issue has involved the status and perceived exploitation of native peoples who inhabit seven of the eight Arctic rim countries (Iceland has no indigenous people of its own). In 1971, President Nixon signed the Alaska Native Claims Settlement Act, which provided Alaska natives with title to forty-four million acres of land and $962.5 million in compensation to eliminate aboriginal title to any additional land in Alaska. Under the act, twelve regional native corporations were established to distribute the funds, but the process opened up claims by indigenous people in other nations as well.

Another source of confrontation has been cultural changes brought by increasing contact between natives and outsiders. In Greenland, for example, the Inuit were subjects of Danish colonialism from 1721 to 1953, but the reforms brought about a drastic restructuring of society and relocation of natives from their settlements into coastal communities. Whites, anxious to modernize the native population, initially brought a radical improvement in health standards, including an end to tuberculosis. But they also brought with them sexually transmitted diseases and alcoholism. Other illnesses previously unknown in the Arctic, such as lung cancer and cardiovascular disease, are now spreading, and a 600 percent increase in sugar consumption during the past twenty years has led to severe dental problems among Arctic peoples.[8] There has been considerable controversy over whether or not the native peoples should be self-ruled or subject to control by a central government that is geographically and culturally distant from them. The Sami of Sweden and Norway began forming associations to fight assimilation policies by their governments just after the turn of the century, and a reform movement in Greenland, which began in 1971, culminated in home rule there in 1979.[9] One of the most significant developments in the history of the indigenous peoples' attempts at self-rule occurred in November 1992 when 70 percent of the Inuit voted to establish their own territory. If approved by the federal government and parliament, the Inuit will be given hunting and fishing rights to Nunavut, or "our land"—an area three times the state of Texas, by 1999. For the first time, the Arctic tundra will be governed by its native inhabitants.

Still, additional problems must be resolved. Conflicts have developed between animal rights activists who decry the natives' traditional practice of harvesting wild animals for food and other necessities of life. Under the 1972 Marine Mammal Protection Act, Alaska natives were granted exceptions for subsistence hunting and other activities, but some groups believe such exceptions are now unnecessary as the natives move toward a cash economy. The most controversial issue has involved Alaska's Inupiat Eskimos, who hunt bowhead whales, the most endangered of the large whales, with only four thousand estimated to still exist.[10] The natives argue the hunt is of cultural significance, and believe their kills do not significantly impact the survival of the species.[11] The Inuit of Greenland are also subsistence hunters and have resisted attempts to restrict whaling in their region.

The debate centers on three issues: biological arguments regarding the viability of species and the causes of population declines, humane treatment arguments, and ethical or moral arguments regarding the rights of humans to kill wild animals. In the mid-1950s, media accounts of the clubbing of baby harp seals brought a storm of protest from animal protection organizations, even though that method is considered to be the quickest and most humane method of killing. Groups like the Canadian Sealers Association, the Aboriginal Trappers Federation of Canada, and Indigenous Survival International have attempted to counter the antiharvesting campaign through the media, and the larger American conservation and environmental groups have distanced themselves from the controversy.[12]

Indigenous groups have also formed their own nongovernmental organizations to serve as a forum for issues of mutual interest. In 1977, the Inuit Circumpolar Conference (ICC) held its first meeting, bringing together for the first time representatives from Alaska, Canada, and Denmark. The group called upon their governments to establish an international Arctic policy, demilitarization of the region, and the establishment of Inuit health care, education, and cultural exchange programs. The ICC remains the only continuing forum for discussion of the future of the Inuit people and was recognized in 1982 as a nongovernmental organization in consultative status by the United Nations.

Although many of the native peoples' conflicts remain unresolved, there is a close tie to the confrontation between environmental groups and the petroleum industry, which sees the Arctic in terms of its energy potential. The 1968 discovery of a pool of at least ten billion barrels of oil and twenty-six trillion cubic feet of gas at Prudhoe Bay on the Alaskan North Slope gave the United States a hint of reduced dependence on Middle Eastern resources. But the discovery also opened up the Pandora's box of how to get the oil to market. The Trans-Alaska Pipeline (TAP) stretches eight hundred miles from Prudhoe Bay to the port of Valdez, and as it was being built, residents were assured the chance

Voyage of the Valdez

On March 23, 1989, the Exxon supertanker *Valdez* left the port loaded with fifty-two million gallons of crude oil, headed for refineries in Long Beach, California. As it navigated through Prince William Sound, it ran aground, tearing eleven holes in the vessel's bottom, releasing the oil in its cargo holds. The oil slick from the vessel began to spread, covering more than one thousand square miles and drifting into the Gulf of Alaska. Miles of shoreline and inaccessible beaches were covered with oil. The U.S. Fish and Wildlife Service officially counted 36,460 dead marine birds, although there is no accurate estimate of how many were actually killed. Over a thousand dead otters were retrieved, and an unknown number of whales and seals also died. Damage also occurred as cleanup crews used steam-cleaning equipment along the rocky shore—a process that affected organisms all along the food chain to an unquantifiable degree. Exxon began cleanup efforts, but the firm was severely criticized by environmentalists and eventually by the state of Alaska as being insufficient for a spill of this magnitude—estimated at eleven million gallons of oil.[14] The company later calculated it was able to recover somewhere between 3 and 13 percent of the spilled oil, with cleanup costs estimated at more than $2 billion. But the lesson learned was critical—no amount of money spent or personnel deployed can control a large oil spill.[15]

Subsequent investigation by the U.S. Coast Guard revealed the captain of the *Valdez*, Joseph Hazelwood, had a blood alcohol level estimated at 0.19—more than double the level at which most states consider a motorist to be legally drunk. Hazelwood was also charged with reckless endangerment for having left his command post to go below ship prior to it having reached open water, violating company policy. Hazelwood's attorneys decided not to have their client testify during his criminal trial, and he was eventually acquitted of the three most serious charges. He was convicted only of the misdemeanor charge of negligent discharge of oil, to which he was sentenced to one thousand hours of cleaning up the Alaska coastline, and to pay $50,000 in restitution. The court suspended a ninety-day jail sentence and a $1,000 fine. Hazelwood's misdemeanor conviction was reversed in July 1992 when the Alaska Court of Appeals ruled the skipper was immune from any charges stemming from the spill because he had followed procedures by reporting to the Coast Guard that the tanker was dead in the water and spilling oil. The state is expected to appeal, and the case will likely be tied up in the judicial system for several more years.[16]

The legacy of the *Valdez* spill continues. Despite Hazelwood's acquittal, Exxon itself was charged criminally and civilly, and only after a year and a half of complex legal negotiations was an initial settlement reached. The company agreed to pay $100 million in criminal penalties and to create a restoration fund of $1 billion in civil penalties over fifteen years. But a federal judge rejected the settlement as being two low, and the parties began to renegotiate. Influenced largely by Alaska governor (and former interior secretary) Walter Hickel, who feared the issue would be tied up in court for decades, the state and Exxon agreed to a second settlement that was identical to the first, except that Exxon would pay $125 million in criminal penalties. Of that money, $50 million would go to the state of Alaska, $50 million to the federal government as restitution for the restoration of Prince William Sound, $12 million to the Department of the Interior to support wetlands for migratory birds in western states, and $13 million to the U.S. Treasury.[17] Environmentalists, however, were outraged at the settlement, particularly after the company announced it would deduct the civil penalties from its tax burden —an outcome that would result in an actual cost of $462.9 million rather than $1.125 billion.[18]

A secondary consequence of the *Valdez* incident was an increase in petroleum prices, as the spill brought a temporary halt to shipments of crude oil out of *Valdez*. West Coast refineries depend upon Alaskan crude for 60 percent of their supply, and consumers faced a jump of ten to twenty cents per gallon at the pump.[19] Aside from the environmental and economic costs of the spill, *Valdez* refocused attention on the energy issue and the development of the Alaskan oil fields. Environmental groups gained momentum in their efforts to preserve the arctic region, and for the first time, the public gained awareness of the impact of such a disaster.

of a major oil spill in Prince William Sound was extremely remote. Throughout the process, impact statements were prepared, and oil tankers docking at Valdez were required to follow extensive safety procedures. The oil companies operating out of the port developed an extensive cleanup plan.

Environmental groups believed, however, that the federal government was not taking the pipeline or the threat of a spill seriously. The first environmental impact statement prepared by the U.S. Department of the Interior was only 6 pages long; the second, in January 1971, was 256 pages; the third and final version, published in six volumes in March 1972, contained 3,736 pages. The difference in size and content was due to the vigilance of environmental groups that monitored the pipeline's construction from the beginning. Friends of the Earth filed suit, as did fishermen, concerned about the impact of a spill on Prince William Sound. Construction began in December 1973, and when completed, the $8 billion pipeline was the most expensive private construction project in history. Tanker traffic along the Northwest Passage and the Arctic coast raised the specter of massive oil spills and pollution, which could devastate the area's marine ecosystem and valuable fishing grounds. Anticipating a potential disaster, Canada enacted the Arctic Waters Pollution Prevention Act in 1970 as a way of regulating shipping, a position that was later accepted multilaterally.[13] Still, no serious accidents had occurred in the Port of Valdez since the loaded first tanker left in August 1977.

THE ARCTIC NATIONAL WILDLIFE REFUGE

The area which encompasses Alaska's Arctic National Wildlife Refuge (ANWR), was first proposed for protection in 1938, but because of World War II, the region was reserved for military purposes. Legislation to protect the area was introduced into law in 1959, and was approved as one of President Dwight Eisenhower's final acts on December 6, 1960, when Interior Secretary Fred Seaton established the preserve under Public Land Order #2214 for the conservation of wildlife and recreation.[20] In 1980, President Jimmy Carter signed the Alaska National Interest Conservation Act, which increased the size of ANWR to nineteen million acres, but excepted from protection a section of the coastal plain (also known as the "1002 area") because of its potential for oil and gas development. The coastal plain, along with the rest of the Arctic Refuge and Canada's Northern Yukon National Park, is one of the largest, most productive intact arctic ecosystems in the world.[21]

The Bush administration sought to open up ANWR for oil and gas exploration in 1991 as part of a massive energy bill as a result of declining domestic oil production. The proposal would have allowed drilling on 12,000 of the 1.5 million acres in the coastal plain area, based on a 1987 study that showed that there was a 46 percent probability of recoverable oil. Interior Secretary Manuel Lujan told Congress the area represented "the most outstanding petroleum exploration target in the onshore United States."[22] If fully recovered, the oil represented about two hundred days worth of U.S. production—and environmentalists believed the small supply was not worth any potential risk to the ecology of the area. They also sought other energy alternatives to drilling, such as an increase in gasoline mileage standards for automobiles and promotion of renewable energy resources.

Environmental groups like Greenpeace testified against the legislation, arguing that the drilling would have a devastating effect on the area's wildlife. The coastal plain area is the prime calving ground for the 180,000 animals that make up the Porcupine caribou herd. The herd is the food supply of the Gwich'in nations of the northern Yukon, Alaska, and Northwest Territories, and is protected by a 1987 treaty signed by both the United States and Canada. In testimony before Congress, U.S. Department of the Interior officials argued oil development and wildlife are compatible, citing the nearby herds at Prudhoe Bay as an example where the species flourishes in the midst of oil-drilling equipment. The department also claimed mitigation measures would ensure that no significant adverse effects would occur.

Congress, however, was unconvinced, and a Senate filibuster in November 1991 dealt a severe blow to President Bush's proposal. Connecticut senator Joseph Lieberman, who opposed the ANWR provisions included in the energy bill, called the Senate's action a clear sign against Arctic drilling: "This was a turning point vote, in my view, for the Alaskan wilderness, for the environment in general, and for American energy policy. We have drawn a line in the tundra."[23] In 1992, the Senate approved the president's energy bill, but only after it had been stripped of the ANWR proposal. The issue of drilling in Alaska's coastal plain appears to have stalled, at least for now.

JAMES BAY

The James Bay hydroelectric project began in 1971 as the "project of the century"—an undertaking that would alter nineteen waterways, create twenty-seven reservoirs, and would cost tens of billions of dollars to expand hydroelectric power in Quebec.[24] There are three phases of the project, built by Hydro Quebec: the completed La Grande complex (the world's largest hydroelectric development), the proposed Great Whale complex, and the proposed Nottaway-Broadback-Rupert complex. Initially, the project had almost universal support, since it was seen as a way of bringing jobs and clean electricity to southern Quebec to stimulate economic development. Substantial opposition soon developed from the Cree and Inuit people who inhabit the region, as well as environmental groups, biologists, and energy experts. More than 17,500 natives live along the shores of Hudson and James bays, and their way of life was threatened by the massive project. The Indians complained that their traditional hunting life-style was altered as a result of the building of project roads linking them with cities to the south, and that social problems like prostitution and alcoholism were increasing.[25] In 1975, the Cree agreed to settle their dispute with Hydro Quebec for $136 million in compensation, plus exclusive hunting, fishing, and trapping rights, and a guaranteed income for Cree hunters living in the bush.[26]

What was unknown at the time, however, was the soil in the lands being flooded by the James Bay dams was heavily contaminated with mercury, and accumulations along the food chain finally made their way to human beings. Tests on Cree who ate fish caught in the region revealed that 47 percent had levels of mercury above World Health Organization standards, and nearly 10 percent had levels high enough to risk developing mercury poisoning—effects that may linger for decades, and possibly as long as one hundred years.[27]

In September, 1991, Quebec premier Robert Bourassa announced a one-year postponement of the Great Whale project, a move likely to mean the end of future James Bay development. The action was triggered by extensive Cree lobbying of New York State officials to cancel their $17 billion power contract, and by a decision by the Canadian government to order a two-year environmental impact study of the project. The study is composed of two phases: first, an analysis of the project's infrastructure (roads and airports) and second, the dams and generating stations.[28] New York's cancellation of its part of the agreement in 1992—carried out without penalty through an escape clause in the contract—pushed the utility's borrowing costs up so it would not be profitable to continue construction and making bond sales difficult to finance the dams and generating plants. The result, as one Ottawa-based newsletter put it, is that "the Great Whale is beached."[29]

A number of factors led to the government's decision to postpone the project. First, the environmental movement in Canada has grown significantly since the James Bay project was proposed in the early 1970s, and its members have effectively lobbied both the Canadian government and other world leaders to halt the project. Second, Canada now requires environmental impact assessments be made of major government projects—a process that did not exist when James Bay was first proposed. Research and technological advances now enable policymakers to better understand the impact of such a massive undertaking. Third, the internationalization of environmental issues has brought many non-Canadians into the policy debate. Hydro Quebec's contracts with New York and Maine became the target of U.S. environmentalists, and the New York–based National Audubon Society released a report that was highly critical of the James Bay project, fueling U.S. opposition to the project.[30] Lastly, there has been a global concern for indigenous peoples' rights, which previously never existed; the Cree and Inuit who lived in the region were never notified of the project when it was initially proposed, a strategy that would be unthinkable today.[31]

Both the ANWR and James Bay projects are an indicator of how effectively environmental organizations have brought pressure to bear on government leaders in an attempt to preserve the Arctic, and the strength of that support. A number of private initiatives have begun to resolve long-standing Arctic conflicts, such as the Working Group on Arctic International Relations, and the 1988 International Conference on Arctic Cooperation, sponsored by Science for Peace. There is also an enhanced effort at multilateral scientific cooperation, such as the UN Northern Science Network and a proposed International Arctic Science Committee (IASC). Cultural exchanges between Alaskans and villagers from Provideniya on the Russian peninsula began in 1988, and an exhibition of Bering Sea region cultural artifacts toured both countries in 1988–89. A flurry of international agreements in 1988 and 1989 have finally brought the Arctic's issues and conflicts to the negotiating table,[32] a step that was improbable just a decade ago.

ANTARCTICA

The most southerly of Earth's continents, Antarctica holds within its 5.5-million-square-mile boundaries 70 percent of Earth's fresh water, and about 10 percent of its land surface. It is the fifth-largest continent on Earth, bigger than the United States and Mexico combined. Nearly 98 percent of the continent is covered by a glacial ice cover that has accumulated over millions of years and varies from twenty-three hundred to four thousand meters in thickness. The only ice-free regions are those along the coastal areas, and these are underlain by permafrost, with conditions perennially below the freezing point. The region is divided into two sections, the larger East Antarctica, and West Antarctica, which is about one-quarter the size of the eastern area. Since there is little melting of the giant ice sheets, there are no river systems, and only poorly developed beaches. Antarctica is dominated by high winds and low temperatures, including a low of minus 88 degrees Celsius, which was recorded in 1960 at the Russian station Vostock.

What makes Antarctica unique is there are no naturally occurring reptiles, mammals, amphibians, plants, or trees on the entire continent. The only sources of life are lichens and mosses, and a few species of insects, worms, and parasites. In contrast, the surrounding Southern Ocean is home to a varied marine ecosystem, including mammals, fish, crustaceans, and plankton, as well as more than fifty species of birds that feed upon them. There are seven species of penguins, which are the most recognizable of the Antarctic birds, with an estimated population of 120 million. The continent is ideal for the study of how organisms adapt and ecosystems function in simple and extreme environments. For example, the antarctic springtail (a small, wingless insect) is able to withstand temperatures as low as minus 60 degrees Celsius, giving researchers insight into natural antifreezes such as polyhydric alcohols and sugars.[33]

There is some controversy about who first discovered Antarctica, although it is known that Captain James Cook discovered the subantarctic island of South Georgia in a 1772–75 circumnavigation of Antarctica after three years of searching for the unknown continent of Terra Australis—a vast southern landmass, which would balance out the northern one. There are reports Antarctica was visited in 1820 by British explorer Edward Bransfield, Russian Thaddeus von Bellingshausen, and American Nathaniel Palmer, who viewed the peninsula from about three miles away. James Eights, a geologist, was the first U.S. scientist to work in Antarctica, conducting investigations along the Peninsula in 1839. Throughout the nineteenth century, various expeditions visited the continent, including Charles Wilkes, who mapped fifteen hundred miles of Antarctic coastline for the U.S. Navy in 1839–40 and James Clark Ross, an Englishman who discovered the Ross Sea, McMurdo Sound, and Mount Erebus.

Besides the explorers, Antarctic waters brought sealers eager to harvest the millions of fur seals inhabiting the southern islands, which led to commercial trading in skins until the 1890s, when they were believed to have become extinct. The whaling industry also moved in at the beginning of the twentieth century, and their harvests pushed several species toward extinction, as well as disrupting the Antarctic food chain.[34] Extensive human intrusion is actually of recent origin, since explorers did not winter over until 1899, and it was not until December 14, 1911, that Norwegian Roald Amundsen (also an Arctic explorer) arrived at the South Pole, followed by noted explorer Capt. Robert F. Scott just over a month later. Scientific exploration did not become extensive until the 1930s, when Richard E. Byrd led two privately sponsored U.S. expeditions, including the first flight over the South Pole. Despite the establishment of two

U.S. Antarctic Service bases in 1939–40, little was known about the continent until 1957.

Commander Matthew Maury of the U.S. Naval Observatory is recognized as one of the major figures who attempted to gain international cooperation among the nine nations with an interest in the area in 1861.[35] Sovereignty issues continued as seven nations—Argentina, Australia, Chile, France, New Zealand, Norway, and the United Kingdom—began to claim portions of the continent, with Argentina and Chile making claims on the basis of geographic proximity. Only the United States and Russia, with numerous explorations into the region, refused to make territorial claims or recognize those of other nations, many of which overlapped.

The years 1957–58 have been called a major turning point in Antarctic history with the organization of the International Geophysical Year (IGY) by the International Conference of Scientific Unions (ICSU). The project included a coordinated accumulation of knowledge about the continent, and by late 1956 to early 1957, twelve countries had established sixty-seven research stations.[36] The IGY culminated in December 1959 when the seven states claiming territory there signed the Antarctic Treaty, whose dual purpose was to maintain the region for peaceful use only and to promote freedom of scientific investigation. The treaty also led to formation of an international Scientific Committee for Antarctic Research (SCAR) a nongovernmental organization of the ICSU. In 1960, SCAR drew up a series of general rules of conduct for expeditions operating in Antarctica. A key provision of the Antarctic Treaty was a prohibition against nuclear testing and the deposition of nuclear waste. Since then, however, the document has been an imperfect model of cooperation, and not all countries have agreed as to whether or not Antarctica is a part of the international commons. Many developing countries have rejected the idea that a tiny minority of rich and technologically advanced nations should manage the region to the exclusion of others.[37]

It can be argued, however, that the treaty has failed in its mission of preservation and protection. In 1962, for example, the United States installed a nuclear reactor at McMurdo, which leaked and required removal (primarily for economic reasons), along with tons of contaminated soil, and in 1983, France constructed an island airstrip, destroying penguin breeding colonies.[38] Three important international conventions sought to further conserve living resources: the 1964 Agreed Measures for the Conservation of Antarctic Fauna and Flora, the 1972 Convention on the Conservation of Antarctic Seals, and the 1980 Convention on the Conservation of Antarctic Marine Living Resources. The latter document grew out of studies of overfishing of Antarctic waters, showing that some finfish are declining to the point where they may never recover.

Human intrusion has brought with it a unique set of problems: The cold climate does not allow biodegradable waste to decompose, so it remains indefinitely preserved in the subfreezing temperatures. Despite efforts to safeguard the environment, the environmental group Greenpeace has documented that the Antarctic Treaty Consultative Parties' Code of Conduct for Waste Disposal is routinely violated by research stations. Tourism has also become a concern, with cruises to the area beginning in 1958, followed by sightseeing flights, which were limited after an Air New Zealand crash in 1979 killed 257 passengers and crew over Mount Erebus. Some two thousand to three thousand tourists visit Antarctica every year (most of them aboard cruise ships) and new regulations have been adopted to avoid disturbing wildlife and to guarantee waste removal. Despite these measures, however, significant environmental degradation has already occurred, and the growing volume of tourism has disrupted national scientific programs. Problems have arisen over the need to offer emergency services (the average age of tourists on one cruise was sixty years old), as well as legal problems concerning insurance, jurisdiction, and liability.[39]

The region's role has changed since the Antarctic Treaty was first signed. Until the 1970s, Antarctica was viewed primarily as a laboratory, rather than as an economic resource, although the 1982 Falklands War between Argentina and Britain accentuated the strategic importance of Antarctica as a reminder that the area is not immune from world conflict. Eight years of negotiations during the 1980s finally resulted in the 1988 signing of the Convention on the Regulation of Antarctic Mineral Resource Activities (CRAMRA), or Wellington Convention, to limit exploration for minerals and oil. Only two minerals have been found in sufficient quantity to make mining even a consideration—coal and iron—but prohibitive mining costs and sufficient sources in more accessible areas make it unlikely as a resource. Surveys by Germany, France, Japan, Britain, and Russia of the continental shelf have provided only circumstantial evidence for the existence of offshore oil and gas, and no deposits have been discovered, but even scientific exploration is a signal of some commercial interest in the area.[40]

Whaling in the Southern Ocean off Antarctica has been an issue since the first station was established in 1904. Initially, whalers killed humpback whales, which swam close to land, but as they were depleted, the main targets became blue, sperm, fin, and sei whales.[41] The International Whaling Commission (IWC) was established in 1946 to regulate the industry. Primarily a whalers' club until 1972, the IWC became the target of environmentalists when it became apparent that whale stocks were rapidly being depleted. During the 1950s and 1960s, when the IWC was supposed to be protecting the species, more whales were killed than ever before, and whales became a symbol of the environmental movement. In 1972, the United Nations proposed a ten-year moratorium on whaling, and a year later, under the Convention on International Trade in Endangered Species (CITES), which became effective in 1975, whales were given various degrees of protection according to their species's status. The IWC voted for a moratorium on all commercial whaling in 1982, but the agreement, which did not take effect until 1986, was viewed as a temporary measure to be reviewed after researchers had time to study whale populations.

Greenpeace, which began its "whale war" in the mid-1970s, began to document violations of the IWC's New Management Procedure, which allowed scientific harvesting of whales for research purposes. Environmentalists argued that the provision was simply an excuse for the continuation of commercial whaling. Japan, which has continued to kill whales under this loophole, has argued that the practice is purely for scientific purposes, and has refused to halt its program. In 1990, Japan and Norway asked the IWC to lift its moratorium on commercial hunting of minke whales, but the body refused. Japan represents the biggest market for whale meat, and as long as that need exists, some whaling will continue.[42] It is estimated that the population of blue whales in now less than 1 percent of the level when whaling began; humpbacks are at 3 percent, and fin whales are at only 20 percent of their original strength.

The moratorium's opponents argue there has never been any scientific assessment of whale stocks, and some species, like the minke whale, could be harvested in substantial quantities for a period without damage to the stocks even though there is no accurate information on the maximum sustained yield.[43] Gradually, the international moratorium on commercial whaling has begun to unravel, with Norway announcing in 1992 the population of North American minke whales had rebounded and Norwegian whalers would resume commercial hunting in 1993. Iceland quit the organization entirely.

Despite the polarization of the IWC (into whalers and antiwhaling interests) whales have continued to be an important, if albeit symbolic part of the movement to protect Antarctic resources. Cynics argue that whales are being protected in the Antarctic because they make excellent fund-raisers, just behind giant pandas and baby seals. There is no doubt that whales have tremendous emotional and political appeal. In 1988, the United States spent $2 million to rescue two California grey whales caught, as grey whales often are, in the ice off Barrow, Alaska.[44] As one critic notes, there may no longer be urgent reasons for conservation for continued pressure to strengthen the controls on whaling, but there are sound financial reasons for groups that depend on public subscriptions to be seen as active in "saving the whale." The Japanese, for example, have accused members of the IWC of cultural imperialism, charging that "Anglo-Saxon nations seem to think their values are the center of the world"— an issue which could easily be applied to other species. In that sense, whales may be "a test case, a trial of strength between those who take because they can, and those who are prepared to exercise a measure of strength."[45] At the very least, the IWC represents a failed regime that has been unable to reach consensus on the ethical, cultural, scientific, economic, and political issues.[46]

Antarctica gained importance for a totally different reason in 1975 when a team of British researchers noticed a precipitous drop in levels of stratospheric ozone during the austral spring. At some altitudes, levels dropped to nearly zero, leading scientists to report there was an "ozone hole" over the region. The appearance of such a hole is important because the ozone layer protects the planet from harmful ultraviolet radiation, a topic that was discussed in Chapter 13. Since the discovery, several expeditions have continued to monitor ozone levels, as well as studies of the upper atmosphere, the aurora, and various astronomical phenomenon.

Various proposals have been advanced as to what the next steps should be to preserve and protect the region and its resources. Environmental organizations like the Antarctica and Southern Ocean Coalition, the Antarctica Project, and Greenpeace have sought to have Antarctica declared a World Park, open only to scientific research, and to ban mineral exploration. In 1986, Greenpeace constructed the first international, nongovernmental research base to monitor human intrusion, especially at the McMurdo base camp. Support for the World Park concept has come from France, New Zealand, and Australia, with the United States, Britain, Uruguay and Argentina initially favoring a less restrictive covenant.[47]

Public pressure and support for a mining ban by the U.S. Environmental Protection Agency resulted in the United States signing the Protocol on Environmental Protection to the Antarctic Treaty in Madrid in 1991. The document builds upon the Antarctic Treaty to provide improved environmental protection measures that can be strengthened in the future if necessary. It establishes an advisory body and incorporates detailed mandatory rules for environmental protection, including prohibition of any activities other than scientific research that relate to Antarctic mineral resources for a minimum of fifty years. Environmentalists believe, however, that they must be constantly vigilant in their efforts to monitor Antarctic development. As the world order goes through a process of change, there is no guarantee that the world leaders of tomorrow will see the same need to protect the region as their predecessors do today.

SUMMARY

Both the Arctic regions and the continent of Antarctica pose a unique environmental challenge even though they are vastly different in resources. Since the Arctic regions are inhabited, the issue of indigenous people is important, where Antarctica is home only for researchers and tourists. Both regions have had their futures decided by a multitude of nations that have made historical and political claim to the area, largely for their strategic value and because of the resources they represent. Public awareness of the fragile nature of these areas was finally awakened when the Exxon supertanker *Valdez* ran aground in Alaskan waters in 1989. Since then, the media has focused attention on the regions' key controversies, including proposed development of Alaska's Arctic National Wildlife Refuge, the James Bay Hydroelectric Project in Quebec, increasing public intrusion into the pristine Antarctic, overfishing, and the whaling harvest. Lastly, the discovery of a hole in the ozone layer over the Antarctic has made the continent the centerpoint of the global warming debate.

NOTES

1. Art Davidson, *In the Wake of the Exxon Valdez: The Devastating Impact of the Alaska Oil Spill* (San Francisco: Sierra Club Books, 1990), xii.
2. For a summary of the migration and culture of the Arctic's native peoples, see

Sam Hall, *The Fourth World: The Heritage of the Arctic and its Destruction* (New York: Knopf, 1987).

3. See, for example, James Gordon Hayes, *Robert Edwin Peary* (London: G. Richards and H. Toulmin, 1929); Jeannette Mirsky, *To the Arctic* (New York: Knopf, 1948); George Pearce, *To The Pacific and Arctic with Beechey* (Cambridge: Cambridge University Press, 1973); Robert E. Peary, *The North Pole* (New York: Frederick A. Stokes, 1910); John Edwards Caswell, *Arctic Frontiers* (Norman: University of Oklahoma Press, 1956).

4. See Vilhjalmur Stefansson, *The Northward Course of Empire* (New York: Harcourt Brace and Company, 1922).

5. See R. J. Sutherland, "The Strategic Significance of the Canadian Arctic," in *The Arctic Frontier*, ed. R. St. J. Macdonald, (Toronto: University of Toronto Press, 1966), 256–78; and Gail Osherenko and Oran R. Young, *The Age of the Arctic: Hot Conflicts and Cold Realities* (Cambridge: Cambridge University Press, 1989), 17–44.

6. Personal communication from Capt. Brian Shoemaker, executive director, Hero Foundation. For a chronology of contemporary U.S. foreign policy in this region, see Samuel Frye, "The Arctic and U.S. Foreign Policy, 1970–90," *U.S. Department of State Dispatch 2*, no. 14 (April 8, 1991): 242–46. See also Pier Horensma, *The Soviet Arctic* (New York: Routledge, 1991).

7. See Franklyn Griffiths, ed., *Politics of the Northwest Passage* (Montreal: McGill-Queen's University Press, 1987). For an analysis of Artic haze, see Marvin S. Soroos, "The Odyssey of Arctic Haze: Towards a Global Atmospheric Regime," *Environment 34*, No. 10 (December 1992): 6–11, 25–26.

8. Hall, *Fourth World*, 129–30.

9. See Osherenko and Young, *Age of the Arctic*, 72–109.

10. See Donald Day, *The Whale War* (San Francisco: Sierra Club Books, 1987), 36–39.

11. See G. Donovan, ed., "Aboriginal/Subsistence Whaling," *Report of the International Whaling Commission*, Special Issue #4 (1982), 1–86.

12. Osherenko and Young, *Age of the Arctic*, 136–39. For an analysis of the two sides of the issue, see Brian Davies, *Savage Luxury: The Slaughter of the Baby Seals* (Toronto: Ryerson Press, 1970); and Alan Herscovici, *Second Nature* (Toronto: CBC Enterprises, 1985).

13. See R. Michael M'Gonigle and Mark Zacher, *Pollution, Politics and International Law: Tankers at Sea* (Berkeley: University of California Press, 1979).

14. For an account of the Exxon incident, see Ken Wells and Marilyn Chase, "Paradise Lost: Heartbreaking Scenes of Beauty Disfigured Follow Alaska Oil Spill," *Wall Street Journal*, March 31, 1989, A-1; George J. Church, "The Big Spill," *Time*, April 10, 1989, 39; and Sharon Begley, "Smothering the Waters," *Newsweek*, April 10, 1989, 56.

15. Davidson, *Wake of the Exxon Valdez*, 297.

16. See "Dry Docked," *U.S. News & World Report*, August 5, 1990, 11; "Suspended, Joseph Hazelwood," *Time*, August 6, 1990, 57; "On and off the Rocks in Alaska," *U.S. News & World Report*, April 2, 1990, 14; Paul A. Witteman, "First Mess Up, Then Mop Up: Hazelwood Is Ordered to Help Cleanse Alaska's Shoreline," *Time*, April 2, 1990, 22; Nora Underwood, "A Captain's Guilt: A Verdict in the Exxon Valdez Oil Spill," *Maclean's*, April 2, 1990, 54. See also John Keeble, *Out of the Channel: The Exxon Valdez Oil Spill in Prince William Sound* (New York: HarperCollins, 1991).

17. See Keith Schneider, "Exxon to Pay Higher Criminal Fines in New Pact to Settle Valdez Claims," *New York Times*, October 1, 1991, A-14.

18. "2nd Settlement to Cost Exxon Less," *New York Times*, October 13, 1991, 1–21.

19. See Rogene A. Buchholz, Alfred A. Marcus, and James E. Post, *Managing Environmental Issues: A Casebook* (Englewood Cliffs, NJ:, Prentice-Hall, 1990), 43–57.

20. See Debbie S. Miller, *Midnight Wilderness* (San Francisco: Sierra Club Books, 1990).

21. For a description of the area's natural resources and beauty, see Paul Rauber, "Last Refuge," *Sierra*, January–February 1992, 37–43.

22. U.S. Congress, Senate, Committee on Environment and Public Works, Subcommittee on Environmental Protection and Subcommittee on Superfund, Ocean and Water Protection, *Joint Hearing on Developing the Coastal Plain of the Alaska National Wildlife Refuge*, 102nd Cong., 1st sess., May 10, 1991 (Washington, DC: U.S. Government Printing Office, 1991), 46.

23. Holly Idelson, "Senate Filibuster Deals Blow to Plan for New Policy," *Congressional Quarterly Weekly Report*, November 2, 1991, 3191. See also Clifford Krause, "Energy Bill Derailed in Senate," *New York Times*, November 2, 1991, 19.

24. For a synopsis of the James Bay project as it was originally planned, see William Hamley, "Hydroelectric Developments in the James Bay Region, Quebec," *The Geographical Review* 73 (January 1983): 110–112. See also, D'Arcy Jenish, "Power to Burn," *Maclean's*, May 21, 1990, 50–54.

25. See D'Arcy Jenish, "Creating a New Way of Life: Changes Threaten Cree Traditions," *Maclean's*, May 21, 1990, 55.

26. Harry Thurston and Stephen Homer, "Power in a Land of Remembrance," *Audubon* 93 (November–December 1991): 52–59.

27. Rae Corelli, "Fateful Consequences: Development Could Take a Heavy Toll," *Maclean's*, May 21, 1990, 56.

28. Barry Came, "Power Plays in Quebec," *Maclean's*, July 22, 1991, 12.

29. Peter C. Newman, "The Beaching of a Great Whale," *Maclean's*, September 16, 1991, 38. See also Peter Quiddington, "Indians Cheer Halt to Canada's Giant Hydro Scheme," *New Scientist*, May 25, 1991, 17.

30. See Dan Burke, "The Southern Campaign," *Maclean's*, May 21, 1991, 54.

31. This case study is best chronicled in Boyce Richardson, *Strangers Devour the Land* (Post Mills, VT: Chelsea Green, 1991).

32. For a summary of these events, see Osherenko and Young, *Age of the Arctic*, 285–95.

33. See Vicky Cullen, *The U.S. Antarctic Programs* (Washington, DC: National Science Foundation, 1990).

34. For a history of the whaling industry in this region, see Arthur James Allen, *A Whaler and Trader in the Arctic* (Anchorage: Northwest, 1978); John R. Bockstoce, *Whales, Ice and Men: The History of Whaling in the Western Arctic* (Seattle: University of Washington Press, 1986); Albert Cook Church, *Whaleships and Whaling* (New York: Norton, 1978); and J.T. Jenkins, *A History of the Whale Fisheries* (London: H.F. and G. Witherby, 1921).

35. For a summary of the early exploration and cooperative efforts, see Peter Beck, *The International Politics of Antarctica* (New York: St. Martin's Press, 1986), 21–45.

36. Richard B. Bilder, "The Present Legal and Political Situation in Antarctica," in *The New Nationalism and the Use of Common Spaces*, ed. Jonathan I. Charney, (Totawa, NJ: Allanheld and Osmun, 1982), 167–205.

37. World Commission on Environment and Development, *Our Common Future* (New York: Oxford University Press, 1987), 280.

38. See John May, *The Greenpeace Book of Antarctica* (New York: Doubleday, 1989).

39. Martin W. Holdgate, "Antarctica: Ice Under Pressure," *Environment* 32, no. 8 (October, 1990): 4–9, 30–33. See also C. Michael Hall, "Tourism in Antarctica: Activities, Impacts and Management," *Journal of Travel Research* 30, no. 4 (Spring, 1992): 2–9.

40. See James H. Zumberge, "Potential Mineral Resource Availability and Possible Environmental Problems in Antarctica," 115–154; and Giulio Pontecorvo, "The

Economics of the Resources of Antarctica," 155–66, both in *The New Nationalism and the use of Common Spaces*, ed. Jonathan I. Charney (Totowa, NJ: Allanheld and Osmun, 1982).

41. For an explanation of the habits and range of each species, see Peter G. H. Evans, *The Natural History of Whales and Dolphins* (New York: Facts on File, 1987).

42. Day, *Whale War*, 112–23.

43. John Gulland, "The End of Whaling?" *New Scientist*, October 29, 1988, 45.

44. For a commentary on the incident, see Debora MacKenzie, "Whales as a Way of Life," *New Scientist*, November 12, 1988, 68.

45. Gulland, "End of Whaling," 42–47. See also "Good Hunting?" *New Scientist*, July 14, 1990, 19.

46. See Fukuzo Nagasaki, "The Case for Scientific Whaling," *Nature* 344 (March 15, 1990): 189–90.

47. Debora MacKenzie, "Antarctica: A Tale of Two Treaties," *New Scientist*, November 17, 1990, 18.

FOR FURTHER READING

Peter Beck. *The International Politics of Antarctica*. New York: St. Martin's Press, 1986.

Grahame Cook. *The Future of Antarctica: Exploitation vs. Preservation*. London: Manchester University Press, 1991.

Sam Hall. *The Fourth World: The Heritage of the Arctic and Its Destruction*. New York: Knopf, 1987.

Pier Horensma. *The Soviet Arctic*. New York: Routledge, 1991.

John Keeble. *Out of the Channel: The Exxon Valdez Oil Spill in Prince William Sound*. New York: HarperCollins, 1991.

John May. *The Greenpeace Book of Antarctica*. New York: Doubleday, 1989.

Debbie S. Miller. *Midnight Wilderness*. San Francisco: Sierra Club Books, 1990.

M. J. Peterson. *Managing the Frozen South*. Berkeley: University of California Press, 1988.

CHAPTER 17

Managing the Human
Population Explosion

> While you are reading these words four people will have died from
> starvation. Most of them children.
> —Dr. Paul R. Ehrlich, *The Population Bomb (1968)*[1]

> In the six seconds it takes you to read this sentence, eighteen more
> people will be added [to the population.]
> —Dr. Paul R. Ehrlich, *The Population Explosion (1990)*[2]

In 1968, when Dr. Paul Ehrlich's book first appeared, most Americans were
shocked. Ehrlich predicted a population explosion accompanied by massive famine and starvation—a prophecy that nevertheless did not come to pass. The
reason? In the mid-1970s there was a slight decline in the global population
growth rate, and it looked as though the population might stabilize at about 10.2
billion toward the end of the next century. Many demographers called Ehrlich an
alarmist, while others argued that population growth was actually a positive
force because it accelerated progress and development, forcing people to use
more ingenuity and resourcefulness. Regardless of the timeliness of the prediction, Ehrlich was correct in pointing out the fact that Earth is a closed system,
with limited resources. At the same time, the world's population is increasing at
a current rate of three people every second—a quarter of a million new mouths
to feed every day. Ehrlich's comments in his 1990 book brought into focus an
issue that has profound economic, ethical, religious, and political implications.
What will happen to the environment if steps are not taken to *manage* the
population?

One of the key phrases often used to answer that question, and one that has
appeared often in this book, is *sustainable development*. The term is used to
describe policies that balance the needs of people today against the resources
that will be needed in the future. It takes into consideration policies related to
agricultural production, energy efficiency, health, a reduction of poverty, and a
reduction in consumption. Individuals practice this concept when they recycle

cans, bottles, newspapers, and plastics. They choose to carpool to work or bicycle instead of commuting in their automobile alone. They may turn their thermostat down to use less electricity, or install a solar heating system in their home. Each of these actions is taken in recognition of the fact that Earth's resources are not unlimited, and that we must restrict our consumption of those resources.

This chapter explores one of the most controversial aspects of sustainable development—the managing of the human population. It is built around the assumption that there are not enough resources available, even with enhanced technology, to provide for the growing number of individuals born each year. It begins by presenting an overview of the scale of the global population boom, and the factors that have caused the problems to be more acute in some areas than others. An overview of global family planning efforts outlines the effectiveness of contraception programs, especially in developing countries where the fertility rate is the highest. It continues by outlining the political aspects of overpopulation, including the efforts by nongovernmental organizations to reduce population and growth, and concludes with a summary of some of the problems faced by policymakers as they attempt to decide what strategies are the most effective and acceptable.

TOO MANY PEOPLE ON TOO SMALL A PLANET

In 1798, Thomas Robert Malthus published "An Essay on the Principle of Population" in which he first argued the "power of population" is indefinitely greater than the power of Earth to produce subsistence for man.[3] One of the ideas that has subsequently dominated the study of demography—the science of population—is demographic transition theory, a term used to describe a three-phase ecological transition that leads to global overpopulation. In the first phase, human demands remain within limits that can be sustained by the environment, so there is enough food, water, and other resources for the needs of the population. In the second phase, human demands begin to exceed a sustainable limit, and continue to grow. In the third phase, the ecosystem is unable to sustain the population as there is little control over birth and death rates, and the system collapses.[4]

Although there has been criticism of the demographic transition theory,[5] there are many demographers who believe Earth has already reached that third stage. The numbers of people already on the planet are staggering, and the projections for the future are even more alarming. The growth in world population is hard to comprehend, especially if we look closely at the past 150 years. Figure 17.1 provides a look at the milestone dates in world population growth from the year 1 C.E. through 1991.

340

Figure 17.1 World Population Growth

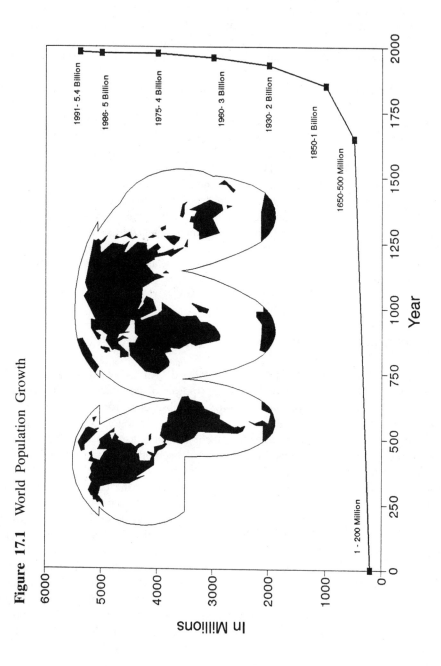

As the growth curve indicates, while it took two hundred years for the global population to double (from 1650 to 1850) from five hundred million to one billion, it took only forty-five years for it to double from two billion to four billion (from 1930 to 1975) and the trend continues. The United Nations Population Division projections through the year 2025 show an even greater increase, as seen in Figure 17.2. The world's total population is expected to grow from a projected 5.6793 billion in 1995 to 6.1271 billion in 2000, and 8.1771 billion by 2025.

A 1991 UN report on world population has identified several critical trends in the growth figures. First, there are differences in the age structure of populations in the industrialized and developing world. By the mid-1990s, about one out of every three persons will be a child; one out of five, a person in the late teens or early twenties. The most significant increase will be in the aged population; one out of sixteen persons will be age sixty-five or older. The median global age will be twenty-four. The implications for these figures is the majority of the population will be of child-bearing age; although women are having fewer children today, there are more women giving birth. This trend is coupled with a dramatic growth in the elderly population; half of the world's elderly live in developing countries, and more than a third of the world's population live in countries where the mortality for young children is greater than one in ten, posing problems for health care, mobility, and productivity.

A second important trend is that the population is also becoming more urbanized, with 45 percent of the world's peoples living in urban areas by mid-1990, 51 percent by the year 2000, and 65 percent by 2025.[6] Urban populations are growing at a much more rapid rate in the less developed regions of the world than they ever did in the industrialized nations, but that growth is due less to people migrating from rural to urban areas than to high birthrates and low death rates in the cities.[7]

Third, the distribution of population varies considerably from continent to continent, which affects the population's economic well-being and impact on the environment. The four largest countries in the world account for virtually half the world's population but only 30 percent of the world's land surface. For example, the richest 15 percent of the world's population consumes more than one-third of Earth's fertilizer and more than half of its energy, while at the other extreme, perhaps one-quarter of the world's population go hungry during at least some seasons of the year. The vast majority of the world's peoples exist on per capita incomes below the official poverty level in the United States.[8]

Similar findings were reported in *The Global 2000 Report to the President*, a U.S. study of global population trends. The study reported populations in sub-Saharan Africa and in the Himalayan hills of Asia have already exceeded their maximum carrying capacity—the number of people who can be sustained by the land—and the entire planet is approaching that level as well. The study goes on to document shortages in water supplies and food, as well as a loss of arable

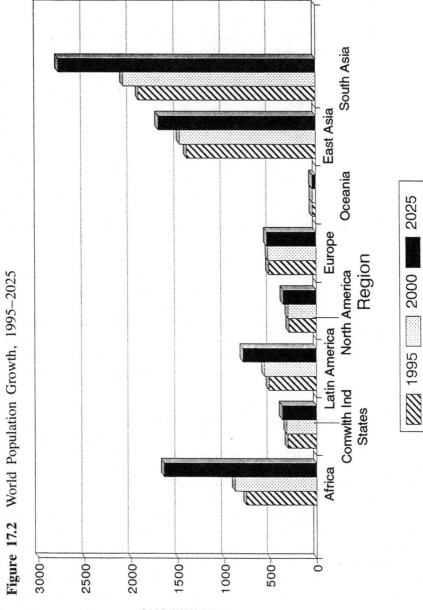

Figure 17.2 World Population Growth, 1995–2025

land, insufficient sources of energy, and massive extinctions of plant and animal species.[9]

Another important aspect of population growth is *where* it takes place. Population growth in the industrialized countries of the world has been relatively modest, rising about 15 percent between 1970 and 1990. In contrast, the population of developing countries grew by almost 55 percent during the same period, and the disparity is expected to grow even larger in the future. The executive director of the UN Population Fund notes that most of the increase in population growth will occur in Southern Asia, which now accounts for about a quarter of the world's population but will have nearly a third of the increase by the end of the century, and Africa, which has 12 percent of the population now but will account for nearly a quarter by 2000. These changes represent a radical shift in population, with areas like Europe and North America growing very slowly, and areas like India, which will overtake China as the world's most populous country by 2030, experiencing rapid growth.[10]

Not all of the forecasters have seen a vision of population doomsday, however. Despite the popularity and acceptance of Ehrlich and similar commentators, others have a much more positive view of man's ability to limit his desire to procreate, or point to errors in the population models that have been used to predict growth rates. There is also a belief that population growth will spur the adoption of existing technology and result in new inventions to solve the need for better food production, requiring us to use our imagination and spirit.[11]

Why has the population rate skyrocketed? Ehrlich and other biologists and demographers have identified a number of factors to which the increases can be attributed. Some of those changes began to occur long ago, while others are more recent in origin. First, there have been dramatic changes in our way of life and ability to survive. Humans' transition from hunting and gathering to the agricultural revolution about eight thousand years ago removed much of the risk of dying from starvation, raising the world's overall standard of living, and high death rates kept the number of people in the world from growing rapidly until the mid-eighteenth century. Second, in the category of more contemporary change, the rapid acceleration in growth after 1750 was due almost entirely to the declines in death rates which occurred with the Industrial Revolution. Rapid advances in science lowered the death rate by finding cures for common diseases that had previously wiped out large segments of the population. The introduction of the pesticide DDT, for example, dramatically reduced deaths from malaria, which is transmitted by mosquitoes, and similar victories reduced deaths due to yellow fever, smallpox, cholera, and other infectious diseases. Similarly, the acknowledgment of the theory that germs were responsible for disease brought about a gradual acceptance of basic sanitary practices like the washing of hands and bathing, which further reduced the spread of disease. The impact of DDT and other health and technological advances can be seen very clearly in Figure 17.1 where the growth curve begins its steep incline.

Advances in medicine have also reduced infant mortality rates to the point where the birthrate continues to exceed the death rate—the bottom line in population growth. The result is that many fewer people die than are born each year. Third, food production has increased, keeping up with population growth until the mid-1950s when food became more scarce and prices began to rise in developing nations. By the mid-1960s, only ten nations grew more food than they consumed: Argentina, Australia, Burma, Canada, France, New Zealand, Romania, South Africa, Thailand, and the United States.[12] Now, demand for food outstrips availability in most of the undeveloped world. The problem is not one of scarcity as much as it is the economic system by which food is distributed.

Fourth, climatic changes may affect the population problem even more. The effects of population growth may be exacerbated by global warming, according to a three-year report published by the Environmental Protection Agency. The study, which was conducted by fifty scientists in eighteen countries, used three computer models, which predicted a doubling, by the year 2060, of the greenhouse gases that may be responsible for a rise in Earth's temperature. If those increases continue, the result may be a decline in crop yields, especially in grain production in developing countries, and an increase in prices from 25 to 150 percent. The reduced supply, together with increased prices, is estimated to increase the numbers of those at risk from hunger in developing countries by between 60 million and 360 million, and to take the total of the world's hungry to 1 billion by 2060. Still unknown is the impact of the AIDS epidemic, which may have an even longer effect on population trends, especially in developing countries. An estimated five million to ten million people are thought to be infected with the human immunodeficiency virus (HIV), about half of whom are in sub-Saharan Africa.

The pictures of starved and dehydrated children in Africa disguise a political reality, however. Although some of the problems associated with famine can be attributed to traditional food scarcity resulting from population increases and drought, some observers believe the real issue is the radicalism of many African governments. One study of Ethiopia, for example, found that a long line of Marxist regimes and massive Soviet aid exacerbated the traditional problems and resulted in persistent famine from 1983 to 1986. Despite $2 billion in worldwide aid, the Ethiopian government used its power to control food and water resources for purely political reasons.[13] In Somalia, millions of people have died because the endless civil war has made it impossible for other nations to safely bring in food and medical supplies. Even with a massive influx of aid in 1992, thousands of Somalis died each day because the country was in a state of virtual anarchy. Relief efforts were thwarted by roving bands of thugs who stole food and supplies as soon as they were brought in to refugee camps. Although the United States intervened alongside UN troops in 1992, many observers believe Somalia's problems are shared with numerous other African nations also suffering from civil strife.

Facts about the Population Crisis

General

- With the world's population now exceeding 5 billion, we will witness three billion young people entering their reproductive years just within the next generation.

- 40 percent of the developing world's population are under age 15 and about to enter their most productive childbearing years.

- By no later than the year 2020, the combined populations of Asia and Africa will be 6 to 8 billion people, significantly more than now live on the entire planet.

- 500 million women want and need family planning but lack either information or means to obtain it.

Health

- 15 million infants under age one will die this year—42,000 each day—many because their mothers did not know how to allow appropriate intervals between pregnancies.

- Nearly 1,500 women die every day because of complications from pregnancy and abortion, many of which might not be necessary if unwanted pregnancies were avoided through family planning.

Security

- Poverty in Central America is a cause of political unrest in the region. There are now 118 million people living on the land between the Rio Grande River and the Isthmus of Panama. By the year 2025, there will be 204 million.

- From the Arab nations in the north to South Africa, the African continent faces internal and external unrest. Today, the continent's population is 680 million and will be 1.65 billion by the year 2020.

- Egypt, a nation of 55 million people and a key force for stability in the Middle East, faces serious economic problems. There will be 69 million Egyptians by the year 2000; 105 million by 2025.

Economy

- Unemployment in many countries of the developing world is as high as 30 percent.

- To accommodate their growing populations, the nations of the world will have to produce 800 million jobs by 2000.

- In 1950, only one city in the developing world had a population greater than 5 million; by the year 2000, there will be 46 such cities.

Environment

- 65 countries that depend on subsistence farming may be unable to feed their populations by the year 2000.

- 25 billion tons of arable topsoil vanish from the world's cropland every year.

- Enough timberland to cover 40 California's will disappear by the end of this century.

- Acute shortages of fuel will affect 350 million people by the year 2000.

- At least 1.7 billion people, nearly one-third of the planet's population, lack an adequate supply of drinking water.

Source: Population Institute, Washington, D.C., September 1992.

GLOBAL FAMILY PLANNING EFFORTS

Information about birth control and access to contraception are known to be major causes of declining fertility, according to a World Bank study that reported that family planning programs account for 39 percent of the decline in developing countries.[14] A historical review of family planning policies shows that such programs have evolved dramatically, considering the fact that artificial birth control was illegal in most countries one hundred years ago. Birth control advocates first spread their doctrine of voluntary fertility in the late nineteenth century, based on the dual concerns of women's health and a rapidly growing poor population. Leaders like Margaret Sanger, Marie Stopes, and Paul Robin were criticized for destroying the family structure, and opponents were successful in lobbying Congress to pass the Comstock Law in 1873, which outlawed advertisements or prescriptions of contraceptives. The federal statute was repealed in 1916, but similar state laws stayed on the books for another fifty years.[15]

Globally, the picture is different. In the early 1960s, when oral contraceptives and intrauterine devices were first becoming available, about sixty million women, or 18 percent of the women of childbearing age in the developing world, were practicing family planning. Nearly three decades later, about one-half of all women in this age group use some means of birth control in developing countries, and about 70 percent in the developed world.[16] Most of the countries that initially adopted family planning programs were Asian, but they included both large and small nations. India became the first country to adopt an official policy to slow population growth in 1951, but no other nations followed suit until nearly a decade later, when Pakistan, the Republic of Korea, China, and Fiji adopted similar policies. Two factors have been identified as the causes behind this growth of an international family planning movement. First, there have been various cultural shifts, such as a growing sense of individualism and a corresponding decline in the perceived need to follow traditional ways. Second, people began to develop an awareness that rapid population growth represented a threat to their economic well-being.[17]

But there are a number of economic, social, and religious reasons why countries have shunned family planning as a way of bringing the birthrate down, especially in centrally planned countries such as China and Cuba. In many of these cultures, families simply *want* more children, even though more babies means more mouths to feed. It may also mean more hands at work in the fields, or more help in caring for aging parents. Population limitation in developing countries is in direct opposition to the teachings of the Catholic Church, which has encouraged procreation and discouraged birth control and abortion, as is the case in most Islamic nations. Many couples refuse to use birth control devices because of rumors and myths about their effectiveness. In India, which has had a government-sponsored family planning program since 1951, women refused to use a loop-shaped intrauterine device when word spread that it would swim through the bloodstream and reach the brain or give the man a shock during intercourse. Vasectomy has been only marginally successful because of fears by men that it reduced their virility. As a result, the use of contraception varies considerably from one nation to another, as shown in Table 17.1.

One trend made clear from the table is that contraception use is highest in the nations of Europe and lowest in Africa—a trend mirrored in population growth rates. Some countries have recognized the problem and have taken steps to make contraception more available and acceptable, while others have made only nominal efforts. In China and Singapore, for example, the use rate is 74 percent; in India, in contrast, the rate is only 34 percent, and in Ethiopia, only 2 percent. With the exception of Lebanon and Turkey, the remainder of the Islamic nations have a contraception use rate of less than 50 percent, with the majority in single digits. Of the African countries, only South Africa (48 percent), Zimbabwe (38 percent) and Botswana (27 percent) have use rates higher than 20 percent. Yet despite the influence of the Catholic Church, every Latin American nation except Haiti has at least a quarter of its women using contraception, led by Argentina at 74 percent and Costa Rica at 69 percent.[18] Generally speaking, economic inequality is the best predictor of fertility rates, however. Residents of poorer nations want more babies because they are a source of labor, while those in midrange economies choose goods over babies. Citizens of rich nations (like the United States) can afford to have both—babies and goods. For them, family planning is less of a priority and there is little incentive to limit family size.

Government-sponsored family planning programs now exist in more than ninety countries, and have been the primary mechanism for population control

Table 17.1   Percentage of Married Women Using Contraception in the World

Top Ten Countries		Bottom Ten Countries	
Czechoslovakia	95%	Somalia	0%
Belgium	91%	Chad	1%
United Kingdom	83%	Mauritania	0%
Finland	80%	North Yemen	1%
France	78%	Angola	1%
Sweden	78%	Tanzania	1%
Italy	78%	Zaire	1%
Germany	77%	Uganda	1%
Bulgaria	76%	Guinea	1%
Poland	75%	Niger	1%
Mauritius	75%	Zambia	1%

United States Use: 68%
Source: Michael J. Sullivan III, *Measuring Global Values: The Ranking of 162 Countries* (New York: Greenwood Press 1991).

in most developing countries. About a dozen nations have established a cabinet-level ministry for population, generally in developing countries where the issue is considered serious enough to require an official program. The commitment is often not very firm, however, in countries with an Islamic or Roman Catholic religious tradition. A 1990 UN Population Fund survey found that sixteen states have absolutely no governmental support for population control: Albania, Bolivia, Cambodia, Gabon, Iraq, Ireland, Kuwait, Laos, Libya, Mongolia, Norway, Oman, Romania, Saudi Arabia, Switzerland, and the United Arab Emirates.[19]

The United Nations has now become the primary agent of family planning programs and has made a number of efforts to address the overpopulation issue. The UN Fund for Population Activities was established as a trust fund in 1967, financed by voluntary contributions from members. During its first fifteen years, it allocated over $1 billion in family planning assistance to member states. Following the 1968 UN Conference on Human Rights, the "Tehran Proclamation" identified the ability to control one's fertility and therefore access to birth control as a basic human right. The UN organization, renamed the United Nations Population Fund (UNPF), has held four world conferences: in Rome (1954), Belgrade (1965), Bucharest (1974), and Mexico City (1984), with a fifth planned for August 1994 in Tunisia. At the Bucharest conference, the UN's World Population Plan of Action was established, led by the United States and other industrialized nations that urged developing countries to set targets for lowering their fertility rates. Many Third World nations and Eastern bloc nations rebelled, accusing the UN of supporting efforts by former colonial masters to suppress emerging nations and limit the strength of their armies. Ten years later, at the Mexico City conference, those misconceptions vanished as leaders committed themselves to a voluntary reduction in population growth and a strong national family planning program.[20]

The United States's role in global population management has been somewhat contradictory. The U.S. Agency for International Development (AID) began promoting large-scale national family programs funded through international aid in the early 1960s, providing health-care workers in many developing countries. Congress first earmarked foreign assistance appropriations in 1968, with nearly $4 billion in assistance allocated through AID over the next two decades. Initially, the United States also supported UN programs for education and family planning. But during the mid-1980s and the Reagan administration, the United States cut off its support (as the major donor) of the UN Population Fund and the International Planned Parenthood Federation, the largest multilateral agency and the largest private voluntary organization providing family planning services in developing countries.

The abrupt policy about-face became tied to the issue of abortion, even though U.S. law (the 1973 Helms amendment to the foreign assistance act) explicitly prohibits government funding for abortion programs overseas, and even though legal abortions are permitted in only twenty-six countries. In 1985, the Kemp-Kasten amendment to the foreign assistance act banned any U.S. contribution to "any organization or program that supports or participates in the management or a program of coercive abortion or involuntary sterilization." The passage of the legislation effectively cut off U.S. support to China's family planning program, which was alleged to have forced women to have abortions, despite denials by the Chinese government. Congressional attempts to restore the UN funding by stipulating that the money not be spent in China were vetoed by President George Bush in November 1989.[21] The Bush administration's position puzzled those who pointed out the fact that by cutting back its aid to the UN Population Fund for family planning, the United States was actually encouraging the demand for abortion in those nations where there are no other alternatives.

A similar situation exists in Romania, which outlawed family planning during the dictatorship of Nicolae Ceausescu, who believed that a high fertility rate was key to building a stable and prosperous nation. When Ceausescu's regime was toppled, women deluged Romanian hospitals seeking abortions at the rate of three thousand a day. Congressional efforts to authorize $1 million for nonabortion family planning efforts in Romania in July 1990 failed when President Bush threatened to veto the aid package. Meanwhile, the abortions continue.[22] This is one issue where the United States stands virtually alone in its refusal to contribute to the United Nations programs. The United States had been the primary donor to the UNPF in 1984, contributing $38 million of the $122 million program budget. But after the U.S. policy change, Germany, Canada, the United Kingdom, Japan, and the Scandinavian countries actually increased their donations, with Japan now the major donor and exceeding what the United States previously contributed.[23]

After Ehrlich's book was published in 1968, several nongovernmental organizations were formed in the United States to try to bring attention to the problems of overpopulation. One of the first was the Washington, DC-based Zero Population Growth, established in 1968, which advocates a sustainable balance of people that basically stays the same from year to year. In contrast, another organization, Negative Population Growth (NPG), which formed in 1972, seeks to slow, halt, and eventually reverse population growth through several extremely controversial measures, including a reduction in legal immigration to the United States to stabilize the population between 100 and 150 million rather than the current 250 million. NPG members seek to limit immigration to 100,000 persons annually, which they believe will encourage developing nations to solve their own environmental and population problems. They also advocate a massive increase in U.S. funding for population assistance programs for Third World countries and the use of noncoercive economic and social incentives for family planning. Their goals are similar to another U.S. organization, Population-Environment Balance, which was founded in 1973 and has lobbied extensively on the immigration issue. Other groups have focused on the direct provision of services rather than on policymaking. In 1957, for exam-

Success Stories

Tunisia, a small nation sandwiched between Algeria and Libya, has managed to reduce its birthrate from an average of 7.15 children per woman in the mid-1960s to just over 3 per woman today, about half the average for all of Africa. Overall, Tunisia's annual population growth rate is less than 1.9 percent, with a projected 1.7 percent by 1996, and 1.6 percent by 2000. What makes the country's efforts so notable, however, is that these results can be attributed to an enlightened population policy, supported by the Tunisian government, which ratified a code of individual rights in 1958 guaranteeing equal status for women. The family planning emphasis has been on contraception (about half of all Tunisian women are covered by free contraceptive services) rather than more controversial methods such as abortion. Two other policies are also of note: Abortions have been free in Tunisia since 1973, and marriage is forbidden to all men under twenty and women under eighteen, a factor held responsible for reducing the number of children per woman.

Zimbabwe has tried another method to reduce its population, currently growing at the rate of 3 percent a year. In male-dominated Africa, the government has focused its outreach efforts on the men who have power over submissive women, educating them about birth control and the virtue of smaller families. Zimbabwean men have been reluctant to use condoms, citing inconvenience and diminished pleasure, and have been misinformed about birth control pills, believing it will affect their virility or cause infertility. But in contrast with Asian women, Zimbabwean women, with one of the highest rates of contraception use in Africa, use birth control pills as a way of spacing their children, rather than limiting family size, resulting in the same number of children being born over a longer period of time.[26]

Both Thailand and Indonesia have made family planning a central element of village life since their first national programs began in the early 1970s. In Indonesia, for example, the National Family Planning Coordinating Board has established tens of thousands of village distribution centers for contraceptive devices and information, mostly in Java and Bali, which are often linked to agricultural cooperatives and health services. Educational programs promote the idea that a family should be small, happy, and prosperous and at five o'clock each evening sirens wail to remind women to take their birth control pill. Since 1972, Indonesia's fertility rate has fallen from 5.6 to 3.4 children per woman; 400,000 couples practiced birth control in 1972, with 18.6 million doing so by 1989. All this has happened in a nation where abortion is illegal.[27]

ple, the Pathfinder Fund began providing family planning services, which include distribution of contraceptives, educational materials, medical kits, and training in developing countries. Currently the group has field offices in nine regions, supporting more than two hundred projects in thirty countries.

The abortion issue has been raised for groups not directly associated with the UN programs or with population management. Prolife groups have also targeted environmental organizations like the National Audubon Society, the National Wildlife Federation, and Trout Unlimited, which had supported a moderate policy of voluntary family planning.[24] Threatened with boycotts of their advertisers and massive letter writing campaigns, the groups have personally witnessed the power and tenacity of the prolife movement.

There are a number of reasons why population management has slipped from the top of the political agenda, both in the United States and globally. Biologist and "population buff" Garrett Hardin, who has been at the forefront of the ethical debate over population management, believes that a change in public attitude is to blame, among other factors. He notes that population is a chronic problem rather than a critical one, with the media preferring the latter to the former. As a result, there is much more media interest in covering "crises" like the fall of the Berlin Wall or the war in the Persian Gulf than the fact that a quarter of a million people were born on the day that Iraq invaded Kuwait. He also points out that many people fail to make the connection between population size and problems like air pollution from too many automobiles. Finally, Hardin believes that population questions bring up issues that might be perceived as being selfish, bigoted, provincial, or even racist—criticisms that he himself has had to bear.[25]

U.S. policies are expected to change dramatically under Clinton administration leadership, however. After more than a decade of having been tangled up in the abortion controversy, Clinton promised to restore U.S. aid to the UNPF, once again bringing the population management issue back to the political agenda.

SUMMARY

One of the most controversial environmental issues—population management—deals with whether Earth's limited resources can sustain the growing number of human beings born each year. The world's population has skyrocketed since the Industrial Revolution due to improved living conditions and scientific advancement, which reduced the number of deaths. Although those declines initially occurred in the more developed countries of the Europe and the United States, technological advances are now available worldwide. In addition, the age structure of the population is changing with the largest segment of the population now of childbearing age. Although the risk of death has been lowered dramatically in developing nations, birthrates have gone down very slowly, with a resulting boom in population growth in those regions. Efforts to reduce fertility have focused on two strategies: providing information about birth control and access to contraception, with varying degrees of success. Although adopted initially by several Asian nations, family planning programs have been stymied for various economic, social, and religious reasons. The ongoing abortion controversy led to an end to U.S. support of UN family planning programs during the Reagan and Bush administrations, but support is likely to resume under President Clinton.

NOTES

1. Paul R. Ehrlich, *The Population Bomb* (New York: Ballantine Books, 1968). The statement is conspicuously placed on the cover of Ehrlich's book.

2. Paul R. Ehrlich and Anne H. Ehrlich, *The Population Explosion* (New York: Simon & Schuster, 1990), 9.

3. See Philip Appleman, ed., *Thomas Robert Malthus: An Essay on the Principle of Population* (New York: Norton, 1976). For biographical material on Malthus and his theories, see Jane S. Nickerson, *Homage to Malthus* (Port Washington, NY: Kennikat Press, 1975); David V. Glass, *Introduction to Malthus* (New York: Wiley, 1953); William Petersen, *Malthus* (Cambridge, MA: Harvard University Press, 1979); and Donald Winch, *Malthus* (New York: Oxford University Press, 1987).

4. See Maurice King, "Health Is a Sustainable State," *The Lancet* 336, no. 8716 (September 15, 1990): 664–67. For a historical perspective on demographic transition theory, see the work of Kingsley Davis, "The World Demographic Transition," *Annals of the American Academy of Political and Social Science* 237 (January 1945): 1–11; and George Stolnitz, "The Demographic Transition: From High to Low Birth Rates and Death Rates," in *Population: The Vital Revolution*, ed. Ronald Freedman, (Garden City, NY: Anchor Books, 1964).

5. See, for example, Ansley Coale, "The History of the Human Population," *Scientific American* 231 (1974): 40–51; and Kingsley Davis, "The Theory of Change and Response in Modern Demographic History," *Population Index* 29, no. 4 (1963): 345–66.

6. "Population Conference Set for 1994," *UN Chronicle* 28, no. 2 (June 1991): 74.

7. See, for example, Richard E. Stren and Rodney R. White, eds., *African Cities in Crisis: Managing Rapid Urban Growth* (Boulder, CO: Westview Press, 1989).

8. William C. Clark, "Managing Planet Earth," *Scientific American* 261 (September 1989): 48.

9. U.S. Executive Office of the President, Council on Environmental Quality, *The Global 2000 Report to the President* (Washington, DC: U.S. Government Printing Office, 1980). For a more contemporary view of the need for a new strategy for sustainable agriculture, see David Norse, "A New Strategy for Feeding a Crowded Planet," *Environment* 34, no. 5 (June 1992): 6.

10. Nafis Sadik, "World Population Continues to Rise," *The Futurist*, March–April 1991, 9–14. See also *World Resources 1992–93* (New York: World Resources Institute, 1992), 76–79.

11. See, for example, Julian L. Simon, "World Population Growth: An Anti-Doomsday View," *Atlantic Monthly*, August 1981, 70–76.

12. Ehrlich, *Population Bomb*, 38.

13. See Steven L. Varnis, *Reluctant Aid or Aiding the Reluctant* (New Brunswick, NJ: Transaction, 1990), 3.

14. Nathan Keyfitz, "The Growing Human Population," *Scientific American* 261 (September 1989): 123.

15. See Peter Fryer, *The Birth Controllers* (New York: Stein and Day, 1965); and James Reed, *From Private Vice to Public Virtue: The Birth Control Movement and American Society Since 1930* (New York: Basic Books, 1978).

16. Peter J. Donaldson and Amy Ong Tsui, "The International Family Planning Movement," *Population Bulletin* 45, no. 3 (November 1990): 4–6.

17. See Ronald Freedman, "Family Planning Programs in the Third World," *Annals of the American Academy of Political and Social Science* 510 (July 1990): 33–43.

18. Michael J. Sullivan III, *Measuring Global Values: The Ranking of 162 Countries* (New York: Greenwood Press, 1991), 172.

19. Ibid., 164.

20. Werner Fornos, "Population Politics," *Technology Review*, February–March 1991, 43–51.

21. Ibid., 64.

22. Ibid., 65.

23. Donaldson and Tsui, "International Family Planning Movement," 14.

24. Frank Graham, Jr., "Thoughts," *Audubon* 92 (January 1990): 8.

25. Garrett Hardin, "Sheer Numbers," *E Magazine* 1, no. 6 (November–December 1990): 40–47.

26. Jane Perlez, "Birth Curbs and the Man of the House," *New York Times*, May 28, 1991, A-8.

27. Keyfitz, "Growing Human Population," 124.

FOR FURTHER READING

Paul R. Ehrlich. *The Population Bomb*. New York: Ballantine Books, 1968.

Paul R. Ehrlich and Anne H. Erlich. *The Population Explosion*. New York: Simon & Schuster, 1990.

Jodi Jacobson. *The Global Politics of Abortion*. Washington, DC: Worldwatch Institute, July 1990.

Donella H. Meadows, Dennis L. Meadows, and Joergen Randers. *Beyond the Limits*. Post Mills, VT: Chelsea Green, 1992.

Thomas W. Merrick. *U.S. Population Assistance: A Continued Priority for the 1990s?* Washington, DC: Population Reference Bureau, 1990.

U.S. Executive Office of the President, Council on Environmental Quality, *The Global 2000 Report to the President*. Washington, DC: U.S. Government Printing Office, 1980.

PART 6

After the Millennia: Environmental Policy in 2000 and Beyond

CHAPTER 18

Emerging Issues
in Environmental Politics

If we do not change the direction we are going, we will end up
where we are headed.
—Old Chinese proverb

The first three sections of this book have focused on environmental issues that
have developed over the past 150 years, the majority of which have made their
way to the political agenda since 1960. The early legislative efforts dealing with
environmental questions have been called the "react and cure" phase of environmental policy. Some environmental problems, such as air and water pollution,
are likely to be around well into the next century in the "anticipate and prevent" stage of policymaking.[1] Many observers believe the framework for environmental legislation has been in place in the United States since the 1970s, and
the past twenty years have seen merely the fine-tuning of those efforts. The
decade of the 1990s has seen an emphasis on the globalization of environmental
issues, with new regimes beginning to be formed to deal with transboundary
pollution and problems like global warming and stratospheric ozone pollution,
described earlier. This last section identifies several of the environmental issues
likely to emerge as we enter the twenty-first century.

FROM GEOPOLITICS TO ECOPOLITICS

The term *geopolitics* was first used in the late nineteenth century to describe the science that conceives the state not as an inanimate body, but as a
geographical organism or as a phenomenon in space. The living state is characterized by its territory and people; its form of government and the economy; its
space, size, and shape; and its relationship to the sea. Early authors described
geopolitics in terms of Darwin's evolutionary theories; states compete with one
another for scarce space, and the laws of natural selection, which favor the most

biologically fit, apply equally to nations as to species.[2] More recently, geopolitics has given way to concerns about the connection between national security and environmental degradation. Why is there a connection between these two disparate issues, and what are the implications for the political agenda in the twenty-first century?

The connection exists because of both ecological and economic linkages. For many countries, national security is threatened by the failure of governments to adequately address issues of overpopulation and resource depletion. It has been argued that the next century will see a redefinition of what constitutes national security, as the previously sharp dividing line between foreign and domestic policy becomes blurred, forcing governments to deal with environmental problems on an international scale, rather than just internally.[3] In addition, the development of an increasing number of trade linkages and the internationalization of the world economy makes the fate of any one nation, developed or developing, dependent upon others as well. Even the national security of the United States is affected by environmental issues in other parts of the world. For example, the Third World now accounts for about 40 percent of U.S. exports and supplies about 40 percent of U.S. imports. American private investment in developing countries has also increased significantly. This gives the United States an important stake in the stable development of the global economy, which is dependent, in large part, to the equally stable development of environmental resources.[4]

There are a number of reasons why these phenomena are already beginning to occur. The burgeoning human population has placed enormous stress on the environment, which has in turn led to an economic decline in many countries around the world. That economic decline is at the root of the kinds of frustration that leads to domestic and civil unrest and makes countries ripe for political upheaval. Political upheaval threatens not only internal order, but the stability of the international political system.

The most acute examples involve refugees. When economic and political problems force citizens to leave their national borders, they spread frustration to surrounding regions. There are several regions where the refugee problem is exemplary of this phenomenon. In Haiti, the government has failed to deal with the problem of expanding population, which has systematically destroyed a landscape that was once heavily forested. The resulting soil erosion which has occurred has limited any attempts at productive agriculture and left the country with only a minimal economic base. In their frustration, thousands of Haitians have attempted to flee their island home for the United States, many of them on board boats with little chance of making the rough sea journey to the mainland. Rescuing the refugees became a politically thorny issue in 1992—the importation of a Haitian environmental problem to the United States. Although several thousand of the refugees said they were seeking political asylum in the United States, a more plausible explanation is that they sought economic sanctuary when their own economy failed. Similarly, desertification, which is believed to affect as much as one-third of the planet's surface, has led to a lack of arable land in several African countries, and led to massive human migrations. Food outputs have fallen behind population growth, leading to famine and starvation. Refugees have fled Chad, Ethiopia, and Uganda for the Ivory Coast and Sudan, exacerbating the impact of those nations' already fragile economic base. Millions of Somalis died of starvation in 1992 when the country's civil war (based largely on who would control the country's economic base) prevented the distribution of donated food and medical supplies from reaching outlying areas. They attempted to flee to other countries whose resources were already tapped out. When nations begin to rely upon imported food sources, they further compromise their sovereignty and destroy their own trade balance. More people means further demands on the economy and further stress the environment's ability to provide enough food and water for residents.

Water scarcity is yet another issue assured of affecting national security in the coming decades. This is particularly true in the Middle East, where fifteen nations depend upon three primary river systems: the Nile, the Jordan, and the Tigris-Euphrates. With high birthrates throughout the region, researchers estimate that all renewable water sources will be depleted by 1995 unless more sustainable development plans are launched. Conflicts over water supplies could lead to increased political instability in many areas, and one study estimated that war could break out as a result of conflicts over dwindling water supplies in ten places in the world.[5] During the closing stages of the Gulf War, Iraqi forces sabotaged Kuwait's desalination plants, cutting off the nation's main supply of fresh water. Mahmoud Abdel-Jawad, head of the Water Desalination Department of the Kuwait Institute for Scientific Research, explains the importance of the facilities to nation's overall security: "These are similar to rivers, lakes and freshwater wells in other countries. If you bomb them, it should be considered a war crime because if you cut water, you cut life."[6]

Tensions over water resources between India and neighboring Bangladesh illustrate another typical problem. Most of Bangladesh's water supply originates in India, and the nations have signed agreements to share water since 1977. Subsequent agreements have now expired, and both governments are uncertain when new ones will be reached. The Bangladesh government feels it is being held hostage by India, especially since an Indian proposal to divert part of the Ganges River flow is being considered. Critics of such massive water management programs point out that if such projects are to succeed, they must take two factors into account. First, because all the water resources within a basin are interrelated (precipitation, agricultural runoff, waters in lakes and streams, and groundwater), all water projects must be evaluated taking into consideration the impact on the entire hydrological system. Second, local people must be integrated into the planning and management of such projects in order to take advantage of indigenous peoples' knowledge, needs, and resources.[7] Despite these considerations, there are few international regimes where water supply is concerned. It is an issue that is literally just under the surface, and that is poised to rise to the top of the global environmental agenda at any moment. Transboundary issues are exacerbated when regional hostilities become intense. An estimated 40 percent of the world's population depend on 214 major river systems shared by two or more countries for drinking water, irrigation, or hydropower. Twelve of these waterways are shared by five or more nations. The Worldwatch Institute has identified sixteen unresolved international water issues, many of them in regions like the Middle East, where political upheaval is a way of life.[8]

Similarly, water quality issues are becoming so acute in some regions of the world that the magnitude of the deaths they cause can no longer be ignored by the industrialized countries. In Africa, for example, the magnitude of waterborne diseases is almost impossible for Westerners to comprehend. Six tropical diseases—malaria, schistosomiasis (caused by a flatworm and carried by snails), sleeping sickness (trypanosomiasis), leishmaniasis (an infection carried by sand flies that is usually fatal within two years), filariasis (which leads to elephantiasis or river blindness), and leprosy—are rampant. In addition, diarrheal illnesses—caused by a variety of intestinal germs and parasites—kill hundreds of thousands of people each year and are the leading cause of death in some countries. These illnesses know no national boundaries, and as more and more tourists visit these areas, there is concern the diseases will be transmitted to developed countries as well.

The current strategy of the United Nations's World Health Organization is to concentrate on those diseases responsible for the greatest mortality and morbidity and for which effective treatment is known. This means control of diarrheal diseases first, followed by respiratory infections and malnutrition second, and with lower priority given to diseases of low prevalence or lengthy/costly care, such as sleeping sickness and leprosy. These are not choices made easily, but they are choices made on the basis of limited resources and incalculable human costs.

Other geopolitical changes are having environmental repercussions as well. In 1992, the United States, Mexico, and Canada announced a free-trade agreement to link the three countries into what would become the world's largest trading area. The agreement, which must be ratified by the U.S. Congress, eliminates all duties, tariffs, and other trade barriers within the three countries over the next fifteen years, allowing goods produced in North America to move freely across national borders. While President Bush heralded the agreement and sought congressional support because it is expected to spur economic growth in all three countries, environmentalists were strongly opposed, as were labor unions. Their concern over the agreement was that U.S. industries would quickly move their operations (which are heavily regulated in this country) to Mexico, whose regulatory framework and enforcement capabilities are not as stringent as that of the United States. The result, in their view, would be more environmental degradation, similar to that which took place when American companies set up *maquiladores* along the Mexican border to avoid California's tough antipollution laws. Other groups argue the agreement is riddled with loopholes and ambiguities and hope President Clinton will support renegotiation of the treaty before it goes to Congress for ratification. Clinton has already announced he will put Vice President Al Gore in charge of negotiations to create a joint U.S.-Mexico environmental protection commission. Canada, which reached agreement with the United States in 1988 to abolish tariffs, is less likely to be affected, and already has relatively strong environmental protection laws in place. It remains to be seen whether the Mexican government (which has been unable to effectively deal with environmental issues thus far) will be able to deal with the expected influx of American firms wanting to capitalize on cheap Mexican labor and less stringent environmental regulations.[9]

The Iraqi invasion of Kuwait on August 2, 1990, further emphasized national security issues in a different way—environmental terrorism. The Gulf region experienced several impacts from the war: destruction of fragile desert ecosystems as a result of the activity of more than a million troops, their equipment and supplies; localized but severe fouling of Kuwait's harbor and Saudi coastline from the deliberate sabotage of oil tanks and U.S. bombing of Iraqi oil tankers anchored nearby; unknown health effects from the smoke and toxic gas produced by 732 burning oil wells; and unquantified loss of marine life, vegetation, wildlife and birds, as well as unknown impacts on crops and farm animals.[10]

Even more important than what appears to be these somewhat localized impacts is the realization that existing international law and regimes have little effect on ecoterrorism. Conventions on the conduct of war proved ineffective, and UN sanctions against Iraq have had questionable utility. The 1991 UN Convention on the Prohibition of Military or Any Other Hostile Use of Environmental Modification Techniques has not yet been ratified by Iraq, nor the majority of the world's states. Even the UN resolution making Iraq financially responsible for the environmental damage it caused Kuwait (an estimated $100 billion, not counting losses to individuals and foreign corporations) is not likely to be complied with.[11]

The next millennium is likely to see a number of developments including a further division between the nations of the North and South. It is somewhat ironic that developing nations (primarily those of the Southern Hemisphere) are now facing environmental protection issues that are due, in some cases at least, to growing consumer demands in the industrialized countries of the North. Even more ironic is the fact the consumers in the South *want* those same goods for themselves. The old battles between the "haves" and the "have-nots" have an added dimension where the environment is concerned. Developing nations with extractive resources (mineral, oil, timber) are loath to give up total control of those resources simply to satisfy the concerns of environmentalists. Natural resources now comprise 30 percent of developing nations' gross national product, generating 60 percent of their employment and 50 percent of their exports. These nations have virtually no choice but to continue development of those resources as a way to help pay for their $1.3 trillion foreign debt.[12]

Environmental organizations in developed regions still have difficulty understanding why Third and Fourth World governments are less eager to absorb the costs of pollution control and limitations on development that are now commonplace in the United States. Why, they ask, can't countries like China, India, and Brazil, which are home to 40 percent of the world's population, agree to sign the Montreal Protocol? Such questions are more than just philosophical—they are at the heart of the debates over who should pay for cleaning up the environment. Developing countries with limited capital and limited technology look to the leaders of the industrialized world, and note that foreign aid has decreased over the past two decades.

Leaders in industrialized countries, saddled with political and economic problems of their own, dislike the "deep pockets" attitude of countries who are unwilling or unable to enact strict environmental protection laws and enforce them. The cost of transferring the technology for chlorofluorocarbon substitutes to developing countries is estimated at between $2 billion and $7 billion over the next 10 years. Who should pick up the tab? Even though developing countries are responsible for less than ten percent of the total industrial carbon dioxide emissions that contribute to global warming, any attempt at reducing emissions by industrialized countries will be negated unless they are also willing to help pay for the cost of reducing greenhouse gases in developing countries as well.

Coupled with the North/South division is an increasing resentment against what some have termed "environmental imperialism" and "environmental racism." This resentment can be seen in the attitudes of the Japanese public, indignant over what is perceived as American hypocrisy over whaling. The United States continues to defend the rights of its native groups to hunt whales for "cultural" reasons, but is critical of the Japanese, who consider whale meat a delicacy for similar "cultural" reasons.

These factors leading to the current rift are contrary to the notion of interdependence, which should be at the center of the political debate over the environment. As an economic and political superpower, the United States is in a unique position to help bridge the gap by initiating global environmental agreements. The United States cannot insulate itself from the environmental degradation that is creeping over its borders, or that its companies are causing in other countries. But the United States has lost its position of environmental leadership to Japan and Germany, as evidenced by the negotiations over biodiversity and carbon dioxide emission limits at the Earth Summit, and by the U.S. failure to fund UN family planning programs. Unless there is a complete reversal of U.S. policy on these issues, other nations will, by default, take over the policy agenda and mold it to fit their national security needs and environmental priorities.

Some observers are calling for the development of what has been called "a new diplomacy"—including new institutions and regulatory regimes. With the increased awareness of the transboundary nature of many environmental problems, such as acid rain, comes an acceptance of the fact that existing strategies for developing international agreements are no longer viable. Some environmental problems cannot withstand the ten- to fifteen-year delays common in building new regimes. The majority of nations, for example, still have not yet signed the 1987 Montreal Protocol, despite almost unanimous scientific agreement that CFCs are depleting Earth's protective ozone layer. Other attempts at regime formation, such as a new Antarctic agreement, will require negotiations among nations like the republics of the former Soviet Union, which themselves are undergoing political upheaval. Nations reluctant to give up their sovereignty have in the past been reluctant to join regimes, fearful they are "giving up" their power. Brazil, for example, resisted a tremendous amount of international pressure (from both governments and nongovernmental organizations) when criticized over the destruction of its rain forests. Brazilian leaders (later joined by other Latin American nations) protested what it considered to be outside interference in their internal affairs.

The new diplomacy may wear a different face entirely. Rather than seeking multilateral acceptance of new regimes (an extremely time-consuming and often unsuccessful process), some nations are simply going ahead on their own and working toward agreements among like-minded countries. Such "environmental alliances" are already beginning to appear, and are likely to grow in the next millennium. The so-called 30-percent Club (originally Canada and nine other European countries) was formed in 1984 to reduce sulfur dioxide emissions, which result in the formation of acid rain; more countries have since joined. In central America, "peace parks" straddling the borders of Costa Rica, El Salvador, Guatemala, Honduras, Nicaragua, and Panama are being developed to preserve rain forests and to help promote sustainable development. In 1989, the International Union for the Conservation of Nature estimated there were sixty-eight border parks involving sixty-six countries, serving not only as nature preserves but also as demilitarized buffer zones. An international "Law of the Air" (similar to the Law of the Sea agreement) was proposed in 1988 by Norway and Canada as a way of protecting the atmosphere, a regime likely to involve years of intense international negotiation.[13]

The internationalization of environmental issues has also led to a call for a world government approach—creation of an institution whose powers go far beyond those of the existing structure of the United Nations. Other observers have called for a rethinking of conventional economic theory so that the emphasis is on balancing the debt between civilization and the biosphere rather than balancing the federal deficit.[14]

Nongovernmental environmental organizations, which will come to play an increasingly important role in the global policy process, are likely to place pressure on governments to use the so-called peace dividend—money previously spent on defense during the cold war—on restoring the environment. The Worldwatch Institute, for example, notes that the $68 billion cost of the U.S. Stealth bomber program could pay two-thirds of the estimated costs to meet U.S. clean water goals by 2000. The $100 billion being spent on the Trident II submarine program and F-16 jet fighter programs could, according to their calculations, pay for the estimated cleanup costs of the three thousand worst hazardous waste dumps in the United States.[15] Whether or not the United States or other industrialized nations are ready to begin a massive economic conversion process is not an issue. Congress in 1991 approved a massive closing of military bases and has begun to phase out various defense programs. The most critical question is whether or not those funds will go to environmental programs.

RISK ASSESSMENT: A QUESTION OF PRIORITIES

An issue that first emerged in the United States in 1969 with the passage of the National Environmental Policy Act is likely to take center stage as policymakers weigh the economic costs of environmental protection. NEPA required that major projects undergo an analysis of their environmental impacts, and one of the tools developed as a part of that process is risk assessment, which has been used extensively by policymakers to justify controls on various toxic substances in the air, in water, and on land. In 1983, the National Research Council defined risk assessment as a technique used to estimate the effects on the health of individuals or populations exposed to certain materials or situations that are regarded as hazardous.[16] Risk assessment consists of four basic steps:

- Hazard identification: determining whether a particular agent is causally linked to certain negative health effects
- Dose-response assessment: determining the relationship between the amount of exposure to the agent and the probability of occurrence of any health effects
- Exposure assessment: determining the extent to which humans are exposed to the agent
- Characterization of risk: describing the nature and the magnitude of risk to humans

Risk assessment has been applied to a wide range of situations, including exposure to various pollutants, occupational exposures to chemicals or radiation, the discovery of chemicals in the environment or in products, and in the disposal of wastes. Naturally, risk from exposure to environmental pollutants must also be put into perspective with the risks that are a part of everyday living, such as riding in a car or airplane, or walking across the street. Some risks, such as making the decision to smoke a cigarette, are voluntary, while others, such as passive exposure to environmental tobacco smoke, are not. For environmental risks like those posed by indoor air pollution, researchers use medical data concerning the effects of the pollutant: time patterns of occurrence of the effect; the distribution of the effects within the population, including age, sex, and racial groups; cofactors, such as diet or occupation that influence the effect; and demographics for exposed and control populations.

Risk assessment performs a valuable function by assisting policymakers and individuals in setting priorities and in comparing new and existing technologies to reduce or mitigate risks. It is expected that risk assessment will play an even more important role in political decision making as the costs of cleaning up prior environmental damage and hazards are calculated and science tells us more about the nature of risk. Economic choices are already beginning to be made. In 1986, the EPA conducted a detailed study of the risks associated with thirty-one "environmental problems" in order to prioritize its resources. The problems ranked highest by the agency included outdoor air pollutants, stratospheric ozone depletion, and pesticide residues on food. Lowest-ranked problems included Resource Conservation and Recovery Act and Superfund sites, underground storage tanks, and municipal nonhazardous waste sites.[17]

Some individuals look at the risks from a purely economic or personal viewpoint. How much will it cost me to remove the old asbestos pipe from my building versus the chance of my employees dying from asbestosis? We each make choices whether to eat foods (such as peanut butter) which are known to contain trace amounts of toxic substances. We measure the likelihood of suffering adverse health effects against our desire to eat. We also know that it is impossible to remove all potential risks from our lives, so we identify those risks we are willing to take and those we are not.

Unfortunately, there is no societal agreement on what constitutes "acceptable risk" so consensus is hard to come by. While one individual might consider the risk of exposure to a toxic waste incinerator to be minimal in light of the costs of other types of disposal, his or her neighbor might not—hence, a political dispute develops. Government agencies have often attempted to establish what is known as *de minimis* risk—a specific level at which the risks are so small that they are usually ignored. Proponents of this concept believe the regulatory agencies should establish *de minimis* levels and regulate only those hazards that pose a risk greater than those levels. Others prefer to rely upon cost-benefit analysis to analyze alternative courses of action. It has the advantage of being a quantifiable method of improving economic efficiency, but critics point out the difficulties of putting a price tag on aesthetics like clear vistas in the Grand Canyon. The problem remains, for the most part, unresolved, with many of these political disputes expected to enter the judicial arena as courts determine what constitutes "reasonable" risk.[18]

Why is risk assessment likely to be an important issue in the next century? Political decision makers are responding to publics who no longer are willing to "pay" for environmental protection unless there is a perceived "benefit." As the costs of other government programs and services (such as health care and interest on the federal deficit) skyrocket, decision makers must choose among competing priorities for limited tax dollars. Unless society perceives that the risks are indeed serious, taxpayers are likely to want to prioritize other needs ahead environmental problems. Those who are truly concerned about risk must make their case to the people in such a way as to enhance that perception. Similarly, efforts toward voluntary pollution reduction efforts are more likely to gain acceptance than costly disincentives and increased governmental regulation.[19]

OTHER EMERGING ISSUES

Green Consumerism

Environmentally friendly. Biodegradable. Earth safe. Cruelty free. Terms like these began showing up on products in the late 1980s as product manufacturers attempted to cash in on what they perceived would be a new marketing trend—consumer demand for products that are not harmful to the environment. A 1989 survey found that 77 percent of Americans say a company's environmental reputation affects what they buy.[20] Suddenly, food and retail companies began changing their packaging and their ingredients, and new products began to appear on supermarket shelves, from organic babyfood in recyclable glass jars to natural pet foods and cosmetics that had never been tested on animals. Environmentally correct apparel, made from 100 percent organic cotton and colored with nontoxic dyes, joined compostable diapers and rainforest crunch as the latest products to jump on the environmental marketing bandwagon.

Even companies with prior negative environmental reputations tried to make redress by publicizing their environmentally responsible activities and products. The oil companies, whose image was further tarnished by the Exxon *Valdez* oil spill in 1989, spent millions of dollars urging drivers to carpool, with ad campaigns focusing on efforts to preserve open space and wildlife habitats. Most environmental groups view the ad campaigns with suspicion, noting that the oil companies' public relations expenditures pale in comparison to the damage caused by a single oil spill. There is no doubt, however, that there is an increased environmental awareness (if not full acceptance) growing in corporate boardrooms.

"Living green" has also been promoted by the media and the entertainment industry, which began to capitalize on the interest in the environment with the film *Chinatown* in the early 1970s to the *Star Trek* movies of the 1990s.[21] A host of television series, from the *National Geographic* specials to *Captain Planet*, focused public attention on environmental issues. More recently, longtime activists Ted Turner and Jane Fonda have used their Turner Broadcasting System to provide coverage of Earth Day observances and the 1992 Earth Summit. Dozens of celebrities have lent their name to the environmental cause, and many work through the Los Angeles–based Earth Communications Office. A partial list of celebrity activists reads like a Hollywood Who's Who: actress Brigitte Bardot (active in France); actor Ed Begley, Jr. (who uses public conveyances or a bicycle for transportation); actor Richard Chamberlain (who works with the group American Rivers); actresses Cher, Meryl Streep, and Goldie Hawn (cofounders of Mothers and Others for the Environment); singer John Denver (founder of the Aspen Institute on Global Change); musician Don Henley (Defenders of Wildlife); singer Madonna (Conservation International); the Muppets (spokespuppets for the National Wildlife Federation); singer Olivia Newton-John (honorary ambassador for the UN Environment Programme); actor Ken Olin (Sierra Club); actor and director Robert Redford (founder of the Sundance Institute); actor Martin Sheen (antinuclear activist); actor Jimmy Stewart (African Wildlife Foundation); and model Cheryl Tiegs (Wilderness Society).

These changes came about as a result of the sharing of issues between the environmental and consumer movements in the early 1980s. The two groups shared ideology, a common constituency, broad public support, a common enemy, and a policy middle ground, the basis of which became the public interest movement.[22] Its member organizations began to use the power of public opinion to put pressure on the pocketbook of American consumers, using traditional strategies like lobbying for guidelines on what constitutes recycled content to boycotts of tuna products. By "piggybacking" onto consumer issues, environmental groups began to raise the political salience of their own agenda.

Those companies most subject to environmental controls have attempted to preempt interest groups' attempts to pressure policymakers who would enact legislation regulating their activities. Typical is the case of McDonald's, which began phasing out foam packaging in 1991, replacing foam and switching to a new, paper-based packaging that is lighter and thinner than foam, reducing overall packaging by 90 percent. The company announced a few months later that it would eliminate 80 percent or more of the garbage created by its eighty-five hundred fast food restaurants in the United States. The action was not the result of a bout of conscience or altruism. McDonald's had been threatened with a boycott by the powerful Environmental Defense Fund and criticism by the Sierra Club. Similarly, the oil industry has attempted to preempt government regulatory action before it was forced upon them, often at the behest of environmental groups. The low emission gasolines introduced in 1989–91 by Amoco, Arco, Exxon, and Shell Oil meet or come close to meeting the 1992 pollution control standards of the 1990 Clean Air Act.[23]

Efforts to promote green consumerism have not been totally successful, however. In 1990, two competing firms, Green Cross Certification Company and Green Seal, began offering their "eco-approval" to companies that made environmental marketing claims. Criticism over the firms' rating systems erupted almost immediately, and it was not long before consumer organizations and industry leaders called upon the Federal Trade Commission (FTC) to issue guidelines for labeling and advertising. Attorneys general from eleven states echoed the call, and made their own recommendations for responsible environmental advertising. They petitioned the FTC to enact guidelines on the use of the terms *recycled*, *degradable*, and *compostable* and recommended that a clear distinction should be made between the environmental attributes of a product and the environmental attributes of its packaging. They were especially critical of claims made about waste management options, since many products were potentially recyclable or compostable, but such options are not universally available.[24]

In 1992, the FTC issued its guidelines, which are not legally enforceable. The agency said environmental claims should be backed up by competent and reliable scientific evidence, and exceptions and qualifications to claims should be explained clearly. Without more stringent federal legislation, however, consumers are still likely to be confused by the companies' advertising claims. The number of green marketing claims has declined for several reasons. Some product manufacturers have found it difficult to comply with conflicting interpretations and a patchwork quilt of state laws and regulations,[25] and studies indicate some consumers are still reluctant to pay a premium for more expensive recycled products. Concerns about potential vulnerability to lawsuits have already caused some manufacturers to drop their green claims, especially after the FTC brought seven cases in 1991 against companies that claimed their products were biodegradable or did not hurt the atmosphere.

Manufacturers hoping to capitalize by "turning green" even faced hostility and backlash from consumers who did not appreciate their attempts at corporate environmental responsibility. For example, the Oregon Lands Coalition, a grassroots group backing northwest loggers, criticized Mattel Toys for its Barbie television commercial supportive of forest protection, and General Mills was similarly censured for its cereal commercials, which critics perceived as negative toward the timber industry. Leading advertising executives still expect that environmental marketing claims will increase, however, now that the FTC guidelines are in place.[26]

While green consumerism has had some impact, it has failed to change the way most products are marketed, and there is little evidence it is the wave of the future so many of its supporters had hoped. A more likely outcome is that corporate America is becoming more conscious about decision making and actions with environmental implications. In September 1989, the Coalition for Environmentally Responsible Economies (CERES) drafted the Valdez Principles, ten corporate commitments to environmental protection that called for companies to reduce waste and market safe products. Although many firms felt that the Valdez Principles were at best an intrusion into their operating policies, there is no doubt the document caused many large companies to take a second look at their environmental practices.[27]

Ecofeminism

Women have historically been active in environmental issues, beginning with the early city beautification and urban sanitation movements of the Progressive Era. Contemporaneously, women have been active in the global peace movement and in efforts to bring about world nuclear disarmament. But in contemporary political history (from the late 1970s onward) these two interests have coalesced. The result is a new term—*ecofeminism*—which has been called the third stage of the women's movement after suffrage in the early part of the century and women's liberation in the 1960s and 1970s. The term usually refers to an analysis of the relationship of women to the status of Earth, and centers on women's presumed universal values of nurturing, healing, and caring for the environment. Ecofeminism is also a very broad term encompassing issues beyond those of the mainstream environmental movement, including women's power as consumers, reproductive rights, international debt and trade, and women and militarism.[28]

With roots in a 1980 Massachusetts conference on Women and Life on Earth, the ecofeminist movement held its first two international gatherings, the Global Assembly of Women and the Environment and the World Women's Congress for a Healthy Planet, in November 1991 in Miami. Organized under the auspices of the UN Environment Programme and a number of nongovernmental organizations, the assembly and the congress that followed brought together fifteen hundred women from eighty-three nations to discuss strategies to protect the environment through ethical, feminist, and antiracist sustainable development. The meetings culminated in the preparation of a Women's Action Agenda, which was brought before the Earth Summit in June 1992. The document makes connections between social and political injustices and environmental destruction, and between the exclusion of women from economic and political decision making and the exploitation of Earth. It makes specific recommendations including equitable gender representation in the United Nations and the creation of a UN Commission on Environment and Development, which would monitor and investigate environmental abuses.[29]

Ecofeminism is not a universally accepted concept for a number of reasons. Some critics argue that there are really no "feminine virtues and masculine vices" and that such a characterization of women as being more concerned about the fate of the planet than men is really sexism in reverse. Others argue that ecofeminism is not particularly intellectually rigorous, while still others believe a more apt term might be "ecospiritualism," since its roots are not those of the mainstream feminist movement at all, but in New Age spiritualism. Still, ecofeminism has its adherents who strongly believe that women can have a special place in solving environmental problems in the twenty-first century.[30]

Ecotourism

Another emerging "ism" that was given considerable attention at the Earth Summit, ecotourism refers to international travel, which minimizes the adverse side effects of recreational activities and environmental and social disruption. Tourism is the second largest industry in the world, according to the World Tourism Organization, an affiliate of the United Nations, comprising 7 percent of the world trade in goods and services. Tourism produces $195 billion annually in domestic and international receipts and creates seventy-four million jobs. The organization predicts that tourism will become the world's largest industry by the year 2000, with ecotourism increasing at the rate of 30 percent a year.[31]

Also known as alternative tourism, several environmental organizations such as the National Audubon Society began offering tours to areas of interest in the U.S. in the 1940s. The concept gained importance during the late 1970s when research began to show an expansion in recreational travel, especially to developing countries, largely as a result of the growing environmental movement, media attention of natural history topics, and enhanced air travel capabilities. Ecotourism developed as concerns grew about the impact of large numbers of visitors (called mass tourism) on environmentally sensitive areas, including heritage sites and in developing regions. A 1979 study by the UN Environment Programme noted that although there are benefits of tourism (notably, income and jobs from tourist spending, preservation of the cultural and natural heritage, increased cultural understanding, and the building of new facilities such as sewage works, which benefit entire communities), there are a number of disadvantages as well. Tourism adds the costs of importing special amenities like buses and snowmobiles, the destruction of the environment when hotels must be built in sensitive areas, the undermining of social standards, abuses of plants and animals and the introduction of alien species, and pollution.

Ecotourism gained credibility after horror stories began to circulate and be publicized by the media—examples where tourists deliberately or inadvertently clashed with the environment. Recreational activities like climbing, caving, riding, sailing, snowmobiling, and dune buggy excursions were causing damage—sometimes irreversible—to fragile ecosystems. Propellers of power boats in Florida have already killed hundreds of endangered manatees; snowmobiles destroy the tunnels of small mammals and reptiles; waterfowl are disturbed by sailboaters; alpine meadows are being trampled by hikers in the Rockies and Sierra Nevada ranges. Even casual wildlife observation can be destructive by distorting normal behaviors through artificial feeding. Animals accustomed to begging for food become more aggressive and often become the target of vigorous control measures. (Remember the bears of Yellowstone and Yosemite National parks?)

The effects of tourists go beyond recreational activities. Support facilities, from hotels and waste disposal facilities to roads, have damaging consequences.

Embankments on roads can be a barrier to family groups of animals that attempt to cross, and there is a real hazard of animals being killed by vehicles on roadways. Sometimes the adverse effects of tourism do not directly affect the host country. There has been a spectacular increase in the incidence of tropical diseases brought back by travelers, including malaria, schistosomiasis, and tick-borne diseases.[32]

In response to these concerns, wildlife organizations and governmental agencies are now taking steps to minimize such disruptions.[33] Some of the solutions are simple and obvious, such as confining observers to locations sited at safe distances from areas where wildlife is likely to appear. Several wildlife refuges, for example, have even constructed artificial waterholes and grazing areas to attract animals without disturbing their natural habits, or built viewing lodges that are screened from view. Other ideas involve trading guns for cameras as a way of "capturing" wildlife on film instead of wall trophies, or setting up tours of ecologically sensitive areas. In central Venezuela for example, the Hato Pinero cattle ranch is both a cattle ranch and refuge for native wildlife as well as an important part of the tourist industry. The ranch enforces a total hunting ban and brings visitors in to tour the ecological resources of the Hato. It is both a source of local pride and revenue.[34]

There has been some discussion, however, that what is really being proposed as alternative tourism is really a disguised form of class prejudice. As one critic puts it, the emphasis on ecotourism means large numbers of middle- and lower-class tourists are not welcome, but small numbers of affluent, well-educated, and well-behaved tourists are invited. The type of tourist who would realistically be attracted to alternative tourism is highly educated, affluent, mature, and probably white.[35] Currently, most ecotourists are from Europe, North America, and Japan, since they have more money and more leisure time than many of their counterparts in developing countries. The average ecotourist is a person familiar with the outdoors, a professional or retiree, between thirty-one and fifty years old, who most likely has had previous experience traveling abroad. One survey found over one-quarter of ecotourists earned over $90,000 a year in family income, with another quarter earning between $30,000 and $60,000.[36]

There are other implications for ecotourism as well that may not be as readily apparent. The concept may lead to a reduction in the number of tourists visiting an area, a change in the type of tourist who visits, and a decline in the amount of revenues an area will receive. For example, the repeat business of tourism may be limited if the Galapagos Islands targets its market at ornithologists, who are likely to move on to a new destination. The resulting economic impact on the region may be devastated if it is heavily dependent upon tourism. What these criticisms mean is that the growth of ecotourism should be seen for what it is—not as an alternative to mass tourism, but rather, an awareness of the environmental and cultural impact of visitors to the Global Commons.[37]

SUMMARY

Although pollution issues are likely to continue to be important as we cross over into the next millennium, those concerns are gradually being eclipsed by more global concerns. This means policymakers will be dealing with the question of transboundary pollution rather than just regional problems, or whether industrialized nations should be held responsible for the cleanup of polluted areas in developing nations. The growing rift between industrialized and developing countries is likely to continue, as attempts are made to find new diplomatic tools to bridge the gaps that have already begun to occur. High on the list of priorities will be questions of cost, with the answers focused on the relative risk posed by an environmental hazard. Policymakers will increasingly be forced to weigh their limited resources (personnel as well as funds) against the harm posed by the problem as more and more environmental threats are identified. A variety of other less critical environmental issues, although important, will face a political agenda crowded by pocketbook problems that are clearly international in scope.

NOTES

1. See Michel Potier, "Towards a Better Integration of Environmental, Economic, and Other Governmental Policies," in *Maintaining a Satisfactory Environment: An Agenda for International Environmental Policy*, ed. Nordal Akerman, (Boulder, CO: Westview Press, 1990), 69–81.

2. For a history of the early geopolitical writers, see Jeremy Rifkin, *Biosphere Politics* (New York: Crown, 1991), 119–23. Among the key works are those of Frederick Ratzel and Ellen Churchill Semple.

3. Jessica Tuchman Mathews, "Redefining Security," *Foreign Affairs* 68, no. 2 (Spring 1989): 162–77.

4. Norman Myers, *Not Far Afield: U.S. Interests and the Global Environment* (Washington, DC: World Resources Institute, June 1987), 9.

5. Gareth Porter and Janet Welsh Brown, *Global Environmental Politics* (Boulder, CO: Westview Press, 1991), 110.

6. Andy Coghlan, "Fresh Water from the Sea," *New Scientist*, August 31, 1991, 37.

7. Kenneth D. Frederick, "Managing Water for Economic, Environmental, and Human Health," *Resources* 106 (Winter, 1992): 25.

8. Michael Renner, *National Security: The Economic and Environmental Dimensions* (Washington, DC: Worldwatch Institute, May 1989), 31–32.

9. See David S. Cloud, "Environmental Groups Look for Ways to 'Green' Trade Agreement," *Congressional Quarterly Weekly Report*, November 28, 1992, 3712–13.

10. See Carl Pope, "War on Earth," *Sierra* May–June 1991, 56; Roy Popkin, "Responding to EcoTerrorism," *EPA Journal* (July–August 1991): 24; and Sir Frederic Warner, "The Environmental Consequences of the Gulf War," *Environment* (June 1991): 9.

11. See U.S. Congress, Senate, Committee on Environment and Public Works, Gulf Pollution Task Force, *The Environmental Aftermath of the Gulf War* (Washington, DC: U.S. Government Printing Office, 1992).

12. See Mustafa Tolba and Rudolf Bahro, "The Ecological Balance of Power," *New Perspectives Quarterly* 7, no. 2 (Spring 1990): 60–62.

13. Renner, *National Security*, 41–44.

14. Rifkin, *Biosphere Politics*, 282–85.

15. Renner, *National Security*, 48–49.

16. See National Research Council, *Risk Assessment in the Federal Government: Managing the Process* (Washington, DC: National Academy Press, 1983).

17. U.S. Environmental Protection Agency, Office of Policy Analysis, *Unfinished Business: A Comparative Assessment of Environmental Problems* (Washington, DC, 1987).

18. See John J. Cohrssen and Vincent T. Covello, *Risk Analysis: A Guide to Principles and Methods for Analyzing Health and Environmental Risks* (Washington, DC: U.S. Government Printing Office, 1989).

19. See William Reilly, "Taking Aim toward 2000: Rethinking the Nation's Environmental Agenda," *Environmental Law* 21, no. 4 (1991): 1359–74. See also Robert F. Blomquist, "The EPA Science Advisory Board's Report on 'Reducing Risk': Some Overarching Observations Regarding the Public Interest," *Environmental Law* 22, no. 1 (1992): 149–88.

20. David Kilpatrick, "Environmentalism: The New Crusade," *Fortune*, February 12, 1990, 44–52.

21. See Craig L. LaMay and Everette E. Dennis, eds., *Media and the Environment* (Washington, DC: Island Press, 1991).

22. See Robert C. Mitchell, "Consumer and Environmentalism in the 1980s: Competitive or Companionable Social Movements?" in *The Future of Consumerism*, ed. P. N. Bloom and R. B. Smith, (Lexington, MA: Lexington Books, 1986), 25–26.

23. Mark Potts, "The Greening of Big Oil," *Washington Post National Weekly Edition*, November 19–25, 1990, 22.

24. *The Green Report II* (Washington, DC: National Association of Attorneys General, May 1991).

25. See "Green Marketing Claims Are Waning Because of Varied State Regulations," *Advertising Age*, March 9, 1992, 1.

26. See "Environmental Marketing Claims Are Expected to Grow Again Now that FTC Has Issued New Guidelines," *Advertising Age*, August 3, 1992, 1.

27. Jack Doyle, "Valdez Principles: Corporate Code of Conduct," *Social Policy* 20 (Winter 1990): 32–34. See also, "Seeing the Green Light," *The Economist*, October 20, 1990, 88–89; "Eco-bucks: Going for the Purse Strings," *Science News*, August 29, 1987, 137; James E. Post, "The Greening of Management," *Issues in Science and Technology* 6 (Summer 1990): 68–71, and Eric Mann, "Environmentalism in the Corporate Climate," *Tikkun* 5 (March–April 1990): 60–65.

28. For an overview of ecofeminism, see Irene Diamond and Gloria Feman Orenstein, *Reweaving the World: The Emergence of Ecofeminism* (San Francisco: Sierra Club Books, 1991); Janet Biehl, *Rethinking Ecofeminist Politics* (Boston: South End Press, 1991); and Judith Plant, *Healing the Wounds: The Promise of Ecofeminism* (Philadelphia: New Society Publishers, 1989).

29. "The Global Assembly of Women and the Environment and the World Women's Congress for a Healthy Planet, *The Ecofeminist Newsletter* 3, no. 1 (Winter 1992): 1–4.

30. For a critique of some of the ecofeminist literature, see Jan Clausen, "Rethinking the World," *The Nation* 253, no. 9 (September 23, 1991): 344–47.

31. Tensie Whelan, ed., *Nature Tourism: Managing for the Environment* (Washington, DC: Island Press, 1991), 4–5.

32. See, generally, John M. Edington and M. Ann Edington, *Ecology, Recreation and Tourism* (Cambridge: Cambridge University Press, 1986).

33. See Elizabeth Boo, *Ecotourism: The Potentials and Pitfalls* (Washington, DC: World Wildlife Fund, 1990).

34. Parisina Malatesta and Jorge Provenza, "Branded for a Balanced Biosphere," *Americas* 43, nos. 5–6 (September–October 1991): 74–83.

35. R. W. Butler, "Alternative Tourism: Pious Hope of Trojan Horse?" *Journal of Travel Research* 28, no. 3 (Winter 1990): 40–45.

36. Whelan, *Native Tourism*, 5–6.

37. See Ruth Norris, "Can Ecotourism Save Natural Areas?" *National Parks* 66, nos. 1–2 (January–February 1992): 30–34; Ann Claire Greiner, "Traveling With Mother Nature," *Technology Review* 93, no. 8 (November–December 1990): 19–20; Lynette Lamb, "Can Ecotourism Spoil What It Seeks to Save?" *Utne Reader* 41 (September–October 1990): 30–32; and Peter A. A. Berle, "The Faces of Eco-Tourism," *Audubon* 92 (March 1990): 6.

FOR FURTHER READING

Janet Biehl. *Rethinking Ecofeminist Politics*. Boston: South End Press, 1991.

Elizabeth Boo. *Ecotourism: The Potentials and Pitfalls*. Washington, DC: World Wildlife Fund-U.S., 1990.

Colin S. Gray. *The Geopolitics of Super Power*. Lexington: University Press of Kentucky, 1988.

Irene Diamond and Gloria Feman Orenstein. *Reweaving the World: The Emergence of Ecofeminism*. San Francisco: Sierra Club Books, 1991.

Michael Renner. *National Security: The Economic and Environmental Dimensions*. Washington, DC: Worldwatch Institute, 1989.

Jeremy Rifkin. *Biosphere Politics*. New York: Crown, 1991.

Arthur H. Westing, ed. *Global Resources and International Conflict*. Oxford: Oxford University Press, 1986.

Tensie Whelan. *Nature Tourism*. Washington, DC: Island Press, 1991.

Index

About the Author

A native of San Diego, Jacqueline Vaughn Switzer is currently associate professor of political science at Southern Oregon State College in Ashland, where she specializes in American government and public policy. She taught previously at the University of Redlands. Professor Switzer holds a Ph.D. in political science from the University of California, Berkeley, where she also attended the Graduate School of Public Policy. Professor Switzer has a broad spectrum of nonacademic experience, including service as an aide to a member of the California state legislature, coordinator of a county-level program providing assistance to victims of crime, as director of a child abuse training program for educators and health-care professionals, and in the public affairs division of Los Angeles' South Coast Air Quality Management District, the nation's largest regional environmental agency. In addition, she has been a partner in a political consulting firm in southern California, and before moving to Oregon in 1990, an environmental policy analyst for Southern California Edison, specializing in the impact of federal, state, and local environmental legislation.